Second edition

Founding Editor-in-Chief
John Sinclair

Publishing Director
Lorna Knight

Editorial Director
Michela Clari

Managing Editor
Maree Airlie

Project Manager
Alison Macaulay

Editor
Maggie Seaton

Editorial Assistance
Sheilagh Wilson

First edition

Editor-in-Chief
John Sinclair

Managing Editor
Gwyneth Fox

Senior Editor
Ramesh Krishnamurthy

Editor
Jenny Watson

Assistant Editors
Christina Rammell
Keith Stuart

Computational Assistance
Tim Lane
Zoe James
Stephen Bullon

Secretarial Staff
Sue Smith
Sue Crawley

HarperCollins Publishers
Annette Capel, Lorna Heaslip, Douglas Williamson

Illustrators
John Batten, Gillian Martin, David Parkins, Clyde Pearson, Peter Shrank

We would like to thank Dave Willis additionally for his valuable contributions to the grammar pages; Sylvia Chalker and Sue Inkster for their detailed comments and suggestions on the text; Annette Capel for writing the key to the Exercises; Richard Fay and Paschalena Groutka for their part in the original drafting of the units; Kirsty Haynes for secretarial assistance during the earlier stages of the project; Sue Inkster, Anthony Harvey, John Curtin, John Dyson, Tom Stableford, Bob Walker, David Evans, and Angus Oliver for their comments on the initial list of Units.

We would also like to thank all the people who contributed to the Collins COBUILD English Grammar, whose original work provided the impetus for this book.

CONTENTS

Note: numbers in **bold** are unit numbers.

Introduction	vii
How to use the Grammar	viii–ix
Guide to the CD-ROM	ix–x
Glossary of grammar terms	xi–xvi

Grammar units

BASIC SENTENCE STRUCTURE

1	Clauses and sentences	2
2	Noun groups	4
3	The verb group	6
4	The imperative and 'let'	8

QUESTIONS

5	Questions	10
6	'Wh'- questions	12
7	Question tags: forms	14
8	Questions tags: uses	16
9	Indirect questions	18
10	Short answers	20

NEGATIVES

11	Sentences with 'not'	22
12	Negative words	24

NOUNS

13	Count nouns	26
14	Singular and plural: singular, plural and collective nouns	28
15	Uncount nouns	30

PRONOUNS AND POSSESSIVES

16	Personal pronouns	32
17	Impersonal subject 'it'	34
18	Impersonal subject 'there'	36
19	Demonstrative pronouns: this, that, these, those, one, ones	38
20	Reflexive pronouns	40
21	Indefinite pronouns	42
22	Possession	44

DETERMINERS

23	Determiners	46
24	Main uses of 'the'	48

25	Other uses of 'the'	50
26	'A' and 'an'	52
27	All, most, no, none	54
28	Both, either, neither	56
29	Quantity 1: much, little, many, few, more, less, fewer	58
30	Quantity 2: some, any, another, other, each, every	60

ADJECTIVES

31	Position of adjectives	62
32	Order of adjectives	64
33	Adjectives with 'to'-infinitive or 'that'-clauses	66
34	'-ing' and '-ed' adjectives	68

COMPARISON

35	Comparison: basic forms	70
36	Comparison: uses	72
37	Other ways of comparing	74

ADVERBIALS

38	Adverbials	76
39	Adverbials of manner	78
40	Adverbials of time	80
41	Adverbials of frequency and probability	82
42	Adverbials of duration – already, yet, still	84
43	Adverbials of degree	86

PREPOSITIONS AND PHRASAL VERBS

44	Prepositions of place and direction	88
45	Prepositions of place – at, in, on	90
46	Prepositions with forms of transport	92
47	Adjective + preposition	94
48	Noun + preposition	96
49	Verb + preposition	98
50	Phrasal verbs	100

TRANSITIVITY: VERBS AND OBJECTS

51	Verbs and objects: transitive and intransitive verbs	102
52	Verbs with two objects	104
53	Reflexive verbs	106
54	Reciprocal verbs	108
55	Ergative verbs	110
56	Common verb + noun patterns	112

CONTENTS

TENSES

57   Auxiliary verbs – be, have, do   114
58   The present tenses 116
59   The past tenses   118
60   The continuous tenses   120
61   The perfect tenses   122
62   Talking about the present   124
63   Talking about the past   126
64   'will' and 'going to'   128
65   Present tenses for future   130

CONDITIONALS AND HYPOTHETICAL SITUATIONS

66   Conditionals using 'if'   132
67   Conditional clauses using modals   134
     and 'unless'
68   'I wish', 'if only', '…as if'   136

-ING CLAUSES AND INFINITIVES

69   Verbs with '-ing' clauses   138
70   Verbs with 'to'-infinitive clauses   140
71   Verbs with 'to'-infinitive or '-ing' clauses   144
72   Verbs with other types of clauses   146
73   Link verbs   148

REPORTED SPEECH

74   Reporting the past   150
75   Reported questions   152
76   Reporting with 'that'-clauses   154
77   Other report structures   156

THE PASSIVE VOICE

78   The passive voice   158

MODALS

79   Introduction to modals   160
80   Introduction to modals 2   162
81   Possibility: can, could, may, might   164
82   Probability and certainty: cannot, can't,   166
     must, ought, should, will
83   Ability: can, could, be able to   168
84   Permission: can, could, may   170
85   Instructions and requests: can, could,   172
     will, would

86   Suggestions: could, may, might, shall   174
87   Offers and invitations: can, could, will,   176
     would
88   Wants and wishes: would like, would
     rather, wouldn't mind   178
89   Obligation and necessity 1: have to,   180
     have got to, must, mustn't
90   Obligation and necessity 2: need to,   182
     needn't, not have to
91   Mild obligation and advice: should,   184
     ought, should/oughtn't to have,
     had better

RELATIVE CLAUSES AND PARTICIPLE CLAUSES

92   Defining relative clauses   186
93   Non-defining relative clauses   188
94   Participle clauses   190
95   Other ways of adding to a noun group   192

OTHER KINDS OF CLAUSES

96   Time clauses   194
97   Purpose and reason clauses   196
98   Result clauses   198
99   Contrast clauses   200
100   Manner clauses   202
101   Changing the focus of a sentence   204
102   Cohesion: making connections in   206
      speech and writing

Bank of further exercises   208

See next page for full details

Appendix: verb forms   240–241

Index   242–249

Key   250–267

Bank of further exercises key   268–272

BANK OF FURTHER EXERCISES CONTENTS

Note: numbers in **bold** are exercise numbers.

BASIC SENTENCE STRUCTURE

1	The Imperative	208

QUESTIONS

2	Questions	208
3	'Wh-' words	208
4	Question tags	209
5	Statements, questions and commands	209
6–8	Review of mood	209

NOUNS

9	plural nouns	210

PRONOUNS AND POSSESSIVES

10	'It' as impersonal subject	210
11	'There as impersonal subject	211
12	Reflexive pronouns	211
13	Possession	211

DETERMINERS

14	Determiners	212
15	'a', 'an', 'the'	212
16	'all of'	212
17	'all', 'none', 'both', 'neither'	213
18–19	Review of determiners	213

ADJECTIVES

20	Position of adjectives	214
21	Adjectives ending in '-ing'	214
22	'-ing' and '-ed' adjectives	214

COMPARISON

23	Comparative adjectives	214
24	Superlative adjectives	215
25	Comparative adjectives and other ways of comparing	215
26	Comparison	216

ADVERBIALS AND PREPOSITIONS

27	Position of adverbials	216
28	Adverbials of time	216
29–30	Adverbials of degree	217
31	Review of adverbials	217
32	Prepositions of place	218
33–34	Review of adverbials	218
35	Nouns with prepositions	219
36–37	Verbs with prepositions	219
38–39	Phrasal verbs	220

TRANSITIVITY: VERBS AND OBJECTS

40	Verbs with two objects	221

41	Common verbs with nouns for actions	221

TENSES

42	Past simple and past perfect	222
43	Past continuous	222
44	Continuous tenses	222
45	Talking about the past	223
46	Review of tenses	223

CONDITIONALS AND HYPOTHETICAL SITUATIONS

47	Conditional clauses	225
48	I wish – wants and wishes	225

'-ING' CLAUSES AND INFINITIVES

49–51	Verbs with '-ing' clauses	225
52–54	Nouns with 'to'-infinitive clauses	226
55	Verbs with 'to'-infinitive or '-ing' clauses	227
56–57	Verbs with other types of clauses	228
58	link verbs	228

REPORTED SPEECH

59–60	Reporting the past	228
61	Reported questions	229
62–63	Reporting	230

REPORTED SPEECH

64	The passive voice	231

MODALS

65	Could - possibility	231
66	Could have, couldn't have – possibility	232
67	Couldn't, couldn't have – possibility	232
68	Must, must have – probability and certainty	232
69	Be able to – ability	233
70	Could have – ability	233
71	Can, can't – ability	233
72	Might – suggestions	234
73	Ought to have – mild obligation	234
74	Had better – mild obligation and advice	234
75–76	Review of modals	235

RELATIVE CLAUSES AND PARTICIPLE CLAUSES

77	Defining relative clauses	235

OTHER KINDS OF CLAUSES

78	Time clauses	236
79–80	Purpose and reason clauses	236
81–82	Result clauses	237
83–84	Contrast clauses	238
85	Changing the focus of a sentence	239

INTRODUCTION

The COBUILD approach to grammar is simple and direct. We study a large collection of English texts, and find out how people are actually using the language. We pick the most important points and we show how the words and phrases are used by quoting actual examples from our text collection. As a student of English, you can be sure that you are presented with real English, as it is actually used.

In this book we give explanations of the most important, frequent, and typical points of English grammar along with a lot of practice material so that you can put the knowledge to use immediately. This makes the book suitable both as a classroom text, and also for private study. This is a grammar of meanings as well as structures. The exercises help you to link the meanings and structures, not just to practice the structures. A key to all the exercises is provided.

The grammar is often very direct and easy to understand. Sometimes English speakers and writers prefer a simple structure and only very advanced students need to know more than that. At other times we give more details, because they are necessary for clear understanding and accurate usage.

This book has been developed from the same database which was used in the Collins COBUILD English Grammar. It is designed for use by anyone who has enough English to understand the explanations, which we expect to be intermediate and above. This new edition is accompanied by a version of the text on a CD-ROM, which also gives you access to a 5-million word corpus of current English so that you can check your understanding of grammatical points with reference to a corpus.

John Sinclair
Founding Editor in Chief, COBUILD
President, The Tuscan Word Centre

HOW TO USE THE GRAMMAR

This book is divided into 102 units, each of which covers a different grammatical area. You may want to study the units in sequence to develop your grammatical understanding systematically. However, if you have problems with particular areas of grammar, you can also select units which relate to these areas.

Finding what you want

Contents
The Units are grouped under various headings to help you, for example 'Nouns', 'Questions' and 'Modals'. There is a complete list of contents on pages iv to v which gives you the numbers and titles of all the Units.

Index
There is an Index at the back of the book on pages 242 to 249. The Index is an alphabetical list of grammar points covered in this book. For each point, the Index gives the Unit number and paragraph number where the point is explained. Grammar terms such as 'adjectives', 'nouns', and 'verbs' are in **bold** letters. The ideas that you can express, such as 'ability' and 'age', are also in bold letters. The actual words and forms explained in the grammar, such as 'able' and 'this', are in *italic* letters.

Glossary
There is a Glossary on pages xi to xvi. The Glossary explains the meaning of the grammar terms used in this book, and illustrates them with examples. The terms are listed in alphabetical order.

Using the grammar units

Each Unit has two parts. The left-hand page contains an explanation in simple English of the grammar rules and patterns. The right-hand page contains practice material, with carefully graded exercises covering the unit material. This allows you to put the grammar into practice and to build on your understanding of the explanations.

Left-hand pages
The left-hand page has two columns. At the top of the first column you will find a box headed 'Main points'. This is a summary of the important information given in the Unit. You will find more detailed information about the point in the numbered paragraphs on the same page.

Each point is illustrated with example sentences printed in italic letters.

When particular words in the example sentences show the point that is being explained, the words are underlined. All of the examples are real English from the Bank of English® corpus, so you can be sure that they show you English as it is really used.

With many rules and patterns, a number of words are used in the same way.

When this is the case, a list of the words is given. For some points, a complete list of the words would be very long, so only the commonest and most useful words are included.

A 'WARNING' label ⊝ WARNING is used before points of English grammar which frequently cause learners to make mistakes.

Sometimes they are exceptions to a rule. Sometimes the rules are different in other languages. You should pay particular attention to these points.

A cross-reference symbol ➤ is used to show you where you can find more information about a particular grammar rule or pattern in another Unit.

Right-hand pages
The right-hand page contains practice material for you to do. There are many different types of exercise, so you should read the instructions carefully.

The 'Bank' symbol ▶ **Bank** indicates that you will find more practice material on the same topic in the 'Bank of further exercises' at the back of the book.

For each exercise, the first answer has been supplied. You can use this as a model for the rest of the exercise.

GUIDE TO THE CD-ROM

Bank of further exercises
The Bank of further exercises is at the back of the book. Some of the exercises relate to a particular Unit, and the Unit or paragraph number is given. Other exercises have been designed to give you more general grammar practice.

Key
A Key to all the exercises is given at the back of the book.

GUIDE TO THE CD-ROM

To the student

Using the **Collins COBUILD Grammar Plus CD-ROM** you can:

- look for detailed information about the grammar and usage of English quickly and easily;
- create your own personal dictionary of new words and find information about these in the Grammar and Usage, along with real examples of usage in the Wordbank;
- find information about a word, even if you are not sure how to spell it.

To the teacher

Using the **Collins COBUILD Grammar Plus CD-ROM** you can:

- access a wealth of reliable information about the grammar and usage of English, including thousands of examples of real English usage from the 5-million word Wordbank;
- cut and paste grammar and usage information directly into your own documents, for example to create a summary of the teaching point at the start of an exercise you have created;
- create cloze tests and other types of exercises and worksheets using real examples of spoken and written English from a wide range of sources: examples from the Wordbank can be cut and pasted easily into your own documents;
- examine the different varieties of English with your learners: Wordbank examples indicate whether the source is spoken or written, British or American English;
- easily create wordbuilding exercises using the Morphological search function to find examples in the Wordbank of inflected forms of a word;
- help your students to develop learner autonomy and good practice by encouraging them to create their own user dictionaries of new words and structures.

Installing your CD-ROM

Insert the CD-ROM into the computer's CD-ROM drive and wait for a few seconds for the installation program to start automatically. If the installation program does not appear after a short time, click the Windows *Start* menu button, then select *Run...*, enter *D:\setup* as the name of the program to open (where 'D' is the drive letter for your computer's CD-ROM drive) and then click the *OK* button.
The installation program allows you to choose:

- The drive and folder where the software will be installed
- To install the full CD-ROM onto your hard disk
- What shortcut icons will be created to start the program.

At the end of the installation program, you will be asked if you wish to start **Collins COBUILD Grammar Plus** straight away. To run **Collins COBUILD Grammar Plus** at any time after installation, either click the icon which was created on your desktop, or else click the *Start* menu button, then select *Programs*, then **Collins COBUILD Grammar Plus CD-ROM**.

The reference texts

The CD-ROM contains three different English reference resources:

- *Grammar*: this contains all of the information that is on the left hand pages in this book.

GUIDE TO THE CD-ROM

● **Usage**: this gives more detailed information about selected words and phrases which often cause some difficulty or confusion. Each entry explains how particular words are used and gives advice about style and accepted usage in modern English.

● **Wordbank**: this is a collection of real texts (spoken as well as written) in which you can see words in their natural contexts as they are actually used in everyday English. The Wordbank contains 5 million words of texts: newspaper articles, books, magazines, conversations, and so on.

Basic searching

Simply enter a word in the Search input line and hit *Return*.

The Search results window has an *Entries* tab which shows the entries matching the search word, and the letter icon on the left shows which reference text the entry comes from: G for Grammar, U for Usage. Search hits from the Wordbank (W) will be listed under the *Full Text* tab, because the Wordbank doesn't have labelled 'entries' – words can only be found in the Wordbank with a Full Text search.

Full text searching

By default, Full Text searching is on. When the software does a Full Text search, it finds your search word across the whole contents of the selected reference texts, not just the labelled entries.

The *Full Text* tab shows search results arranged into sections (*Entries, Definitions, Extras, Examples*). The contents of each section can be opened or closed by clicking on the [+] or [-] symbol to the left of the section name.

Getting examples from the Wordbank

After entering a word in the *Search* input line, hitting *Return*, then selecting the *Full Text* tab in the Search results window, you can click on the *Examples* section to open it and see a summary of the number of example phrases and sentences which contain the word. These examples may be in the Grammar, Usage, or Wordbank. The *G*, *U*, and *W* icons indicate which resource the examples come from.

The examples from the Wordbank are not selected and edited by Collins' lexicographers – they are real examples found from 5 million words of modern English text samples. So you can see how the word is actually used by native English speakers in everyday writing and speech.

Morphological search

You can set the software to search automatically for the inflected forms of your search word (e.g. if you enter the word **broken,** the software searches for **break, breaks, breaking, broke** and **broken**). Click on *Entry* from the Menu Bar, select *Search…* and when the Search dialogue box appears click the checkbox marked *Morphological search*. If the Morphological search is switched off, then only the word form that you typed in will be matched.

Search for misspelled words

This option is useful if you are not sure how a word is spelled in English. If you misspell a word and no results are given, click the *Suggestions* button, and the software will suggest various close matches.

User dictionary

You can create your own supplementary dictionary to add notes, new words that you have learned, or any other personal vocabulary entries. These entries will be searched along with the other reference texts on the CD-ROM. To add or modify entries in the User dictionary, click on *Edit* from the Menu Bar, select *User dictionary* and use the new window which appears to create your own entries or modify entries that you have previously saved. The user dictionary is denoted in the Entries window with a smiling face icon.

Setting options for display and searching

Under the *Full text* tab you can set which sections of the reference texts will be searched: for example, if you are only interested in finding authentic example sentences for your search word, then you can go to the *Full text* options tab and set only the *Examples* checkbox. Then when you enter the next search word, only the *Examples* section will appear under the *Full text* tab in the Search results window.

GLOSSARY OF GRAMMAR TERMS

abstract noun a noun used to refer to a quality, idea, feeling, or experience, rather than a physical object; **eg** *size, reason, joy*.
➤ See Units 15, 70, 73

active voice verb groups such as 'gives', 'took', 'has made', which are used when the subject of the verb is the person or thing doing the action or responsible for it. Compare with **passive voice**.
➤ See Unit 78

adjective a word used to tell you more about a person or thing, such as their appearance, colour, size, or other qualities; **eg** …*a pretty blue dress*.
➤ See Units 31–36, 47

adjunct another name for **adverbial**.

adverb a word that gives more information about when, how, where, or in what circumstances something happens; **eg** *quickly, now*.
➤ See Units 21, 36–44, 95

adverbial an adverb, or an adverb phrase, prepositional phrase, or noun group which does the same job as an adverb; **eg** *then, very quickly, in the street, the next day*.
➤ See Units 38–46

adverbial of degree an adverbial which indicates the amount or extent of a feeling or quality; **eg** *She felt* **extremely** *tired*.
➤ See Unit 43

adverbial of duration an adverbial which indicates how long something continues or lasts; **eg** *He lived in London* **for six years**.
➤ See Unit 42

adverbial of frequency an adverbial which indicates how often something happens; **eg** *She* **sometimes** *goes to the cinema*.
➤ See Unit 41

adverbial of manner an adverbial which indicates the way in which something happens or is done; **eg** *She watched* **carefully**.
➤ See Unit 39

adverbial of place an adverbial which gives more information about position or direction; **eg** *They are* **upstairs**… *Move* **closer**.
➤ See Unit 44–45

adverbial of probability an adverbial which gives more information about how sure you are about something; **eg** *I realized I'd* **probably** *lost it*.
➤ See Unit 41

adverbial of time an adverbial which gives more information about when something happens; **eg** *I saw her* **yesterday**.
➤ See Unit 40

adverb phrase two adverbs used together; **eg** *She spoke* **very quietly**… *He did not play* **well enough** *to win*.
➤ See Unit 38

affirmative a clause or sentence in the affirmative is one which does not contain a negative word such as 'not' and which is not a question.
➤ See Units 21, 29–30, 41–42

apostrophe s an ending ('s) added to a noun to indicate possession; **eg** …*Harriet's daughter*… *the professor's husband*… *the Managing Director's secretary*.
➤ See Units 21–22

article See **definite article, indefinite article**.

auxiliary another name for **auxiliary verb**.

auxiliary verb one of the verbs 'be', 'have', and 'do' when they are used with a main verb to form tenses, negatives, and questions. Some grammars include modals in the group of auxiliary verbs.
➤ See Units 3, 5, 7, 9–11, **57**

base form the form of a verb without any endings added to it, which is used in the 'to'–infinitive and for the imperative; **eg** *walk, go, have, be*. The base form is the form you look up in a dictionary.
➤ See Units 3, 72, 79

cardinal number a number used in counting; **eg** *one, seven, nineteen*.
➤ See Units 2, 13, 23, 26, 30–31

clause a group of words containing a verb. See also **main clause** and **subordinate clause**.
➤ See Unit 1

collective noun a noun that refers to a group of people or things, which can be used with a singular or plural verb; **eg** *committee, team, family*.
➤ See Unit 14

comparative an adjective or adverb with '–er' on the end or 'more' in front of it; **eg** *slower, more important, more carefully*.
➤ See Units 35–36

complement a noun group or adjective, which comes after a link verb such as 'be', and gives more information about the subject of the clause; **eg** *She is a* **teacher**… *She is* **tired**.
➤ See Units 1–3, 73

complex sentence a sentence consisting of a main clause and a subordinate clause; **eg** *She wasn't thinking very quickly because she was tired*.
➤ See Unit 1

compound sentence a sentence consisting of two or more main clauses linked by 'and', 'or' or 'but'; **eg** *They picked her up and took her straight into the house*.
➤ See Unit 1

conditional clause a subordinate clause, usually starting with 'if' or 'unless', which is used to talk about possible situations and their results; **eg** *They would be rich* **if they had taken my advice**… *We'll go to the park,* **unless it rains**.
➤ See Units 66–67

GLOSSARY OF GRAMMAR TERMS

conjunction a word such as 'and', 'because', or 'nor', that links two clauses, groups, or words.
➤ See Units 1, 97, 102

continuous tense a tense which contains a form of the verb 'be' and a present participle; eg *She was laughing… They had been playing* badminton. See **tense**.
➤ See Unit 60

contrast clause a subordinate clause, usually introduced by 'although' or 'in spite of the fact that', which contrasts with a main clause; eg *Although I like her, I find her hard to talk to.*
➤ See Unit 99

coordinating conjunction a conjunction such as 'and', 'but', or 'or', which links two main clauses.
➤ See Unit 102

countable noun another name for **count noun**.

count noun a noun which has both singular and plural forms; eg *dog/dogs, foot/feet lemon/lemons.*
➤ See Units 13, 24, 26–27, 29–30

declarative another name for **affirmative**.

defining relative clause a relative clause which identifies the person or thing that is being talked about; eg *…the lady **who lives next door**… I wrote down everything **that she said**.* Compare with **non-defining relative clause**.
➤ See Unit 92

definite article the determiner 'the'.
➤ See Units 24–25

delexical verb a common verb such as 'give', 'have', 'make', or 'take', which has very little meaning in itself and is used with a noun as object that describes the action; eg *She **gave** a small cry… I've just **had** a bath.*
➤ See Unit 56

demonstrative one of the words 'this', 'that', these', and 'those'; eg *…**this** woman. …**that** tree… **That** looks interesting… **This** is fun.*
➤ See Unit 19

descriptive adjective an adjective which describes a person or thing, for example indicating their size, age, shape, or colour, rather than expressing your opinion of that person or thing. Compare with **opinion adjective**.
➤ See Unit 32

determiner one of a group of words including 'the', 'a', 'some', and 'my', which are used at the beginning of a noun group.
➤ See Units 2, 13–14, 23–30

direct object a noun group referring to the person or thing affected by an action, in a clause with a verb in the active voice; eg *She wrote **her name**… I shut **the windows**.*
➤ See Units 16, 20, 51–53

direct speech the actual words spoken by someone.
➤ See Units 74–77

ditransitive verb another name for a verb with two objects, such as 'give', 'take', or 'sell'; eg *She **gave** me a kiss.*
➤ See Unit 52

double-transitive verb another name for a **ditransitive verb**.

'-ed' adjective an adjective which has the same form as the '–ed' form of a regular verb, or the past participle of an irregular verb; eg *…**boiled** potatoes….a **broken** wing.*
➤ See Unit 34

'-ed' form the form of a regular verb used for the past simple and for the past participle.
➤ See Units 3, 57, 94

ellipsis the leaving out of words when they are obvious from the context.

emphasizing adverb an adverb such as 'absolutely' or 'utterly', which modifies adjectives that express extreme qualities, such as 'astonishing' and 'wonderful'; eg *You were **absolutely** wonderful.*
➤ See Unit 43

ergative verb a verb which is both transitive and intransitive in the same meaning. The object of the transitive use is the subject of the intransitive use; eg *He **boiled** a kettle… The kettle **boiled**.*
➤ See Unit 55

first person see **person**.

future tense see **tense**.

gerund another name for the '–ing' form when it is used as a noun.
➤ See Units 69, 71–72

'if'-clause see **conditional clause**.

imperative the form of a verb used when giving orders and commands, which is the same as its base form; eg ***Come** here… **Take** two tablets every four hours… **Enjoy** yourself.*
➤ See Units **4**, 8, 12, 66

impersonal 'it' 'it' used as an impersonal subject to introduce new information; eg ***It's** raining… **It's** ten o'clock.*
➤ See Units 16–17, 33, 47, 73, 76, 96, 101

indefinite adverb a small group of adverbs including 'anywhere' and 'somewhere' which are used to indicate place in a general way.
➤ See Unit 21

indefinite article the determiners 'a' and 'an'.
➤ See Unit 26

indefinite pronoun a small group of pronouns including 'someone' and 'anything' which are used to refer to people or things without saying exactly who or what they are.
➤ See Units **21**, 94–95

indirect object an object used with verbs that take two objects. For example, in 'I gave him the pen' and 'I gave

the pen to him', 'him' is the indirect object and 'pen' is the direct object. Compare with **direct object**.
➤ See Units 16, 20, 52

indirect question a question used to ask for information or help; eg *Do you know **where Jane is?**… I wonder **which hotel it was***.
➤ See Unit 9

indirect speech the words you use to report what someone has said, rather than using their actual words. Also called **reported speech**.
➤ See Units 74–77

infinitive the base form of a verb; eg *I wanted to **go**… She helped me **dig** the garden*. The infinitive is the form you look up in a dictionary.
➤ See Units 11, 33–34, 65, 70, 73, 76–77, 79, 82, 91, 95, 97–98

'-ing' adjective an adjective which has the same form as the present participle of a verb; eg *…a **smiling** face. …a **winning** streak*.
➤ See Unit 34

'-ing' form a verb form ending in '-ing' which is used to form verb tenses, and as an adjective or a noun. Also called the **present participle**.
➤ See Units 3, 34, 69, 71–72, 94

interrogative pronoun one of the pronouns 'who', 'whose', 'whom', 'what', and 'which', when they are used to ask questions.
➤ See Unit 6

interrogative sentence a sentence in the form of a question.
➤ See Unit 5

intransitive verb a verb which does not take an object; eg *She arrived… I was yawning*. Compare with **transitive verb**.
➤ See Unit 51

irregular verb a verb that has three or five forms, or whose forms do not follow the normal rules.
➤ See Unit 3 and appendix of verb tables

link verb a verb which takes a complement rather than an object; eg *be, become, seem, appear*.
➤ See Unit 73

main clause a clause which does not depend on another clause, and is not part of another clause.
➤ See Unit 1

main verb all verbs which are not auxiliaries or modals.
➤ See Units 3, 5, 57

manner clause a subordinate clause which describes the way in which something is done, usually introduced with 'as' or 'like'; eg *She talks **like her mother used to***.
➤ See Units 68, 100

modal a verb such as 'can', 'might', or 'will', which is always the first word in a verb group and is followed by the

base form of a verb. Modals are used to express requests, offers, suggestions, wishes, intentions, politeness, possibility, probability, certainty, obligation, and so on.
➤ See Units 7–8, 18, 60–61, 64, 67, **79–91**, 97

mood the mood of a clause is the way in which the verb forms are used to show whether the clause is a statement, command, or question.

negative a negative clause, question, sentence, or statement is one which has a negative word such as 'not', and indicates the absence or opposite of something, or is used to say that something is not the case; eg *I don't know you… I'll never forget*. Compare with **positive**.
➤ See Units 4, **11–12**, 57, 80

negative word a word such as 'never', 'no', 'not', 'nothing', or 'nowhere', which makes a clause, question, sentence, or statement negative.
➤ See Units 3–4, 7–8, 10–**12**, 21, 23, 27, 30, 80

non-defining relative clause a relative clause which gives more information about someone or something, but which is not needed to identify them because we already know who or what they are; eg *That's Mary, **who was at university with me***. Compare with **defining relative clause**.
➤ See Unit 93

non-finite clause a 'to'–infinitive clause, '–ed' clause, or '–ing' clause.
➤ See Units 69–73, 94

noun a word which refers to people, things, ideas, feelings, or qualities; eg *woman, Harry, guilt*.
➤ See Units 2, **13–15**, 23–31, 48, 56, 94–95

noun group a group of words which acts as the subject, complement, or object of a verb, or as the object of a preposition.
➤ See Units 1–**2**, 38–40, 44

object a noun group which refers to a person or thing that is affected by the action described by a verb or preposition. Compare with **subject**.
➤ See Units 16, 20, **51–56**

object pronoun one of a set of pronouns including 'me', 'him', and 'them', which are used as the object of a verb or preposition. Object pronouns are also used as complements after 'be'; eg *I hit **him**… It's **me***.
➤ See Unit 16

opinion adjective an adjective which you use to express your opinion of a person or thing, rather than just describing them. Compare with **descriptive adjective**.
➤ See Unit 32

ordinal number a number used to indicate where something comes in an order or sequence; eg *first, fifth, tenth, hundredth*.

participle a verb form used for making different tenses.

Verbs have two participles, a present participle and a past participle.
➤ See Units 3, 34, 57, 69, 71–72, 94

particle an adverb or preposition which combines with verbs to form phrasal verbs.
➤ See Unit 50

passive voice verb groups such as 'was given', 'were taken', 'had been made', which are used when the subject of the verb is the person or thing that is affected by the action. Compare with **active voice**.
➤ See Units 70, **78**

past form the form of a verb, often ending in '–ed', which is used for the past simple tense.
➤ See Units 3, 59

past participle a verb form which is used to form perfect tenses and passives. Some past participles are also used as adjectives; **eg** *watched, broken.*
➤ See Units 3, 57, 70, 94

past tense see **tense**.

perfect tense see **tense**.

person one of the three classes of people who can be involved in something that is said. The person or people who are speaking or writing are called the first person ('I', 'we'). The person or people who are listening or reading are called the second person ('you'). The person, people or things that are being talked about are called the third person ('he', 'she', 'it', 'they').

personal pronoun one of the group of words including 'I', 'you', and 'me', which are used to refer back to yourself, the people you are talking to, or the people or things you are talking about. See also **object pronoun** and **subject pronoun**.
➤ See Units **16**, 102

phrasal verb a combination of a verb and a particle, which together have a different meaning to the verb on its own; **eg** *back down, hand over, look forward to.*
➤ See Units **50**, 69

plural the form of a count noun or verb, which is used to refer to or talk about more than one person or thing; **eg** *Dogs have ears… The women were outside.*
➤ See Units 2, 13–14

plural noun a noun which is normally used only in the plural form; **eg** *trousers, scissors.*
➤ See Unit 14

positive a positive clause, question, sentence, or statement is one which does not contain a negative word such as 'not'. Compare with **negative.**
➤ See Units 21, 29–30, 41–42

possessive one of the determiners 'my', 'your', 'his', 'her', 'its', 'our', or 'their', which is used to show that one person or thing belongs to another; **eg** *…your car.*
➤ See Units 22–23

possessive adjective another name for **possessive**.
➤ See Units **22**–23

possessive pronoun one of the pronouns 'mine', 'yours', 'hers', 'his', 'ours', or 'theirs'.
➤ See Units **22**, 37

preposition a word such as 'by', 'with' or 'from', which is always followed by a noun group.
➤ See Units 5, 16, 20, **44–50**, 52, 54, 92

prepositional phrase a structure consisting of a preposition followed by a noun group as its object; **eg** *on the table, by the sea.*
➤ See Units 22, 34, 36, 38–40, 43, 46–49, 97

present participle see **'-ing' form**.

present tense see **tense**.

progressive tense another name for **continuous tense**.
➤ See Unit 60

pronoun a word which you use instead of a noun, when you do not need or want to name someone or something directly; **eg** *it, you, none.*
➤ See Units 6, **16–17**, 19–22, 37, 92–95, 102

proper noun a noun which is the name of a particular person, place, organization, or building. Proper nouns are always written with a capital letter; **eg** *Nigel, Edinburgh, the United Nations, Christmas.*
➤ See Unit 25

purpose clause a subordinate clause which is used to talk about the intention that someone has when they do something; **eg** *I came here **in order to ask you out to dinner**.*
➤ See Unit 97

qualifier a word or group of words, such as an adjective, prepositional phrase, or relative clause, which comes after a noun and gives more information about it; **eg** *…the person **involved**. …a book **with a blue cover**. …the shop **that I went into**.*
➤ See Units 22, 92–94

question a sentence which normally has the verb in front of the subject, and which is used to ask someone about something; **eg** *Have you any money?*
➤ See Units **5–10**, 11, 58, 75, 80

question tag an auxiliary or modal with a pronoun, which is used to turn a statement into a question. **eg** *He's very friendly, **isn't he?**… I can come, **can't I?***
➤ See Units 7–8

reason clause a subordinate clause, usually introduced by 'because', 'since', or 'as', which is used to explain why something happens or is done; **eg** *Since you're here, we'll start.*
➤ See Unit 97

reciprocal verb a verb which describes an action which involves two people doing the same thing to each other; **eg** *I **met** you at the dance… We've **met** one another*

*before… They **met** in the street.*
➤ See Unit 54

reflexive pronoun a pronoun ending in '–self' or '–selves', such as 'myself' or 'themselves', which you use as the object of a verb when you want to say that the object is the same person or thing as the subject of the verb in the same clause; **eg** *He hurt **himself**.*
➤ See Unit 20

reflexive verb a verb which is normally used with a reflexive pronoun as object; **eg** *He **contented himself** with the thought that he had the only set of keys to the car.*
➤ See Unit 53

regular verb a verb that has four forms, and follows the normal rules.
➤ See Unit 3

relative clause a subordinate clause which gives more information about someone or something mentioned in the main clause. See also **defining relative clause** and **non-defining relative clause**.
➤ See Units **92–93**, 95

relative pronoun 'that' or a 'wh'–word such as 'who' or 'which', when it is used to introduce a relative clause; **eg** *…the girl **who** was carrying the bag.*
➤ See Units 92–93

reported clause the clause in a report structure which indicates what someone has said; **eg** *She said **that I couldn't see her**.*
➤ See Units 74–77

reported question a question which is reported using a report structure rather than the exact words used by the speaker. See also **indirect question**.
➤ See Unit 75

reported speech the words you use to report what someone has said, rather than using their actual words. Also called **indirect speech**.
➤ See Units 74–77

reporting clause the clause in a report structure which contains the reporting verb.
➤ See Units 74, 76

reporting verb a verb which describes what people say or think; **eg** *suggest, say, wonder.*
➤ See Units 74, 76–77

report structure a structure which is used to report what someone says or thinks, rather than repeating their exact words; **eg** *She told me she'd be late.*
➤ See Units 74–77

result clause a subordinate clause introduced by 'so', 'so…that', or 'such…(that)', which indicates the result of an action or situation; **eg** *I don't think there's any more news, **so I'll finish**.*
➤ See Unit 98

second person see **person**.

semi-modal a term used by some grammars to refer to the verbs 'dare', 'need', and 'used to', which behave like modals in some structures.
➤ See Units 63, 72, 90

sentence a group of words which express a statement, question, or command. A sentence usually has a verb and a subject, and may be a simple sentence with one clause, or a compound or complex sentence with two or more clauses. In writing, a sentence has a capital letter at the beginning and a full–stop, question mark, or exclamation mark at the end.
➤ See Units 1, 66, 92–93, 96–102

short form a form in which one or more letters are omitted and two words are joined together, for example an auxiliary or modal and 'not', or a subject pronoun and an auxiliary or modal; **eg** *aren't, couldn't, he'd, I'm, it's, she's.*
➤ See Unit 11

simple tense a present or past tense formed without using an auxiliary verb; **eg** *…I **wait**. …she **sang**.* See **tense**.
➤ See Units 58–63, 65

singular the form of a count noun or verb which is used to refer to or talk about one person or thing; **eg** *A **dog** **was** in the car… That **woman is** my **mother**.*
➤ See Units 13–14

singular noun a noun which is normally used only in the singular form; **eg** *the sun, a bath.*
➤ See Unit 14

strong verb another name for **irregular verb**.

subject the noun group in a clause that refers to the person or thing who does the action expressed by the verb; **eg** ***We** were going shopping.* Compare with **object**.
➤ See Units 1, 3, 5, 9–10, 13, 15–18, 21, 25, 38, 53, 55, 69–71, 75–77, 80, 102

subject pronoun one of the set of pronouns including 'I', 'she', and 'they', which are used as the subject of a verb.
➤ See Unit 16

subordinate clause a clause which must be used with a main clause and is not usually used alone, for example a time clause, conditional clause, relative clause, or result clause, and which begins with a subordinating conjunction such as 'because' or 'while'.
➤ See Units 1, 66–68, 92–93, 96–100, 102

subordinating conjunction a conjunction such as 'although', 'as if', 'because' or 'while', which you use to begin a subordinate clause; **eg** *He laughed **as if** he'd said something funny.*
➤ See Unit 102

superlative an adjective or adverb with '–est' on the end or 'most' in front of it; **eg** *thinnest, quickest, most beautiful.*
➤ See Units 32, **35–36**, 70

tag question a statement to which a question tag has

been added; **eg** *She's quiet, isn't she?... You've got a car, haven't you?*
➤ See Units 7–8

tense the form of a verb which shows whether you are referring to the past, present, or future.
➤ See Units 57–65

future 'will' or 'shall' with the base form of the verb, used to refer to future events; **eg** *She **will come** tomorrow... I **shall** ask her as soon as I see her.*
➤ See Unit 64

future continuous 'will' or 'shall' with 'be' and a present participle, used to refer to future events; **eg** *She **will be going** soon.*
➤ See Units 60, 64

future perfect 'will' or 'shall' with 'have' and a past participle, used to refer to future events; **eg** *I **shall have finished** by tomorrow.*
➤ See Units 61, 64

future perfect continuous 'will' or 'shall' with 'have been' and a present participle, used to refer to future events; **eg** *I **will have been walking** for three hours by then.*
➤ See Units 60–61, 64

past simple the past form of a verb, used to refer to past events; **eg** *They **waited**.*
➤ See Units 59, 63, 74

past continuous 'was' or 'were' with a present participle, usually used to refer to past events; **eg** *They **were worrying** about it all day yesterday.*
➤ See Units 59–60, 63

past perfect 'had' with a past participle, used to refer to past events; **eg** *She **had finished** her meal.*
➤ See Units 59, 61, 63

past perfect continuous 'had been' with a present participle, used to refer to past events; **eg** *He **had been waiting** for hours.*
➤ See Units 59–61, 63

present simple the base form and the third person singular form of a verb, usually used to refer to present events; **eg** *I **like** bananas... My sister **hates** them.*
➤ See Units 58, 62, 65, 74

present continuous the present simple of 'be' with a present participle, usually used to refer to present events; **eg** *Things **are improving**... She **is working**.*
➤ See Units 58, 60, 62, 65

present perfect 'have' or 'has' with a past participle, used to refer to past events which exist in the present; **eg** *She **has loved** him for over ten years.*
➤ See Units 58, 61, 63, 65

present perfect continuous 'have been' or 'has been' with a present participle, used to refer to past events which continue in the present; **eg** *We **have been sitting** here for hours.*

➤ See Units 58, 60–61, 63

'that'-clause a clause starting with 'that', used mainly when reporting what someone has said; **eg** *She said **that she'd wash up for me**.*
➤ See Units 33–34, 76–77, 95

third person see **person**.

time clause a subordinate clause which indicates the time of an event; **eg** *I'll phone you **when I get back**.*
➤ See Unit 96

time expression a noun group used as an adverbial of time; **eg** *last night, the day after tomorrow, the next time.*
➤ See Unit 40

'to'-infinitive the base form of a verb preceded by 'to'; **eg** *to go, to have, to jump.*
➤ See Units 11, 33–34, 65, 70–73, 76–77, 79, 82, 91, 95, 97–98

transitive verb a verb which takes an object; **eg** *She's **wasting** her money.* Compare with **intransitive verb**.
➤ See Unit 51

uncountable noun another name for **uncount noun**.

uncount noun a noun which has only one form, takes a singular verb, and is not used with 'a' or numbers. Uncount nouns often refer to substances, qualities, feelings, activities, and abstract ideas; **eg** *coal, courage, anger, help, fun.*
➤ See Units **15**, 24, 27, 29–30

verb a word which is used with a subject to say what someone or something does, or what happens to them; **eg** *sing, spill, die.*
➤ See Units 3–4, 10, 49–65, 69–78

verb group a main verb, or a main verb with one or more auxiliaries, a modal, or a modal and an auxiliary, which is used with a subject to say what someone does, or what happens to them; **eg** *I'll **show** them... She's **been** sick.*
➤ See Units 1, **3**, 5, 11–12, 57, 79

'wh'-question a question which expects the answer to give more information than just 'yes' or 'no'; **eg** *What happened next?... Where did he go?* Compare with **'yes/no'-question**.
➤ See Units 5–**6**, 9, 75

'wh'-word one of a group of words starting with 'wh-', such as 'what', 'when' or 'who', which are used in 'wh'–questions. 'How' is also called a 'wh'–word because it behaves like the other 'wh'–words.
➤ See Units 5–**6**, 70, 75, 77, 92–93

'yes/no'-question a question which can be answered by just 'yes' or 'no', without giving any more information; **eg** *Would you like some more tea?* Compare with **'wh'-question**.
➤ See Units 5, 7, 10, 75

GRAMMAR UNITS

Clauses and sentences

Main points

Simple sentences have one clause.

Clauses usually consist of a noun group as the subject, and a verb group.

Clauses can also have another noun group as the object or complement.

Clauses can have an adverbial, also called an adjunct.

Changing the order of the words in a clause can change its meaning.

Compound sentences consist of two or more main clauses. Complex sentences always include a subordinate clause, as well as one or more main clauses.

1 A simple sentence has one clause, beginning with a noun group called the subject. The subject is the person or thing that the sentence is about. This is followed by a verb group, which tells you what the subject is doing, or describes the subject's situation.

> *I waited.*
> *The girl screamed.*

2 The verb group may be followed by another noun group, which is called the object. The object is the person or thing affected by the action or situation.

> *He opened <u>the car door.</u>*
> *She married <u>a young engineer.</u>*

After link verbs like 'be', 'become', 'feel', and 'seem', the verb group may be followed by a noun group or an adjective, called a complement. The complement tells you more about the subject.

> *She was <u>a doctor.</u>*
> *He was <u>angry.</u>*

3 The verb group, the object, or the complement can be followed by an adverb or a prepositional phrase, called an adverbial. The adverbial tells you more about the action or situation, for example how, when, or where it happens. Adverbials are also called adjuncts.

> *They shouted <u>loudly.</u>*
> *She won the competition <u>last week.</u>*
> *He was a policeman <u>in Birmingham.</u>*

4 The word order of a clause is different when the clause is a statement, a question, or a command.

> *<u>He speaks</u> English very well.* (statement)
> *<u>Did she win</u> at the Olympics?* (question)
> *<u>Stop</u> her.* (command)

Note that the subject is omitted in commands, so the verb comes first.

5 A compound sentence has two or more main clauses: that is, clauses which are equally important. You join them with 'and', 'but', or 'or'.

> *He met Jane at the station <u>and</u> went shopping.*
> *I wanted to go <u>but</u> I felt too ill.*
> *You can come now <u>or</u> you can meet us there later.*

Note that the order of the two clauses can change the meaning of the sentence.

> *He went shopping <u>and</u> met Jane at the station.*

If the subject of both clauses is the same, you usually omit the subject in the second clause.

> *I wanted to go <u>but felt</u> too ill.*

6 A complex sentence contains a subordinate clause and at least one main clause. A subordinate clause gives information about a main clause, and is introduced by a conjunction such as 'because', 'if', 'that', or a 'wh'-word. Subordinate clauses can come before, after, or inside the main clause.

> *<u>When he stopped,</u> no one said anything.*
> *<u>If you want,</u> I'll teach you.*
> *They were going by car <u>because it was more comfortable.</u>*
> *I told him <u>that nothing was going to happen to me.</u>*
> *The car <u>that I drove</u> was a Ford.*
> *The man <u>who came into the room</u> was small.*

Practice

A **Change the meaning of these sentences by changing the subject and the object.**

1 John loves Mary. / Mary loves John.
2 Charlie Brown kicked the horse. / The Horse kicked Charlie Brown
3 A big fish ate Jonah. / Jonah ate a big fish
4 Mrs Jackson taught my father. / My father taught Mrs Jackson
5 The giant killed Jack. / Jack killed the giant

B **Put these words and phrases in the right order to make sentences. The letters in brackets show the structure of your sentences. S stands for Subject, V for Verb, O for Object, and A for Adverbial.**

1 a bone / the dog / ate. / (S + V + O) The dog ate a bone.
2 everybody / hard / worked. / (S + V + A) Everybody worked hard
3 the cat / the mouse / caught. / (S + V + O) The cat caught the mouse
4 children / kittens / love. / (S + V + O) The children love kittens
5 the answer / nobody / knows. / (S + V + O) Nobody knows the answer
6 a new dress / Mary / bought / yesterday. / (S + V + O + A)
7 the film / all of us / last night / enjoyed. / (S + V + O + A)
8 John Black / to the supermarket / went. / (S + V + A)
9 her car / Janet Black / to the airport / drove. / (S + V + O + A)
10 a cup of coffee / Mike / after lunch / drank. / (S + V + O + A)

C **Read the following sentences and write down their structure using the letters S (for Subject), V (for Verb), O (for Object), and A (for Adverbial).**

1 The dog bit Peter very badly. / S + V + O + A
2 Bill ran fast. /
3 I ate some fish and chips for supper. /
4 We all went home. /
5 Most of my friends enjoyed the game last week. /
6 John saw Fred yesterday. /

D **Change these sentences from negative statements to negative questions.**

1 They don't live near here. / Don't they live near here?
2 You didn't see Jill last Friday. / Didn't you see Jill last Friday
3 They haven't arrived yet. / Haven't they arrived yet
4 Peter won't help you. / Won't Peter help you
5 Henry can't speak French. / Can't Henry speak French
6 He doesn't smoke any more. / Doesn't he smoke any more
7 They didn't understand him. / Didn't they understand him
8 John hasn't met Mary yet. / Hasn't John met Mary yet

3

Noun groups

Main points

Noun groups can be the subject, object, or complement of a verb, or the object of a preposition.

Noun groups can be nouns on their own, but often include other words such as determiners, numbers, and adjectives.

Noun groups can also be pronouns.

Singular noun groups take singular verbs, plural noun groups take plural verbs.

1 Noun groups are used to say which people or things you are talking about. They can be the subject or object of a verb.

> *Strawberries are very expensive now.*
> *Keith likes strawberries.*

A noun group can also be the complement of a link verb such as 'be', 'become', 'feel', or 'seem'.

> *She became champion in 1964*
> *He seemed a nice man.*

A noun group can be used after a preposition, and is often called the object of the preposition.

> *I saw him in town.*
> *She was very ill for six months.*

2 A noun group can be a noun on its own, but it often includes other words. A noun group can have a determiner such as 'the' or 'a'. You put determiners at the beginning of the noun group.

> *The girls were not in the house.*
> *He was eating an apple.*

3 A noun group can include an adjective. You usually put the adjective in front of the noun.

> *He was using blue ink.*
> *I like living in a big city.*

Sometimes you can use another noun in front of the noun.

> *I like chocolate cake.*
> *She wanted a job in the oil industry.*

A noun with 's (apostrophe s) is used in front of another noun to show who or what something belongs to or is connected with.

> *I held Sheila's hand very tightly.*
> *He pressed a button on the ship's radio.*

4 A noun group can also have an adverbial, a relative clause, or a 'to'-infinitive clause after it, which makes it more precise.

> *I spoke to a girl in a dark grey dress.*
> *She wrote to the man who employed me.*
> *I was trying to think of a way to stop him.*

A common adverbial used after a noun is a prepositional phrase beginning with 'of'.

> *He tied the rope to a large block of stone.*
> *The front door of the house was wide open.*

Participles and some adjectives can also be used after a noun.
▶ See Units 31 and 94.

> *She pointed to the three cards lying on the table.*
> *He is the only man available.*

5 Numbers come after determiners and before adjectives.

> *I had to pay a thousand dollars.*
> *Three tall men came out of the shed.*

6 A noun group can also be a pronoun. You often use a pronoun when you are referring back to a person or thing that you have already mentioned.

> *I've got two boys, and they both enjoy playing football.*

You also use a pronoun when you do not know who the person or thing is, or do not want to be precise.

> *Someone is coming to mend it tomorrow.*

7 A noun group can refer to one or more people or things. Many nouns have a singular form referring to one person or thing, and a plural form referring to more than one person or thing. ▶ See Unit 13.

> *My dog never bites people.*
> *She likes dogs.*

Similarly, different pronouns are used in the singular and in the plural.

> *I am going home now.*
> *We want more money.*

When a singular noun group is the subject, it takes a singular verb. When a plural noun group is the subject, it takes a plural verb.

> *His son plays football for the school.*
> *Her letters are always very short.*

Practice

A Expand the noun group in these sentences by adding the words given.

1 There's a man.
  ...There's an old man................... *(old)*
  ...There's an old man standing by the bus stop.............. *(standing by the bus stop)*
  ...There's an old man with an umbrella standing by the bus stop............. *(with an umbrella)*

2 There's a dog.
  .... *(big)*
  ....*(running out of the shop)*
  .... *(carrying a bone)*

3 There's a man.
  ....*(fat)*
  ....*(with a knife in his hand)*
  .... *(running after the dog)*

4 There's a woman.
  ....*(young)*
  .... *(with long hair)*
  .... *(standing outside the shop)*

B Complete the following by adding these 'to'-infinitives.

| to carry | to catch | to do | to drive through | to wear | to meet |
| to post | to play | to read | to visit | to eat | |

1 I'm hungry. I haven't had anything ...*to eat.*...................
2 He's very busy. He has a lot of work ...*to do*...................
3 It's a wonderful place for children ...*to play*...................
4 I mustn't be late. I have some important people .....*to meet*...................
5 Can you call at the post office? There are a few letters ....*to post*...................
6 When I am travelling I always take a good book ....*to read*...................
7 If I'm going to the party I must buy a new dress ....*to wear*...................
8 I'll have to take a taxi. I've got too much luggage .....*to carry*...................
9 I'll have to leave now. I have a train ....*to catch*...................
10 Oxford is a wonderful place ....*to visit*..............., but it's a dreadful place
  ....*to drive through*

5

The verb group

Main points

In a clause, the verb group usually comes after the subject and always has a main verb.

The main verb has several different forms.

Verb groups can also include one or two auxiliaries, or a modal, or a modal and one or two auxiliaries.

The verb group changes in negative clauses and questions.

Some verb groups are followed by an adverbial, a complement, an object, or two objects.

1 The verb group in a clause is used to say what is happening in an action or situation. You usually put the verb group immediately after the subject. The verb group always includes a main verb.

> I _waited._
> They _killed_ the elephants.

2 Regular verbs have four forms: the base form, the third person singular form of the present simple, the '-ing' form or present participle, and the '-ed' form used for the past simple and for the past participle.

ask	asks	asking	asked
dance	dances	dancing	danced
reach	reaches	reaching	reached
try	tries	trying	tried
dip	dips	dipping	dipped

Irregular verbs may have three forms, four forms, or five forms.
Note that 'be' has eight forms.

cost	costs	costing		
think	thinks	thinking	thought	
swim	swims	swimming	swam	swum
be	am/is/are	being	was/were	been

➤ See Appendix for details of verb forms.

3 The main verb can have one or two auxiliaries in front of it.

> I _had met_ him in Zermatt.
> The car _was being repaired._

The main verb can have a modal in front of it.

> You _can go_ now.
> I _would like_ to ask you a question.

The main verb can have a modal and one or two auxiliaries in front of it.

> I _could have spent_ the whole year on it.
> She _would have been delighted_ to see you.

4 In negative clauses, you have to use a modal or auxiliary and put 'not' after the first word of the verb group.

> He _does not speak_ English very well.
> I _was not smiling._
> It _could not have been_ wrong.

Note that you often use short forms rather than 'not'.

> I _didn't_ know that.
> He _couldn't_ see it.

5 In 'yes/no' questions, you have to put an auxiliary or modal first, then the subject, then the rest of the verb group.

> _Did_ you _meet_ George?
> _Couldn't_ you _have been_ a bit quieter?

In 'wh'-questions, you put the 'wh'-word first. If the 'wh'-word is the subject, you put the verb group next.

> Which _came_ first?
> Who _could have done_ it?

If the 'wh'-word is the object or an adverbial, you must use an auxiliary or modal next, then the subject, then the rest of the verb group.

> What _did_ you _do?_
> Where _could_ she _be going?_

6 Some verb groups have an object or two objects after them.
➤ See Units 51 and 52.

> He closed _the door._
> She sends _you her love._

Verb groups involving link verbs, such as 'be', have a complement after them.
➤ See Unit 73.

> They were _sailors._
> She felt _happy._

Some verb groups have an adverbial after them.

> We walked _through the park._
> She put the letter _on the table._

Practice

A **Underline the main verbs in these sentences. The number in brackets tells you how many main verbs there are.**

1 Jack will <u>kill</u> the giant. (1)
2 We can come round tomorrow. (1)
3 I haven't heard from her since she went on holiday. (2)
4 I would have told her, if she had asked. (2)
5 Did you walk to school, or did you go on your bike? (2)
6 You could have stayed with us, if we had known you were coming. (3)
7 He said he didn't know who was coming. (3)
8 They woke up when they heard the noise. (2)
9 You must do what the boss tells you. (2)
10 Do you always do what the boss tells you? (2)

B **Underline the auxiliaries.**

1 I <u>don't</u> speak English very well. (1)
2 We haven't seen them. They weren't at home when we called. (1)
3 We were playing tennis when the storm started. (1)
4 They are coming as soon as they have finished work. (2)
5 John had seen Mary just twice before. (1)
6 Do you live here or are you just visiting? (2)
7 Do you know each other or haven't you met before? (2)
8 Will you be coming early or are you arriving later? (2)
9 This cup has been broken. (2)
10 They will have been found by now. (2)

C **Underline the modals.**

1 You <u>will</u> get a good seat if you get there early. (1)
2 I'll ask Fred if he can help. (2)
3 Ken will certainly come if he can find the time. (2)
4 Could you keep quiet while we are trying to listen to the music? (1)
5 I would help you if I could. (2)
6 I suppose you should tell her as soon as you can. (2)
7 They might agree but on the other hand they might not. (2)
8 I think they may come if they can find the time. (2)
9 You should have known that Jack would try to make trouble. (2)
10 They would probably have done it if they could have found the money. (2)

The imperative and 'let'

Main points

The imperative is the same as the base form of a verb.

You form a negative imperative with 'do not', 'don't', or 'never'.

You use the imperative to ask or tell someone to do something, or to give advice, warnings, or instructions on how to do something.

You use 'let' when you are offering to do something, making suggestions, or telling someone to do something.

1 The imperative is the same as the base form of a verb. You do not use a pronoun in front of it.

> *Come* to my place.
> *Start* when you hear the bell.

2 You form a negative imperative by putting 'do not', 'don't', or 'never' in front of the verb.

> *Do not write* in this book.
> *Don't go* so fast.
> *Never open* the front door to strangers.

3 You use the imperative when you are:

- asking or telling someone to do something

> *Pass* the salt.
> *Hurry up!*

- giving someone advice or a warning

> *Mind* your head.
> *Take* care!

- giving someone instructions on how to do something

> *Put* this bit over here, so it fits into that hole.
> *Turn* right off Broadway into Caxton Street.

4 When you want to make an imperative more polite or more emphatic, you can put 'do' in front of it.

> *Do have* a chocolate biscuit.
> *Do stop* crying.
> *Do be* careful.

5 The imperative is also used in written instructions on how to do something, for example on notices and packets of food, and in books.

> *To report faults, dial 6666.*
> *Store in a dry place.*
> *Fry the chopped onion and pepper in the oil.*

Note that written instructions usually have to be short. This means that words such as 'the' are often omitted.

> *Turn off switch.*
> *In case of fire, break glass.*

Written imperatives are also used to give warnings.

> *Reduce speed now.*

6 You use 'let me' followed by the base form of a verb when you are offering to do something for someone.

> *Let me take your coat.*
> *Let me give you a few details.*

7 You use 'let's' followed by the base form of a verb when you are suggesting what you and someone else should do.

> *Let's go outside.*
> *Let's look at our map.*

Note that the form 'let us' is only used in formal or written English.

> *Let us consider a very simple example.*

You put 'do' before 'let's' when you are very keen to do something.

> *Do let's get a taxi.*

The negative of 'let's' is 'let's not' or 'don't let's'.

> *Let's not talk about that.*
> *Don't let's actually write it in the book.*

8 You use 'let' followed by a noun group and the base form of a verb when you are telling someone to do something or to allow someone else to do it.

> *Let me see it.*
> *Let Philip have a look at it.*

A **Where might you find these instructions? Choose the right answer from the list below.**

1 Once opened keep in fridge and eat within 3 days. ....*A jar of meat paste*...........................

2 Do not spray directly on food. Keep in a safe place away from young children. ....

3 Adults: Take 1 teaspoonful every two or three hours. ....

4 Brush regularly and thoroughly – ideally after every meal. ....

5 Dilute to taste. ....

6 Cut out this coupon and save 15p on your next packet of cornflakes. ....

7 If pouring oil back into bottle, allow it to cool first. ....

8 Shake well before opening. ....

9 Store in a cool dry place. ....

a packet of breakfast cereal	a bottle of cooking oil	a box of cheese biscuits
a tin of milk	an insect spray	a jar of meat paste
a bottle of orange squash	a tube of toothpaste	a bottle of cough mixture

B **These instructions appear in public telephone boxes in Britain. Can you put them in the correct order?**

1 Give the address where help is needed.   a ...*Dial 999 for emergency*...................

2 Wait for the emergency service to answer.   b ....

3 Dial 999 for emergency.   c ....

4 Tell the operator which service you want.   d ....

5 Give any other necessary information.   e ....

6 Give the telephone number shown on the phone. f ....

Check the answer then complete this short paragraph.

First you ....*dial 999*.............. , ... , and ....

Then you give .... , ... , and

....

C **Rewrite the suggestions and requests in bold, starting with 'don't'.**

1 **You shouldn't touch that.** It's very hot. / ......*Don't touch that.*............................

2 She's very tired. **I hope you won't wake her up.** / Please ....

3 He'll be in a hurry. **You mustn't keep him waiting.** / ....

4 It's a secret. **You mustn't tell anyone.** / ....

5 **You mustn't bother me now.** I'm much too busy. / ....

D **Make each of the following sentences into an offer with 'let me', or a suggestion with 'let's'.**

1 I'll take your coat. / ...*Let me take your coat.*...

2 I think we should go home now. / ...*Let's go home now.*...

3 Can I carry that bag for you? / ....

4 We could telephone for help. / ....

5 I'll help you. / ....

6 I think we should start now. / ....

▶ **Bank**

Questions

Main points

In most questions the first verb comes before the subject.

'Yes/no'-questions begin with an auxiliary or a modal.

'Wh'-questions begin with a 'wh'-word.

[1] Questions which can be answered 'yes' or 'no' are called 'yes/no'-questions.

> *'Are you ready?'* – 'Yes.'
> *'Have you read this magazine?'* – 'No.'

If the verb group has more than one word, the first word comes at the beginning of the sentence, before the subject. The rest of the verb group comes after the subject.

> *Is he* coming?
> *Can John* swim?
> *Will you* have finished by lunchtime?
> *Couldn't you* have been a bit quieter?
> *Has he* been working?

[2] If the verb group consists of only a main verb, you use the auxiliary 'do', 'does', or 'did' at the beginning of the sentence, before the subject. After the subject you use the base form of the verb.

> *Do the British* take sport seriously?
> *Does that* sound like anyone you know?
> *Did he* go to the fair?

Note that when the main verb is 'do', you still have to add 'do', 'does', 'did' before the subject.

> *Do they* do the work themselves?
> *Did you* do an 'O' Level in German?

[3] If the main verb is 'have', you usually put 'do', 'does', or 'did' before the subject.

> *Does anyone have* a question?
> *Did you have* a good flight?

When 'have' means 'own' or 'possess', you can put it before the subject, without using 'do', 'does', or 'did', but this is less common.

> *Has he* any idea what it's like?

[4] If the main verb is the present simple or past simple of 'be', you put the verb at the beginning of the sentence, before the subject.

> *Are you* ready?
> *Was it* lonely without us?

[5] When you want someone to give you more information than just 'yes' or 'no', you ask a 'wh'-question, which begins with a 'wh'-word:

what	when	where	which	who
whom	whose	why	how	

Note that 'whom' is only used in formal English.

[6] When a 'wh'-word is the subject of a question, the 'wh'-word comes first, then the verb group. You do not add 'do', 'does', or 'did' as an auxiliary.

> *What* happened?
> *Which* is the best restaurant?
> *Who* could have done it?

[7] When a 'wh'-word is the object of a verb or preposition, the 'wh'-word comes first, then you follow the rules for 'yes/no'-questions, adding 'do', 'does', or 'did' where necessary.

> *How many* are there?
> *Which* do you like best?

If there is a preposition, it comes at the end. However, you always put the preposition before 'whom'.

> *What's* this *for?*
> *With whom* were you talking?

Note that you follow the same rules as for 'wh'-words as objects when the question begins with 'when', 'where', 'why', or 'how'.

> *When* would you be coming down?
> *Why* did you do it?
> *Where* did you get that *from?*

[8] You can also use 'what', 'which', 'whose', 'how many', and 'how much' with a noun.

> *Whose idea* was it?
> *How much money* have we got in the bank?

You can use 'which', 'how many', and 'how much' with 'of' and a noun group.

> *Which of* the suggested answers was the correct one?
> *How many of* them bothered to come?

➤ See Unit 6 for more information on 'wh'-words.

Practice

A **Expand the 'What about…?' phrases to make 'yes/no'-questions.**

1 John can swim. What about Henry? / .... *Can Henry swim?* ....

2 I've read the newspaper. What about you? / ....

3 I often go for a walk in the park. What about you? / ....

4 Helen lives near here. What about Becky? / ....

5 My kids have gone back to school. What about your children? / ....

6 I'll be home for lunch. What about Sally and Peter? / ....

7 I could have eaten a bit more. What about you? / ....

8 John will have arrived by noon. What about Sandra? / ....

9 I never learned German at school. What about you? / ....

10 I do most of the cooking at home. What about you? / ....

11 Peter's here. What about Joe? / ....

12 John and Jean are here. What about Alan and Tina? / ....

B **Rearrange the parts of the sentences to make questions with 'wh'-words as subject.**

1 How many people / to the party / next week / will be coming? / ..... *How many people will be* .....
coming to the party next week?

2 Which team / first prize / won / at the weekend? / ....

3 What / when you were late / happened / this morning / for work? / ....

4 Who / the answer / told you / to the exam question? / ....

5 Who / next door / lives / to you? / ....

6 What / to this question / the right answer / is? / ....

7 Whose car / that red one / over there / is? / ....

8 How many students / to your English class / come? / ....

C **Expand the 'What about…?' phrases to make questions with 'wh'-words as object.**

1 I've written twenty letters. What about you? / How many ... *letters have you written?* ....

2 I like soft chocolates best. What about you? / Which ....

3 Jack came on his bike. What about you? / How ....

4 Karen can swim over ten kilometres. What about Jim? / How far ....

5 We got hundreds of cards. What about you? / How many ....

6 We'll be there at about six o'clock. What about Mary and Bill? / What time ....

7 John arrived at about eight. What about Kathy? / When ....

8 I will have finished work by five. What about you? / ....

D **Now do these questions starting and finishing with the words given.**

1 My wife works in the maths department. What about you? / Which ... *department do you work* ... in?

2 I'm going to the dance with Sandy. What about you? / Who .... with?

3 My letter is from Fred. What about yours? / Who .... from?

4 My sister goes to Birmingham University. What about your brother? / Which university .... to?

5 This morning's lecture is about Shakespeare. What about the afternoon lecture? / What ....
.... about?

▶ **Bank**

Main points

You use 'who', 'whom', and 'whose' to ask about people, and 'which' to ask about people or things.

You use 'what' to ask about things, and 'what for' to ask about reasons and purposes.

You use 'how' to ask about the way something happens.

You use 'when' to ask about times, 'why' to ask about reasons, and 'where' to ask about places and directions.

---

1 You use 'who', 'whom', or 'whose' in questions about people. 'Who' is used to ask questions about the subject or object of the verb, or about the object of a preposition.

> _Who_ discovered this?
> _Who_ did he marry?
> _Who_ did you dance with?

In formal English, 'whom' is used as the object of a verb or preposition. The preposition always comes in front of 'whom'.

> _Whom_ did you see?
> _For whom_ were they supposed to do it?

You use 'whose' to ask which person something belongs to or is related to. 'Whose' can be the subject or the object.

> _Whose_ is nearer?
> _Whose_ did you prefer, hers or mine?

2 You use 'which' to ask about one person or thing, out of a number of people or things. 'Which' can be the subject or object.

> _Which_ is your son?
> _Which_ does she want?

3 You use 'what' to ask about things, for example about actions and events. 'What' can be the subject or object.

> _What_ has happened to him?
> _What_ is he selling?
> _What_ will you talk about?

You use 'what...for' to ask about the reason for an action, or the purpose of an object.

> _What_ are you going there _for?_
> _What_ are those lights _for?_

4 You use 'how' to ask about the way in which something happens or is done.

> _How_ did you know we were coming?
> _How_ are you going to get home?

You also use 'how' to ask about the way a person or thing feels or looks.

> _'How_ are you?' – 'Well, _how_ do I look?'

5 'How' is also used:

• with adjectives to ask about the degree of quality that someone or something has

> _How good_ are you at Maths?
> _How hot_ shall I make the curry?

• with adjectives such as 'big', 'old', and 'far' to ask about size, age, and distance

> _How old_ are your children?
> _How far_ is it to Montreal from here?

Note that you do not normally use 'How small', 'How young', or 'How near'.

• with adverbs such as 'long' and 'often' to ask about time, or 'well' to ask about abilities

> _How long_ have you lived here?
> _How well_ can you read?

• with 'many' and 'much' to ask about the number or amount of something

> _How many_ were there?
> _How much_ did he tell you?

6 You use 'when' to ask about points in time or periods of time, 'why' to ask about the reason for an action, and 'where' to ask about place and direction.

> _When_ are you coming home?
> _When_ were you in London?
> _Why_ are you here?
> _Where_ is the station?
> _Where_ are you going?

You can also ask about direction using 'which direction...in' or 'which way'.

> _Which direction_ did he go _in?_
> _Which way_ did he go?

Practice

A Use the 'wh'-words below to complete the questions which follow. Look at Unit 5 as well as Unit 6.

what	when	where	which	who	whose	why	how

1 *What* .... time do you finish work?
2 *Who* .... lives in that big house?
3 *Which* .... of these coats belong to you?
4 *What* .... advice would you give to someone about to leave school?
5 *How* .... old is your daughter now?
6 *Where* .... exactly did you buy that lovely dress? In London?
7 I haven't seen George for ages. .... *When* .... did you last see him?
8 .... *Whose* .... bag is this? It's not yours, is it?
9 About .... *How* .... long does it take to get to Birmingham?
10 .... *How* .... do you get to the post office from here?
11 .... *Where* .... did you live before you came to London?
12 But .... *Why* .... can't you come? Are you busy?
13 .... *Which* .... day does Dad get home?
14 I don't know. .... *Why* .... do you ask?

B Make questions from these sentences by using 'who' or 'what' instead of the words in bold.

1 **George** bought her that necklace. / Who *bought her that necklace?*
2 George bought her **a necklace** . / What *did George buy her?*
3 They have invited **Mary** and **Philip** . / Who ....
4 I've lent that book to **Bill** . / Who ....
5 They gave **the keys** to Peter. / What ....
6 **My daughter** answered the telephone. / Who ....
7 The manager said **no** . / What ....
8 I asked **Andrew** to help. / Who ....
9 We can send **a bunch of flowers** . / What ....
10 **The children** will be at home. / Who ....

C Make questions from these words to complete the story. The replies to the questions are given.

1 Where / your young brother / playing? He had been playing outside. / *Where had your young brother been playing?*
2 How long / your young brother / playing outside? All morning. / ....
3 What / he / ask for? He asked for something to eat. / ....
4 What / you / give him? Bread and peanut butter. / ....
5 How / he / hold the bread? He held it in both hands. / ....
6 Why / he / look so puzzled? Because he couldn't open the door. / ....
7 Why / he / not open the door? He couldn't open the door because his hands were full. / ....
....
8 What / he / do with the bread? He ate it. / ....
9 Where / he / go then? Out into the garden to play. / ....

▶ **Bank**

Question tags: forms

Main points

You add a question tag to a statement to turn it into a question.

A question tag consists of a verb and a pronoun. The verb in a question tag is always an auxiliary, a modal, or a form of the main verb 'be'.

With a positive statement, you usually use a negative question tag containing a short form ending in '-n't'.

With a negative statement, you always use a positive question tag.

1 A question tag is a short phrase that is added to the end of a statement to turn it into a 'yes/no'-question. You use question tags when you want to ask someone to confirm or disagree with what you are saying, or when you want to sound more polite. Question tags are rarely used in formal written English.

> He's very friendly, _isn't he?_
> You haven't seen it before, _have you?_

2 You form a question tag by using an auxiliary, a modal, or a form of the main verb 'be', followed by a pronoun. The pronoun refers to the subject of the statement.

> David's school is quite nice, _isn't it?_
> She made a remarkable recovery, _didn't she?_

3 If the statement contains an auxiliary or modal, the same auxiliary or modal is used in the question tag.

> Jill's coming tomorrow, _isn't she?_
> You _didn't_ know I was an artist, _did_ you?
> You've never been to Benidorm, _have_ you?
> You _will_ stay in touch, _won't_ you?

4 If the statement does not contain an auxiliary, a modal, or 'be' as a main verb, you use 'do', 'does', or 'did' in the question tag.

> You _like_ it here, _don't_ you?
> Sally still _works_ there, _doesn't_ she?
> He _played_ for Ireland, _didn't_ he?

5 If the statement contains the present simple or past simple of 'be' as a main verb, the same form of the verb 'be' is used in the question tag.

> It _is_ quite warm, _isn't_ it?
> They _were_ really rude, _weren't_ they?

6 If the statement contains the simple present or simple past of 'have' as a main verb, you usually use 'do', 'does', or 'did' in the question tag.

> He _has_ a problem, _doesn't_ he?

You can also use the same form of 'have' in the question tag, but this is not very common.

> She _has_ a large house, _hasn't_ she?

7 With a positive statement you normally use a negative question tag, formed by adding '-n't' to the verb.

> You _like_ Ralph a lot, _don't_ you?
> They _are_ beautiful, _aren't_ they?

Note that the negative question tag with 'I' is 'aren't'.

> _I'm_ a fool, _aren't I?_

8 With a negative statement you always use a positive question tag.

> It _doesn't_ work, _does_ it?
> You _won't_ tell anyone else, _will_ you?

Practice

A Here are some of the things people say at parties. Match the statements with the question tags. Look at Unit 8 as well as Unit 7.

1 It's a bit noisy, …
2 We haven't met before, …
3 You're Henry's brother, …
4 Pass this plate round, …
5 Don't drop it, …
6 You live next door, …
7 You're not leaving, …
8 You can stay a bit later, …
9 You'll come again, …
10 That was fun, …

a …will you?
b …don't you?
c …isn't it?
d …aren't you?
e …will you?
f …have we?
g …wasn't it?
h …won't you?
i …can't you?
j …are you?

B Mark and Jenny went into the travel agent's to book a holiday. These are some of the questions that were asked. Add the question tags.

1 It's a lovely place. You haven't been there before, …have you………………………………………?
2 It's a bit expensive. You haven't got anything cheaper, ……………………………………………?
3 You can't give us a discount, ………………………………………………………………………?
4 You haven't had a holiday with us before, ………………………………………………………?
5 That won't be too expensive, ………………………………………………………………………?
6 We went there a couple of years ago, but we didn't like it very much, …………………………?
7 Oh dear. We don't have to fly on a Saturday, ……………………………………………………?
8 And we don't have to pay extra for the coach, …………………………………………………?
9 There won't be any other extras to pay for, ………………………………………………………?

C Mark and Jenny were showing some family photographs to a friend. Here are some of the questions that were asked. Complete the questions by adding the question tags.

1 That's a lovely picture of Sally. She looks just like Mary, …doesn't she……………………………?
2 I think you've seen this one before, ………………………………………………………………?
3 This one was taken in Scotland, ……………………………………………………………………?
4 We took this one on holiday, ………………………………………………………………………?
5 We'll be going there again next year, ……………………………………………………………?
6 You can see the sea in the distance, ………………………………………………………………?
7 That must be Jenny's mother and father, …………………………………………………………?
8 The weather was lovely, ……………………………………………………………………………?
9 Yes, then it started to rain, …………………………………………………………………………?
10 Those mountains look very high, …………………………………………………………………?
11 Yes. We walked right to the top, …………………………………………………………, Jenny?
12 Yes. We'd never done anything like that before, …………………………………………………?
13 Nearly everyone's asleep in this one, ……………………………………………………………?
14 There's something wrong with this one, …………………………………………………………?
15 That's me. I'm looking awfully fat, ………………………………………………………………?

Question tags: uses

Main points

You can use negative statements with positive question tags to make requests.

You use positive statements with positive question tags to show reactions.

You use some question tags to make imperatives more polite.

1 You can use a negative statement and a positive question tag to ask people for things, or to ask for help or information.

> You _wouldn't_ sell it to me, _would you?_
> You _won't_ tell anyone else this, _will you?_

2 When you want to show your reaction to what someone has just said, for example by expressing interest, surprise, doubt, or anger, you use a positive statement with a positive question tag.

> You've been to North America before, _have you?_
> You _fell_ on your back, _did you?_
> I borrowed your car last night. – Oh, you _did, did you?_

3 When you use an imperative, you can be more polite by adding one of the following question tags.

will you	won't you	would you

> _See_ that she gets safely back, _won't you?_
> _Look_ at that, _would you?_

When you use a negative imperative, you can only use 'will you' as a question tag.

> _Don't_ tell Howard, _will you?_

'Will you' and 'won't you' can also be used to emphasize anger or impatience. 'Can't you' is also used in this way.

> Oh, hurry up, _will you!_
> For goodness sake be quiet, _can't you!_

4 You use the question tag 'shall we' when you make a suggestion using 'let's'.

> _Let's_ forget it, _shall we?_

You use the question tag 'shall I' after 'I'll'.

> _I'll_ tell you, _shall I?_

5 You use 'they' in question tags after 'anybody', 'anyone', 'everybody', 'everyone', 'nobody', 'no one', 'somebody' or 'someone'.

> _Everyone_ will be leaving on Friday, won't _they?_
> _Nobody_ had bothered to plant new ones, had _they?_

You use 'it' in question tags after 'anything', 'everything', 'nothing', or 'something'.

> _Nothing_ matters now, does _it?_
> _Something_ should be done, shouldn't _it?_

You use 'there' in question tags after 'there is', 'there are', 'there was', or 'there were'.

> _There's_ a new course out now, isn't _there?_

6 When you are replying to a question tag, your answer refers to the statement, not the question tag.

If you want to confirm a positive statement, you say 'yes'. For example, if you have finished a piece of work and someone says to you 'You've finished that, haven't you?', the answer is 'yes'.

> 'It _became_ stronger, didn't it?' – _'Yes,_ it did.'

If you want to disagree with a positive statement, you say 'no'. For example, if you have not finished your work and someone says 'You've finished that, haven't you?', the answer is 'no'.

> You've just _seen_ a performance of the play, haven't you? – _No,_ not yet.

If you want to confirm a negative statement, you say 'no'. For example, if you have not finished your work and someone says 'You haven't finished that, have you?', the answer is 'no'.

> 'You _didn't know_ that, did you?' – _'No.'_

If you want to disagree with a negative statement, you say 'yes'. For example, if you have finished a piece of work and someone says 'You haven't finished that, have you?', the answer is 'yes'.

> 'You _haven't been_ there, have you?' – _'Yes,_ I have.'

Practice

A **Rewrite these requests using question tags.**

1 Could you open the door, please? / ......You couldn't open the door, could you?......
2 Do you know what time the next train leaves? / ....
3 Would you look after the children for us, please? / ....
4 Could you tell me what to do? / ....
5 Would you lend me your car, please? / ....
6 Could you come round tomorrow? / ....
7 Have you got time to help me out? / ....
8 Could you do the shopping while you are out? / ....

Now do these.

9 Please don't be late. / ......You won't be late, will you?......
10 Please don't spend too much. / ....
11 Please don't drive too fast. / ....
12 Please don't be angry with him. / ....

B **Complete these questions with the appropriate question tags.**

1 I see, you've crashed the car, ...have you...... ?
2 Oh, so you just borrowed it, ... ?
3 You were going to see some friends, ... ?
4 It was only a couple of miles, ... ?
5 You were driving very carefully, ... ?
6 The other car just ran into you, ... ?
7 You forgot to write down the car's number, ... ?
8 Oh, you're very sorry, ... ?
9 And you'll pay for the damage, ... ?
10 And you'll be more careful next time, ... ?

▶ **Bank**

Indirect questions

Main points

You use indirect questions to ask for information or help.

In indirect questions, the subject of the question comes before the verb.

You can use 'if' or 'whether' in indirect questions.

1 When you ask someone for information, you can use an indirect question beginning with a phrase such as 'Could you tell me…' or 'Do you know…'.

> _Could you tell me_ how far it is to the bank?
> _Do you know_ where Jane is?

2 When you want to ask someone politely to do something, you can use an indirect question after 'I wonder'.

> _I wonder_ if you can help me.
> _I was wondering_ whether you could give me some information.

You also use 'I wonder' followed by an indirect question to indicate what you are thinking about.

> _I wonder_ what she'll look like.
> _I wonder_ which hotel it was.
> I just _wonder_ what you make of all that.

3 In indirect questions, the subject of the question comes before the verb, just as it does in affirmative sentences.

> Do you know where _Jane is?_
> I wonder if _you can help me._

4 You do not normally use the auxiliary 'do' in indirect questions.

> Can you remember when _they open_ on Sundays?
> I wonder what _he feels_ about it.

The auxiliary 'do' can be used in indirect questions, but only for emphasis, or to make a contrast with something that has already been said. It is not put before the subject as in direct questions.

> I was beginning to wonder if he _does_ do anything.
> He wondered whether it really _did_ make any difference to the outcome.

5 You use 'if' or 'whether' to introduce indirect questions.

> I wonder _if you'd_ give the children a bath?
> I'm writing to ask _whether_ you would care to come and visit us.

'Whether' is used especially when there is a choice of possibilities.

> I wonder _whether_ it is the police or just a neighbour.
> I wonder _whether_ that's good for him or not.

Note that you can put 'or not' immediately after 'whether', but not immediately after 'if'.

> I wonder _whether or not_ we are so different from our ancestors.
> Even optimists wonder _if_ property prices can keep on rising.

Practice

A The questions below start with 'could you tell me' and 'I wonder'. Rewrite them to start with a 'wh'-word.

1 Could you tell me what time I have to start work? / *What time do I have to start work?* ....

2 I wonder where Tom and Mary live. / ....

3 I wonder what work Tom does. / ....

4 Could you tell me how I can get to the post-office? / ....

5 I wonder how old she is. / ....

6 Could you tell me who is in charge here? / ....

7 Could you tell me what I have to do? / ....

8 I wonder who has left his car in front of our house. / ....

9 I wonder where they've gone. / ....

10 Could you tell me when they'll be here? / ....

B Rewrite these as 'yes/no'-questions.

1 I wonder if George is at home. / *Is George at home?* ....

2 Could you tell me if the shop is still open? / ....

3 Do you know whether Mary will be coming? / ....

4 I want to know if I can book a room. / ....

5 Do you know if this seat is free? / ....

6 I'd like to know whether anyone has left any messages for me. / ....

7 Could you tell me if you will be staying long? / ....

8 Do you know if Bill called this evening? / ....

C Rewrite the following as polite questions using an indirect form.

1 How long will you be staying here? / Could you tell me ...*how long you will be staying here*....... ?

2 Where do Bill and Tessa live? / Do you know .... ?

3 Would you look after the children this evening? / I wonder ....

4 Where is the nearest post office? / Could you tell me .... ?

5 Could you give me Peter's address? / I wonder ....

6 Where will Simon be staying? / Do you know .... ?

7 Why did Jack and Jill leave so suddenly? / I wonder ....

8 Do the shops open at the weekend? / Can you tell me .... ?

9 What would he like for his birthday? / Do you know .... ?

10 Would you like to come round for a cup of coffee sometime? / I wonder ....

▸ **Bank**

Short answers

Main points

A short answer uses an auxiliary, a modal, or the main verb 'be'.

A short answer can be in the form of a statement or a question.

1 Short answers are very common in spoken English. For example, when someone asks you a 'yes/no'-question, you can give a short answer by using a pronoun with an auxiliary, modal, or the main verb 'be'. You usually put 'yes' or 'no' before the short answer.

> '*Does she still want to come?*' – 'Yes, *she does.*'
> '*Can you imagine what it might feel like?*' – 'No, *I can't.*'
> '*Are you married?*' – '*I am.*'

Note that a short answer such as 'Yes, I will' is more polite or friendly than just 'Yes', or than repeating all the words used in the question. People often repeat all the words used in the question when they feel angry or impatient.

> '*Will you have finished by lunchtime?*' – 'Yes, I will have finished by lunchtime.'

2 You can also use short answers to agree or disagree with what someone says.

> '*You don't like Joan?*' – 'No, *I don't.*'
> '*I'm not coming with you.*' – 'Yes, *you are.*'

If the statement that you are commenting on does not contain an auxiliary, modal, or the main verb 'be', you use a form of 'do' in the short answer.

> '*He never comes on time.*' – 'Oh yes *he does.*'

3 You often reply to what has been said by using a short question.

> '*He's not in Japan now.*' – 'Oh, *isn't he?*'
> '*He gets free meals.*' – '*Does he?*'

Note that questions like these are not always asked to get information, but are often used to express your reaction to what has been said, for example to show interest or surprise.

> '*Dad doesn't help me at all.*' – '*Doesn't he?* Why not?'
> '*Penny has been climbing before.*' – 'Oh, *has she?* When was that?'

4 If you want to show that you definitely agree with a positive statement that someone has just made, you can use a negative short question.

> '*Well, that was very nice.*' – 'Yes, *wasn't it?*'

5 When you want to ask for more information, you can use a 'wh'-word on its own or with a noun as a short answer.

> '*He saw a snake.*' – '*Where?*'
> '*He knew my cousin.*' – '*Which cousin?*'

You can also use 'Which one' and 'Which ones'.

> '*Can you pass me the cup?*' – '*Which one?*'

6 Sometimes a statement about one person also applies to another person. When this is the case, you can use a short answer with 'so' for positive statements, and with 'neither' or 'nor' for negative statements, using the same verb that was used in the statement. There is no difference between 'neither' and 'nor' in this use.

You use 'so', 'neither', or 'nor' with an auxiliary, modal, or the main verb 'be'. The verb comes before the subject.

> '*You were different then.*' – '*So were you.*'
> '*I don't normally drink at lunch.*' – '*Neither do I.*'
> '*I can't do it.*' – '*Nor can I.*'

You can use 'not either' instead of 'neither' or 'nor', in which case the verb comes after the subject.

> '*He doesn't understand.*' – '*We don't either.*'

7 You often use 'so' in short answers after verbs such as 'think', 'hope', 'expect', 'imagine', and 'suppose', when you think that the answer to the question is 'yes'.

> '*You'll be home at six?*' – '*I hope so.*'
> '*So it was worth doing?*' – '*I suppose so.*'

You use 'I'm afraid so' when you are sorry that the answer is 'yes'.

> '*Is it raining?*' – '*I'm afraid so.*'

With 'suppose', 'think', 'imagine', or 'expect' in short answers, you also form negatives with 'so'.

> '*Will I see you again?*' – '*I don't suppose so.*'
> '*Is Barry Knight a golfer?*' – 'No, *I don't think so.*'

However, you say 'I hope not' and 'I'm afraid not'.

> '*It isn't empty, is it?*' – '*I hope not.*'

Practice

A Write short answers to these question tags. Look at Unit 8 as well as Unit 10.
1   Columbus discovered India, didn't he? / ....No, he didn't... .
2   Milan isn't the capital of Italy, is it? / ....
3   John Kennedy was President of the USA, wasn't he? / ....
4   It'll be Wednesday tomorrow, won't it? / ....
5   You don't live in London, do you? / ....
6   You're studying English, aren't you? / ....
7   You don't enjoy learning English, do you? / ....
8   Vienna is in Germany, isn't it? / ....
9   Albert Einstein wasn't an American, was he? / ....
10   You haven't answered all these correctly, have you? / ....

B Match statements and short questions.
1   We don't live there anymore.   a   Do you really?
2   I know your sister Mary very well.   b   Won't they?
3   Jack and Jill will be coming.   c   Haven't they?
4   I don't think your parents will like this very much.   d   Wouldn't you?
5   The children have been here before.   e   Don't you?
6   Most people haven't arrived yet.   f   Will they?
7   I wouldn't do that if I were you.   g   Have they really?
8   I'm sure they would come if they could.   h   Would they?

C Match statements and short answers.
1   I always enjoy a good night out.   a   So do I.
2   My husband is never on time.   b   Neither did we.
3   I didn't get a holiday this year.   c   So will Sue.
4   Amanda will be at University next year.   d   So would I.
5   I haven't written to Jane yet.   e   So am I.
6   George would be furious if he found out.   f   Neither is my wife.
7   John can't stand pop music.   g   Nor have I.
8   The children are tired out.   h   Nor can I.

D Answer these questions in the affirmative using the words given.
1   Have you been here before? (*think*) / ......I think so... .
2   Will there be any tickets left? (*expect*) / ....
3   Do we have to pay the full price? (*suppose*) / ....
4   Was he very angry? (*be afraid*) / ....
5   Will there be lots of people there? (*imagine*) / ....
6   Is Jenny coming home for the holiday? (*hope*) / ....

E Answer these questions in the negative using the words given.
1   Do you think it'll take very long? (*think*) / ...I don't think so............................. .
2   Do you think it's going to rain? (*hope*) / ....
3   Will the train be on time? (*expect*) / ....
4   Will Becky do as she's told? (*suppose*) / ....
5   Do you get an extra day off on Monday? (*be afraid*) / ....

Sentences with 'not'

Main points

'Not' is often shortened to '-n't' and added to some verbs.

You put 'not' after the first verb in the verb group, or you use a short form.

1 In spoken and in informal written English, 'not' is often shortened to '-n't' and added to an auxiliary, a modal, or a form of the main verb 'be'.

> I *haven't* heard from her recently.
> I *wasn't* angry.

Here is a list of short forms.

isn't	haven't	don't	can't	shan't	daren't
aren't	hasn't	doesn't	couldn't	shouldn't	needn't
wasn't	hadn't	didn't	mightn't	won't	
weren't			mustn't	wouldn't	
			oughtn't		

If the verb is already shortened, you cannot add '-n't'.

> It's *not* easy.
> I've *not* had time.

You cannot add '-n't' to 'am'. You use 'I'm not'.

> I'm *not* excited.

2 If the verb group has more than one word, you put 'not' after the first word, or you use a short form.

> I *was not* smiling.
> He *hadn't* attended many meetings.
> They *might not* notice.
> I *haven't* been playing football recently.

3 If the sentence only contains a main verb other than 'be', you use the auxiliary 'do'.
You use 'do not', 'does not', 'did not', or a short form, followed by the base form of the main verb.

> They *do not need* to talk.
> He *does not speak* English very well.
> I *didn't know* that.

Note that if the main verb is 'do', you still use a form of 'do' as an auxiliary.

> They *didn't do* anything about it.

4 If the main verb is the present or past simple of 'be', you put 'not' immediately after it, or you use a short form.

> It *is not* difficult to understand.
> It's *not* the same, is it?
> He *wasn't* a bad actor actually.

5 If the main verb is 'have', you usually use a form of 'do' as an auxiliary.

> They *don't have* any money.

You can also use a short form, or you can put 'not' after the verb but this is not very common.

> He *hadn't* enough money.

Note that in the present tense, 'have got' is often used instead of 'have', especially in British English. When 'have got' is used, 'have' is used like an auxiliary.

> I *haven't got* any money left.
> Gregory *hasn't got* enough time to make the changes.

6 You can put 'not' in front of an '-ing' form or a 'to'-infinitive.

> We stood there, *not knowing* what to do.
> Try *not to worry*.

7 In negative questions, you use a short form.

> Why *didn't* she win at the Olympics?
> *Hasn't* he put on weight?
> *Aren't* you bored?

8 You can use a negative question:

• to express your feelings, for example to show that you are surprised or disappointed

> Hasn't he done it yet?

• in exclamations

> Isn't the weather awful!

• when you think you know something and you just want someone to agree with you

> 'Aren't you Joanne's brother?' – 'Yes, I am.'

9 Note the meaning of 'yes' and 'no' in answers to negative questions.

> *Isn't* Tracey going to get a bit bored in Birmingham?'
> – 'Yes.' (She is going to get bored.)
> – 'No.' (She is not going to get bored.)

Practice

A **Make these sentences negative.**

1 He works in Manchester now. / ...He doesn't work in Manchester now.....................

2 We have been there often. / ....

3 Mary was very happy. / ....

4 English is easy to understand. / ....

5 I've been to San Francisco. / ....

6 We might be late. / ....

7 He knows her name. / ....

8 They'll be arriving in time for lunch. / ....

9 We can go by train. / ....

10 John may be coming with his wife. / ....

B **Now do the same with these.**

1 Bill might have left a message. / ...Bill mightn't have left a message.............

2 They will probably have telephoned. / ....

3 Mary should have told you. / ....

4 I could have arrived earlier. / ....

5 You should have asked Peter. / ....

C **Rewrite these sentences using 'do' as an auxiliary.**

1 We hadn't any time to spare. / ....We didn't have any time to spare.............

2 She hasn't any friends in London. / ....

3 He hasn't any brothers or sisters. / ....

4 I haven't any money. / ....

5 They hadn't any new clothes to wear. / ....

6 We haven't anything to eat. / ....

D **Add a negative question to show surprise.**

1 They'll arrive before ten. / .....Won't they arrive..................... before then?

2 He earns about £100 a week. / .... more than that?

3 They gave us five pounds. / .... more than that?

4 We can stay until eleven o'clock. / .... later than that?

5 I have met Fred. / .... his brother too?

E **Complete the answers to these negative questions.**

1 Doesn't John live somewhere round here? / Yes, ...he does....................

2 Didn't you go to school with Peter? / No, ...

3 Haven't you finished yet? / No, I'm afraid ....

4 Won't they be back soon? / Yes, ...

5 Can't you come. / Yes, I think ....

6 Hasn't she told you? / No, ...

7 Aren't you pleased? / Yes, ...

8 Hadn't you heard? / No, ...

23

Negative words

Main points

A negative sentence contains a negative word.
You do not normally use two negative words in the same clause.

1 Negative statements contain a negative word.

not	nobody	neither
never	no one	nor
no	nothing	
none	nowhere	

➤ See Unit 11 for negative statements using 'not'.

2 You use 'never' to say that something was not the case at any time, or will not be the case at any time.

If the verb group has more than one word, you put 'never' after the first word.

I've never had such a horrible meal.
He could never trust her again.

3 If the only verb in the sentence is the present simple or past simple of any main verb except 'be', you put 'never' before the verb.

She never goes abroad.
He never went to university.

If the only verb in the sentence is the simple present or simple past of the main verb 'be', you normally put 'never' after the verb.

He's never late.
There were never any people in the house.

You can also use 'never' at the beginning of an imperative sentence.

Never walk alone late at night.

4 You use 'no' before a noun to say that something does not exist or is not available.

He has given no reason for his decision.
The island has no trees at all.

Note that if there is another negative word in the clause, you use 'any', not 'no'.

It won't do any good.

5 You use 'none' or 'none of' to say that there is not even one thing or person, or not even a small amount of something.

You can't go to a college here because there are none in this area.
'Where's the coffee?' – 'There's none left.'
None of us understood the play.

➤ See Unit 27 for more information on 'none' and 'none of'.

6 You also use 'nobody', 'no one', 'nothing', and 'nowhere' in negative statements.
You use 'nobody' or 'no one' to talk about people.

Nobody in her house knows any English.
No one knew.

'No one' can also be written 'no-one'.

There's no-one here.

You use 'nothing' to talk about things.

There's nothing you can do.

You use 'nowhere' to talk about places.

There's almost nowhere left to go.

➤ See Unit 21 for more information about these words.

7 You do not normally use two negative words in the same clause. For example, you do not say 'Nobody could see nothing'. You say 'Nobody could see anything'.

You use 'anything', 'anyone', 'anybody', and 'anywhere' instead of 'nothing', 'no one', 'nobody', and 'nowhere' when the clause already contains a negative word.

No-one can find Howard or Barbara anywhere.
I could never discuss anything with them.

8 The only negative words that are often used together in the same clause are 'neither' and 'nor'.

You use 'neither' and 'nor' together to say that two alternatives are not possible, not likely, or not true.

Neither Margaret nor John was there.
They had neither food nor money.

Practice

A Answer the questions below using one of the words in brackets.

1 How often have you been to Oxford?

I've ………………never……………………… been. I'd like to go one day, though. (*never / none / nowhere*)

2 How many books did you buy?

……………………………I had ……………… money left. (*No / None / Nothing*) (*no / none / nothing*)

3 What did you do?

……………………………………………… . I was too tired to do anything. (*No / None / Nothing*)

4 Where did you find the money?

………………………… . We looked everywhere but we couldn't find it at all. (*None / Nothing / Nowhere*)

5 Who did you talk to at the party?

………………………………… . There were lots of people there but ………………… of them spoke

English. (*Nobody / None / Nothing*) (*no / neither / none*)

6 Who won the prize, Jill or Helen?

…………………………………………… of them. Mary finally won quite easily. (*Neither / None / No one*)

7 Have you seen John lately?

I'm afraid not. He …………………………………… comes to visit us nowadays. (*never / not / no*)

8 Was that the postman?

No. I answered the door but there was ………………………… there. (*no-one / nothing / none*)

9 Did you both go to the show last night?

No, ………………………………… of us managed to go. We were too busy. (*neither / none / no*)

10 Did you see John and Mary yesterday?

No. ………………… John ………………… Mary came to the meeting. (*no / neither*) (*nor / not*)

B Complete these sentences using one of the words in brackets.

1 I looked everywhere for Jane but I couldn't find her ……………anywhere.…… (*anywhere / somewhere / nowhere*)

2 There were lots of people there but I didn't meet ……………………… I knew. (*anybody / nobody / somebody*)

3 I asked lots of people but ……………………………… knew the answer. (*anyone / no one / someone*)

4 I asked Bill for help but he couldn't do ……………………………… . (*anything / nothing / something*)

5 I asked Bill if he could do ……………………… to help but he said he couldn't. (*anything / nothing / something*)

6 I haven't ………………………………… heard of him before. (*ever / never / not*)

7 I've met Frank but I've ……………………………………… met his brother. (*ever / never*)

8 I wanted some coffee but there wasn't …………………………………… left. (*any / none / some*)

9 I wanted a biscuit but there were …………………………………… left. (*any / none / some*)

10 I knocked at the door but there was ………………………… at home. (*anybody / nobody / somebody*)

Count nouns

In English, some things are thought of as individual items that can be counted directly. The nouns which refer to these countable things are called count nouns. Most nouns in English are count nouns.

➤ See Unit 15 for information on uncount nouns.

1 Count nouns have two forms. The singular form refers to one thing or person.

  …*a book* … …*the teacher.*

The plural form refers to more than one thing or person.

  … *books* … …*some teachers.*

2 You add '-s' to form the plural of most nouns.

book	→ books	school	→ schools

You add '-es' to nouns ending in '-ss', '-ch', '-s', '-sh', or '-x'.

class	→ classes	watch	→ watches
gas	→ gases	dish	→ dishes
fox	→ foxes		

Some nouns ending in '-o' add '-s', and some add '-es'.

photo	→ photos	piano	→ pianos
hero	→ heroes	potato	→ potatoes

Nouns ending in a consonant and '-y' change to '-ies'.

country	→ countries	lady	→ ladies
party	→ parties	victory	→ victories

Nouns ending in a vowel and '-y' add an '-s'.

boy	→ boys	day	→ days
key	→ keys	valley	→ valleys

Some common nouns have irregular plurals.

child	→ children	foot	→ feet
man	→ men	mouse	→ mice
tooth	→ teeth	woman	→ women

⊖ WARNING: Some nouns that end in '-s' are uncount nouns, for example 'athletics' and 'physics'.
➤ See Unit 15.

3 Count nouns can be used with numbers.

  … *one table*…

  … *two cats*…

  … *three hundred pounds.*

4 Singular count nouns cannot be used alone, but always take a determiner such as 'a', 'another', 'every', or 'the'.

  We've killed a pig.

  He was eating another apple.

  She had read every book on the subject.

  I parked the car over there.

5 Plural count nouns can be used with or without a determiner. They do not take a determiner when they refer to things or people in general.

  Does the hotel have large rooms?

  The film is not suitable for children.

Plural count nouns do take a determiner when they refer precisely to particular things or people.

  Our computers are very expensive.

  These cakes are delicious.

➤ See Unit 23 for more information on determiners.

6 When a count noun is the subject of a verb, a singular count noun takes a singular verb.

  My son likes playing football.

  The address on the letter was wrong.

A plural count noun takes a plural verb.

  Bigger cars cost more.

  I thought more people were coming.

➤ See also Unit 14 on collective nouns.

Practice

A **Give the plurals of the following nouns.**

cow ....cows....   child ....   tooth ....

glass ....   wish ....   lorry ....

story ....   friend ....   bus ....

tomato ....   parent ....   monkey ....

box ....   piano ....   house ....

mouse ....   key ....   way ....

B **Rewrite these sentences in the plural.**

1 A train is much quicker than a bus. / ......Trains are much quicker than buses.....................

2 A lion is a dangerous animal. / ....

3 A lawyer generally earns more than a teacher. /...

4 A computer is an expensive piece of equipment. / ....

5 A student has to work hard. / ....

6 A policeman only does what he is told. / ....

7 A cat is supposed to have nine lives. / ....

8 A bus is the best way of getting into town. / ....

9 A woman tends to live longer than a man. / ....

10 A good book helps to pass the time. / ....

C **Complete these sentences with a singular or plural count noun.**

1 The ....bus............... stops right outside our house. (*bus / buses*)

2 The .... were waiting for me. (*child / children*)

3 The .... are in the cupboard. (*dish / dishes*)

4 The .... have gone bad. (*tomato / tomatoes*)

5 The .... is full. (*box / boxes*)

6 Do you know the .... that lives next door? (*man / men*)

7 The .... who were here have gone home. (*person / people*)

8 The dentist pulled out the .... that was hurting. (*tooth / teeth*)

9 Have you washed the .... that were in the kitchen? (*dish / dishes*)

10 Do you know the .... that delivers the newspapers? (*boy / boys*)

D **Complete these sentences with a singular or a plural verb.**

1 The children ......are getting....................... ready for school. (*is getting / are getting*)

2 My brother .... in the army. (*is / are*)

3 The cake .... delicious. (*smell / smells*)

4 The mice .... the cheese. (*has eaten / have eaten*)

5 The books we bought .... very expensive. (*was / were*)

6 Did you notice the picture that .... on the wall? (*was hanging / were hanging*)

7 The young man you met .... to college with my sister. (*go / goes*)

8 The letters you posted .... wrongly addressed. (*was / were*)

9 The woman they were meeting .... telephoned to say she can't come. (*has / have*)

10 Mary and Peter, the couple I met last week, ... invited us to dinner. (*has / have*)

Singular and plural

Main points

Singular nouns are used only in the singular, always with a determiner.

Plural nouns are used only in the plural, some with a determiner.

Collective nouns can be used with singular or plural verbs.

[1] Some nouns are used in particular meanings in the singular with a determiner, like count nouns, but are not used in the plural with that meaning. They are often called 'singular nouns'.

Some of these nouns are normally used with 'the' because they refer to things that are unique.

air	country	countryside	dark	daytime
end	future	ground	moon	past
sea	seaside	sky	sun	wind
world				

> *The sun was shining.*
> *I am scared of the dark.*

Other singular nouns are normally used with 'a' because they refer to things that we usually talk about one at a time.

bath	chance	drink	fight	go	jog
move	rest	ride	run	shower	
smoke	snooze	start	walk	wash	

> *I went upstairs and had a wash.*
> *Why don't we go outside for a smoke?*

[2] Some nouns are used in particular meanings in the plural with or without determiners, like count nouns, but are not used in the singular with that meaning. They are often called 'plural nouns'.

> *His clothes looked terribly dirty.*
> *Troops are being sent in today.*

Some of these nouns are always used with determiners.

activities	authorities	feelings	likes
pictures	sights	travels	

> *I went to the pictures with Tina.*
> *You hurt his feelings.*

Some are usually used without determiners.

airs	expenses	goods	refreshments	riches

> *Refreshments are available inside.*
> *They have agreed to pay for travel and expenses.*

⊖ WARNING: 'Police' is a plural noun, but does not end in '-s'.

> *The police were informed immediately.*

[3] A small group of plural nouns refer to single items that have two linked parts. They refer to tools that people use or things that people wear.

binoculars	glasses	jeans	knickers	pincers
pants	pliers	pyjamas	scales	scissors
shears	shorts	tights	trousers	tweezers

> *She was wearing brown trousers.*
> *These scissors are sharp.*

You can use 'a pair of' to make it clear you are talking about one item, or a number with 'pairs of' when you are talking about several items.

> *I was sent out to buy a pair of scissors.*
> *Liza had given me three pairs of jeans.*

Note that you also use 'a pair of' with words such as 'gloves', 'shoes', and 'socks' that you often talk about in twos.

[4] With some nouns that refer to a group of people or things, the same form can be used with singular or plural verbs, because you can think of the group as a unit or as individuals. Similarly, you can use singular or plural pronouns to refer back to them. These nouns are often called 'collective nouns'.

army	audience	committee	company	crew
data	enemy	family	flock	gang
government	group	herd	media	navy
press	public	staff	team	

> *Our little group is complete again.*
> *The largest group are the boys.*
> *Our family isn't poor any more.*
> *My family are perfectly normal.*

The names of many organizations and sports teams are also collective nouns, but are normally used with plural verbs in spoken English.

> *The BBC is showing the programme on Saturday.*
> *The BBC are planning to use the new satellite.*
> *Liverpool is leading 1-0.*
> *Liverpool are attacking again.*

Practice

A Use the singular nouns below to complete the sentences which follow.

| a bath | a go | a drink | a fight | a jog | a rest | a shower | a move | a walk | a wash | a ride |

1 I need some fresh air. I think I'll go out for .... *a walk* ....
2 I'm going to lie down and have ....
3 I haven't time for .... I'll just have .... instead.
4 The children are covered in dirt. They need a ....
5 Can I have .... on your bike?
6 He keeps fit by going for .... every evening.
7 This is thirsty work. Let's stop for ....
8 Bill's in trouble. He started .... and got himself arrested.
9 You can't succeed if you don't have ....
10 It's time to go. Let's make ....

B Use these plural nouns to complete the sentences that follow.

| belongings | clothes | expenses | feelings | goods | holidays | pictures | papers | refreshments | sights |

1 If I spend a lot of money, can I claim .... *expenses* .... ?
2 Britain needs to export more ....
3 There was a short break for ....
4 My .... are soaking wet. I need to change.
5 He's very unhappy. You must have hurt his ....
6 The kids aren't at home. They're on their ....
7 What's on at the cinema? I haven't been to the .... for ages.
8 You're famous. I saw your picture in the ....
9 He carries all his .... with him in an old suitcase.
10 We took some time off to walk around the town and see the ....

C Use these collective nouns to complete the sentences that follow.

| audience | crew | enemy | family | gang | government | media | public | staff | team |

1 Take cover. The .... *enemy* .... are attacking.
2 Do you think Liverpool are the best .... in Europe?
3 Dad is out but the rest of the .... are at home.
4 The .... has decided to increase taxes.
5 The ship sank but the .... are safe.
6 The office is closed. The .... are on strike.
7 The house was surrounded and the .... were arrested.
8 The .... is much bigger than at last night's performance.
9 The railways should provide a better service for the travelling ....
10 Some sports stars are very badly treated by the newspapers and other ....

▸ **Bank**

29

Uncount nouns

Main points

Uncount nouns have only one form, and take a singular verb.

They are not used with 'a', or with numbers.

Some nouns can be both uncount nouns and count nouns.

1 English speakers think that some things cannot be counted directly. The nouns which refer to these uncountable things are called uncount nouns. Uncount nouns often refer to:

substances:	coal food ice iron rice steel water
human qualities:	courage cruelty honesty patience
feelings:	anger happiness joy pride relief respect
activities:	aid help sleep travel work
abstract ideas:	beauty death freedom fun life luck

The donkey needed <u>food</u> and <u>water.</u>
Soon, they lost <u>patience</u> and sent me to Durban.
I was greeted with shouts of <u>joy.</u>
All prices include <u>travel</u> to and from London.
We talked for hours about <u>freedom.</u>

▶ See Unit 13 for information on count nouns.

2 Uncount nouns have only one form. They do not have a plural form.

I needed <u>help</u> with my homework.
The children had great <u>fun</u> playing with the puppets.

⊝ WARNING Some nouns which are uncount nouns in English have plurals in other languages.

advice	baggage	equipment	furniture
homework	information	knowledge	luggage
machinery	money	news	traffic

We want to spend more <u>money</u> on roads.
Soldiers carried so much <u>equipment</u> that they were barely able to move.

3 Some uncount nouns end in '-s' and therefore look like plural count nouns. They usually refer to:

subjects of study:	mathematics	physics
activities:	athletics	gymnastics
games:	cards	darts
illnesses:	measles	mumps

<u>Mathematics</u> is too difficult for me.
<u>Measles</u> is in most cases a harmless illness.

4 When an uncount noun is the subject of a verb, it takes a singular verb.

Electricity <u>is</u> dangerous.
Food <u>was</u> very expensive in those days.

5 Uncount nouns are not used with 'a'.

They resent having to pay <u>money</u> to people like me.
My father started <u>work</u> when he was ten.

Uncount nouns are used with 'the' when they refer to something that is specified or known.

I am interested in <u>the education of young children.</u>
She buried <u>the money that Hilary had given her.</u>

6 Uncount nouns are not used with numbers. However, you can often refer to a quantity of something which is expressed by an uncount noun, by using a word like 'some'. ▶ See Unit 23.

Please buy <u>some bread</u> when you go to town.
Let me give you <u>some advice.</u>

Some uncount nouns that refer to food or drink can be count nouns when they refer to quantities of the food or drink.

Do you like <u>coffee?</u> (uncount)
We asked for <u>two coffees.</u> (count)

Uncount nouns are often used with expressions such as 'a loaf of', 'packets of', or 'a piece of', to talk about a quantity or an item. 'A bit of' is common in spoken English.

I bought <u>two loaves of bread</u> yesterday.
He gave me <u>a</u> very good <u>piece of advice.</u>
They own <u>a bit of land</u> near Cambridge.

7 Some nouns are uncount nouns when they refer to something in general and count nouns when they refer to a particular instance of something.

<u>Victory</u> was now assured. (uncount)
In 1960, the party won <u>a convincing victory.</u> (count)

Practice

A Use these uncount nouns to complete the sentences below.

advice	electricity	equipment	happiness	help
information	knowledge	luggage	money	traffic

1 We've got a lot of ....luggage................... but it's not too heavy.
2 At that time my .... of German was minimal.
3 I'd like some .... about trains, please.
4 They exported a million dollars' worth of stereo ....
5 Do you have any .... on you?
6 If you want my .... , I think you ought to start all over again.
7 There's always a lot of .... in the rush hour.
8 Do you cook by gas or .... ?
9 You can always telephone, if you need any ....
10 Money doesn't always bring ....

B Look at the following pairs of sentences. In one the noun in bold is used as a count noun and in the other as an uncount noun. Mark the sentences C for count or U for uncount.

1 Shakespeare's **language** is magnificent. ...U....................................
   It's easier to work with someone who speaks your own **language.** ...C....................................
2 She's had nine months' **experience** as a secretary. ....
   The funeral was a painful **experience.** ....
3 People spend their **lives** worrying about money. ....
   How's **life?** ....
4 Are you in San Francisco for **business** or pleasure? ....
   He set up a small travel **business.** ....
5 She never completely gave up **hope.** ....
   Ken has high **hopes** of a promotion before the end of the year. ....
6 There was general **agreement** on the problem. ....
   We hope to come to a general **agreement** on future action. ....

C Use these phrases with 'the' and an uncount noun to complete the sentences which follow.

the news about Bill	the furniture in the sitting room	the traffic in London
the advice you gave me	the information you need	the strength to go on

1 I liked ......the furniture in the sitting room...... . I thought it looked very smart.
2 I'd like to thank you for ....
3 I'm tired out. I haven't got ....
4 You can find .... in any good grammar book.
5 .... is dreadful – particularly in the rush hour.
6 Have you heard .... ?

Personal pronouns

Main points

You use personal pronouns to refer back to something or someone that has already been mentioned.

You also use personal pronouns to refer to people and things directly.

There are two sets of personal pronouns: subject pronouns and object pronouns.

You can use 'you' and 'they' to refer to people in general.

1 When something or someone has already been mentioned, you refer to them again by using a pronoun.

> John took <u>the book</u> and opened <u>it.</u>
> He rang <u>Mary</u> and invited <u>her</u> to dinner.
> 'Have you been to <u>London</u> ?' – 'Yes, <u>it</u> was very crowded.'
> <u>My father</u> is fat – <u>he</u> weighs over fifteen stone.

In English, 'he' and 'she' normally refer to people, occasionally to animals, but very rarely to things.

2 You use a pronoun to refer directly to people or things that are present or are involved in the situation you are in.

> Where shall <u>we</u> meet, Sally?
> <u>I</u> do the washing; <u>he</u> does the cooking; <u>we</u> share the washing-up.
> Send <u>us</u> a card so <u>we</u>'ll know where <u>you</u> are.

3 There are two sets of personal pronouns, subject pronouns and object pronouns. You use subject pronouns as the subject of a verb.

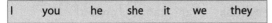

I	you	he	she	it	we	they

Note that 'you' is used for the singular and plural form.

> <u>We</u> are going there later.
> <u>I</u> don't know what to do.

4 You use object pronouns as the direct or indirect object of a verb.

me	you	him	her	it	us	them

Note that 'you' is used for the singular and plural form.

> The nurse washed <u>me</u> with cold water.
> The ball hit <u>her</u> in the face.
> John showed <u>him</u> the book.
> Can you give <u>me</u> some more cake?

Note that, in modern English, you use object pronouns rather than subject pronouns after the verb 'be'.

> 'Who is it?' – 'It<u>'s me.</u>'
> There <u>was</u> only John, Baz, and <u>me</u> in the room.

You also use object pronouns as the object of a preposition.

> We were all sitting in a cafe <u>with him.</u>
> Did you give it <u>to them?</u>

5 You can use 'you' and 'they' to talk about people in general.

> <u>You</u> have to drive on the other side of the road on the continent.
> <u>They</u> say she's very clever.

6 You can use 'it' as an impersonal subject in general statements which refer to the time, the date, or the weather.
➤ See Unit 17.

> 'What time is <u>it?</u>' '<u>It</u>'s half past three.'
> <u>It</u> is January 19th.
> <u>It</u> is rainy and cold.

You can also use 'it' as the subject or object in general statements about a situation.

> <u>It</u> is too far to walk.
> I like <u>it</u> here. Can we stay a bit longer?

7 A singular pronoun usually refers back to a singular noun group, and a plural pronoun to a plural noun group. However, you can use plural pronouns to refer back to:

● indefinite pronouns, even though they are always followed by a singular verb

> If <u>anybody comes,</u> tell <u>them</u> I'm not in.

● collective nouns, even when you have used a singular verb

> His <u>family was</u> waiting in the next room, but <u>they</u> had not yet been informed.

Practice

A **Complete these sentences by adding the names given.**

Mr Brown	Mr and Mrs Jackson	Mary	Tom and Jane

1 I spoke to ....Mr Brown.......................... yesterday. He said he'd call me back.
2 .... says she'll see you tomorrow.
3 .... said we should meet them at their house.
4 Good morning sir. Good morning madam. You must be .... You have a
   reservation, haven't you?

B **Now do the same with these.**

Mr Brown	Mr and Mrs Jackson	Mary	Tom and Jane

1 ....Mary......... 's feeling much better. I spoke to her in the hospital this morning.
2 If you see .... , give them my love.
3 .... ? This way please. The room is ready for you.
4 Is .... in ? I have a message for him.

C **Look at the picture and add personal pronouns to complete the story.**

The other day when I was shopping a woman stopped ....me........... and asked ... ...
.... the way to the post office. ....
gave her directions and .... thanked ....
politely, then ran off quickly in the opposite direction. .... put
my hand in my pocket and found that my wallet was missing. ....
must have taken it while .... were talking. ....
shouted and ran after .... but .... was
no good. .... had disappeared in the crowd.

Impersonal subject 'it'

Main points

You use impersonal 'it' as the subject of a sentence to introduce new information.

You use 'it' to talk about the time or the date.

You use 'it' to talk about the weather.

You use 'it' to express opinions about places, situations, and events.

'It' is often used with the passive of reporting verbs to express general beliefs and opinions.

1 'It' is a pronoun. As a personal pronoun it refers back to something that has already been mentioned.

> *They learn to speak <u>English</u> before they learn to read <u>it</u>.*
> *<u>Maybe he changed his mind,</u> but I doubt <u>it</u>.*

You can also use 'it' as the subject of a sentence when it does not refer back to anything that has already been mentioned. This impersonal use of 'it' introduces new information, and is used particularly to talk about times, dates, the weather, and personal opinions.

2 You use impersonal 'it' with a form of 'be' to talk about the time or the date.

> *<u>It is</u> nearly one o'clock.*
> *<u>It's</u> the sixth of April today.*

3 You use impersonal 'it' with verbs which refer to the weather:

drizzle	hail	pour	rain	sleet	snow	thunder

> *<u>It's</u> still <u>raining</u>.*
> *<u>It snowed</u> steadily through the night.*
> *<u>It was pouring</u> with rain.*

You can describe the weather by using 'it' followed by 'be' and an adjective with or without a noun.

> *It's a lovely day.*
> *It was very bright.*

You can describe a change in the weather by using 'it' followed by 'get' and an adjective.

> *It was getting cold.*
> *It's getting dark.*

4 You use impersonal 'it', followed by a form of 'be' and an adjective or noun group, to express your opinion about a place, a situation, or an event. The adjective or noun group can be followed by an adverbial or by an '-ing' clause, a 'to'-infinitive clause, or a 'that'-clause.

> *<u>It was</u> terribly <u>cold in the trucks.</u>*
> *<u>It's fun working</u> for him.*
> *<u>It was a pleasure to be</u> there.*
> *<u>It's strange that</u> it hasn't been noticed before.*

5 You use 'it' followed by a verb such as 'interest', 'please', 'surprise', or 'upset' which indicates someone's reaction to a fact, situation, or event. The verb is followed by a noun group, and a 'that'-clause or a 'to'-infinitive clause.

> *<u>It pleases me that</u> he should want to talk about his work.*
> *<u>It surprised him to realize</u> that he hadn't thought about them until now.*

6 You can also use 'it' with the passive of a reporting verb and a 'that'-clause when you want to suggest that an opinion or belief is shared by many people. This use is particularly common in news reports, for example in newspapers, on the radio, or on television.

> *<u>It was said that</u> he could speak their language.*
> *Nowadays <u>it is believed that</u> the size is unimportant.*
> *<u>It is thought that</u> about a million puppies are born each year.*

Note that the passive of reporting verbs can also be used without impersonal 'it' to express general opinions.

> *<u>The factories were said to be</u> much worse.*
> *<u>They are believed to be</u> dangerous.*

➤ See Units 76 and 77 for more information on reporting verbs.

A The word 'it' has been left out of these sentences. The number in brackets tells you how many times it should occur. Show where it should be.

1 A: What's the house like? Is it big or small? B: It Is quite big. It Has four bedrooms. (3)

2 We live in Hagley. Is a village near Birmingham. (1)

3 I'm learning Chinese, but is very difficult to understand. (1)

4 There's a new restaurant in the High Street. Opened about a month ago. We went there last week but was very expensive and we didn't like very much. (3)

5 A: Where's the tin opener? B: I think is in the kitchen. I put back in the drawer. (2)

6 She was very frightened but she tried not to show. (1)

7 A: Did you see the film about Japan on TV last night? I really enjoyed. B: Yes, I enjoyed too. I thought was very interesting. C: I didn't see. I went to bed before started. (5)

B Make ten sentences from this table.

It	is can be	interesting difficult fun nice expensive awful boring	learning English. going abroad on holiday. meeting new people. travelling in the rush hour. going to school. buying new clothes. going shopping.

1 ....It can be boring going to school...

2 ....

3 ....

4 ....

5 ....

6 ....

7 ....

8 ....

9 ....

10 ....

C Rewrite these sentences with 'It' and a 'to'-infinitive clause.

1 Driving over 70 mph is illegal. / ...It's illegal to drive over 70 mph...........................

2 Missing a train is very annoying. / ....

3 Getting a letter from an old friend is nice. / ....

4 Going for a good night out is fun. / ....

5 Learning another language is interesting. / ....

6 Eating too much is unhealthy. / ....

7 Looking after young children is tiring. / ....

8 Driving too fast is very dangerous. / ....

▸ **Bank**

Impersonal subject 'there'

1 'There' is often an adverb of place.

> *Are you comfortable <u>there</u>?*
> *The book is <u>there</u> on the table.*

You can also use 'there' as the impersonal subject of a sentence when it does not refer to a place. In this case you use 'there' to introduce new information and to focus upon it. After 'there' you use a form of 'be' and a noun group.

> *<u>There is work</u> to be done.*
> *<u>There will be a party</u> tonight.*
> *<u>There was no damage.</u>*
> *<u>There have been two telephone calls.</u>*

Note that the impersonal subject 'there' is often pronounced without stress, whereas the adverb is almost always stressed.

2 You use 'there' as the impersonal subject to talk about:

● the existence or presence of someone or something

> *There are two people who might know what happened.*
> *There are many possibilities.*
> *There is plenty of bread.*

● something that happens

> *There was a general election that year.*
> *There's a meeting every week.*
> *There was a fierce battle.*

● a number or amount

> *There are forty of us, I think.*
> *There is a great deal of anger about his decision.*
> *There were a lot of people camped there.*

3 When the noun group after the verb is plural, you use a plural verb.

> *<u>There are many reasons</u> for this.*
> *<u>There were two men</u> in the room.*

You also use a plural verb before phrases such as 'a number (of)', 'a lot (of)', and 'a few (of)'.

> *<u>There were a lot of</u> people camped there.*
> *<u>There are</u> only <u>a few</u> left.*

4 When the noun group after the verb is singular or uncountable, you use a singular verb.

> *<u>There is one point</u> we must add here.*
> *<u>There isn't enough room</u> in here.*

You also use a singular verb when you are mentioning more than one person or thing and the first noun after the verb is singular or uncountable.

> *<u>There was a man</u> and a woman.*
> *<u>There was a sofa</u> and two chairs.*

5 You can also use 'there' with a modal, followed by 'be' or 'have been'.

> *<u>There could be</u> a problem.*
> *<u>There should be</u> a change in government.*
> *<u>There can't have been</u> anybody outside.*
> *<u>There must have been</u> some mistake.*

6 In spoken and informal written English, short forms of 'be' or a modal are normally used after 'there'.

> *<u>There's</u> no danger.*
> *<u>There'll</u> always <u>be</u> a future for music.*
> *I knew <u>there'd be</u> trouble.*
> *<u>There's been</u> quite a lot of research into it.*
> *I didn't even know <u>there'd been</u> a murder.*

7 You can also use 'there' with 'appear' or 'seem', followed by 'to be' or 'to have been'.

> *<u>There appears to be</u> a vast amount of confusion on this point.*
> *<u>There don't seem to be</u> many people on campus.*
> *<u>There seems to have been</u> some carelessness.*

Practice

A Use the 'to'-infinitive clauses below to complete the sentences which follow.

to ask	to drink	to do	to eat	to help	to read	to see	to sleep	to spare	to watch

1 I was thirsty, but there was nothing ..*to drink*.. .
2 I was tired out, but there was nowhere ....
3 We were all hungry, but there wasn't very much ....
4 We were late setting off, so there was no time ....
5 I couldn't do it alone, and there was no one ....
6 The children were bored. They said there was nothing ....
7 There were no books or newspapers, nothing ....
8 I couldn't find my way, and there was no one ....
9 I switched on the TV, but there wasn't really anything ....
10 We had a walk round the town, but there wasn't anything interesting ....

B Rewrite these sentences to begin with 'There' as an impersonal subject.

1 Two general elections took place that year. / ....*There were two general elections that year.*....
2 We have a class every Friday. / ....
3 A meeting will be held at three o'clock on Tuesday. / ....
4 Lots of children will be at the concert. / ....
5 A few friends will be coming round. / ....
6 People give lots of parties at Christmas. / ....
7 An accident will happen if you're not careful. / ....
8 You must have made a mistake. / ....

C Rewrite these sentences beginning with 'There seems ...' or 'There appears ...'.

1 I think there is a problem here.
   ...*There appears to be a problem here.*...
   (or) .*There seems to be a problem here.*..
2 I think there has been a mistake.
   ...*There appears to have been a mistake.*..
   (or) .*There seems to have been a mistake.*..
3 I think there is something wrong with the engine. / ....
4 I think there's nothing left. / ....
5 I think there has been an accident. / ....
6 I think there was a lot of trouble. / ....
7 I think there is no one at home. / ....
8 I think there has been a fire. / ....

▶ **Bank**

Demonstrative pronouns

Main points

You use the demonstrative pronouns 'this', 'that', 'these', and 'those' when you are pointing to physical objects or identifying people.

You use 'one' or 'ones' instead of a noun that has been mentioned or is known.

1 You use the demonstrative pronouns 'this', 'that', 'these', and 'those' when you are pointing to physical objects. 'This' and 'these' refer to things near you, 'that' and 'those' refer to things farther away.

> *This is a list of rules.*
> *'I brought you these'. Adam held out a bag of grapes.*
> *That looks interesting.*
> *Those are mine.*

You can also use 'this', 'that', 'these', and 'those' as determiners in front of nouns.
▶ See Unit 23.

> *This book was a present from my mother.*
> *When did you buy that hat?*

2 You use 'this', 'that', 'these', and 'those' when you are identifying or introducing people, or asking who they are.

> *Who's this?*
> *These are my children, Susan and Paul.*
> *Was that Patrick on the phone?*

3 You use 'this', 'that', 'these', and 'those' to refer back to things that have already been mentioned.

> *That was an interesting word you used just now.*
> *More money is being pumped into the education system, and we assume this will continue.*
> *'Let's go to the cinema.' – 'That's a good idea.'*
> *These are not easy questions to answer.*

You also use 'this' and 'these' to refer forward to things you are going to mention.

> *This is what I want to say: it wasn't my idea.*
> *These are the topics we will be looking at next week: how the accident happened, whether it could have been avoided, and who was to blame.*
> *This is the important point: you must never see her again.*

4 You use 'one' or 'ones' instead of a noun that has already been mentioned or is known in the situation, usually when you are adding information or contrasting two things of the same kind.

> *My car is the blue one.*
> *Don't you have one with buttons instead of a zip?*
> *Are the new curtains longer than the old ones?*

You can use 'which one' or 'which ones' in questions.

> *Which one do you prefer?*
> *Which ones were damaged?*

You can say 'this one', 'that one', 'these ones', and 'those ones'.

> *I like this one better.*
> *We'll have those ones, thank you.*

You can use 'each one' or 'one each', but note that there is a difference in meaning. In the following examples, 'each one' means 'each brother' but 'one each' means 'one for each child'.

> *I've got three brothers and each one lives in a different country.*
> *I bought the children one each.*

5 In formal English, people sometimes use 'one' to refer to people in general.

> *One has to think of the practical side of things.*
> *One never knows what to say in such situations.*

6 There are several other types of pronoun, which are dealt with in other units.

▶ See Unit 22 for information on possessive pronouns.

▶ See Unit 6 for information on 'who', 'whom', 'whose', 'which', and 'what' as interrogative pronouns.

▶ See Units 92 and 93 for information on 'that', 'which', 'who', 'whom', and 'whose' as relative pronouns.

Most determiners, except 'the', 'a', 'an', 'every', 'no', and the possessives, are also pronouns.
▶ See Units 27 to 30.

A Each of the pronouns in bold below refers back to a clause. Underline the clause in each case.

1 <u>I'm tired out.</u> **That**'s why I'm going home early.
2 He's always complaining and **this** is why nobody likes him.
3 George had just got a new job. **That**'s why he was so pleased with himself.
4 I've mended the radiator. I hope **this** will solve the problem.
5 Finally, Mary told him she was tired of him. I think **that**'s what really annoyed him.
6 George likes Mary, but she doesn't like him. **That**'s what annoys him.
7 The engine's all right but the brakes are useless. **That**'s why it needs to go into the garage.
8 Even when they go to bed late the children sometimes stay awake all night. **That**'s why they get so tired.
9 The traffic was dreadful even though we left home early. **That**'s why we're late.
10 The engine starts and after a few seconds the light goes on. **That**'s when you press the button.

B Look at the picture and complete the answers to these questions using 'one' or 'ones'.

1 How many cars are there?
Five. Three big ……*ones*……………… and two small ….*ones*……………… .
2 What colour are they?
There are three white ……………………………… and two black ………………… .
3 How many small cars are there?
Two. A black ……………………………… and a white ……………………………… .
4 How many big cars are there?
Three. Two white ………………………… and one black ……………………………… .
5 Where is the small white car?
Between the small black ……………………………… and the big black ……………………………… .

C Here is a puzzle.

There are some books on a shelf. There are three big ones and two small ones. One of the big ones is red. There is a small green book. There are two green ones altogether and two blue ones. Only one of the small books is green.

1 How many books are there altogether? …………………………………………………………
2 What colour are the big books? …………………………………………………………………
3 What colour are the small ones? …………………………………………………………………

Reflexive pronouns

Main points

Reflexive pronouns can be direct or indirect objects.

Most transitive verbs can take a reflexive pronoun as object.

Reflexive pronouns can be the object of a preposition.

Reflexive pronouns can emphasize a noun or pronoun.

1 The reflexive pronouns are:

| singular: | myself yourself himself herself itself |
| plural: | ourselves yourselves themselves |

Note that, unlike 'you' and 'your', there are two forms for the second person: 'yourself' in the singular and 'yourselves' in the plural.

2 You use reflexive pronouns as the direct or indirect object of the verb when you want to say that the object is the same person or thing as the subject of the verb in the same clause.

For example, 'John taught himself' means that John did the teaching and was also the person who was taught, and 'Ann poured herself a drink' means that Ann did the pouring and was also the person that the drink was poured for.

She stretched herself out on the sofa.
The men formed themselves into a line.
He should give himself more time.

Note that although the subject 'you' is omitted in imperatives, you can still use 'yourself' or 'yourselves'.

Here's the money, go and buy yourself an ice cream.

3 Most transitive verbs can take a reflexive pronoun.

I blame myself for not paying attention.
He introduced himself to me.

⊖ WARNING: Verbs which describe actions that people normally do to themselves do not take reflexive pronouns in English, although they do in some other languages.

I usually shave before breakfast.
She washed very quickly and rushed downstairs.

▶ See Unit 53 for more information.

4 You use a reflexive pronoun as the object of a preposition when the object of the preposition refers to the same person or thing as the subject of the verb in the same clause.

I was thoroughly ashamed of myself.
They are making fools of themselves.
Tell me about yourself.

Note that you use personal pronouns, not reflexive pronouns, when referring to places and after 'with' meaning 'accompanied by'.

You should have your notes in front of you.
He would have to bring Judy with him.

5 You use reflexive pronouns after nouns or pronouns to emphasize the person or thing that you are referring to.

The town itself was so small that it didn't have a bank.
I myself have never read the book.

6 You use a reflexive pronoun at the end of a clause to emphasize that someone did something without any help from anyone else.

She had printed the card herself.
I'll take it down to the police station myself.
Did you make these yourself?

7 You use reflexive pronouns with 'by' to say:

• that someone does something without any help from other people

…when babies start eating their meals by themselves.
She was certain she could manage by herself.

• that someone is alone

He went off to sit by himself.
I was there for about six months by myself.

You can also use 'on my own', 'on your own', and so on, to say that someone is alone or does something without any help.

We were in the park on our own.
They managed to reach the village on their own.

You can use 'all' for emphasis.

Did you put those shelves up all by yourself?
We can't solve this problem all on our own.

⊖ WARNING: 'One another' and 'each other' are not reflexive pronouns.

▶ See Unit 54 for more information on 'one another' and 'each other'.

Practice

A Choose a personal pronoun or a reflexive pronoun to complete these sentences correctly.

1 He was tired out but he forced ....*himself*... to go on.

2 I could hear someone walking along behind ....*me*.. .

3 She had cut .... so badly she had to be rushed to hospital.

4 She realised that the car in front of .... had stopped suddenly.

5 They built .... a garage behind the house.

6 He boiled .... a couple of eggs for breakfast.

7 Put it down in front of ....

8 If you've got a sleeping bag bring it with ....

9 They had promised .... a summer holiday abroad.

10 On Sunday mornings the children were left to take care of ....

B Change the phrases 'on my own' etc to 'by myself' etc.

1 It looked extremely heavy. I knew I couldn't lift it **on my own.** / ....*by myself.*.........

2 She hated being in the house **on her own.** / ....

3 If the rest of you can't help we'll have to do it **on our own.** / ....

4 You can't expect them to do everything **on their own.** / ....

5 Mothers had to go out to work and leave children in the house **on their own.** / ....

6 If there are three of you, you should be able to manage **on your own.** / ....

7 I hate living **on my own.** / ....

8 It's a horror film so children aren't allowed to see it **on their own.** / ....

9 John had to walk home **on his own.** / ....

10 It's too difficult for me. I can't do it all **on my own.** / ....

C Use the correct reflexive pronouns to complete the following sentences.

1 The chairman announced the news ....*himself*..

2 Helen will be very upset. I'll have to tell her the news ....

3 We built most of the house ....

4 The president .... appeared on television. She spoke for about ten minutes.

5 The children .... did most of the work for the school play.

D Rewrite the following sentences to start with the words given.

1 It was the BBC correspondent himself who told me. / I was told *by the BBC correspondent himself.*

2 This picture can't have been painted by Rembrandt himself. / It can't have been ....

3 There can be no doubt that Shakespeare himself wrote this play. / There can be no doubt that this play ....

4 The captain himself scored the winning goal. / The winning goal was scored ....

▸ **Bank**

Indefinite pronouns

Main points

Indefinite pronouns refer to people or things without saying exactly who or what they are.

When an indefinite pronoun is the subject, it always takes a singular verb.

You often use a plural pronoun to refer back to an indefinite pronoun.

1 The indefinite pronouns are:

anybody	everybody	nobody	somebody
anyone	everyone	no one	someone
anything	everything	nothing	something

Note that 'no one' is written as two words, or sometimes with a hyphen: 'no-one'.

2 You use indefinite pronouns when you want to refer to people or things without saying exactly who or what they are. The pronouns ending in '-body' and '-one' refer to people, and those ending in '-thing' refer to things.

> *I was there for over an hour before <u>anybody</u> came.*
> *It had to be <u>someone</u> with a car.*
> *Jane said <u>nothing</u> for a moment.*

3 When an indefinite pronoun is the subject, it always takes a singular verb, even when it refers to more than one person or thing.

> *<u>Everyone knows</u> that.*
> *<u>Everything was</u> fine.*
> *<u>Is anybody</u> there?*

When you refer back to indefinite pronouns, you use plural pronouns or possessives, and a plural verb.

> *Ask <u>anyone. They</u>'ll tell you.*
> *Has <u>everyone</u> eaten as much as <u>they</u> want?*
> *You can't tell <u>somebody</u> why <u>they</u>'ve failed.*

⊖ WARNING: Some speakers prefer to use singular pronouns. They prefer to say 'You can't tell somebody why he or she has failed'.

4 You can add apostrophe s ('s) to indefinite pronouns that refer to people.

> *She was given a room in <u>someone's</u> studio.*
> *That was <u>nobody's</u> business but mine.*

⊖ WARNING: You do not usually add apostrophe s ('s) to indefinite pronouns that refer to things. You do not say 'something's value', you say 'the value of something'.

5 You use indefinite pronouns beginning with 'some-' in:

- affirmative clauses

> *<u>Somebody</u> shouted.*
> *I want to introduce you to <u>someone</u>.*

- questions expecting the answer 'yes'

> *Would you like <u>something</u> to drink?*
> *Can you get <u>someone</u> to do it?*

6 You use indefinite pronouns beginning with 'any-':

- as the subject or object in statements

> *<u>Anyone</u> knows that you need a licence.*
> *You still haven't told me <u>anything</u>.*

You do not use them as the subject of a negative statement. You do not say 'Anybody can't come in'.

- in both affirmative and negative questions

> *Does <u>anybody</u> agree with me?*
> *Won't <u>anyone</u> help me?*

7 If you use an indefinite pronoun beginning with 'no-', you must not use another negative word in the same clause. You do not say 'There wasn't nothing'.

> *There was <u>nothing</u> you could do.*
> *<u>Nobody</u> left, <u>nobody</u> went away.*

8 You use the indefinite adverbs 'anywhere', 'everywhere', 'nowhere', and 'somewhere' to talk about places in a general way. 'Nowhere' makes a clause negative.

> *I thought I'd seen you <u>somewhere</u>.*
> *No-one can find Howard or Barbara <u>anywhere</u>.*
> *There was <u>nowhere</u> to hide.*

9 You can use 'else' after indefinite pronouns and adverbs to refer to people, things, or places other than those that have been mentioned.

> *<u>Everyone else</u> is downstairs.*
> *I don't like it here. Let's go <u>somewhere else</u>.*

Practice

A Complete each of the sentences below using one of the indefinite pronouns in brackets.

1 ......Everybody... arrived in good time and the meeting started promptly at 3.30. (*Anybody / Everybody / Nobody*)

2 .... in the village went to the party but .... enjoyed it very much. (*Everyone / No one / Someone*) (*anybody/somebody/nobody*)

3 When the show finished there was complete silence. .... clapped. (*Everyone / No one / Someone*)

4 Mohammed Ali is .... I have always admired. (*everybody / nobody / somebody*)

5 .... heard anything. (*Everyone / Nobody / Somebody*)

6 'Who shall I give this one to?' – 'You can give it to .... It doesn't matter.' (*anybody / nobody / somebody*)

7 That's a very easy job. .... can do it. (*Anybody / Nobody / Somebody*)

B Complete these sentences using the correct form of the verb in brackets.

1 I don't know why everybody .... hates .... me. (*hate*)

2 Let me know as soon as anyone .... (*arrive*)

3 Nobody .... being poor. (*like*)

4 It's no good if everyone .... to get their own way. (*want*)

5 The house is deserted. Nobody .... there now. (*live*)

6 If anybody .... , you can tell them I'll be back soon. (*ask*)

C Complete the following sentences with 'they', 'them', or 'their'.

1 Has everybody collected .... their .... luggage?

2 Tell everyone I'll wait for .... here.

3 If somebody had called, ... would have left a message.

4 Nobody offered to help. .... probably didn't have the time.

5 If anybody wants to know, tell .... to phone this number.

D Complete these sentences using 'something', 'nothing', 'everything', or 'anything'.

1 Excuse me, you've dropped .... something .... Yes, look, it's your passport.

2 I agree with most of what he said, but I don't agree with ....

3 It's all finished. I'm afraid there's .... left.

4 Did you turn the oven off? I think I can smell .... burning.

5 'Can I have whatever I want?' 'Yes, ... you like.'

E Complete the following sentences by using one of the indefinite pronouns given in brackets.

1 The box was completely empty. There was .... nothing .... in it. (*nothing / anything*)

2 I heard a noise, but I didn't see .... (*anyone / no one*)

3 I'm sorry, but there's .... at home. (*anybody / nobody*)

4 It's too late. We can't do .... to help. (*anything / nothing*)

5 No, I don't want .... , thanks. I'm not hungry. (*anything / nothing*)

6 It was very disappointing. Absolutely .... happened. (*anything/nothing*)

7 I didn't meet .... new. (*anybody / nobody*)

8 He claimed to be an expert, but he knew almost .... about it. (*anything / nothing*)

9 .... knew what to do next. (*Anybody / Nobody*)

▶ **Bank**

43

Possession

Main points

Possessives and possessive pronouns are used to say that one person or thing belongs to another or is connected with another.

You use apostrophe s ('s) to say who something belongs to.

You use phrases with 'of' to say that one person or thing belongs to another or is connected with another.

1 You use possessives to say that a person or thing belongs to another person or thing or is connected with them. The possessives are sometimes called 'possessive adjectives'.

my	your	his	her	its	our	their

Note that 'your' is both singular and plural.

> *I'd been waiting a long time to park my car.*
> *They took off their shoes.*

🔴 WARNING: The possessive 'its' is not spelled with an apostrophe. The form 'it's' with an apostrophe is the short form for 'it is' or 'it has'.

2 You put numbers and adjectives after the possessive and in front of the noun.

> *Their two small children were playing outside.*
> *She got a bicycle on her sixth birthday.*

3 You use a possessive pronoun when you want to refer to a person or thing and to say who that person or thing belongs to or is connected with. The possessive pronouns are:

mine	yours	his	hers	ours	theirs

Note that 'yours' is both singular and plural.

> *Is that coffee yours or mine ?*
> *It was his fault, not theirs.*

🔴 WARNING: There is no possessive pronoun 'its'.

4 You can also say who or what something belongs to or is connected with by using a noun with apostrophe s ('s). For example, if John owns a motorbike, you can refer to it as 'John's motorbike'.

> *Sylvia put her hand on John's arm.*
> *I like the car's design.*

You add apostrophe s ('s) to singular nouns and irregular plural nouns, usually referring to people rather than things.

> *I wore a pair of my sister's boots.*
> *Children's birthday parties can be boring.*

With plural nouns ending in '-s' you only add the apostrophe (').

> *It is not his parents' problem.*

You add apostrophe s ('s) to people's names, even when they end in '-s'.

> *Could you give me Charles's address?*

Note that when you use two or more names linked by 'and', you put the apostrophe s ('s) after the last name.

> *They have bought Sue and Tim's car.*

5 When you want to refer to someone's home, or to some common shops and places of work, you can use apostrophe s ('s) after a name or noun on its own.

> *He's round at David's.*
> *He bought it at the chemist's.*
> *She must go to the doctor's.*

6 You can also use apostrophe s ('s) with some expressions of time to identify something, or to say how much time is involved.

> *Did you see the cartoon in yesterday's newspaper?*
> *They have four weeks' holiday per year.*

7 You can use a prepositional phrase beginning with 'of' to say that one person or thing belongs to or is connected with another.

> *She is the mother of the boy who lives next door.*
> *Ellen aimlessly turned the pages of her magazine.*

After 'of' you can use a possessive pronoun, or a noun or name with apostrophe s ('s).

> *He was an old friend of mine.*
> *That word was a favourite of your father's.*
> *She's a friend of Stephen's.*

8 You can add 'own' after a possessive, or a noun or name with apostrophe s ('s), for emphasis.

> *My own view is that there are no serious problems.*
> *The professor's own answer may be unacceptable.*

Practice

A Complete these sentences by adding a possessive.

1 I left .... my .... car in the garage.
2 Mary hung .... coat on the peg.
3 Jack had .... hair cut.
4 Neil and David ate .... supper.
5 I hope you enjoy .... holiday.
6 We'll invite you round to .... house sometime.

And complete these by adding a possessive with 'own'.

7 You must make up .... your own .... mind.
8 The children had to cook .... supper.
9 Bill borrowed Jenny's car. .... car was being repaired.
10 I'll bring .... sheets and towels.
11 Every dog had .... special basket to sleep in.
12 You should do .... washing up.

B Complete the sentences by adding apostrophe or an apostrophe s ('s) to the noun group in brackets.

1 They're having a .... children's .... party on Saturday. (*children*)
2 This is my .... house. (*parents*)
3 You know John? He's .... father. (*David and Neil*)
4 I borrowed .... bike. (*James*)
5 I'll be staying in my .... flat. (*friends*)
6 That looks like .... car. (*John and Jean*)
7 This is .... coat, isn't it? (*Sylvia*)
8 We're going away for .... holiday. (*a week*)
9 You need .... rest. (*a couple of days*)
10 We usually have .... holiday in summer. (*two weeks*)

C Rewrite the replies to these questions.

1 A: Is this Becky's coat?
   B: No, it belongs to Jenny. / No, it's Jenny's. ....
2 A: Whose keys are these?
   B: They belong to me. / ....
3 A: Is this your money?
   B: No, I think it belongs to you. / ....
4 A: Is this John's pen?
   B: Yes, I think it belongs to him. / ....
5 A: Is this Jane's book?
   B: Yes, I'm sure it belongs to her. / ....
6 A: Is that Neil and David's car?
   B: Yes, it belongs to them. / ....

▶ **Bank**

Determiners

Main points

Determiners are used at the beginning of noun groups.

You use specific determiners when people know exactly which things or people you are talking about.

You use general determiners to talk about people or things without saying exactly who or what they are.

1 When you use a determiner, you put it at the beginning of a noun group, in front of numbers or adjectives.

I met _the two Swedish girls_ in London.
Our main bedroom is through there.
Have you got _another red card?_
Several young boys were waiting.

2 When the people or things that you are talking about have already been mentioned, or the people you are talking to know exactly which ones you mean, you use a specific determiner.

The man began to run towards _the_ boy.
Young people don't like _these_ operas.
Her face was very red.

The specific determiners are:

the definite article:	the
demonstratives:	this that these those
possessives:	my your his her its our their

Note that 'your' is used both for the singular and plural possessive.

➤ See Unit 19 for 'this', 'that', 'these', and 'those' as pronouns.

3 When you are mentioning people or things for the first time, or talking about them generally without saying exactly which ones you mean, you use a general determiner.

There was _a_ man in the lift.
We went to _an_ art exhibition.
You can stop at _any_ time you like.
There were _several_ reasons for this.

The general determiners are:

a	all	an	another	any
both	each	either	enough	every
few	fewer	less	little	many
more	most	much	neither	no
other	several	some		

4 Each general determiner is used with particular types of noun, such as:

• singular count nouns

a	an	another	any	each
either	every	neither	no	

I got _a postcard_ from Susan.
He opened _another shop_.
Any big tin container will do.

• plural count nouns

all	any	both	enough	few
fewer	many	more	most	no
other	several	some		

There were _few doctors_ available.
Several projects were postponed.
He spoke _many different languages._

• uncount nouns

all	any	enough	less	little
more	most	much	no	some

There was _little applause._
He did not speak _much English._
We need _more information_

⊖ WARNING: The following general determiners can never be used with uncount nouns.

a	an	another	both	each
either	every	few	many	
neither	several			

5 Most of the determiners are also pronouns, except 'the', 'a', 'an', 'every', 'no' and the possessives.

I saw _several_ in the woods last night.
There is _enough_ for all of us.
Have you got _any_ that I could borrow?

You use 'one' as a pronoun instead of 'a' or 'an', 'none' instead of 'no', and 'each' instead of 'every'.

Have you got _one?_
There are _none_ left.
Each has a separate box and number.

Practice

Unit 23

A Underline the determiners in the following sentences. The numbers in brackets tell you how many determiners there are.

1 <u>My</u> friend Alec works in <u>a</u> hotel on <u>the</u> corner of <u>this</u> street. (*4*)
2 There weren't many people at the match. But it was very exciting and our team scored twice in each half. (*4*)
3 Would you like another piece of this cake, or would you prefer a chocolate biscuit? (*3*)
4 Most young people like this sort of music. (*2*)
5 Every child at the party was given a present to take home. (*3*)
6 Thank you for your letter and the lovely flowers. (*2*)
7 We live in a small village in the country. It's a quiet, comfortable place with several useful shops. (*4*)
8 I hope to spend another month in your country sometime this summer. (*3*)
9 There was little information at the airport. Few people seemed to have any idea what time the flight was likely to leave. (*5*)
10 Can you give me another call at the office? I don't have much time to spare right now. (*3*)

B Now do these. Remember that a determiner comes at the front of a noun phrase.

1 <u>These</u> oranges cost ten pence each. (*1*)
2 Each orange costs ten pence. (*1*)
3 A: Is this your coat? (*1*)
   B: No, I'm fairly sure it belongs to that man over there in the corner. I left my coat in the cloakroom. (*4*)
4 Most students read both books, but they didn't find either very useful. (*2*)
5 There were several people at the meeting earlier, but most of them left early so there aren't many left now. (*2*)
6 This is what I always have for my breakfast. (*1*)
7 If I haven't any books, I can't do my homework. (*2*)
8 There's another bottle of milk in the fridge. Help yourself to a glass if you'd like some. (*3*)
9 Have you finished that glass of milk? There's plenty more in the fridge if you'd like another. (*2*)
10 Most people enjoyed the show, but I was definitely the one who enjoyed it most. (*3*)

47

Main uses of 'the'

Main points

You can use 'the' in front of any noun.

You use 'the' when the person you are talking to knows which person or thing you mean.

You use 'the' when you are referring back to someone or something.

You use 'the' when you are specifying which person or thing you are talking about.

You use 'the' when you are referring to something that is unique.

You use 'the' when you want to use one thing as an example to say something about all things of the same type.

1 'The' is called the definite article, and is the commonest determiner. You use 'the' when the person you are talking to knows which person or thing you mean. You can use 'the' in front of any noun, whether it is a singular count noun, an uncount noun, or a plural count noun.

> She dropped <u>the can.</u>
> I remembered <u>the fun</u> I had with them.
> <u>The girls</u> were not at home.

2 You use 'the' with a noun when you are referring back to someone or something that has already been mentioned.

> I called for <u>a waiter</u> …
> … <u>The waiter</u> with a moustache came.
> I have bought <u>a house</u> in Wales…
> … <u>The house</u> is in an agricultural area.

3 You use 'the' with a noun and a qualifier, such as a prepositional phrase or a relative clause, when you are specifying which person or thing you are talking about.

> I've no idea about <u>the geography of Scotland.</u>
> <u>The book that I recommended</u> now costs over three pounds.

4 You use 'the' with a noun when you are referring to something of which there is only one in the world.

> They all sat in <u>the sun.</u>
> We have landed men on <u>the moon.</u>
> <u>The sky</u> was a brilliant blue.

You also use 'the' when you are referring to something of which there is only one in a particular place.

> Mrs Robertson heard that <u>the church</u> had been bombed.
> He decided to put some words on <u>the blackboard.</u>

5 You can use 'the' with a singular count noun when you want to make a general statement about all things of that type. For example, if you say 'The whale is the largest mammal in the world', you mean all whales, not one particular whale.

> <u>The computer</u> allows us to deal with a lot of data very quickly.
> My father's favourite flower is <u>the rose.</u>

6 You can use 'the' with a singular count noun when you are referring to a system or service. For example, you can use 'the phone' to refer to a telephone system and 'the bus' to refer to a bus service.

> I don't like using <u>the phone.</u>
> How long does it take on <u>the train?</u>

7 You can use 'the' with the name of a musical instrument when you are talking about someone's ability to play the instrument.

> 'You play <u>the guitar,</u> I see,' said Simon.
> Geoff plays <u>the piano</u> very well.

Practice

A Read this passage.

Three learned Christian monks were travelling through Turkey hoping to meet (1) **the** wisest **man** in (2) **the** whole **country**. (3) **The monks** explained that they wanted to meet him because they each had a question to ask him. (4) **The sultan** sent for Nasreddin Hodja who came to (5) **the palace** at once. (6) **The** first **monk** stepped up and asked his question.

'Where is (7) **the centre** of (8) **the earth?'** 'At this moment the centre of the earth is exactly below (9) **the** front right **foot** of my donkey.'

'How can you possibly know that?' asked (10) **the monk.**

'If you measure the earth carefully you will find that I am correct,' replied Hodja.

(11) **The** second **monk** stepped up and asked his question.

'How many stars are there in (12) **the sky?'**

'As many as there are hairs on my donkey,' replied Hodja. 'As you will see if you count them.'

(13) **The** third **monk** came forward. 'How many hairs are there in my beard?' he asked.

'That is easy,' said Hodja. 'As many as there are hairs in (14) **the** donkey's **tail** . If you do not believe me step forward and we can pull out (15) **the hairs** from your beard and (16) **the hairs** from (17) **the** donkey's **tail** one by one and count them.'

The third monk was not very keen on this idea so he had to admit he was beaten, so everyone could see that Hodja was (18) **the** wisest **man** of all.

Look at the 18 phrases with 'the' above. How do you know in each case which person or thing the writer is talking about?

Now answer these questions:

1 Which man? ....The wisest man...
2 Which country? ....
3 Which monks? ....
4 Which sultan? ....
5 Which palace? ....
6 Which monk? ....
7 Which centre? ....
9 Which foot? ....
10 Which monk? ....
11 Which monk? ....
13 Which monk? ....
14 Which donkey? ....
15 Which hairs? ....
16 Which hairs? ....
17 Which tail? ....

What about (8), (12), and (18)? How do you know which one the writer means in each case?

8 ....
12 ....
18 ....

▶ **Bank**

Other uses of 'the'

Main points

You do not normally use 'the' with proper nouns referring to people. You do use 'the' with many proper nouns referring to geographical places.

You use 'the' with some adjectives to talk about groups of people.

1 You do not normally use 'the' with proper nouns that are people's names. However, if you are talking about a family, you can say 'the Browns'.

You use 'the' with some titles, such as 'the Queen of England', and with the names of some organizations, buildings, newspapers, and works of art.

  … _the United Nations_…   … _the Taj Mahal_.
  … _the Times_…   … _the Mona Lisa_.

2 You do use 'the' with some proper nouns referring to geographical places.

  … _the Bay of Biscay_…   … _the Suez Canal_.
  … _the Arabian Gulf_…   … _the Pacific_.

You use 'the' with countries whose names include words such as 'kingdom', 'republic', 'states', or 'union'.

  … _the United Kingdom_…   … _the Soviet Union_.

You use 'the' with countries that have plural nouns as their names.

  … _the Netherlands_…   … _the Philippines_.

Note that you do not use 'the' with countries that have singular nouns as their names, such as 'China', 'Italy', or 'Turkey'.

You use 'the' with names of mountain ranges and groups of islands.

  … _the Canaries_…   … _the Himalayas_.

Note that you do not use 'the' with the names of individual mountains such as 'Everest' or 'Etna', or the names of individual islands such as 'Sicily', 'Minorca', or 'Bali'.

You use 'the' with regions of the world, or regions of a country that include 'north', 'south', 'east', or 'west'.

  … _the Middle East_…   … _the north of England_

Note that there are some exceptions.

  … _North America_…   … _South-East Asia_.

You do not use 'the' with 'northern', 'southern', 'eastern', or 'western' and a singular name.

  … _northern England_…   … _western Africa_.

You use 'the' with the names of areas of water such as seas, oceans, rivers, canals, gulfs, and straits.

  … _the Mediterranean Sea_… … _the Atlantic_.
  … _the river Ganges_…   … _the Panama Canal_.
  … _the Gulf of Mexico_…   … _the straits of Gibraltar_.

Note that you do not use 'the' with lakes.

  … _Lake Geneva_…   … _Lake Superior_.

Note that you do not use 'the' with continents, cities, streets, or addresses.

  … _Asia_…   … _Tokyo_.
  … _Oxford Street_…   … _15 Park Street_.

3 You use 'the' with adjectives such as 'rich', 'poor', 'young', 'old', and 'unemployed' to talk about a general group of people. You do not need a noun.

  Only the rich could afford his firm's products.
  They were discussing the problem of the unemployed.

When you use 'the' with an adjective as the subject of a verb, you use a plural verb.

  In the cities the poor are as badly off as they were in the villages.

4 You use 'the' with some nationality adjectives to talk about the people who live in a country.

  They will be increasingly dependent on the support of the French.
  The Spanish claimed that the money had not been paid.

With other nationalities, you use a plural noun.

  … _Germans_…   … _the Americans_.

When you use 'the' with a nationality adjective as the subject of a verb, you use a plural verb.

  The British are worried.

5 You use 'the' with superlatives.

  He was the cleverest man I ever knew.
  He was the youngest.
  His shoulders hurt the worst.
  It was the most exciting summer of their lives.

Practice

A In each of the following sentences the word 'the' has been left out at least once. Read the sentences and mark where 'the' should be. The number in brackets tells you how many times 'the' occurs. In 1, for example, you need to put 'the' in twice.

1 I have been to **the** United Kingdom, Germany, and **the** Soviet Union, but never to Poland. (2)
2 Amazon in Brazil is the longest river in South America. (1)
3 Japan and United States are separated by Pacific Ocean. (2)
4 Liverpool is in north of England, fairly close to Wales. (1)
5 I would love to go to Jamaica, Bahamas or somewhere else in Caribbean. (2)
6 Suez Canal flows through north of Egypt from Port Said to Suez, joining Mediterranean to Gulf of Suez and Red Sea. (5)
7 Lake Windermere in north-west of England is one of the largest lakes in British Isles. (2)
8 Mont Blanc is in Alps on the border between France and Italy. (1)
9 Biarritz stands on the mouth of Adour river which flows into Gulf of Gascony in Bay of Biscay. (3)

B Now do the same with these sentences.

1 While we were in London we stayed at **the** Royal Hotel in Albert Street near Trafalgar Square. (1)
2 On the first morning we went to British Museum and had lunch at MacDonald's in Church Street. (1)
3 In the evening we went to a pub off Leicester Square, then we went to a play at National Theatre. (1)
4 Next day we went to Houses of Parliament and Westminster Abbey and had lunch at Peking Restaurant. (2)
5 We looked in Evening Standard newspaper and found there was a good film at Odeon cinema near Piccadilly Circus. (2)

C Complete the sentences below using 'the' with these adjectives.

| blind | dead | disabled | poor | rich | unemployed |

1 It is said that we should never speak ill of ....the dead............................... .
2 Buildings should be specially designed so they can be used by ....
3 It is only fair that .... should pay higher taxes than ....
4 In St John's Park there is a special garden for .... with strongly scented flowers.
5 Life is bound to be difficult for ....

51

'A' and 'an'

Unit 26

Main points

You only use 'a' or 'an' with singular count nouns.

You use 'a' or 'an' to talk about a person or thing for the first time.

1 You only use 'a' or 'an' with singular count nouns. 'A' and 'an' are called the indefinite article.

> *I got a postcard from Susan.*
> *He was eating an apple.*

Remember that you use 'a' in front of a word that begins with a consonant sound even if the first letter is a vowel, for example 'a piece, a university, a European language'. You use 'an' in front of a word that begins with a vowel sound even if the first letter is a consonant, for example 'an exercise, an idea, an honest man'.

2 You use 'a' or 'an' when you are talking about a person or thing for the first time.

> *She picked up a book.*
> *After weeks of looking, we eventually bought a house.*

Note that the second time you refer to the same person or thing, you use 'the'.

> *She picked up a book …*
> *… The book was lying on the table.*
> *After weeks of looking, we bought a house …*
> *… The house was in a village.*

3 After the verb 'be' or another link verb, you can use 'a' or 'an' with an adjective and a noun to give more information about someone or something.

> *His brother was a sensitive child.*
> *He seemed a worried man.*
> *It was a really beautiful house.*

You can also use 'a' or 'an' with a noun followed by a qualifier, such as a prepositional phrase or a relative clause, when you want to give more information about someone or something.

> *The information was contained in an article on biology.*
> *I chose a picture that reminded me of my own country.*

4 You use 'a' or 'an' after the verb 'be' or another link verb when you are saying what someone is or what job they have.

> *He became a school teacher.*
> *She is a model and an artist.*

5 You use 'a' or 'an' to mean 'one' with some numbers.

You can use 'a' or 'an' with nouns that refer to whole numbers, fractions, money, weights, or measures.

| a hundred | a quarter | a pound | a kilo |
| a thousand | a half | a dollar | a litre |

6 You do not use 'a' or 'an' with uncount nouns or plural count nouns. You do not need to use a determiner at all with plural count nouns, but you can use the determiners 'any', 'a few', 'many', 'several', or 'some'.

> *I love dogs.*
> *Do you have any dogs?*
> *Many adults don't listen to children.*
> *I have some children like that in my class.*

Note that if you do not use a determiner with a plural count noun, you are often making a general statement about people or things of that type. For example, if you say 'I love dogs', you mean all dogs. However, if you say 'There are eggs in the kitchen', you mean there are some eggs. If you do use a determiner, you mean a number of people or things but not all of them, without saying exactly how many.

> *I have some friends coming for dinner.*
> *He has bought some plants for the house.*
> *I have some important things to tell them.*

Practice

A Rewrite the sentences using singular nouns with 'a' or 'an' instead of the plural nouns in bold.

1 **Dogs** make good **pets.** / ....A dog makes a good pet.....................

2 **Lawyers** usually earn more than **policemen.** / ....

3 I love reading good **books.** / ....

4 You don't often see good **programmes** on TV nowadays. / ....

5 **Sons** are always a lot more trouble than **daughters.** / ....

6 I often have **eggs** for breakfast. / ....

7 Nowadays you can buy computer-controlled **washing machines.** / ....

8 I hate to hear **babies** crying or **dogs** barking. / ....

B Where you find a noun phrase with a singular count noun but no determiner, put in 'a' or 'an'.

1 In English ᵃ noun phrase with ᵃ singular count noun can hardly ever stand on its own.

2 We have just bought new house with large garden.

3 My brother is teacher and I have cousin who works with young children as well.

4 Would you like biscuit or piece of cake?

5 I spoke to official and he gave me very good advice.

C Look at the following pairs of sentences. For each pair fill one blank with 'a' or 'an', and the other with 'the'.

1 I wrote ....ᵃ............... long letter to Jenny this morning.

  Did I show you ....the.......... letter I got from Peter this morning?

2 My uncle used to be .... dentist before he retired.

  Arthur Brown is .... dentist who lives next door to my parents.

3 Is there .... bookshop on the High Street?

  I bought this at .... bookshop in the High Street.

4 Has anyone seen .... newspaper I left in the sitting room?

  I usually buy .... newspaper on my way to work.

5 London is easily .... biggest city in Britain.

  Manchester is .... big city in the north of England.

6 It's not easy to learn .... foreign language which is very
  different from your own language.

  Japanese is certainly .... most difficult language I have tried to learn.

7 Agatha Christie was .... well known writer of detective stories.

  Agatha Christie was .... writer who invented Hercule Poirot.

8 The police are looking for .... young man aged about 23.

  .... young man the police are looking for is about 23.

9 Last night I saw .... interesting TV programme about Eastern Europe.

  I really enjoyed .... programme about Eastern Europe last night.

10 I learned to drive .... car when I was eighteen.

  Dad, can I borrow .... car tonight?

▶ **Bank**

All, most, no, one

Main points

You use 'all' with plural count nouns and uncount nouns. You use 'all' to talk about every person or thing in the world, or in the group you are talking about.

You use 'most' with plural count nouns and uncount nouns. You use 'most' to talk about nearly all of a number of people or things, or nearly all of a quantity of something.

You use 'no' with singular and plural count nouns and uncount nouns. You use 'no' to say that something does not exist or is not present.

1 You use 'all' with plural count nouns and uncount nouns to talk about every person or thing in the world or in the group that you are talking about.

> *All children should complete the primary course.*
> *All important decisions were taken by the government.*
> *He soon lost all hope of becoming a rock star.*
> *All luggage will be searched.*

2 You use 'most' with plural count nouns and uncount nouns to talk about nearly all of a number of people or things, or nearly all of a quantity of something.

> *The method was suitable for most purposes.*
> *Most good drivers stop at zebra crossings.*
> *Most milk is still delivered to people's houses.*
> *He ignored most advice, and did what he thought best.*

3 You use 'no' with singular count nouns, plural count nouns, and uncount nouns to say that something does not exist or is not present.

> *There was no chair for me to sit on.*
> *They had no immediate plans to change house.*
> *No money was available for the operation.*

Note that if there is another word in the clause that makes it negative, you use 'any', not 'no'.

> *It hasn't made any difference.*
> *He will never do any work for me again.*

4 'All' and 'most' are also pronouns, so you can say 'all of' and 'most of'. 'No' is not a pronoun, so you must say 'none of'.

> *He spent all of the money on a new car.*
> *Most of my friends live in London.*
> *None of those farmers had ever driven a tractor.*

Note that you use 'all of', 'most of', and 'none of' with an object pronoun.

> *All of us were sleeping.*
> *I had seen most of them before.*
> *None of them came to the party.*

Note that if the clause is already negative, you use 'any of', not 'none of'.

> *I hadn't eaten any of the biscuits.*

When 'none of' is followed by a plural noun or pronoun, the verb is usually plural, but can be singular.

> *None of us are the same.*
> *None of them has lasted very long.*

5 You can use 'all the' with a plural count noun or an uncount noun. There is no difference in meaning between 'all the' and 'all of the'.

> *All the girls think it's great.*
> *All the best jokes came at the end of the programme.*
> *Thank you for all the help you gave me.*

⊖ WARNING: You cannot say 'most the' or 'none the'. You must say 'most of the' or 'none of the'.

6 You can use 'all' after a noun or pronoun to emphasize that the noun or pronoun refers to everyone or everything that has been mentioned or is involved.

Note that you can use 'all' to emphasize the subject or the object.

> *The band all live together in the same house.*
> *I enjoyed it all.*

A Use the phrases below to complete the sentences which follow.

all alcoholic drinks	all banks	all cars	all children	all doctors	all old people

1 .... All children .... must go to school until the age of 16.
2 .... must be licensed.
3 .... receive a pension from the state.
4 There is a tax on ....
5 .... are closed on Sunday.
6 .... must have at least five years' training.

All these sentences are true for Britain. How many are true for your country?

B Choose phrases from the list to say where you might see the notices given below.

at an airport	in a bank	in a hotel	at a railway station	in a department store
in a library	in a park	in a restaurant		

1 All dogs must be kept on a lead. ....In a park....................
2 All books must be returned within three weeks. ....
3 All customers should wait to be seated. ....
4 All goods must be taken to the cash desk. ....
5 All luggage must be checked at the security desk. ....
6 All traveller's cheques must be signed and dated. ....
7 All passengers must have a valid ticket. ....
8 All bills must be paid before guests check out. ....

C Rewrite the following sentences using 'all of' or 'most of'.

1 The children were all fast asleep. / ....All of the children were fast asleep...................
2 The children were nearly all fast asleep. / ....
3 Nearly all the students passed the exam. / ....
4 All my friends came to the party. / ....
5 The clothes were all very expensive. / ....
6 Nearly all the seats were booked. / ....
7 The ice cream was nearly all finished. / ....
8 The garden was nearly all full of weeds. / ....

D Rewrite these sentences using 'no'.

1 I haven't any free time this week. / ....I have no free time this week.......................
2 John didn't have any money left. / ....
3 He hasn't any friends. / ....
4 There isn't any milk in the fridge. / ....
5 We didn't get any letters today. / ....
6 There weren't any girls in the class. / ....

▶ **Bank**

Both, either, neither

1 You use 'both', 'either', and 'neither' when you are saying something about two people or things that have been mentioned, or are known to the person you are talking to.

> *There were excellent performances from <u>both actresses</u>.*
> *Denis held his cocoa in <u>both hands</u>.*
> *No argument could move <u>either man</u> from this decision.*
> *<u>Neither report</u> mentioned the Americans.*

2 You use 'both' when you think of the two people or things as a group. You use 'both' with a plural noun.

> *<u>Both children</u> were happy with their presents.*
> *<u>Both policies</u> make good sense.*

3 You use 'either' when you think of the two people or things as individuals. You use 'either' with a singular noun.

> *<u>Either way</u> is acceptable.*
> *She could not see <u>either man</u>.*

4 You use 'neither' when you are thinking of the two people or things as individuals and you are making a negative statement about them. You use 'neither' with a singular noun.

> *In reality, <u>neither party</u> was enthusiastic.*
> *<u>Neither man</u> knew what he was doing.*

5 You can use 'both' with a specific determiner such as 'the', 'these', or 'my'.

> *<u>Both the young men</u> agreed to come.*
> *<u>Both these books</u> have been recommended to us.*
> *<u>Both her parents</u> were dead.*

🔵 WARNING: You cannot use 'either' or 'neither' with a specific determiner.

6 You can use 'both of', 'either of', or 'neither of' with a plural noun or pronoun.

Note that when 'both of', 'either of', and 'neither of' are followed by a noun rather than a pronoun, you must use a specific determiner such as 'the', 'these', or 'her' before the noun.

> *<u>Both of these restaurants</u> are excellent.*
> *<u>Either of them</u> could have done the job.*
> *<u>Neither of our boys</u> was involved.*

Note that 'neither of' is normally used with a singular verb but it can be used with a plural verb.

> *Neither of us <u>was having</u> any luck.*
> *Neither of the children <u>were</u> there.*

7 Remember that you can also use 'both', 'either', and 'neither' as conjunctions. You use 'both...and' to give two alternatives and say that each of them is possible or true.

> *I am looking for opportunities <u>both</u> in this country <u>and</u> abroad.*
> *<u>Both</u> my wife <u>and</u> I are aged 40.*

You use 'either...or' to give two alternatives and say that only one of them is possible or true.

> *You can have <u>either</u> fruit <u>or</u> ice cream.*
> *I was expecting you <u>either</u> today <u>or</u> tomorrow.*
> *You <u>either</u> love him <u>or</u> hate him.*

You also use 'neither...nor' to give two alternatives and say that each of them is not possible or is not true.

> *<u>Neither</u> Margaret <u>nor</u> John was there.*
> *He did it <u>neither</u> quickly <u>nor</u> well.*

Practice

A Choose the correct form of the verb in brackets to complete these sentences.

1 Both my brothers ……………………… *live* ……………………… in London. (*lives / live*)
2 Neither of his parents ……………………………………………… alive. (*is / are*)
3 Neither John nor Mary …………………………………………… at home. (*was / were*)
4 We both …………………………………… football but neither of us …………………………
   tennis. (*likes / like*) (*likes / like*)
5 Both Peter and Michael …………………………………………… here quite often but neither of
   them …………………………………………… us much help. (*comes / come*) (*gives / give*)
6 Both of us …………………………………………… been to Paris but neither of us ………………
   been to Rome. (*has / have*) (*has / have*)

B Which of the cities below do the following sentences refer to?

London	Milan	New York	Rome	Washington

1 Neither is a capital city. ……………… *Milan and New York.* ………………
2 Both of them are in America. ……………………………………………………………
3 None of them is in America. …………………………………………………………
4 All of them are capital cities. ………………………………………………………
5 They are both in Italy. …………………………………………………………
6 They are all in Europe. …………………………………………………………

C Complete the sentences about the cities, choosing suitable phrases from the table below.

All Neither Both None	of them	is are

1 Birmingham and Manchester.
   ……… *Both of them are* ……… in Britain. / ……… *Neither of them is* ……… in Asia.
2 Valencia and Hiroshima.
   ……………………………………………… a capital city.
3 Hong Kong, Singapore, and Peking.
   …………………………… in Asia. / …………………………………………… in Europe.
4 San Francisco, Bangkok, and Canberra.
   ……………………………………… in Europe.
5 Bangkok, Tokyo, and Athens.
   …………………………… capital cities. / …………………………………… in America.
6 Marseilles and Lyons.
   ………………………… in France. / ………………………… the capital of France.

▸ **Bank**

Quantity 1

Main points

You use 'much' and 'little' with uncount nouns to talk about a quantity of something.

You use 'many' and 'few' with plural nouns to talk about a number of people or things.

You use 'much' in negative sentences and questions, and 'a lot of' or 'plenty of' rather than 'much' in affirmative sentences.

You use 'more' and 'less' with uncount nouns, and 'more' and 'fewer' with plural count nouns.

1 You use 'much' to talk about a large quantity of something, and 'little' to talk about a small quantity of something. You only use 'much' and 'little' with uncount nouns.

> I haven't got <u>much time.</u>
> We've made <u>little progress.</u>

2 You use 'many' to talk about a large number of people or things, and 'few' to talk about a small number of people or things. You can only use 'many' and 'few' with plural count nouns.

> He wrote <u>many novels.</u>
> There were <u>few visitors</u> to our house.

3 You normally use 'much' in negative sentences and questions.

> He did <u>not</u> speak <u>much</u> English.
> Why haven<u>'t</u> I given <u>much</u> attention to this problem?

In affirmative sentences you do not use 'much', you use 'a lot of', 'lots of', or 'plenty of' instead. You can use them with both uncount nouns and plural nouns.

> He demanded <u>a lot of attention.</u>
> I make <u>a lot of mistakes.</u>
> They spent <u>lots of time</u> on the project.
> He saw a large room with <u>lots of windows.</u>
> I've got <u>plenty of money.</u>
> There are always <u>plenty of jobs</u> to be done.

Note that you can use 'so much' and 'too much' in affirmative sentences.

> She spends <u>so much time</u> here.
> There is <u>too much chance</u> of error.

4 You use 'so much' to emphasize that a large quantity of something is involved.

> I have <u>so much work</u> to do.
> They have <u>so much money</u> and we have so little.

You use 'too much' and 'too many' to say that the quantity of something, or the number of people or things, is larger than is reasonable or necessary.

> He has <u>too much work.</u>
> <u>Too many people</u> still smoke.

You use 'very many' to emphasize that a large number of people or things are involved.

> <u>Very many old people</u> live alone.

Note that 'very much' is used with nouns and verbs.

> There isn't <u>very much time.</u>
> I <u>liked</u> it <u>very much.</u>

5 You use 'few' and 'little' to emphasize that only a small quantity of something or a small number of people or things are involved. They can be used with 'very' for greater emphasis.

> The town has <u>few monuments.</u>
> I have <u>little time</u> for anything but work.
> <u>Very few cars</u> had reversing lights.
> I had <u>very little money</u> left.

Note that 'a few' and 'a little' just indicate that a quantity or number is small.

> He spread <u>a little honey</u> on a slice of bread.
> I usually do <u>a few jobs</u> for him in the house.

6 You use 'more' with uncount nouns and plural count nouns to refer to a quantity of something or a number of people or things that is greater than another quantity or number.

> His visit might do <u>more harm</u> than good.
> He does <u>more hours</u> than I do.

You use 'less' with uncount nouns to refer to an amount of something that is smaller than another amount.

> The poor have <u>less access</u> to education.
> This machinery uses <u>less energy.</u>

You use 'fewer', or 'less' in informal English, with plural nouns to refer to a number of people or things that is smaller than another number.

> There are <u>fewer trees</u> here.
> They have sold <u>less computers</u> this year.

Practice

A Complete these sentences using the determiners given in brackets.

1 She speaks …*a lot of*……… English but she doesn't speak…*much*……… French. (*a lot of / much*)
2 He didn't sell very …………… books. That's why he never made …………… money. (*many / much*)
3 There weren't ………… trains to Birmingham, but there were …………… buses. (*plenty of / many*)
4 Very …………… people could manage to live on so …………………… money. (*few / little*)
5 There's ………………… work to do, so we haven't ………………… time to spare. (*a lot of / much*)
6 If you can spare me ………………… time, I'd like to make …………… suggestions. (*a few / a little*)
7 He spends so ……………… time playing football that he has ………………… time for anything else. (*little / much*)
8 There are …………… cars in the city centre at rush hour, but very ……… late at night. (*few / lots of*)

B Complete these sentences using 'little' or 'few'.

1 He is very successful even though he has very ………………*little*……………… education.
2 …………………………………………… people really understood what the lecture was about.
3 Diana tried hard but she was very …………………………………………… help.
4 He made so …………………………………………… mistakes that he came top in the exam.
5 I can't do much I'm afraid. I have so …………………………………………… time.

C Complete these using 'a little' or 'a few'.

1 Would you like ……………*a little*………………………… cake?
2 Would you like ………………………………………… apples?
3 I have to see ………………………………………… people this afternoon.
4 Could you give me ………………………………………… help?
5 I don't know the answer, but I've got ………………………………………… ideas.

D Complete these sentences using 'very few', 'a few', 'very little' or 'a little'.

1 There are lots of boys in our class, but …………………*very few*………………… girls.
2 He's an expert on languages, but he knows …………………………………… about mathematics.
3 There are lots of cinemas in town as well as …………………………………… good theatres.
4 I took plenty of sugar and …………………………………… milk.
5 When I'm busy, I always do …………………………………… work before breakfast.
6 I come home so tired that I can do …………………………………… work in the evenings.
7 Jack is very helpful. He's sure to have …………………………………… good ideas.
8 Jack is usually very helpful but he had …………………………………… advice for us this time.
9 …………………………………… unskilled jobs are well paid, but not very many.
10 I was tired and hungry, but fortunately I had …………………………………… money left.

Quantity 2

Main points

You use 'some' to talk about a quantity or number without being precise.

You use 'any' to talk about a quantity or number that may or may not exist.

You use 'another', or 'another' and a number, to talk about additional people or things.

You use 'each' and 'every' to talk about all the members of a group of people or things.

1 You use 'some' with uncount nouns and plural nouns to talk about a quantity of something or a number of people or things without being precise.

> *I have left <u>some food</u> for you in the fridge.*
> *<u>Some trains</u> are running late.*

You normally use 'some' in affirmative sentences.

> *There's <u>some chocolate cake</u> over there.*
> *I had <u>some good ideas.</u>*

You use 'some' in questions when you expect the answer to be 'yes', for example in offers or requests.

> *Would you like <u>some coffee?</u>*
> *Could you give me <u>some examples?</u>*

You can use 'some' with a singular noun when you do not know which person or thing is involved, or you think it does not matter.

> *<u>Some</u> man phoned, but didn't leave his number.*
> *Is there <u>some</u> problem?*

2 You use 'any' in front of plural and uncount nouns to talk about a quantity of something that may or may not exist. You normally use 'any' in questions and negative sentences.

> *Are there <u>any jobs</u> men can do but women can't?*
> *It hasn't made <u>any difference.</u>*

You use 'any' with a singular noun to emphasize that it does not matter which person or thing is involved.

> *<u>Any</u> container will do.*

You can use 'no' with an affirmative verb instead of 'not any'.

> *There weren<u>'t any tomatoes</u> left.*
> *There <u>were no tomatoes</u> left.*

You can also use 'not' and 'any', or 'no', with a comparative.

> *Her house was<u>n't any better</u> than ours.*
> *Her house was <u>no better</u> than ours.*

3 You use 'another' with singular nouns to talk about an additional person or thing.

> *Could I have <u>another cup of coffee?</u>*
> *He opened <u>another shop</u> last month.*

You can also use 'another' with a number and a plural noun to talk about more people or things.

> *<u>Another four years</u> passed before we met again.*
> *I've got <u>another three books</u> to read.*

You use 'other' with plural nouns and 'the other' with singular or plural nouns.

> *I've got <u>other things</u> to think about.*
> *<u>The other</u> man has gone.*
> *<u>The other</u> European countries have beaten us.*

4 You use 'each' or 'every' with a singular noun to talk about all the members of a group of people or things. You use 'each' when you are thinking about the members as individuals, and 'every' when you are making a general statement about all of them.

> *<u>Each county</u> is subdivided into several districts.*
> *<u>Each applicant</u> has five choices.*
> *<u>Every child</u> would have milk <u>every day.</u>*
> *She spoke to <u>every person</u> at that party.*

You can modify 'every' but not 'each'.

> *He spoke to them <u>nearly every day.</u>*
> *We went out <u>almost every evening.</u>*

5 You can use 'some of', 'any of', or 'each of', and a noun group to talk about a number of people or things in a group of people or things.

> *<u>Some of the information</u> has already been analysed.*
> *It was more expensive than <u>any of the other magazines.</u>*
> *He gave <u>each of us</u> advice about our present goals.*

You can use 'each of' and a plural noun group but 'every' must be followed by 'one of'.

> *<u>Each of the drawings</u> is different.*
> *<u>Every one of them</u> is given a financial target.*

Note that you can also use 'each' with 'one of'.

> *This view of poverty influences <u>each one of us.</u>*

Practice

A Complete these sentences by using 'some' or 'any'.

1 I've met ....*some*.......... people, but I don't have ....*any*.................. real friends yet.

2 I'd like to make .... friends, but I haven't met .... young people yet.

3 A: Is there .... petrol in the tank?
   B: Well, I filled it yesterday. There must be .... left.

4 There are .... biscuits left, but there isn't .... cake.

5 I know you speak .... French, but do you speak .... German?

6 A: Have you got .... matches?
   B: Yes, I think I've got .... in my pocket.

7 I thought I had met .... of the people here but I don't know .... of them.

8 Have you .... idea what time it is?

B Rewrite these sentences using 'some' or 'any'.

1 **All** children can learn to read and write. (*any*) / ..*Any child can learn to read and write.*..........

2 **Not all** of the children understood. (*some*) / ....

3 I will be free **every** day next week.(*any*) / ....

4 **All** the buses will take you to the city centre. (*any*) / ....

5 **A few** people said that they would be late. (*some*) / ....

6 You can buy it at **all** good bookshops. (*any*) / ....

7 I'd like to give you **a bit of** advice. (*some*) / ....

8 **One** of the guides will show you the way. (*any*) / ....

9 **A few** of the children missed the bus. (*some*) / ....

10 I like **all** fruit except bananas. (*any*) / ....

C Choose which determiner in brackets best completes each sentence.

1 There are ....*plenty*..... of chocolate biscuits. Would you like another one? (*some / a few / plenty*)

2 I have .... books with me. I've read most of them, but I
   haven't read .... one. (*a few / any / plenty*) (*another / any / every*)

3 He gave .... of the children a small gift. (*any / each / every*)

4 You can ask the doctor if you want .... advice. (*any / every / another*)

5 I wanted .... pound of meat but there wasn't
   .... left. (*another / other / each*) (*any / other / some*)

6 We hadn't .... oil left, but ....
   .... people lent us some. (*any / some*) (*another / other*)

7 I'd like to ask you for .... advice. (*another / any / some*)

8 I see Jack at work almost .... day. (*any / each / every*)

9 There was a prize for .... one of the competitors. (*any / every / some*)

10 Jenny was older than .... of the other girls. (*any / every*)

61

Unit 31

Main points

There are two main positions for adjectives: in front of a noun, or as the complement of a link verb.

Most adjectives can be used in either of these positions, but some adjectives can only be used in one.

1 Most adjectives can be used in a noun group, after determiners and numbers if there are any, in front of the noun.

> He had a _beautiful smile._
> She bought a loaf of _white bread._
> There was no _clear evidence._

2 Most adjectives can also be used after a link verb such as 'be', 'become', or 'feel'.

> _I'm cold._
> I _felt angry._
> Nobody _seemed amused._

3 Some adjectives are normally used only after a link verb.

afraid	alive	alone	asleep	aware
content	due	glad	ill	ready
sorry	sure	unable	well	

For example, you can say 'She was glad', but you do not talk about 'a glad woman'.

> I wanted to _be alone._
> We were _getting ready_ for bed.
> _I'm_ not quite _sure._
> He didn't know whether to _feel glad_ or _sorry._

4 Some adjectives are normally used only in front of a noun.

atomic	countless	digital	eastern
existing	indoor	introductory	maximum
neighbouring	northern	occasional	outdoor
southern	western		

For example, you talk about 'an atomic bomb', but you do not say 'The bomb was atomic'.

> He sent _countless letters_ to the newspapers.
> This book includes a good _introductory chapter_ on forests.

5 When you use an adjective to emphasize a strong feeling or opinion, it always comes in front of a noun.

absolute	complete	entire	outright
perfect	positive	pure	real
total	true	utter	

> Some of it was _absolute rubbish._
> He made me feel like a _complete idiot._

6 Some adjectives that describe size or age can come after a noun group consisting of a number or determiner and a noun that indicates the unit of measurement.

deep	high	long	old	tall	thick	wide

> He was about _six feet tall._
> The water was _several metres deep._
> The baby is _nine months old._

Note that you do not say 'two pounds heavy', you say 'two pounds in weight'.

7 A few adjectives are used alone after a noun.

designate	elect	galore	incarnate

> She was now the _president elect._
> There are empty _houses galore._

8 A few adjectives have a different meaning depending on whether they come in front of or after a noun.

concerned	involved	present	proper
responsible			

For example, 'the concerned mother' means a mother who is worried, but 'the mother concerned' means the mother who has been mentioned.

> It's one of those incredibly _involved stories._
> The _people involved_ are all doctors.
> I'm worried about the _present situation._
> Of the 18 _people present,_ I knew only one.
> Her parents were trying to act in a _responsible manner._
> We do not know the _person responsible_ for his death.

Practice

A Rewrite the phrases by putting one of these adjectives in front of the appropriate noun.

atomic	countless	digital	eastern	indoor	introductory	maximum
neighbouring	northern	outdoor				

1 … the region in the east of the country. / ....the eastern region. ....
2 … power produced by nuclear fission. / ....
3 … a watch which uses figures to show the time. / ....
4 … the first paragraph in a piece of writing. / ....
5 … the largest number possible. / ....
6 … the border to the north of the country. / ....
7 … countries on the borders. / ....
8 … a party held in the open air. / ....
9 … plants which can be kept in the house. / ....
10 … a huge number of people. / ....

B Complete the definitions using the adjectives below.

afraid	asleep	aware	content	due	glad	ready	sorry	sure	unable

1 If you are ....afraid....................... to do something, you feel fear because you think it will hurt you in some way.
2 If you are .... about something, you are pleased and happy about it.
3 If you are .... to do something, it is impossible for you to do it.
4 If something is .... at a particular time, it is expected to happen or arrive at that time.
5 If you feel .... about something, you are sad or disappointed about it.
6 If you say that someone is .... of himself or herself, you mean that they are very confident.
7 If you are .... of something, you know that it exists or that it is important.
8 If you are half .... , you are not listening or paying attention because you are very tired.
9 If you are .... to do something, you are willing to do it.
10 If you are .... , you are fairly happy.

C Match the phrases and definitions below. The first has been done for you.

1 Someone who is very stupid is …   a … an utter disaster.
2 Someone who is very troublesome is …   b … a real problem.
3 Something which is extremely unfortunate and tragic is … c … a positive menace.
4 Something which is quite ridiculous is …   d … a champion.
5 Someone who wins a sports competition is … e … a true friend.
6 Something which will cause a lot of difficulties is … f … a total failure.
7 Someone who is always loyal is …   g … a perfect nuisance.
8 Something that does not work at all is …   h … a complete fool.
9 Something which is extremely dangerous is … i … absolute nonsense.

▶ **Bank**

Order of adjectives

Main points

You put opinion adjectives in front of descriptive adjectives.

You put general opinion adjectives in front of specific opinion adjectives.

You can sometimes vary the order of adjectives.

If you use two or more descriptive adjectives, you put them in a particular order.

If you use a noun in front of another noun, you put any adjectives in front of the first noun.

1 You often want to add more information to a noun than you can with one adjective. In theory, you can use the adjectives in any order, depending on the quality you want to emphasize. In practice, however, there is a normal order.

When you use two or more adjectives in front of a noun, you usually put an adjective that expresses your opinion in front of an adjective that just describes something.

> *You live in a <u>nice big</u> house.*
> *He is a <u>naughty little</u> boy.*
> *She was wearing a <u>beautiful pink</u> suit.*

2 When you use more than one adjective to express your opinion, an adjective with a more general meaning such as 'good', 'bad', 'nice', or 'lovely' usually comes before an adjective with a more specific meaning such as 'comfortable', 'clean', or 'dirty'.

> *I sat in a <u>lovely comfortable</u> armchair in the corner.*
> *He put on a <u>nice clean</u> shirt.*

3 You can use adjectives to describe various qualities of people or things. For example, you might want to indicate their size, their shape, or the country they come from.

Descriptive adjectives belong to six main types, but you are unlikely ever to use all six types in the same noun group. If you did, you would normally put them in the following order:

size	age	shape	colour	nationality	material

This means that if you want to use an 'age' adjective and a 'nationality' adjective, you put the 'age' adjective first.

> *We met some <u>young Chinese</u> girls.*

Similarly, a 'shape' adjective normally comes before a 'colour' adjective.

> *He had <u>round black</u> eyes.*

Other combinations of adjectives follow the same order.
Note that 'material' means any substance, not only cloth.

> *There was a <u>large round wooden</u> table in the room.*
> *The man was carrying a <u>small black plastic</u> bag.*

4 You usually put comparative and superlative adjectives in front of other adjectives.

> *Some of the <u>better English</u> actors have gone to live in Hollywood.*
> *These are the <u>highest monthly</u> figures on record.*

5 When you use a noun in front of another noun, you never put adjectives between them. You put any adjectives in front of the first noun.

> *He works in the <u>French</u> film industry.*
> *He receives a <u>large weekly</u> cash payment.*

6 When you use two adjectives as the complement of a link verb, you use a conjunction such as 'and' to link them. With three or more adjectives, you link the last two with a conjunction, and put commas after the others.

> *The day was <u>hot and dusty.</u>*
> *The room was <u>large but square.</u>*
> *The house was <u>old, damp and smelly.</u>*
> *We felt <u>hot, tired and thirsty.</u>*

Practice

A Put the adjectives in the following list into the correct box below, according to whether they are opinion adjectives or descriptive adjectives.

golden	wood	tiny	young	good	ugly	plastic
modern	Japanese	triangular	lovely	enormous	square	handsome

Opinion adjectives   Descriptive adjectives

B Take adjectives from the phrases below and put them into the columns given. The first phrase has been done for you. You should finish with three adjectives in column 1; four in column 2; four in 3; two in 4; three in 5; two in 6; three in 7; and four in 8.

Opinion adjectives   Descriptive adjectives

1	2	3	4	5	6	7	8
general	specific	size	shape	age	colour	nationality	material
1 lovely	comfortable						leather

1 … a lovely comfortable leather armchair.
2 … a large round wooden table.
3 … a nice intelligent young man.
4 … an old Spanish song.
5 … a big square metal box.
6 … a horrible stinking fish.
7 … a small brown paper bag.
8 … a valuable ancient Egyptian manuscript.
9 … a huge red American automobile.

C Put the adjectives in brackets in the correct order in the gap in each sentence.

1 Tex McCrary collected us in a .... big American .... car. (*American, big*)
2 It is an .... microscope, fitted with special lenses. (*green, German, old*)
3 The intricately carved pegs were added by the .... violin maker Jean-Baptiste Vuillaume. (*famous, French, nineteenth-century*)
4 A .... visitor centre has been built at Sutton Hoo. (*timber, new, big*)
5 Anna used to have .... hair. (*brown, wavy, long*)
6 Is this the best .... necklace you have? (*black, big, round, pearl*)

65

Adjective + 'to' or 'that'

Main points

Adjectives used after link verbs are often followed by 'to'-infinitive clauses or 'that'-clauses.

Some adjectives are always followed by 'to'-infinitive clauses.

You often use 'to'-infinitive clauses or 'that'-clauses after adjectives to express feelings or opinions.

You often use 'to'-infinitive clauses after adjectives when the subject is impersonal 'it'.

1 After link verbs, you often use adjectives that describe how someone feels about an action or situation. With some adjectives, you can add a 'to'-infinitive clause or a 'that'-clause to say what the action or situation is.

afraid	anxious	ashamed	disappointed
frightened	glad	happy	pleased
proud	sad	surprised	unhappy

If the subject is the same in both clauses, you usually use a 'to'-infinitive clause. If the subject is different, you must use a 'that'-clause.

> I was <u>happy to see</u> them again.
> He was <u>happy that</u> they were coming to the party.

You often use a 'to'-infinitive clause when talking about future time in relation to the main clause.

> I am <u>afraid to go</u> home.
> He was <u>anxious to leave</u> before it got dark.

You often use a 'that'-clause when talking about present or past time in relation to the main clause.

> He was <u>anxious that</u> the passport was missing.
> They were <u>afraid that</u> I might have talked to the police.

2 You often use 'sorry' with a 'that'-clause. Note that 'that' is often omitted.

> I'm very <u>sorry that</u> I can't join you.
> I'm <u>sorry</u> I'm so late.

3 Some adjectives are not usually used alone, but have a 'to'-infinitive clause after them to say what action or situation the adjective relates to.

able	apt	bound	due
inclined	liable	likely	prepared
ready	unlikely	unwilling	willing

> They were <u>unable to help</u> her.
> They were not <u>likely to forget</u> it.
> I am <u>willing to try.</u>
> I'm <u>prepared to say</u> I was wrong.

4 When you want to express an opinion about someone or something, you often use an adjective followed by a 'to'-infinitive clause.

difficult	easy	impossible	possible	right	wrong

> She had been <u>easy to deceive.</u>
> The windows will be almost <u>impossible to open.</u>
> Am I <u>wrong to stay</u> here?

Note that in the first two examples, the subject of the main clause is the object of the 'to'-infinitive clause. In the third example, the subject is the same in both clauses.

5 With some adjectives, you use a 'that'-clause to express an opinion about someone or something.

awful	bad	essential	extraordinary
funny	good	important	interesting
obvious	sad	true	

> I was <u>sad that</u> people had reacted in this way.
> It is <u>extraordinary that</u> we should ever have met!

6 You can also use adjectives with 'to'-infinitive clauses after 'it' as the impersonal subject. You use the preposition 'of' or 'for' to indicate the person or thing that the adjective relates to.

> It was <u>easy to find</u> the path.
> It was <u>good of John to help</u> me.
> It was <u>difficult for her to find</u> a job.

➤ See Unit 17 for 'it' as impersonal subject.

➤ See Unit 47 for more information about adjectives followed by 'of' or 'for'.

Practice

A Rewrite each pair of sentences, using a 'to'-infinitive clause in one and a 'that'-clause in the other.

1 a I didn't go home. I was afraid. / ....I was afraid to go home...............................

   b We might be late. I was worried. / ....I was worried that we might be late.........................

2 a I met George again. I was happy. / ....

   b George was waiting to meet me. I was pleased. / ....

3 a Mary was ill. I was sorry. / ....

   b Mary heard the news. She was unhappy. / ....

4 a We saw them. We were surprised. / ....

   b Everyone enjoyed the picnic. We were delighted. / ....

5 a Peter missed the match. He was disappointed. / ....

   b Anne missed the match. Peter was disappointed. / ....

6 a She didn't tell the children. She was ashamed. / ....

   b The children didn't tell her. She was ashamed. / ....

B Use these adjectives to complete the sentences below.

bound	due	important	impossible	likely	unlikely	willing	wrong

1 He will probably win. / He is ....likely.................................... to win.

2 You must arrive on time. / It is .... to arrive on time.

3 They probably won't come. / They are .... to come.

4 I am certain he will agree. / He is .... to agree.

5 Michael has offered to lend you the money. / Michael is .... to lend you the money.

6 The plane is expected at 7.30. / The plane is .... to land at 7.30.

7 Nobody can read his writing. / His writing is .... to read.

8 You ought not to have done that. / You were .... to do that.

C Rewrite these sentences to begin with 'it' as the impersonal subject.

1 You shouldn't have lost the money. That was stupid. / It was stupid of you to lose the money......

2 They stopped the thief. That was brave. / ....

3 You forgot to lock the door. That was very careless. / ....

4 She looked after the children. That was kind. / ....

5 Mary paid the bill. That was very generous. / ....

6 You solved the problem. That was clever. / ....

7 Joe sent us the flowers. That was kind. / ....

8 He kept everything for himself. That was mean. / ....

D Rewrite these sentences to begin wit 'it' as the impersonal subject.

1 We can help you. It will be easy. ...It will be easy for us to help you..............................

2 They must succeed. It's very important. / ....

3 I don't think I can do it. It will be very difficult. / ....

4 They often complain. It's very common. / ....

5 I'll give you a lift. It's very easy. / ....

6 You don't need to come early. It's unnecessary. / ....

'-ing' and '-ed' adjectives

Main points

Many adjectives ending in '-ing' describe the effect that something has on someone's feelings.

Some adjectives ending in '-ing' describe a process or state that continues over a period of time.

Many adjectives ending in '-ed' describe people's feelings.

1 You use many '-ing' adjectives to describe the effect that something has on your feelings, or on the feelings of people in general. For example, if you talk about 'a surprising number', you mean that the number surprises you.

alarming	amazing	annoying	astonishing
boring	charming	confusing	convincing
depressing	disappointing	embarrassing	exciting
frightening	interesting	shocking	surprising
terrifying	tiring	worrying	welcoming

He lives in a <u>charming</u> house just outside the town.
She always has a warm <u>welcoming</u> smile.

Most '-ing' adjectives have a related transitive verb.
➤ See Unit 51 for information on transitive verbs.

2 You use some '-ing' adjectives to describe something that continues over a period of time.

ageing	booming	decreasing	dying
existing	increasing	living	remaining

Britain is an <u>ageing</u> society.
<u>Increasing</u> prices are making food very expensive.

These adjectives have related intransitive verbs.
➤ See Unit 51 for information on intransitive verbs.

3 Many '-ed' adjectives describe people's feelings. They have the same form as the past participle of a transitive verb and have a passive meaning. For example, 'a frightened person' is a person who has been frightened by something.

alarmed	amused	astonished
bored	delighted	depressed
disappointed	excited	frightened
interested	satisfied	shocked
surprised	tired	worried

She looks <u>alarmed</u> about something.
A <u>bored</u> student complained to his teacher.
She had big blue <u>frightened</u> eyes.

Note that the past participles of irregular verbs do not end in '-ed', but can be used as adjectives.
➤ See Appendix for a list of irregular past participles.

The bird had a <u>broken</u> wing.
His coat was dirty and <u>torn.</u>

4 Like other adjectives, '-ing' and '-ed' adjectives can be:

• used in front of a noun

They still show <u>amazing</u> loyalty to their parents.
The <u>worried</u> authorities cancelled the match.

• used after link verbs

It's <u>amazing</u> what they can do.
He felt <u>satisfied</u> with all the work he had done.

• modified by adverbials such as 'quite', 'really', and 'very'

The film was <u>quite boring.</u>
There is nothing <u>very surprising</u> in this.
She was <u>quite astonished</u> at his behaviour.
He was a <u>very disappointed</u> young man.

• used in the comparative and superlative

His argument was <u>more convincing</u> than mine.
He became even <u>more depressed</u> after she died.
This is one of <u>the most boring books</u> I've ever read.
She was <u>the most interested</u> in going to the cinema.

5 A small number of '-ed' adjectives are normally only used after link verbs such as 'be', 'become', or 'feel'. They are related to transitive verbs, and are often followed by a prepositional phrase, a 'to'-infinitive clause, or a 'that'-clause.

convinced	delighted	finished	interested
involved	pleased	prepared	scared
thrilled	tired	touched	

The Brazilians are <u>pleased</u> with the results.
He was always <u>prepared</u> to account for his actions.
She was <u>scared</u> that they would find her.

A Use the '-ing' adjectives below to complete the sentences which follow.

ageing	existing	growing	increasing	living	rising

1 The main problem is ....rising................. prices. Things are getting much too expensive.

2 Factories in Japan are becoming even more automated, making .... use of robots.

3 Things will have to change. The .... system simply doesn't work.

4 Mohammed Ali, the former heavyweight champion of the world, has been described as a
.... legend.

5 The young folk have all gone. There is no one left in the village apart from a few .... people.

6 Unemployment is on the increase. A .... number of young
people, in particular, are finding themselves out of work.

B Use the '-ed' adjectives below to complete the definitions which follow.

alarmed	amused	astonished	bored	depressed	satisfied

1 When you find something funny, you are ....amused...................... by it.

2 If something makes you sad and unhappy, you feel ....

3 If you are .... , you feel very surprised.

4 If something makes you very worried, you are .... by it.

5 If you are reasonably content with something, you feel ....

6 When you are .... , you feel tired and impatient because you have nothing to do.

C Complete the following pairs of sentences using the correct form of the verb in brackets.
You must use the '-ed' form for one sentence in each pair and the '-ing' form for the other.

1 a I had nothing to do. I was ....bored............................ and lonely.

   b I had only one book with me but I didn't read it. It was so .....boring........................... . (*bore*)

2 a I enjoyed Dr Brown's visit. He is a very .... speaker.

   b We invited them to join us, but they weren't really .... (*interest*)

3 a The bad news was very ....

   b It was a bad day. We were all thoroughly .... (*depress*)

4 a I enjoyed the film. The monster was absolutely ....

   b We were told there was a bomb in the building. Everyone was absolutely .... (*terrify*)

5 a We were rather .... with the results.

   b The results were very .... (*disappoint*)

6 a We were dreadfully late. It was very ....

   b George made a perfect fool of himself. He was awfully .... (*embarrass*)

7 a Jack looked even more .... than he felt.

   b She is a brilliant woman. She has the most .... ideas. (*amaze*)

8 a Have you heard what's happened? Isn't it .... ?

   b Mary looked calm, but inside she felt really .... (*excite*)

▸ **Bank**

Comparison: basic forms

Main points

You add '-er' for the comparative and '-est' for the superlative of one-syllable adjectives and adverbs.

You use '-er' and '-est' with some two-syllable adjectives.

You use 'more' for the comparative and 'most' for the superlative of most two-syllable adjectives, all longer adjectives, and adverbs ending in '-ly'.

Some common adjectives and adverbs have irregular forms.

1 You add '-er' for the comparative form and '-est' for the superlative form of one-syllable adjectives and adverbs. If they end in '-e', you add '-r' and '-st'.

cheap	→	cheaper	→	cheapest
safe	→	safer	→	safest

close	cold	fast	hard	large
light	nice	poor	quick	rough
small	weak	wide	young	

They worked <u>harder</u>.
I've found a <u>nicer</u> hotel.

If they end in a single vowel and consonant (except '-w'), double the consonant.

big	→	bigger	→	biggest

fat	hot	sad	thin	wet

The day grew <u>hotter</u>.
Henry was the <u>biggest</u> of them.

2 With two-syllable adjectives and adverbs ending in a consonant and '-y', you change the '-y' to '-i' and add '-er' and '-est'.

happy	→	happier	→	happiest

angry	busy	dirty	easy	friendly
funny	heavy	lucky	silly	tiny

It couldn't be <u>easier</u>.
That is the <u>funniest</u> bit of the film.

3 You use 'more' for the comparative and 'most' for the superlative of most two-syllable adjectives, all longer adjectives, and adverbs ending in '-ly'.

careful	→	more careful	→	most careful
beautiful	→	more beautiful	→	most beautiful
seriously	→	more seriously	→	most seriously

Be <u>more careful</u> next time.
They are the <u>most beautiful</u> gardens in the world.
It affected Clive <u>most seriously</u>.

Note that for 'early' as an adjective or adverb, you use 'earlier' and 'earliest', not 'more' and 'most'.

4 With some common two-syllable adjectives and adverbs you can either add '-er' and '-est', or use 'more' and 'most'.

common	cruel	gentle	handsome	likely
narrow	pleasant	polite	simple	stupid

Note that 'clever' and 'quiet' only add '-er' and '-est'.

It was <u>quieter</u> outside.
He was the <u>cleverest</u> man I ever knew.

5 You normally use 'the' with superlative adjectives in front of a noun, but you can omit 'the' after a link verb.

It was <u>the happiest</u> day of my life.
I was <u>happiest</u> when I was on my own.

⊖ WARNING: When 'most' is used without 'the' in front of adjectives and adverbs, it often means almost the same as 'very'.

This book was <u>most interesting</u>.
I object <u>most strongly</u>.

6 A few common adjectives and adverbs have irregular comparative and superlative forms.

good/well	→	better	→	best
bad/badly	→	worse	→	worst
far	→	farther/further	→	farthest/furthest
old	→	older/elder	→	oldest/eldest

She would ask him when she knew him <u>better</u>.
She sat near the <u>furthest</u> window.

Note that you use 'elder' or 'eldest' to say which brother, sister, or child in a family you mean.

Our <u>eldest</u> daughter couldn't come.

Practice

A Put the adjectives below into two columns.

| black | careful | certain | difficult | fashionable | great | intelligent | long | old | short |
| slow | small | useful | warm | | | | | | |

One syllable adjectives with comparative
in '-er' and superlative in '-est'
..black.......................................

....

Adjectives of two or more syllables
using 'more' and 'most'
..careful....................................

....

Write down the comparative and superlative forms of three adjectives from each column.
..blacker, blackest......................

....

....

..more careful, most careful..........

....

....

B Look at these adjectives and underline those ending in '-y'. All of these form the
comparative and superlative with '-ier' and '-iest'.

| crafty | disappointed | funny | helpful | important | interesting |
| pretty | silly | unhappy | unlucky | unusual | valuable |

**Look at the remaining adjectives. Do they all have two or more syllables? How do they
form the comparative and superlative? Write the comparative and superlative of the
following adjectives.**

1 unhappy ..unhappier, unhappiest........................

2 valuable ....

3 important ....

4 funny ....

C Write the comparative and superlative of the following adjectives.

1 bad ...worst, worst..............   5 good ....

2 fine ....   6 hot ....

3 big ....   7 white ....

4 fit ....   8 slim ....

D Review exercises A to C above and write down the comparative and superlative form of
these adjectives.

1 tiny ..tinier, tiniest....................   7 fat ....

2 simple ....   8 thin ....

3 angry ....   9 slender ....

4 convenient ....   10 generous ....

5 cold ....   11 friendly ....

6 wide ....   12 gentle ....

Comparison: uses

Main points

Comparative adjectives are used to compare people or things.

Superlative adjectives are used to say that one person or thing has more of a quality than others in a group or others of that kind.

Comparative adverbs are used in the same way as adjectives.

1 You use comparative adjectives to compare one person or thing with another, or with the same person or thing at another time. After a comparative adjective, you often use 'than'.

> She was much _older than_ me.
> I am _happier than_ I have ever been.

2 You use a superlative to say that one person or thing has more of a quality than others in a group or others of that kind.

> Tokyo is Japan's _largest city._
> He was _the tallest person_ there.
> Buses are often _the cheapest way of travelling._

3 You can use comparative and superlative adjectives in front of a noun.

> I was _a better writer_ than he was.
> He had _more important things_ to do.
> It was _the quickest route_ from Rome to Naples.

You can also use comparative and superlative adjectives after link verbs.

> My brother is _younger_ than me.
> He feels _more content_ now.
> The sergeant was _the tallest._
> This book was _the most interesting._

4 You can use adverbs of degree in front of comparative adjectives.

| a bit | far | a great/good deal | a little |
| a lot | much | rather | slightly |

> This car's _a bit more expensive._
> Now I feel _a great deal more confident._
> It's _a rather more complicated_ story than that.

You can also use adverbs of degree such as 'by far', 'easily', 'much', or 'quite' in front of 'the' and superlative adjectives.

> It was _by far the worst hospital_ I had ever seen.
> She was _easily the most intelligent person_ in the class.

Note that you can put 'very' between 'the' and a superlative adjective ending in '-est'.

> It was of _the very highest quality._

5 When you want to say that one situation depends on another, you can use 'the' and a comparative followed by 'the' and another comparative.

> _The smaller_ it is, _the cheaper_ it is to post.
> _The larger_ the organisation is, _the greater_ the problem of administration becomes.

When you want to say that something increases or decreases, you can use two comparatives linked by 'and'.

> It's getting _harder and harder_ to find a job.
> Cars are becoming _more and more expensive._

6 After a superlative adjective, you can use a prepositional phrase to specify the group you are talking about.

> Henry was _the biggest of them._
> These cakes are probably _the best in the world._
> He was _the most dangerous man in the country._

7 You use the same structures in comparisons using adverbs as those given for adjectives:

• 'than' after comparative adverbs

> Prices have been rising _faster than_ incomes.

• 'the' and a comparative adverb followed by 'the' and another comparative adverb

> _The quicker_ we finish, _the sooner_ we will go home.

• two comparative adverbs linked by 'and'

> He sounded _worse and worse._
> He drove _faster and faster_ till we told him to stop.

Practice

A Make sentences with a comparative adjective and 'than', using the words given.

1 Tokyo – big – New York. / Tokyo is bigger than New York. ....

2 My sister – old – me. / ....

3 Our new house – big – the one we used to live in. / ....
   ....

4 Travelling by train – comfortable – travelling by bus. / ....
   ....

5 Shopping at a supermarket – cheap – going to the local shops. / ....
   ....

B Complete these sentences using the comparative of the adjectives in brackets and 'than'.

1 You certainly look much ....happier than........................... you did yesterday. (*happy*)

2 He is obviously .... in sport .... I am. (*interested*)

3 The game will certainly be much .... it was last year. (*exciting*)

4 Children nowadays seem to be much .... they used to be. (*noisy*)

5 She's actually a good deal .... she looks. (*old*)

C Form the comparative of the adjectives in these phrases and use the phrases in the sentences below.

| a good idea | a big house | a healthy climate | a young man | a good job |

1 California certainly has ....a healthier climate............... than New York.

2 I'm getting too old. This is a job for ....

3 When the children get a bit older we'll really need ....

4 I'm sure it won't work. Can't you come up with .... ?

5 Perhaps we could afford it if I could get ....

D Complete these sentences using a superlative adjective in each one.

1 I've never heard a more ridiculous story.
   That's ....the most ridiculous story........... I've ever heard.

2 We had never stayed in a more expensive hotel.
   It was .... we had ever stayed in.

3 I had never had such a tiring journey before.
   It was .... I had ever had.

4 I've never had nearly such a tasty meal before.
   That was .... I have ever had.

5 It's years since I saw a game as good as that.
   That's .... I've seen for years.

▶ **Bank**

Other ways of comparing

Main points

This includes words like: 'as…as', 'the same (as)' and 'like'.

You use 'as…as…' to compare people or things.

You can also compare people or things by using 'the same (as)'.

You can also compare people or things by using a link verb and a phrase beginning with 'like'.

1 You use 'as…as…' to compare people or things that are similar in some way.
You use 'as' and an adjective or adverb, followed by 'as' and a noun group, an adverbial, or a clause.

> You're <u>as bad as your sister.</u>
> The airport was <u>as crowded as ever.</u>
> I am <u>as good as she is.</u>
> Let us examine it <u>as carefully as we can.</u>

2 You can make a negative comparison using 'not as…as…' or 'not so…as…'.

> The food was<u>n't as</u> good <u>as</u> yesterday.
> They are <u>not as</u> clever <u>as</u> they appear to be.
> He is <u>not so</u> old <u>as</u> I thought.

3 You can use the adverbs 'almost', 'just', 'nearly', or 'quite' in front of 'as…as…'.

> He was <u>almost as</u> fast <u>as</u> his brother.
> Mary was <u>just as</u> pale <u>as</u> before.
> She was <u>nearly as</u> tall <u>as</u> he was.

In a negative comparison, you can use 'not nearly' or 'not quite' before 'as…as…'.

> This is <u>not nearly as</u> complicated <u>as</u> it sounds.
> The hotel was <u>not quite as</u> good <u>as</u> they expected.

4 When you want to say that one thing is very similar to something else, you can use 'the same as' followed by a noun group, an adverbial, or a clause.

> Your bag is <u>the same as</u> mine.
> I said <u>the same as</u> always.
> She looked <u>the same as</u> she did yesterday.

If people or things are very similar or identical, you can also say that they are 'the same'.

> Teenage fashions are <u>the same</u> all over the world.
> The initial stage of learning English is <u>the same</u> for many students.

You can use some adverbs in front of 'the same as' or 'the same'.

| almost | exactly | just | more or less |
| much | nearly | roughly | virtually |

> He did <u>exactly the same as</u> John did.
> You two look <u>almost the same.</u>

You can use 'the same' in front of a noun group, with or without 'as' after the noun group.

> They reached almost <u>the same height.</u>
> It was painted <u>the same colour as</u> the wall.

5 You can also compare people or things by using a link verb such as 'be', 'feel', 'look', or 'seem' and a phrase beginning with 'like'.

> It <u>was like</u> a dream.
> He still <u>feels like</u> a child.
> He <u>looked like</u> an actor.
> The houses <u>seemed like</u> mansions.

You can use some adverbs in front of 'like'.

a bit	a little	exactly	just
least	less	more	most
quite	rather	somewhat	very

> He looks <u>just like</u> a baby.
> Of all his children, she was the one <u>most like</u> me.

6 If the noun group after 'as' or 'like' in any of these structures is a pronoun, you use an object pronoun or possessive pronoun.

> Jane was as clever as <u>him.</u>
> His car is the same as <u>mine.</u>

7 You can also use 'less' and 'least' to make comparisons with the opposite meaning to 'more' and 'most'.

> They were <u>less fortunate</u> than us.
> He was <u>the least skilled</u> of the workers.
> We see him <u>less frequently</u> than we used to.

Practice

A Rewrite these sentences using 'as .... as ....'.

1 John's father is handsome and so is John. / John is as handsome as his father.
2 Jean's mother is generous and so is Jean. / ....
3 Neil's brother is mischievous and so is Neil. / ....
4 Mary drives fast and so does Helen. / ....
5 Our home is comfortable and so is yours. / ....
6 Last summer was very hot and so is this summer. / ....
7 Jenny works hard and so does Becky. / ....
8 Jack can run fast and so can Jill. / ....

B Use these adjectives and adverbs to complete the sentences that follow.

| cheap clever cold hard long much quick well |

1 I'm getting old. I can't work .... as hard as .... I used to.
2 Prices have gone up. Things aren't .... they used to be.
3 Have you been ill? You're not looking .... you usually do.
4 Jack's doing well at school. He's nearly .... his sister.
5 It's freezing. It must be nearly .... last winter.
6 Joe still plays tennis. He says he enjoys it .... ever.
7 The bus wasn't .... the train. It took over two hours.
8 Cats don't usually live .... dogs.

C Write sentences using 'the same'. Here are some nouns to help you.

| age length size height weight |

1 Mary and Jan are both 17. / They're the same age.
2 John is six feet tall and so is Henry. / ....
3 I weigh seventy five kilos and so does Jack. / ....
4 This box is exactly as big as that one. / ....
5 This piece of string is just as long as that one. / ....

D Match these sentences. The first has been done for you.

1 It was an enormous house.
2 The dog gave a dreadful growl.
3 The city centre is dreadfully crowded.
4 This cheese is awful.
5 I recognised Eleanor easily.
6 This is lovely soft cotton.

a It sounded like a tiger.
b It smells like bad eggs.
c It feels like silk.
d She looks just like her sister.
e It looked like a castle.
f It's just like London.

▸ **Bank**

Adverbials

Main points

Adverbials are usually adverbs, adverb phrases, or prepositional phrases.

Adverbials of manner, place, and time are used to say how, where, or when something happens.

Adverbials usually come after the verb, or after the object if there is one.

The usual order of adverbials is manner, then place, then time.

1 An adverbial is often one word, an adverb.

Sit there quietly, and listen to this music.

However, an adverbial can also be a group of words:

• an adverb phrase

He did not play well enough to win.

• a prepositional phrase

The children were playing in the park.

• a noun group, usually a time expression

Come and see me next week.

2 You use an adverbial of manner to describe the way in which something happens or is done.

They looked anxiously at each other.
She listened with great patience as he told his story.

You use an adverbial of place to say where something happens.

A plane flew overhead.
No birds or animals came near the body.

You use an adverbial of time to say when something happens.

She will be here soon.
He was born on 3 April 1925.

3 You normally put adverbials of manner, place, and time after the main verb.

She sang beautifully.
The book was lying on the table.
The car broke down yesterday.

If the verb has an object, you put the adverbial after the object.

I did learn to play a few tunes very badly.
Thomas made his decision immediately.
He took the glasses to the kitchen.

If you are using more than one of these adverbials in a clause, the usual order is manner, then place, then time.

They were sitting quite happily in the car. (manner, place)
She spoke very well at the village hall last night. (manner, place, time)

4 You usually put adverbials of frequency, probability, and duration in front of the main verb.

She occasionally comes to my house.
You have very probably heard the news by now.
They had already given me the money.

A few adverbs of degree also usually come in front of the main verb.

She really enjoyed the party.

5 When you want to focus on an adverbial, you can do this by putting it in a different place in the clause:

• you can put an adverbial at the beginning of a clause, usually for emphasis

Slowly, he opened his eyes.
In September I travelled to California.
Next to the coffee machine stood a pile of cups.

Note that after adverbials of place, as in the last example, the verb can come in front of the subject.

• you can sometimes put adverbs and adverb phrases in front of the main verb for emphasis, but not prepositional phrases or noun groups

He deliberately chose it because it was cheap.
I very much wanted to go with them.

• you can change the order of adverbials of manner, place, and time when you want to change the emphasis

They were sitting in the car quite happily. (place, manner)
At the meeting last night, she spoke very well. (place, time, manner)

Practice

A You are given the parts of a sentence in brackets below. Write the sentences in the normal order, without any special emphasis.

1 (*the children / happily / in the garden / were playing*)
   The children ......*were playing happily in the garden.*....................

2 (*last night / the concert / we enjoyed / very much*)
   We enjoyed ....

3 (*Mary / yesterday / in the supermarket / I met*)
   I met ....

4 (*in Greece / last year / we had / a holiday*)
   Last year ....

5 (*in London / most people / about nine o'clock / start work*)
   In London ....

6 (*very late / this morning / to work / I got*)
   This morning ....

7 (*a new school / they are building / next year / in our town*)
   Next year ....

8 (*most things / cheaply / you can buy / in the supermarket*)
   You can buy ....

9 (*Andreas / five languages / fluently / speaks*)
   ....

10 (*at the meeting / yesterday / Jack / very angrily / spoke*)
   ....

11 (*very heavily / it rained / last night / in London*)
   ....

12 (*neatly / his name / at the bottom of the page / he wrote*)
   ....

B Make the adverbials in these sentences emphatic by putting them at the front of the sentence.

1 They visit their grandparents every weekend. / *Every weekend they visit their grandparents.*

2 He opened the door quietly. / ....

3 I have tried to call you several times. / ....

4 We waited for him for over an hour. / ....

5 He posted the wrong letter by mistake. / ....

6 She drove to town as quickly as possible. / ....

7 He folded the paper carefully. / ....

8 I spoke to him about it only yesterday. / ....

9 There are some wonderful paintings in the National Gallery. / ....
   ....

10 He walked out of the room angrily. / ....

▸ **Bank**

Adverbials of manner

Main points

Most adverbs of manner are formed by adding '-ly' to an adjective, but sometimes other spelling changes are needed.

You cannot form adverbs from adjectives that end in '-ly'.

Some adverbs have the same form as adjectives.

You do not use adverbs after link verbs, you use adjectives.

Adverbials of manner are sometimes prepositional phrases or noun groups.

1 Adverbs of manner are often formed by adding '-ly' to an adjective.

Adjectives:	bad	beautiful	careful
	quick	quiet	soft
Adverbs:	badly	beautifully	carefully
	quickly	quietly	softly

2 Adverbs formed in this way usually have a similar meaning to the adjective.

> *She is as clever as she is beautiful.*
> *He talked so politely and danced so beautifully.*
> *'We must not talk. We must be quiet,' said Sita.*
> *She wanted to sit quietly, to relax.*

3 There are sometimes changes in spelling when an adverb is formed from an adjective.

'-le' changes to '-ly':	gentle	→	gently
'-y' changes to '-ily':	easy	→	easily
'-ic' changes to '-ically':	automatic	→	automatically
'-ue' changes to '-uly':	true	→	truly
'-ll' changes to '-lly':	full	→	fully

Note that 'public' changes to 'publicly', not 'publically'.

⊖ WARNING: You cannot form adverbs from adjectives that already end in '-ly'. For example, you cannot say 'He smiled at me friendlily'. You can sometimes use a prepositional phrase instead: 'He smiled at me in a friendly way'.

4 Some adverbs of manner have the same form as adjectives and have similar meanings, for example 'fast', 'hard', and 'late'.

> *I've always been interested in fast cars. (adjective)*
> *The driver was driving too fast. (adverb)*

Note that 'hardly' and 'lately' are not adverbs of manner and have different meanings from the adjectives 'hard' and 'late'.

> *It was a hard decision to make.*
> *I hardly had any time to talk to her.*
> *The train was late as usual.*
> *Have you seen John lately?*

5 The adverb of manner related to the adjective 'good' is 'well'.

> *He is a good dancer.*
> *He dances well.*

Note that 'well' can sometimes be an adjective when it refers to someone's health.

> *'How are you?' – 'I am very well, thank you.'*

6 You do not use adverbs after link verbs such as 'be', 'become', 'feel', 'get', 'look', and 'seem'. You use an adjective after these verbs. For example, you do not say 'Sue felt happily'. You say 'Sue felt happy'.

▶ See Unit 73 for more information on link verbs.

7 You do not often use prepositional phrases or noun groups as adverbials of manner. However, you occasionally need to use them, for example when there is no adverb form available. The prepositional phrases and noun groups usually include a noun such as 'way', 'fashion', or 'manner', or a noun that refers to someone's voice.

> *She asked me in such a nice manner that I couldn't refuse.*
> *He did it the right way.*
> *They spoke in angry tones.*

Prepositional phrases with 'like' are also used as adverbials of manner.

> *I slept like a baby.*
> *He drove like a madman.*

Practice

A Use the adjective or adverb in brackets to complete each of the following pairs of sentences correctly.

1 It's an .... *easy* .... question.
  You should be able to answer it quite .... *easily* .... (*easy / easily*)

2 I can type a bit but I'm very ....
  I'm afraid I can only type very .... (*slow / slowly*)

3 Mr Robbins shouted .... at the children.
  The children made Mr Robbins very .... (*angry / angrily*)

4 Use this chair if you want to sit ....
  Use this chair. It's very .... (*comfortable / comfortably*)

5 Mary sang .... at the concert last night. Mary sang a
  .... song at the concert last night. (*beautiful / beautifully*)

6 There's no need to feel ....
  Peter answered the questions .... (*nervous / nervously*)

7 What was wrong with Bill? He looked very ....
  Bill shook his head .... (*sad / sadly*)

8 The children played together very ....
  The children looked very .... as they played together. (*happy / happily*)

9 I'm afraid you have done this piece of work ....
  I'm afraid your work has been very .... (*careless / carelessly*)

10 The letter I received this morning was quite ....
  I received a letter this morning quite .... (*unexpected / unexpectedly*)

B Fill each of the gaps below with one of the following adverbs. You will need to use some more than once.

anxiously	badly	carefully	fast	hard	late	lately	quietly	slowly	suddenly	well

1 We had to work very .... *hard* .... to finish in time.

2 I play the piano, but I don't play it very ....

3 You should drive very .... in wet weather. It's dangerous to
  drive ....

4 He drove very .... to Liverpool, but he still arrived too
  .... for the meeting.

5 It'll take us hours to get there. Chris always drives so ....

6 Could you speak .... please. The baby is sleeping.

7 He didn't work very .... That's why he did so
  .... in the exam.

8 The exams were over and everyone was waiting ....

9 Do you know how David is? I haven't heard anything ....

10 We got a dreadful shock. We were just sitting here .... and
  .... there was a loud knock at the door.

Adverbials of time

Main points

Adverbials of time can be time expressions such as 'last night'.

Adverbials of time can be prepositional phrases with 'at', 'in', or 'on'.

'For' refers to a period of time in the past, present, or future.

'Since' refers to a point in past time.

1 You use adverbials of time to say when something happens. You often use noun groups called time expressions as adverbials of time.

yesterday	today	tomorrow
last night	last year	next Saturday
next week	the day after tomorrow	
the other day		

Note that you do not use the prepositions 'at', 'in', or 'on' with time expressions.

> *One of my children wrote to me today.*
> *So, you're coming back next week?*

You often use time expressions with verbs in the present tense to talk about the future.

> *The plane leaves tomorrow morning.*
> *They're coming next week.*

2 You can use prepositional phrases as adverbials of time:

• 'at' is used with:

clock times:	at eight o'clock, at three fifteen
religious festivals:	at Christmas, at Easter
mealtimes:	at breakfast, at lunchtimes
specific periods:	at night, at the weekend, at weekends, at half-term

• 'in' is used with:

seasons:	in autumn, in the spring
years and centuries:	in 1985, in the year 2000, in the nineteenth century
months:	in July, in December
parts of the day:	in the morning, in the evenings

Note that you also use 'in' to say that something will happen during or after a period of time in the future.

> *I think we'll find out in the next few days.*

• 'on' is used with:

days:	on Monday, on Tuesday morning
special days:	on Christmas Day, on my birthday
dates:	on the twentieth of July, on June 21st

3 You use 'for' with verbs in any tense to say how long something continues to happen.

> *He is in Italy for a month.*
> *I remained silent for a long time.*
> *I will be in London for three months.*

⊖ WARNING: You do not use 'during' to say how long something continues to happen. You cannot say 'I went there during three weeks'.

4 You use 'since' with a verb in the present perfect or past perfect tense to say when something started to happen.

> *Marilyn has lived in Paris since 1984.*
> *I had eaten nothing since breakfast.*

5 You can use many other prepositional phrases as adverbials of time. You use:

• 'during' and 'over' for a period of time in which something happens

> *I saw him twice during the holidays.*
> *Will you stay here over Christmas?*

• 'from…to/till/until' and 'between…and' for the beginning and end of a period of time

> *The building is closed from April to May.*
> *She worked from four o'clock till ten o'clock.*
> *Can you take the test between now and June?*

• 'by' when you mean 'not later than'

> *By eleven o'clock, Brody was back in his office.*
> *Can we get this finished by tomorrow?*

• 'before' and 'after'

> *I saw him before the match.*
> *She left the house after ten o'clock.*

'Since', 'till', 'until', 'after', and 'before' can also be conjunctions with time clauses. ▶ See Unit 96.

> *I've been wearing glasses since I was three.*

6 You use the adverb 'ago' with the past simple to say how long before the time of speaking something happened. You put 'ago' after the period of time.

> *We saw him about a month ago.*
> *John's wife died five years ago.*

⊖ WARNING: You do not use 'ago' with the present perfect tense. You cannot say 'We have gone to Spain two years ago'.

Practice

A **Complete these sentences using 'at', 'in', 'on', or nothing at all.**

1 I'll come round ....*at*............ six o'clock.
2 The Second World War began .... September 1939 and ended .... 1945.
3 It's my birthday .... Friday.
4 The meeting is .... half past two .... the afternoon .... next Monday.
5 This house gets dreadfully cold .... winter, especially
   .... night. We nearly froze to death .... last Christmas.
6 It's our anniversary next month. We were married 1966,
   .... the 17th of September.
7 Come round .... lunchtime and have something to eat. We
   normally start lunch .... about one o'clock .... the weekend.
8 The programme is .... six o'clock .... Saturday evening.
9 In Europe we have our weekend break .... Saturday and
   Sunday, but .... the Middle East the weekend is .... Thursday and Friday.
10 In Scotland the main winter celebration is not .... Christmas but ....
   New Year, or Hogmanay as the Scots call it. There are lots of parties .... New Year's Eve
   and .... midnight everyone joins hands to sing Auld Lang Syne.

B **Complete the following sentences using 'ago', 'for', or 'since'.**

1 Columbus discovered America about six hundred years .... *ago* ....
2 Ghana has been an independent country .... 1957.
3 Russia has been a republic .... over seventy years.
4 Oxford has been a centre of learning .... more than a thousand years.
5 Most British universities were founded less than a hundred years ....
6 There has been a university in Birmingham .... about 1900.
7 William Shakespeare was born about four hundred years ....
8 It is over four hundred years .... Shakespeare's birth.
9 Two thousand years .... Britain was part of the Roman Empire.
10 England and Scotland have been united .... 1707.

C **Use the prepositions and adverbs in brackets to complete the following sentences.**

1 I had to work ....*during*............... the summer holidays, ... the beginning
   of July .... the end of August. (*during / from / until*)
2 We got married .... 1970 so we have been married
   .... more than twenty years now. (*for / in*)
3 I should have handed in my homework a week .... .My
   teacher isn't very pleased. She says I must finish it .... six
   o'clock .... Monday at the latest. (*ago / by / on*)
4 The last time we went to England was .... 1996, that's nearly
   ten years .... .We haven't been back ....
   then even though our friends have often invited us. (*ago / in / since*)
5 My parents lived in Liverpool .... 1960 .... 1975.
   .... 1978, when I was born, they had moved to Birmingham. (*by / from / until*)

▶ **Bank**

Frequency and probability

Main points

This includes words like: 'always', 'ever', 'never', 'perhaps', 'possibly' and 'probably'.

Adverbials of frequency are used to say how often something happens.

Adverbials of probability are used to say how sure you are about something.

These adverbials usually come before the main verb, but they come after 'be' as a main verb.

1 You use adverbials of frequency to say how often something happens.

a lot	always	ever	frequently
hardly ever	never	normally	occasionally
often	rarely	sometimes	usually

> We _often_ swam in the sea.
> She _never_ comes to my parties.

2 You use adverbials of probability to say how sure you are about something.

certainly	definitely	maybe	obviously
perhaps	possibly	probably	really

> I _definitely_ saw her yesterday.
> The driver _probably_ knows the quickest route.

3 You usually put adverbials of frequency and probability before the main verb and after an auxiliary or a modal.

> He _sometimes works_ downstairs in the kitchen.
> You _are definitely wasting_ your time.
> I _have never had_ such a horrible meal!
> I _shall never forget_ this day.

Note that you usually put them after 'be' as a main verb.

> He _is always_ careful with his money.
> You _are probably_ right.

'Perhaps' usually comes at the beginning of the sentence.

> _Perhaps_ the beaches are cleaner in the north.
> _Perhaps_ you need a membership card to get in.

'A lot' always comes after the main verb.

> I go swimming _a lot_ in the summer.

4 'Never' is a negative adverb.

> She _never_ goes abroad.
> I've _never_ been to Europe.

You normally use 'ever' in questions, negative sentences, and 'if'-clauses.

> Have you _ever_ been to a football match?
> Don't _ever_ do that again!
> If you _ever_ need anything, just call me.

Note that you can sometimes use 'ever' in affirmative sentences, for example after a superlative.

> She is the _best_ dancer I have _ever_ seen.

You use 'hardly ever' in affirmative sentences to mean almost never.

> We _hardly ever_ meet.

_The bus is _always_ late._

Perhaps it has broken down

_It's _probably_ stuck in traffic_

Practice

A Choose one of the following adverbials to add to each of these sentences so that they are true for you.

never	hardly ever	rarely	occasionally	sometimes
often	usually	always	nearly	always

1 I .... *sometimes* .... watch TV in the evening.
2 I .... take a holiday in the summer.
3 I .... go shopping at the weekend.
4 I .... do the cooking at home.
5 I .... do the washing up.
6 I .... go out somewhere at the weekend.
7 I .... go to bed before eleven.

B Give true replies to the following questions using one of these adverbials for each answer.

definitely	certainly	probably	possibly	probably not	definitely not

1 Will you enjoy your next English lesson? .... *Definitely.* ....
2 Will you do your next piece of homework on time? ....
3 Do you think you will visit England within the next year? ....
4 Will you ever be very rich? ....
5 Will you be moving to a new house within the next year? ....
6 Do you think you will learn to speak English really fluently? ....
7 Do you think the best way of learning a language is by living in a country where that language is spoken? ....
8 Do you think that reading a lot in English is a good way to improve your English? ....

C Rewrite the sentences below to include the adverbials in brackets.

1 I go swimming. / ....*I usually go swimming at the weekend.*............ (*usually / at the weekend*)
2 My brother goes swimming. / .... (*normally / twice a week*)
3 Peter went to visit his grandparents. / .... (*on Sundays / often*)
4 The British are talking about the weather. / .... (*always*)
5 I'll be back. / .... (*in a couple of minutes / probably*)
6 He will be at home. / .... (*probably / at lunchtime*)
7 He should have telephoned. / .... (*by now / certainly*)
8 I locked the door. / .... (*last night / definitely*)
9 He phoned home. / .... (*usually / every day*)
10 They didn't get there. / .... (*in time / perhaps*)
11 We go to the theatre. / .... (*hardly ever / nowadays*)
12 John will call round. / .... (*tomorrow / probably*)

Adverbials of duration

Main points

'Already' is used to say that something has happened earlier than expected.

'Still' is used to say that something continues to happen until a particular time.

'Yet' is used to say that something has not happened before a particular time.

'Any longer', 'any more', 'no longer', and 'no more' are used to say that something has stopped happening.

[1] You use adverbials of duration to say that an event or situation is continuing, stopping, or is not happening at the moment.

> She _still_ lives in London.
> I couldn't stand it _any more._
> It isn't dark _yet._

[2] You use 'already' to say that something has happened sooner than it was expected to happen. You put 'already' in front of the main verb.

> He had _already bought_ the cups and saucers.
> I've _already seen_ them.
> The guests were _already coming_ in.

You put 'already' after 'be' as a main verb.

> Julie was _already_ in bed.

You can also use 'already' to emphasize that something is the case, for example when someone else does not know or is not sure.

> I am _already_ aware of that problem.

You do not normally use 'already' in negative statements, but you can use it in negative 'if'-clauses.

> Show it to him _if he hasn't already seen it._

You can put 'already' at the beginning or end of a clause for emphasis.

> _Already_ he was calculating the profit he could make.
> I've done it _already._

[3] You use 'still' to say that a situation continues to exist up to a particular time in the past, present, or future. You put 'still' in front of the main verb.

> We _were still waiting_ for the election results.
> My family _still live_ in India.
> You _will still get_ tickets, if you hurry.

You put 'still' after 'be' as a main verb.

> Martin's mother died, but his father _is still_ alive.

You can use 'still' after the subject and before the verb group in negative sentences to express surprise or impatience.

> You _still_ haven't given us the keys.
> He _still_ didn't say a word.
> It was after midnight, and he _still_ wouldn't leave.

Remember that you can use 'still' at the beginning of a clause with a similar meaning to 'after all' or 'nevertheless'.

> _Still,_ he is my brother, so I'll have to help him.
> _Still,_ it's not too bad. We didn't lose all the money.

[4] You use 'yet' at the end of negative sentences and questions to say that something has not happened or had not happened up to a particular time, but is or was expected to happen later.

> We haven't got the tickets _yet._
> Have you joined the swimming club _yet?_
> They hadn't seen the baby _yet._

Remember that 'yet' can also be used at the beginning of a clause with a similar meaning to 'but'.

> I don't miss her, _yet_ I do often wonder where she went.
> They know they won't win. _Yet_ they keep on trying.

[5] You use 'any longer' and 'any more' at the end of negative clauses to say that a past situation has ended and does not exist now or will not exist in the future.

> I wanted the job, but I couldn't wait _any longer._
> He's not going to play _any more._

In formal English, you can use an affirmative clause with 'no longer' and 'no more'. You can put them at the end of the clause, or in front of the main verb.

> He could stand the pain _no more._
> He _no longer_ wanted to buy it.

Practice

A Fill the blanks with 'yet' or 'any longer/any more'.

1 I've started learning French but I haven't learned very much ....*yet*.. .

2 Time is running out. We can't wait ....

3 We aren't ready to start .... Let's wait a little longer.

4 Mary posted the letter last week but I haven't got it ....

5 You mustn't leave .... The party is only just beginning.

6 If you stand there talking .... we'll miss our train.

B Fill the blanks with 'still' or 'already'.

1 You needn't tell Harry. He ....*already*................................ knows.

2 I didn't know you were .... working at Brown's. You've been there for ages.

3 Joe .... lives in Manchester, where he was born.

4 I'm .... trying to finish my homework. I've .... been at it for three hours.

5 The children are grown up now but they .... like to come home for the holidays.

6 I've .... seen that film and I don't want to see it again.

C Complete these sentences using 'still', 'yet', 'already', 'any longer', or 'any more'.

1 John doesn't live in London ....*any more*.......................... . He's moved to Bristol.

2 The children haven't gone to bed .... They're .... watching television.

3 A: Is Anne .... here?

   B: No, she has .... left.

4 Becky hasn't gone to university .... She's .... at school.

5 Have you started your new job .... or are you .... working in London?

6 Tom had eaten well but he was .... hungry.

7 Since her accident, Susan .... plays golf but she doesn't play tennis ....

8 I offered to help Joe with the car but he had .... mended it.

9 Thanks for your help. I won't trouble you ....

10 A: Have you finished your homework .... , or are you .... working on it?

   B: I've .... finished it.

Adverbials of degree

1 You use adverbs of degree to modify verbs. They make the verb stronger or weaker.

> I *totally disagree.*   I can *nearly swim.*

2 Some adverbs can come in front of a main verb, after a main verb, or after the object if there is one.

badly	completely	greatly
seriously	strongly	totally

> Mr Brooke *strongly* criticized the Bank of England.
> I disagree *completely* with John Taylor.
> That argument doesn't convince me *totally.*

Some adverbs are mostly used in front of the verb.

almost	largely	nearly	really	quite

> He *almost* crashed into a lorry.

Note that 'really' is used at the beginning of a clause to express surprise, and at the end of a clause as an adverb of manner.

> *Really,* I didn't know that!
> He wanted it *really,* but was too shy to ask.

'A lot' and 'very much' come after the main verb if there is no object, or after the object.

> She helped *a lot.*
> We liked him *very much.*

'Very much' can come after the subject and in front of verbs like 'want', 'prefer', and 'enjoy'.

> I *very much* wanted to take it with me.

3 Some adverbs of degree go in front of adjectives or other adverbs and modify them.

awfully	extremely	fairly	pretty
quite	rather	really	very

> …a *fairly large* office, with filing space.

Note that you can use 'rather' before or after 'a' or 'an' followed by an adjective and a noun.

> Seaford is *rather a* pleasant town.
> It is *a rather* complicated story.

When 'quite' means 'fairly', you put it in front of 'a' or 'an' followed by an adjective and a noun.

> My father gave me *quite a large sum* of money.

However, when 'quite' means 'extremely', you can put it after 'a'. You can say 'a quite enormous sum'.

4 You use some adverbs of degree to modify clauses and prepositional phrases.

entirely	just	largely
mainly	partly	simply

> Are you saying that *simply because I am here?*
> I don't think it's worth going *just for a day.*

5 You use 'so' and 'such' to emphasize a quality that someone or something has. 'So' can be followed by an adjective, an adverb, or a noun group beginning with 'many', 'much', 'few', or 'little'.

> John is *so interesting* to talk to.
> Science is changing *so rapidly.*
> I want to do *so many* different things.

'Such' is followed by a singular noun group with 'a', or a plural noun group.

> There was *such a noise* we couldn't hear.
> They said *such nasty things.*

⊖ WARNING 'So' is never followed by a singular noun group with 'a' or a plural noun group.

6 You use 'too' when you mean 'more than is necessary' or 'more than is good'. You can use 'too' before adjectives and adverbs, and before 'many', 'much', 'few', or 'little'.

> The prices are *too high.*
> I've been paying *too much* tax.

You use 'enough' after adjectives and adverbs.

> I waited until my daughter was *old enough* to read.
> He didn't work *quickly enough.*

Note that 'enough' is also a determiner.

> We've got *enough money* to buy that car now.

7 You use emphasizing adverbs to modify adjectives such as 'astonishing', 'furious', and 'wonderful', which express extreme qualities.

absolutely	completely	entirely	perfectly	purely
quite	really	simply	totally	utterly

> I think he's *absolutely wonderful.*

A Look at the pairs of sentences below. Each sentence has an adverb of degree that is modifying a verb. In each case, say whether the adverb of degree is in the right place or not.

1 I **really** enjoyed our visit to the art gallery. .... Right. ....

I enjoyed **really** our visit to the art gallery. .... Wrong. ....

2 I have finished **nearly** . I'll be with you in a minute. ....

I have **nearly** finished. I'll be with you in a minute. ....

3 He wanted to find a new job **very badly.** ....

Very badly he wanted to find a new job. ....

4 Jack **completely** forgot to sign the cheque. ....

Jack forgot to sign the cheque **completely.** ....

5 It was a dreadful accident but fortunately nobody was **seriously** injured. ....

It was a dreadful accident but fortunately nobody **seriously** was injured. ....

B Here are some adverbs of degree that modify phrases or clauses. Put them in the right place in their sentences.

1 It was   mainly   because of Henry that we were invited. (*mainly*)
         ⌄

2 His success was the result of hard work. (*largely*)

3 They finally came to an agreement because they were tired of arguing. (*simply*)

4 You can often get what you want by asking. (*simply*)

5 He usually disagreed with the majority to make things difficult. (*just*)

6 I missed my flight to Cairo owing to a traffic hold-up. (*partly*)

7 He finally got what he wanted, but it was by good luck. (*mainly*)

8 He used to play the fool to annoy his father. (*just*)

C Rewrite these sentences with 'rather a/an' or 'quite a/an'.

1 The book was rather interesting. / It was .... rather an interesting book. ....

2 The house we lived in was quite big. / We lived in ....

3 The film was quite exciting. / It was ....

4 My childhood was rather sad. / I had ....

5 The car was rather expensive. / It was ....

6 The school is quite good. / It is ....

7 I met a man who was quite interesting. / I met ....

8 When she was a child she was rather naughty. / She was ....

9 The problem was rather difficult. / It was ....

10 The letter she wrote him was quite rude. / She wrote him ....

Now rewrite sentences 1, 4, 5, and 9 with 'a rather'.

1 ...... It was a rather interesting book. ....

4 ....

5 ....

9 ....

▶ **Bank**

Place and direction

Main points

This includes words like: 'above', 'below', 'down', 'from', 'to', 'towards' and 'up'.

You normally use prepositional phrases to say where a person or thing is, or the direction they are moving in.

You can also use adverbs and adverb phrases for place and direction.

Many words are both prepositions and adverbs.

1 You use prepositions to talk about the place where someone or something is. Prepositions are always followed by a noun group, which is called the object of the preposition.

above	among	at	behind	below
beneath	beside	between	in	inside
near	on	opposite	outside	over
round	through	under	underneath	

> He stood _near_ the door.
> Two minutes later we were safely _inside_ the taxi.

Note that some prepositions consist of more than one word.

in between	in front of	next to	on top of

> There was a man standing _in front of_ me.
> The books were piled _on top of_ each other.

2 You can also use prepositions to talk about the direction that someone or something is moving in, or the place that someone or something is moving towards.

across	along	back to	down
into	onto	out of	past
round	through	to	towards
up			

> They dived _into_ the water.
> She turned and rushed _out of_ the room.

3 Many prepositions can be used both for place and direction.

> The bank is just _across_ the High Street. (place)
> I walked _across_ the room. (direction)

> We live in the house _over_ the road. (place)
> I stole his keys and escaped _over_ the wall. (direction)

4 You can also use adverbs and adverb phrases for place and direction.

abroad	away	downstairs	downwards
here	indoors	outdoors	there
underground	upstairs	anywhere	everywhere
nowhere	somewhere		

> Sheila was _here_ a moment ago.
> Can't you go _upstairs_ and turn the bedroom light off?

Note that a few noun groups can also be used as adverbials of place or direction.

> Steve lives _next door_ at number 23.
> I thought we went _the other way_ last time.

5 Many words can be used as prepositions and as adverbs, with no difference in meaning. Remember that prepositions have noun groups as objects, but adverbs do not.

> Did he fall _down the stairs?_
> Please do sit _down._
> I looked _underneath the bed,_ but the box had gone!
> Always put a sheet of paper _underneath._

Practice

A Look at the picture carefully, then look at the following pairs of sentences. In each case one sentence is true and the other is not true. Write 'True' or 'Not True' for each.

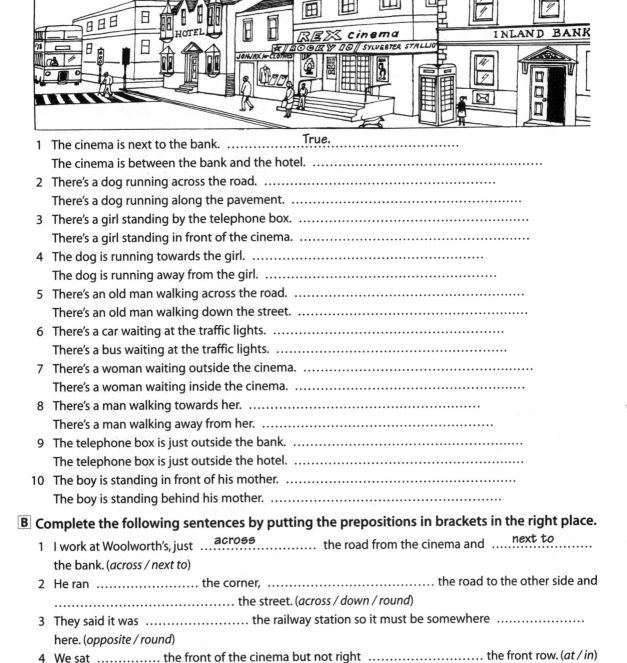

1 The cinema is next to the bank. ....True..........................

   The cinema is between the bank and the hotel. ....

2 There's a dog running across the road. ....

   There's a dog running along the pavement. ....

3 There's a girl standing by the telephone box. ....

   There's a girl standing in front of the cinema. ....

4 The dog is running towards the girl. ....

   The dog is running away from the girl. ....

5 There's an old man walking across the road. ....

   There's an old man walking down the street. ....

6 There's a car waiting at the traffic lights. ....

   There's a bus waiting at the traffic lights. ....

7 There's a woman waiting outside the cinema. ....

   There's a woman waiting inside the cinema. ....

8 There's a man walking towards her. ....

   There's a man walking away from her. ....

9 The telephone box is just outside the bank. ....

   The telephone box is just outside the hotel. ....

10 The boy is standing in front of his mother. ....

   The boy is standing behind his mother. ....

B Complete the following sentences by putting the prepositions in brackets in the right place.

1 I work at Woolworth's, just ......*across*...... the road from the cinema and ......*next to*......

   the bank. (*across / next to*)

2 He ran .... the corner, ... the road to the other side and

   .... the street. (*across / down / round*)

3 They said it was .... the railway station so it must be somewhere ....

   here. (*opposite / round*)

4 We sat .... the front of the cinema but not right .... the front row. (*at / in*)

5 Jill sat in the front .... the driver and I sat .... her. (*behind / next to*)

6 My office is .... town, ... the post office. (*close to / in the middle of*)

Place – 'at', 'in', 'on'

Main points

You use 'at' to talk about a place as a point.

You use 'in' to talk about a place as an area.

You use 'on' to talk about a place as a surface.

1 You use 'at' when you are thinking of a place as a point in space.

> She waited _at the bus stop_ for over twenty minutes.
> 'Where were you last night?' – '_At Mick's house._'

2 You also use 'at' with words such as 'back', 'bottom', 'end', 'front', and 'top' to talk about the different parts of a place.

> Mrs Castle was waiting _at the bottom_ of the stairs.
> They escaped by a window _at the back_ of the house.
> I saw a taxi _at the end_ of the street.

You use 'at' with public places and institutions. Note that you also say 'at home' and 'at work'.

> I have to be _at the station_ by ten o'clock.
> We landed _at a small airport._
> A friend of mine is _at Training College._
> She wanted to stay _at home._

You say 'at the corner' or 'on the corner' when you are talking about streets.

> The car was parked _at the corner_ of the street.
> There's a telephone box _on the corner._

You say 'in the corner' when you are talking about a room.

> She put the chair _in the corner_ of the room.

3 You use 'in' when you are talking about a place as an area. You use 'in' with:

• a country or geographical region

> When I was _in Spain,_ it was terribly cold.
> A thousand homes _in the east of Scotland_ suffered power cuts.

• a city, town, or village

> I've been teaching at a college _in London._

• a building when you are talking about people or things inside it

> They were sitting having dinner _in the restaurant._

You also use 'in' with containers of any kind when talking about things inside them.

> She kept the cards _in a little box._

4 Compare the use of 'at' and 'in' in these examples.

> I had a hard day _at the office._ ('at' emphasizes the office as a public place or institution)
> I left my coat behind _in the office._ ('in' emphasizes the office as a building)
> There's a good film _at the cinema._ ('at' emphasizes the cinema as a public place)
> It was very cold _in the cinema._ ('in' emphasizes the cinema as a building.)

5 When talking about addresses, you use 'at' when you give the house number, and 'in' when you just give the name of the street.

> They used to live _at 5, Weston Road._
> She got a job _in Oxford Street._

Note that American English uses 'on':

> He lived _on Penn Street._

You use 'at' when you are talking about someone's house.

> I'll see you _at Fred's house._

6 You use 'on' when you are talking about a place as a surface. You can also use 'on top of'.

> I sat down _on the sofa._
> She put her keys _on top of the television._

You also use 'on' when you are thinking of a place as a point on a line, such as a road, a railway line, a river, or a coastline.

> Scrabster is _on the north coast._
> Oxford is _on the A34_ between Birmingham and London.

➤ See Unit 40 for information on 'at', 'in', and 'on' in adverbials of time.

Practice

A **Look at the pictures and use these words to complete the sentences below.**

back	bottom	bus	car	corner (2)	door	flat
floor	front row	Park Street	left	phone box	picture	table

1 There's someone at the ....*door*...................................
2 There's a .... on the wall above the TV set in a .... of the room.
3 I waited at the .... of the queue.
4 I wanted to use the phone on the .... of the street but there
   was an old lady in the ....
5 I had a seat on the .... in the ....
6 Jack lives in a .... in .... on the third ....
7 There was a note on the .... It was from Elsie. She had
   signed her name at the ....
8 Jenny went to work in the .... and I went home on the ....

B **Complete the following sentences using 'at', 'in', or 'on'.**

1 They live ....*in*.................... Coronation Street ....*at*..................... number 32.
2 Jack works .... Oxford .... the University.
3 I've left my briefcase .... the office. I think I left it .... the chair .... the
   corner.
4 Meet me .... the bus-stop .... the end of Bristol Road.
5 They live .... Seal, a small village .... the road to Folkestone.
6 When we were .... the south we stayed .... a small hotel .... the coast.
7 My diary is .... the table .... the sitting room.
8 Sign your name .... the dotted line .... the bottom of the page.
9 Meet me .... the entrance to the Supermarket .... the High Street.
10 I've applied for a job .... the United Nations .... Geneva.
11 Hello. This is Gina. I'm .... Athens .... the Acropolis Hotel.

▸ **Bank**

Transport prepositions

Main points

This includes phrases like: 'by bus', 'in a car', 'on the plane', and 'off the train'.

You can use 'by' with most forms of transport.

You use 'in', 'into', and 'out of' with cars.

You normally use 'on', 'onto', and 'off' with other forms of transport.

1 When you talk about the type of vehicle or transport you use to travel somewhere, you use 'by'.

by bus	by bicycle	by car
by coach	by plane	by train

> She had come *by car* with her husband and her four children.
> I left Walsall in the afternoon and went *by bus and train* to Nottingham.

⊖ WARNING: If you want to say you walk somewhere, you say you go 'on foot'. You do not say 'by foot'.

> Marie decided to continue *on foot.*

2 You use 'in', 'into', and 'out of' when you are talking about cars, vans, lorries, taxis, and ambulances.

> I followed them *in my car.*
> The carpets had to be collected *in a van.*
> Mr Ward happened to be getting *into his lorry.*
> She was carried *out of the ambulance* and up the steps.

3 You use 'on', 'onto', and 'off' when you are talking about other forms of transport, such as buses, coaches, trains, ships, and planes.

> Why don't you come *on the train* with me to New York?
> Peter Hurd was already *on the plane* from California.
> The last thing he wanted was to spend ten days *on a boat* with Hooper.
> He jumped back *onto the old bus,* now nearly empty.
> Mr Bixby stepped *off the train* and walked quickly to the exit.

You can use 'in', 'into', and 'out of' with these other forms of transport, usually when you are focusing on the physical position or movement of the person, rather than stating what form of transport they are using.

> The passengers *in the plane* were beginning to panic.
> He got back *into the train* quickly, before Batt could stop him.
> We jumped *out of the bus* and ran into the nearest shop.

Practice

A **Use these pairs of phrases to complete the sentences below.**

by bullet train	on a bullet train
by luxury liner	on a luxury liner
by fighter plane	on a jumbo jet
by bus	on a double-decker bus
by coach	in an air-conditioned coach
by car ferry	on a car ferry

1 a The fastest way of getting from Kyoto to Tokyo is ....by bullet train...........

   b I've been on an express train, but I've never been ....on a bullet train............ .

2 a The most comfortable way of travelling is ....

   b I'd love to spend a holiday ....

3 a A fighter plane is very fast, but you are more comfortable ....

   b You could take a jumbo jet, but it's quicker ....

4 a You can get about sixty passengers ....

   b For short journeys it's covenient to travel ....

5 a We drove to the airport ....

   b We were taken to the airport ....

6 a If you are taking the family, it's cheaper to go ....

   b You can relax and take it easy ....

B **Complete the following sentences using 'by', 'in', 'off', 'on', or 'out of'.**

1 I usually go back home ....by........ bus. It's much cheaper than going .... train.

2 It gets so crowded in the rush hour that it's quicker to go .... foot than .... car.

3 We can take five people .... the car and the others will have to go .... the train.

4 It takes about half an hour to get home .... my bike and

   about twenty minutes .... the bus.

5 I have often travelled .... plane but I've never been .... a jumbo jet.

6 Since I broke my leg I have to travel .... bus because I can't get .... the car.

7 I have to get .... the train at the next stop.

8 Let me help you get your things .... the car.

9 The journey is uphill all the way so it's very tiring .... bike. I prefer to go .... foot.

10 We went for a trip up the Nile .... a big boat called a felucca.

93

Adjective + preposition

Main points

Some adjectives used after link verbs can be used alone or followed by a prepositional phrase.

Some adjectives must be followed by particular prepositions.

Some adjectives can be followed by different prepositions to introduce different types of information.

1 When you use an adjective after a link verb, you can often use the adjective on its own or followed by a prepositional phrase.

➜ See Unit 33 for other patterns.

>*He was <u>afraid.</u>*
>*He was <u>afraid of</u> his enemies.*

2 Some adjectives cannot be used alone after a link verb. If they are followed by a prepositional phrase, it must have a particular preposition:

aware of	accustomed to	unaware of
unaccustomed to	fond of	used to

>*I've always been terribly <u>fond of</u> you.*
>*He is <u>unaccustomed to</u> the heat.*

3 Some adjectives can be used alone, or followed by a particular preposition:

● used alone, or with 'of' to specify the cause of a feeling

afraid	ashamed	convinced	critical
envious	frightened	jealous	proud
scared	suspicious	terrified	tired

>*They may feel <u>jealous of</u> your success.*
>*I was <u>terrified of</u> her.*

● used alone, or with 'of' to specify the person who has a quality

brave	careless	clever	generous
good	intelligent	kind	nice
polite	sensible	silly	stupid
thoughtful	unkind	unreasonable	wrong

>*That was <u>clever of</u> you!*
>*I turned the job down, which was <u>stupid of</u> me.*

● used alone or used with 'to', usually referring to:

similarity:	close equal identical related similar
marriage:	married engaged
loyalty:	dedicated devoted loyal
rank:	junior senior

>*My problems are very <u>similar to</u> yours.*
>*He was <u>dedicated to</u> his job.*

● used alone, or followed by 'with' to specify the cause of a feeling

bored	content	displeased	dissatisfied
impatient	impressed	pleased	satisfied

>*I could never be <u>bored with</u> football.*
>*He was <u>pleased with</u> her.*

● used alone, or with 'at', usually referring to:

strong reactions:	alarmed amazed astonished shocked surprised
ability:	bad excellent good hopeless useless

>*He was <u>shocked at</u> the hatred they had known.*
>*She had always been <u>good at</u> languages.*

● used alone, or with 'for' to specify the person or thing that a quality relates to

common	difficult	easy	essential
important	necessary	possible	unnecessary
unusual	usual		

>*It's <u>difficult for young people</u> on their own.*
>*It was <u>unusual for them</u> to go away at the weekend.*

4 Some adjectives can be used alone, or used with different prepositions.

● used alone, with an impersonal subject and 'of' and the subject of the action, or with a personal subject and 'to' and the object of the action.

cruel	friendly	generous	good
kind	mean	nasty	nice
polite	rude	unfriendly	unkind

>*It was <u>rude of</u> him to leave so suddenly.*
>*She was <u>rude to</u> him for no reason.*

● used alone, with 'about' to specify a thing or 'with' to specify a person

angry	annoyed	delighted	disappointed
fed up	furious	happy	upset

>*She was still <u>angry about</u> the result.*
>*They're getting pretty <u>fed up with</u> him.*

Practice

A Use the adjectives below to complete the sentences that follow.

| bored | delighted | different | fond | proud |
| responsible | senior | stupid | surprised | used |

1 My brother did well. I was .... proud .... of him.
2 He made a silly mistake. It was very .... of him.
3 I can't stand the heat. I'm not .... to it.
4 Things have changed. Life is very .... from what it used to be.
5 I'm .... at you. I can't understand the way you behaved.
6 I'm .... with the result. It's exactly what I wanted.
7 Who is .... for this mess? Who left all these things lying around?
8 Jack is .... with school. He wants to leave as soon as possible.
9 Mary is an old friend of mine. I'm very .... of her.
10 In the army, a sergeant is .... to a corporal.

B Complete these definitions by adding the adjective with the right meaning. Use a different adjective in each sentence. See the lists on the opposite page for adjectives to use.

1 If something makes you very frightened you are .... terrified .... of it.
2 If you continue to support someone who is in trouble you are .... to them.
3 If two things are almost the same one is .... to the other.
4 If two things are exactly the same one is .... to the other.
5 If you buy someone an expensive present they might say 'That's very .... of you.'
6 Someone who is a fine athlete is .... at games.

C Complete the definitions using one of the adjectives below with the correct preposition.

| engaged | furious | jealous | kind | sensible | suspicious | upset |

1 If something makes you very worried and unhappy, you are very ...upset about.................. it.
2 If someone makes you very angry, you are .... them.
3 If you make a wise decision, someone might say 'That's very .... you'.
4 If you feel that you do not trust someone, you are .... them.
5 If someone else has something and you wish you had it, you are .... them.
6 If you treat someone very well, you are being .... them.
7 If you have agreed to marry someone, you are .... them.

D Rewrite the sentences below using an adjective, the appropiate preposition, and 'way'.

1 He drives dangerously. It makes me terrified. / I'm .... terrified of the way he drives..............
2 She played very well. I was proud of her. / I was ....
3 He behaved badly. Everyone was very critical. / ....
4 They looked lovely. I was delighted. / ....
5 They treated us very well. We were very happy. / ....

Noun + preposition

Main points

'Of' can be used to add many different types of information, 'with' is used to specify a quality or possession.

Some nouns are always followed by particular prepositions.

1 You can give more information about a noun by adding a prepositional phrase after it.

> Four men _on holiday_ were in the car.
> A sound _behind him_ made him turn.

2 You often use the preposition 'of' after a noun to add various kinds of information. For example, you can use 'of' to indicate:

- what something is made of or consists of

> ...a wall _of stone._
> A feeling _of panic_ was rising in him.

- what the subject matter of speech, writing, or a picture is

> She gave a brief account _of her interview._
> There was a picture _of them both_ in the paper.

- what a person or thing belongs to or is connected with

> She was the daughter _of the village priest._
> The boys sat on the floor _of the living room._

- what qualities a person or thing has

> She was a woman _of energy and ambition._
> They faced problems _of great complexity._

3 After nouns referring to actions, you use 'of' to indicate the subject or object of the action.

> ...the arrival _of the police._
> ...the destruction _of their city._

After nouns referring to people who perform an action, you use 'of' to say what the action involves or is aimed at.

> ...supporters _of the hunger strike._
> ...a student _of English._

Note that you often use two nouns, rather than a noun and a prepositional phrase. For example, you say 'bank robbers', not 'robbers of the bank'.

4 After nouns referring to measurement, you use 'of' to give the exact figure.

> ...an average annual temperature _of 20 degrees._
> ...a speed _of 25 kilometres an hour._

You can use 'of' after a noun to give someone's age.

> Jonathan was a child _of seven_ when it happened.

5 You use 'with' after a noun to say that a person or thing has a particular quality, feature, or possession.

> ...a girl _with red hair._
> ...the man _with the gun._

Note that you use 'in' after a noun to say what someone is wearing.

> ...a grey-haired man _in a raincoat._
> ...the man _in dark glasses._

6 Some nouns are usually followed by a particular preposition. Here are some examples of:

- nouns followed by 'to'

alternative	answer	approach	attitude
introduction	invitation	reaction	reference
reply	resistance	return	solution

> This was my first real _introduction to_ Africa.

- nouns followed by 'for'

admiration	cure	demand	desire
dislike	need	reason	recipe
respect	responsibility	room	search
substitute	sympathy	taste	thirst

> Their _need for_ money is growing fast.

- nouns followed by 'on'

agreement	attack	comment	decision	effect	tax

> She had a dreadful _effect on_ me.

- nouns followed by 'with' or 'between'

connection	contact	link	relationship

> His illness had some _connection with_ his diet.

- nouns followed by 'in'

decrease	difficulty	fall	increase	rise

> They demanded a large _increase in_ wages.

Practice

A Use the nouns below to complete the sentences which follow.

> contribution   cure   damage   demand   invitation   recipe   reply   room   solution   sympathy

1 In the last storm there was a lot of ....damage... to the roof.
2 They asked me for a .... to the church so I gave them £25.
3 What did you say in your .... to David's letter?
4 They were kind enough to send me an .... to the wedding.
5 I'm afraid I can't offer any .... to the problem.
6 Do you think they will ever find a .... for the common cold?
7 Sit here. We can make .... for another one.
8 I have no .... for people who get into trouble through dangerous driving.
9 Can I have the .... for that lovely cake?
10 There's not much .... for firewood nowadays.

B Now do these in the same way. Use a dictionary to help you if necessary.

> advantage   cause   comment   contact   decision   difference   difficulty   relationship   increase   tax

1 The government is going to increase the ....tax................................. on cigarettes.
2 I'd like to make just one .... on your answer.
3 She has always had a very close .... with her father.
4 I haven't heard from Angela for ages. I've almost lost .... with her.
5 There is always a big .... in sales just before Christmas.
6 Heart disease is the commonest .... of death in industrialised societies.
7 The main .... of air travel is that it's so quick.
8 I always have great .... in getting up early in the morning.
9 Have you reached a .... on whether or not to sell your house?
10 What's the .... between a house and a bungalow?

C Complete these sentences using the correct prepositions.

1 Some people have a very strange attitude ....to................................. animals.
2 The Sunday Times made a fierce attack .... the Prime Minister.
3 There was a sharp rise .... prices last month.
4 People used to believe that air pollution was the cause .... malaria.
5 You should try to have more sympathy .... other people.
6 Surely we can come to some agreement .... the price.
7 In the long run there is no alternative .... hard work.
8 We should have respect .... other people's beliefs.
9 The main disadvantage .... air travel is the high cost.
10 Our school has close links .... several schools overseas.

▸ **Bank**

Verb + preposition

Main points

Some verbs do not take an object and are normally followed by a preposition.

Some verbs take an object followed by a particular preposition.

Some verbs can take either an object or a preposition.

1 Many verbs that are used without an object are normally followed by a prepositional phrase. Some verbs take a particular preposition:

belong to	consist of	hint at	hope for
insist on	lead to	listen to	pay for
qualify for	refer to	relate to	sympathize with

The land _belongs to_ a rich family.
She then _referred to_ the Minister's report.

2 With other verbs that are used without an object, the choice of a different preposition may alter the meaning of the clause.

agree on/with	appeal for/to	apologize for/to
conform to/with	result from/in	suffer from/with

They _agreed on_ a plan of action.
You _agreed with_ me that we should buy a car.
His failure _resulted from_ lack of attention to details.
The match _resulted in_ a draw.

3 With verbs that are used without an object, different prepositions are used to introduce different types of information.

• 'about' indicates the subject matter

care	complain	dream	explain	hear
know	speak	talk	think	write

We will always _care about_ freedom.
Tonight I'm going to _talk about_ engines.

• 'at' indicates direction

glance	glare	grin	laugh
look	shout	smile	stare

I don't know why he was _laughing at_ that joke.
'Hey!' she _shouted at_ him.

• 'for' indicates purpose or reason

apologize	apply	ask	look	wait

He wanted to _apologize for_ being late.
I'm going to _wait for_ the next bus.

• 'into' indicates the object involved in a collision

bump	crash	drive	run

His car _crashed into_ the wall.
She _drove into_ the back of a lorry.

• 'of' indicates facts or information

hear	know	speak	talk	think

I've _heard of_ him but I don't know who he is.
Do you _know of_ the new plans for the sports centre?

• 'on' indicates confidence or certainty

count	depend	plan	rely

You can _count on_ me.
You can _rely on_ him to be polite.

• 'to' indicates the listener or reader

complain	explain	listen	say	speak	talk	write

They _complained to_ me about the noise.
Mary turned her head to _speak to_ him.

• 'with' indicates someone whose opinion is the same or different

agree	argue	disagree	side

Do you _agree with_ me about this?
The daughters _sided with_ their mothers.

4 Some verbs have an object, but are also followed by a preposition.

The police _accused_ him _of_ murder.
They _borrowed_ some money _from_ the bank.

Some verbs can take either an object or a prepositional phrase with no change in meaning.

He had to fight _them_.
He was fighting _against history._

Practice

A Use these verbs and prepositions in the sentences below. Use the correct form of the verbs.

appeal to/for	belong to	depend on	hope for	insist on
pay for	refer to	result in	suffer from	sympathize with

1 If you don't understand any of these words, you could always ....refer to........... a dictionary.
2 All last winter he .... coughs and colds.
3 The accident on the A41 sadly .... the death of a child.
4 The police are .... witnesses to come forward.
5 The poor driver – I really .... him, it wasn't his fault.
6 It wasn't his car. In fact I don't know who it ....
7 The buses are often late, so you can't .... them.
8 We are still .... improvements in the bus service.
9 Nurses are very badly paid. I think they should .... higher rates of pay.
10 Keep enough money to .... your ticket.

B Read the sentences, then use 'about' and 'to' in each one, as appropriate.

1 I want to talk ....to................... the group ....about............... their exams.
2 When will you write .... Bill .... your plans?
3 Have you heard .... what happened to those prisoners? Or don't you care .... them?
4 I said .... you I was thinking .... going to
   work in Africa, didn't I? Well, I actually dreamt .... Africa last night!
5 If the service is really so dreadful, you ought to complain .... it .... the manager.
6 She listened .... me talking .... the bad
   service, and then complained .... the problems they were having with staffing.

C Use 'at' or 'into' in these sentences.

1 The brakes failed and the bus ran ....into.............................. the wall of a house.
2 People started to shout .... the driver.
3 Who was the boy you were all laughing ....?
4 I bumped .... an old friend the other day.
5 I saw somebody staring .... me from the other side of the road.

D Use 'with' or 'for' in these sentences.

1 He was always arguing ....with.......................... his brothers.
2 I agree .... you that we should wait a bit longer .... her.
3 She never apologizes .... arriving late.
4 I thought we should look .... someone else to do the job,
   but the boss disagreed .... me.
5 If you want to travel, that would be a good job to apply ....

▶ **Bank**

Phrasal verbs

Main points

A phrasal verb is a combination of a verb and an adverb or preposition.

The usual meaning of the verb is normally altered.

Phrasal verbs are used in four main structures.

1 Phrasal verbs are verbs that combine with adverbs or prepositions. The adverbs and prepositions are called particles, for example 'down', 'in', 'off', 'out', and 'up'.

> She _turned off_ the radio.
> Mr Knight offered to _put_ him _up._

2 Phrasal verbs extend the usual meaning of the verb or create a new meaning. For example, if you 'break' something, you damage it, but if you 'break out of' a place, you escape from it.

> They _broke out of_ prison on Thursday night.
> The pain gradually _wore off._

3 Phrasal verbs are normally used in one of four main structures. In the first structure, the verb is followed by a particle, and there is no object.

break out	catch on	check up	come in
get by	give in	go away	grow up
look in	ring off	start out	stay up
stop off	wait up	watch out	wear off

> War _broke out_ in September.
> You'll have to _stay up_ late tonight.

4 In the second structure, the verb is followed by a particle and an object.

fall for	feel for	grow on	look after
part with	pick on	set about	take after

> She _looked after_ her invalid mother.
> Peter _takes after his father_ but John is more like me.

5 In the third structure, the verb is followed by an object and a particle.

answer back	ask in	call back	catch out
count in	invite out	order about	tell apart

> I _answered him back_ and took my chances.
> He loved to _order people about._

6 Some phrasal verbs can be used in both the second structure and the third structure: verb followed by a particle and an object, or verb followed by an object and a particle.

add on	bring up	call up	fold up
hand over	knock over	point out	pull down
put away	put up	rub out	sort out
take up	tear up	throw away	try out

> It took ages to _clean up the mess._
> It took ages to _clean the mess up._
> There was such a mess. It took ages to _clean it up._

⊖ WARNING: If the object is a pronoun, it must go in front of the particle. You cannot say 'He cleaned up it'.

7 In the fourth structure, the verb is followed by a particle and a preposition with an object.

break out of	catch up with	come down with
get on with	go down with	keep on at
look forward to	make off with	miss out on
play around with	put up with	run away with
stick up for	talk down to	walk out on

> You go on ahead. I'll _catch up with_ you later.
> Children have to learn to _stick up for_ themselves.

8 A very few verbs are used in the structure: verb followed by an object, a particle, and a preposition with its object.

do out of	let in for	put down to
put up to	take out on	talk out of

> I'll _take you up on_ that generous invitation.
> Kroop tried to _talk her out of_ it.

Practice

A Use the following phrasal verbs to complete the sentences below.

catch up	cool off	fall behind	give in	grow up
keep up	speak up	stay on	watch out	wait up

1 He still behaves like a child. I wish he'd ....*grow up*.............................. .
2 Come to the party on Friday and .... for the weekend.
3 I won't be back until late. Will you .... for me?
4 He was exhausted but he still kept going. He just wouldn't ....
5 Please don't go so fast. I just can't ....
6 Could you .... a bit? I can hardly hear you.
7 .... ! Oh dear. Didn't you see that car coming?
8 You look hot and sticky. Come and sit in the shade and ....
9 You go on ahead and I'll ....
10 Wait for me. I don't want to ....

B Complete the following sentences using the phrasal verb in brackets and a personal pronoun. The pronoun must come between the verb and the particle.

1 I am in charge here. Don't ....*answer me back*............................ . (*answer back*)
2 We're very cold out here. Aren't you going to .... ? (*ask in*)
3 I'd like to speak to him again. Will you please .... ? (*call back*)
4 They were fighting so fiercely that it took two of us to .... (*pull apart*)
5 I'm afraid we're just on our way out, so I can't .... (*invite in*)
6 I'm afraid the money is lost. We'll never .... (*get back*)
7 She knows all the answers. Nobody can .... (*catch out*)
8 They took us to dinner last month. It's our turn to .... for a meal. (*invite out*)
9 It certainly is a difficult problem. I just can't .... (*work out*)
10 It's difficult to find your way out. Wait a minute and I'll ask someone to .... (*show out*)

C Complete the following sentences using the phrasal verb and object given in brackets.

1 I have to ring off now. I'll ....*call you back*.................... this evening. (*you / call back*)
2 It's an obvious trick. Nobody but a fool would ....*fall for that*.................... . (*that / fall for*)
3 I .... on my way to work yesterday. (*an old friend / bumped into*)
4 It's hard work having a full time job and .... as well. (*the house / looking after*)
5 Let's ring Tom and Molly and .... for dinner. (*them / invite out*)
6 Everybody tells me I .... (*my mother / take after*)

▸ **Bank**

Verbs and objects

Main points

Intransitive verbs do not have an object.

Transitive verbs have an object.

Some verbs can be used with or without an object, depending on the situation or their meaning.

1 Many verbs do not normally have an object. They are called 'intransitive' verbs. They often refer to:

existence: appear die disappear happen live remain

the human body: ache bleed blush faint shiver smile

human noises: cough cry laugh scream snore speak yawn

light, smell, vibration: glow shine sparkle stink throb vibrate

position, movement: arrive come depart fall flow go kneel run sit sleep stand swim wait walk work

An awful thing <u>has happened.</u>
The girl <u>screamed.</u>
I <u>waited.</u>

Note that intransitive verbs cannot be used in the passive.

2 Many verbs normally have an object. These verbs are called 'transitive' verbs. They are often connected with:

physical objects: build buy carry catch cover cut destroy hit own remove sell use waste wear

senses: feel hear see smell taste touch

feelings: admire enjoy fear frighten hate like love need prefer surprise trust want

facts, ideas: accept believe correct discuss expect express forget include know mean remember report

people: address blame comfort contact convince defy kill persuade please tease thank warn

He <u>hit the ball</u> really hard.
She <u>reported the accident</u> to the police.
Don't <u>blame me.</u>

Note that transitive verbs can be used in the passive.

They <u>were blamed</u> for everything.

⊖ WARNING: 'Have' is a transitive verb, but cannot be used in the passive. You can say 'I have a car' but not 'A car is had by me'.

3 Often, the people you are talking to know what the object is because of the situation, or because it has already been mentioned. In this case you can omit the object, even though the verb is transitive.

accept	answer	change	choose
clean	cook	draw	drive
eat	explain	forget	help
iron	know	learn	leave
paint	park	phone	read
remember	ride	sing	steal
study	type	understand	wash
watch	write		

I don't own a car. I can't <u>drive.</u>
You don't <u>smoke,</u> do you?
I asked a question and George <u>answered.</u>
Both dresses are beautiful. It's difficult to <u>choose.</u>

4 Many verbs have more than one meaning, and are transitive in one meaning and intransitive in another meaning. For example, the verb 'run' is intransitive when you use it to mean 'move quickly' but transitive when you use it to mean 'manage or operate'.

call	fit	lose	manage	miss
move	play	run	show	spread

The hare <u>runs</u> at enormous speed.
She <u>runs a hotel.</u>
She <u>moved</u> gracefully.
The whole incident <u>had moved her</u> profoundly.

5 A few verbs are normally intransitive, but can be used with an object that is closely related to the verb.

dance (a dance)	die (a death)	dream (a dream)
laugh (a laugh)	live (a life)	sigh (a sigh)
smile (a smile)		

Steve <u>smiled his thin, cruel smile.</u>
I once <u>dreamed a very nice dream.</u>

Note that you normally add more information about the object, for example by using adjectives in front of the noun.

Practice

A In each pair of sentences below one sentence has a transitive verb and the other an intransitive verb. Mark the sentences T (transitive) or I (intransitive). In the sentences which have a transitive verb, underline the object.

1 The postman calls at about 7 am every morning. .... I ....

They are going to call <u>the new town</u> Skelmersdale. .... T ....

2 You're not allowed to drive a car until you're seventeen. ....

She learned to drive when she was eighteen. ....

3 I've never deliberately hurt anyone. ....

My leg was beginning to hurt quite a lot. ....

4 You look just the same. You haven't changed a bit. ....

You can't change human nature. ....

5 We are running a course for English teachers. ....

I can't run as fast as I used to. ....

6 She is studying for a law degree. ....

He had studied chemistry at university. ....

7 He turned to Joan and began to explain. ....

He turned the handle and pushed the door open. ....

8 I don't think we've met before, have we? ....

Dan came to the airport to meet me. ....

9 He's only young, but he's learning fast. ....

What did you learn at school today? ....

10 Could you stop the bus, please. I want to get off. ....

Do you think you could stop in front of the post office? ....

B Use the correct form of the verbs below to complete the sentences which follow.

accept choose forget hear know leave phone remember understand watch

1 He offered me a drink and I .... *accepted* ....

2 There were so many good things to eat it was almost impossible to ....

3 He asked me for an answer but I just didn't ....

4 I hadn't time to write a letter so I decided to ....

5 No matter how I tried to .... , I just couldn't think of his name.

6 I kept thinking of the tragic accident, no matter how much I wanted to ....

7 He explained to me how to do the problem and I did my best to ....

8 We wanted to get home early so at half past two we decided it was time to ....

9 It looked as if it would be an exciting game so we stayed to ....

10 If I had .... the question, I might have been able to answer it.

Verbs with two objects

Main points

Some verbs have two objects, a direct object and an indirect object.

The indirect object can be used without a preposition, or after 'to' or 'for'.

1 Some verbs have two objects after them, a direct object and an indirect object. For example, in the sentence 'I gave John the book', 'the book' is the direct object. 'John' is the indirect object. Verbs that have two objects are sometimes called 'ditransitive' verbs or 'double-transitive' verbs.

> His uncle had <u>given</u> him books on India.
> She <u>sends</u> you her love.
> I <u>passed</u> him the cup.

2 When the indirect object is a pronoun, or another short noun group such as a noun with 'the', you put the indirect object in front of the direct object.

> Dad gave <u>me</u> a car.
> You promised <u>the lad</u> a job.
> He had lent <u>my cousin</u> the money.
> She bought <u>Dave and me</u> an ice cream.

3 You can also use the prepositions 'to' and 'for' to introduce the indirect object. If you do this, you put the preposition and indirect object after the direct object.

> He handed his room key <u>to the receptionist.</u>
> Bill saved a piece of cake <u>for the children.</u>

When the indirect object consists of several words, you normally use a preposition to introduce it.

> She taught physics and chemistry <u>to pupils at the local school.</u>
> I made that lamp <u>for a seventy-year-old woman.</u>

You often use a preposition when you want to emphasize the indirect object.

> Did you really buy that <u>for me?</u>

4 With some verbs you can only use 'for', not 'to', to introduce the indirect object.

book	buy	cook	cut
find	keep	leave	make
paint	pour	prepare	save
win			

> They booked a place <u>for me.</u>
> He had found some old clothes <u>for the beggar.</u>
> They bought a present <u>for the teacher.</u>
> She painted a picture <u>for her father.</u>

5 With some verbs you normally use 'to' to introduce the indirect object.

give	lend	offer	pass	pay	post
promise	read	sell	send	show	teach
tell					

> I had lent my bicycle <u>to a friend.</u>
> Ralph passed a message <u>to Jack.</u>
> They say they posted the letter <u>to me</u> last week.
> He sold it <u>to me.</u>

Note that you can use 'for' with these verbs, but it has a different meaning. 'For' indicates that one person does something on behalf of another person, so that the other person does not have to do it.

> His mother paid the bill <u>for him.</u>
> If you're going out, can you post this <u>for me,</u> please?

Practice

A Rewrite the sentences below putting the indirect object after the verb and using the preposition 'to' or 'for'.

1 He made his wife a cup of tea. / .... *He made a cup of tea for his wife.* ....

2 John sold Mary his old car. / ....

3 Could you show your grandfather those old photographs? / ....

4 Save the rest of us something to eat. / ....

5 I'm going to book your guests a really good table. / ....

6 We've prepared you a light snack. / ....

7 We'll leave you some food in the fridge. / ....

8 I taught Peter's children French when they were younger. / ....

9 I'll try to find you those books. / ....

10 We must remember to send George and Alice a card. / ....

B Rewrite these sentences by changing the indirect object (in bold) to 'him', 'her', or 'them' and putting it in front of the direct object.

1 I bought a present for **my little brother.** / .... *I bought him a present.* ....

2 She cooked a wonderful meal for **her visitors.** / ....

3 He passed the money to **the man behind the counter.** / ....

4 Cut some bread for **the children at that table.** / ....

5 Give this letter to **the lady at the desk.** / ....

6 She used to teach arithmetic to **the children at the village school.** / ....

7 I'd like to keep something for **the people who arrive late.** / ....

8 You must show these papers to **the police officers on the border.** / ....

9 He always reads a story to **his youngest daughter** before she goes to sleep. / ....

10 I'm going to write a short note to **the girl I met on holiday last year.** / ....

C Rearrange the parts of sentences given below to make sentences with two objects.

1 a long letter / her friend / wrote / she / to.
She wrote a long letter to her friend.
....

2 for / some money / left / Mrs Brown / the milkman.

....

3 sent a Christmas card / to / on holiday / we / the people we met.

....

4 her / some flowers / on her birthday / he gave.

....

5 Jack and Mary / the children / promised / a day at the seaside.

....

6 us / what to do/ told / Nobody.

....

▸ **Bank**

Reflexive verbs

Main points

Transitive verbs are used with a reflexive pronoun to indicate that the object is the same as the subject, for example: 'I hurt myself'.

Some verbs which do not normally have a person as the object can have reflexive pronouns as the object.

1 You use a reflexive pronoun after a transitive verb to indicate that the object is the same as the subject.

> He blamed <u>himself</u> for his friend's death.
> I taught <u>myself</u> French.

➤ See Unit 20 for more information on reflexive pronouns.

2 In theory, most transitive verbs can be used with a reflexive pronoun. However, you often use reflexive pronouns with the following verbs.

amuse	blame	cut	dry	help
hurt	introduce	kill	prepare	repeat
restrict	satisfy	teach		

> Sam <u>amused himself</u> by throwing branches into the fire.
> 'Can I borrow a pencil?' – 'Yes, <u>help yourself.</u>'
> <u>Prepare yourself</u> for a shock.
> He <u>introduced himself</u> to me.

3 Verbs like 'dress', 'shave', and 'wash', which describe actions that people do to themselves, do not usually take reflexive pronouns in English, although they do in some other languages. With these verbs, reflexive pronouns are only used for emphasis.

> I usually <u>shave</u> before breakfast.
> He prefers to <u>shave himself,</u> even with that broken arm.
> She <u>washed</u> very quickly and rushed downstairs.
> Children were encouraged to <u>wash themselves.</u>

4 'Behave' does not normally take an object at all, but can take a reflexive pronoun as object.

> If they don't <u>behave,</u> send them to bed.
> He is old enough to <u>behave himself.</u>

5 Some verbs do not normally have a person as object, because they describe actions that you do not do to other people. However, these verbs can have reflexive pronouns as object, because you can do these actions to yourself.

apply	compose	distance	enjoy
excel	exert	express	strain

> I really <u>enjoyed</u> the party.
> Just go out there and <u>enjoy yourself.</u>
> She <u>expressed</u> surprise at the news.
> Professor Dale <u>expressed himself</u> very forcibly.

6 When 'busy' and 'content' are used as verbs, they always take a reflexive pronoun as their direct object. They are therefore true 'reflexive verbs'.

> He had <u>busied himself</u> in the laboratory.
> I had to <u>content myself</u> with watching the little moving lights.

Practice

A Use the verbs below with a reflexive pronoun to complete the sentences which follow.

behave blame describe enjoy excel express find help introduce kill repeat teach

1 The children realized that they were all alone in the forest.
   The children .... *found themselves* .... all alone in the forest.
2 Have another drink.
   .... to another drink.
3 They don't know how to behave properly.
   They don't know how to ....
4 He kept on saying the same thing again and again.
   He kept ....
5 I'm afraid I didn't have a very good time.
   I'm afraid I didn't .... very much.
6 I'd like to tell you about myself.
   I'd like to ....
7 She's learning French at home, without a teacher.
   She's .... French.
8 I wouldn't really say that I'm lazy.
   I wouldn't .... as lazy.
9 You shouldn't think it's your fault.
   You shouldn't ....
10 He is difficult to understand.
   He doesn't .... very clearly.
11 They have done better than anyone expected.
   They have ....
12 She was so unhappy, she tried to commit suicide.
   She was so unhappy, she tried to ....

B Rewrite these sentences putting in a verb with a reflexive pronoun wherever you can.

1 He's still very ill but he can wash and shave.
   ...*He's still very ill, but he can wash himself and shave himself.*.........................
2 You ought to behave better than that.
   ....
3 You must learn to adapt to new ideas.
   ....
4 The children tried to hide in the cupboard.
   ....
5 You can dry on that towel.
   ....
6 Billy undressed before going to bed.
   ....

107

Reciprocal verbs

Main points

Some verbs describe two people or two groups of people doing the same thing to each other, for example: 'We met', 'I met you', 'We met each other'.

You use 'each other' or 'one another' for emphasis.

With some verbs, you use 'each other' or 'one another' after 'with'.

1 Some verbs refer to actions that involve two people or two groups of people doing the same thing to each other. These verbs are sometimes called 'reciprocal' verbs.

>*We met in Delhi.*
>*Jane and Sarah told me that <u>they met you.</u>*
>*<u>They met each other</u> for the first time last week.*

2 The two people or groups of people involved in the action are often mentioned as the plural subject of the verb, and the verb does not have an object. For example, 'John and Mary argued' means that John argued with Mary and Mary argued with John.

argue	clash	coincide	combine
compete	fight	kiss	marry
match	meet		

>*The pair of you <u>have argued</u> about that for years.*
>*We <u>competed</u> furiously.*
>*Their children <u>are always fighting.</u>*
>*They <u>kissed.</u>*

3 When you want to emphasize that both people or groups of people are equally involved, you can use the pronouns 'each other' or 'one another' as the object of the verb. Verbs that refer to actions in which there is physical contact between people are often used with 'each other' or 'one another'.

cuddle	embrace	fight	hug	kiss	touch

>*We embraced <u>each other.</u>*
>*They fought <u>one another</u> desperately for it.*
>*They kissed <u>each other</u> in greeting.*
>*It was the first time they had touched <u>one another.</u>*

4 Some verbs do not take an object, so you use a preposition before 'each other' or 'one another'.

>*They <u>parted from each other</u> after only two weeks.*
>*We <u>talk to one another</u> as often as possible.*

5 With some verbs you have a choice of preposition before 'each other' or 'one another'. For example, you can 'fight with' one another or 'fight against' one another.

with/against:	compete fight
with/from:	part
with/to:	correspond relate talk

>*Many countries are <u>competing with each other.</u>*
>*Did you <u>compete against each other</u> in yesterday's race?*
>*Stephen and I <u>parted with one another</u> on good terms.*
>*They <u>parted from one another</u> quite suddenly.*

6 With some verbs, you can only use 'with' before 'each other' or 'one another'.

Note that most of these verbs refer to people talking or working together.

agree	argue	clash
collide	communicate	co-operate
disagree	quarrel	

>*We do <u>agree with each other</u> sometimes.*
>*Have they <u>communicated with each other</u> since then?*
>*The two lorries <u>collided with one another</u> on the motorway.*

7 If you want to focus on one of the people involved, you make them the subject of the verb and make the other person the object.

>*<u>She</u> married <u>a young engineer.</u>*
>*<u>You</u> could meet <u>me</u> at the restaurant.*

If the verb cannot take an object, you mention the other person after a preposition.

>*Youths clashed <u>with police</u> in Belfast.*
>*She was always quarrelling <u>with him.</u>*

Practice

A Use the correct form of the verbs below to complete the sentences which follow.

| argue attack bump communicate cooperate fight hurt part talk |

1 Watch what you're doing with those sticks. You'll ....*hurt*........................ each other if you're not careful.

2 We have to keep these dogs separate. They .... each other on sight.

3 The children won't play peacefully together. They always .... each other.

4 I wish Jack and Jill could work together but they just refuse to .... with one another.

5 They can never agree. They .... with one another about everything.

6 They've had a dreadful quarrel. Now they won't even .... to one another.

7 I met Sally yesterday. We .... into each other on the train.

8 Neither of us is on the phone so we find it difficult to .... with one another.

9 They're twins and they hate to .... from one another.

B Complete the following sentences by adding 'at', 'into', 'of', 'on', 'to' or 'with'.

1 John and Helen looked ....*at*........................ each other and smiled.

2 The children quarrel a lot but they're very fond .... each other.

3 They both talk at the same time. They never seem to listen .... each other.

4 They have been corresponding .... one another since they left school.

5 They were so angry they just stood and shouted .... each other.

6 They were both very sorry. They apologised .... each other.

7 The two cars just crashed .... each other.

8 We could just see one another so we waved .... each other across the park.

9 They are both very well known but they hadn't heard .... each other.

10 It was so funny. They just sat and laughed .... each other.

11 We can rely .... one another.

12 They knew that they could depend .... each other.

C Complete these sentences using 'themselves' or 'each other'.

1 They always send ....*each other*.................... a card at Christmas.

2 They really enjoyed ....*themselves*............................ on holiday.

3 Fred and Charles hadn't met .... before.

4 Jane and Mary went shopping together and locked .... out of the house.

5 Neither John nor Peter would take responsibility for the accident. They both blamed

   ....

6 John and Peter were dreadfully sorry about the accident. They blamed ....

   for it.

7 The two children smiled happily at ....

8 A lot of people injure .... doing jobs about the house.

Ergative verbs

Main points

Ergative verbs are both transitive and intransitive. The object of the transitive use is the subject of the intransitive use, for example: 'I opened the door'; 'The door opened'.

A few verbs are only ergative with particular nouns.

A few of these verbs need an adverbial when they are used without an object.

1 Some verbs can be used as transitive verbs to focus on the person who performs an action, and as intransitive verbs to focus on the thing affected by the action.

> When _I opened the door,_ there was Laverne.
> Suddenly _the door opened._

Note that the object of the transitive verb, in this case 'the door', is the subject of the intransitive verb. Verbs like these are called 'ergative' verbs.

2 Ergative verbs often refer to:

● changes

begin	break	change	crack	dry
end	finish	grow	improve	increase
slow	start	stop	tear	

> I _broke_ the glass.
> The glass _broke_ all over the floor.
> The driver _stopped_ the car.
> A big car _stopped._

● cooking

bake	boil	cook	defrost
fry	melt	roast	simmer

> I _'ve boiled_ an egg.
> The porridge _is boiling._
> I _'m cooking_ spaghetti.
> The rice _is cooking._

● position or movement

balance	close	drop	move	open
rest	rock	shake	stand	turn

> She _rested_ her head on his shoulder.
> Her head _rested_ on the table.
> An explosion _shook_ the hotel.
> The whole room _shook._

● vehicles

back	crash	drive	fly	reverse
run	sail			

> He _had crashed_ the car twice.
> Her car _crashed_ into a tree.
> She _sailed_ her yacht round the world.
> The ship _sailed_ on Monday.

3 Some verbs can be used in these two ways only with a small set of nouns. For example, you can say 'He fired a gun' or 'The gun fired'. You can do the same with other words referring to types of gun, 'cannon', 'pistol', or 'rifle'. However, although you can say 'He fired a bullet', you cannot say 'The bullet fired'.

catch:	belt, cloth, clothing, dress, shirt, trousers
fire:	cannon, gun, pistol, rifle
play:	guitar, music, piano, violin
ring:	alarm, bell
show:	anger, disappointment, emotions, fear, joy
sound:	alarm, bell, horn

> I _caught_ my dress on the fence.
> My tights _caught_ on a nail.
> A car _was sounding_ its horn.
> A horn _sounded_ in the night.

4 A few verbs can be used in both ways, but need an adverbial when they are used without an object.

clean	freeze	handle	mark	polish	sell
stain	wash				

> He _sells_ books.
> This book _is selling well._
> She _had handled_ a machine gun.
> This car _handles very nicely._

Practice

A Complete the sentences below using the correct form of the following verbs.

begin boil cook crack handle increase open ring sell tear stop wash

1 The door ....*opened*............ and a young man came out.
2 Be careful with that paper. It'll .... easily.
3 The glass will probably .... if you pour boiling water in it.
4 Has the kettle .... yet?
5 Those jeans are very good value. They should .... really quickly.
6 The bus .... right outside the house.
7 The meat will .... quite quickly. It'll be ready in half an hour.
8 The meeting .... with a short welcome from the new chairman.
9 The doorbell .... several times before anyone answered.
10 This shirt is dreadful. It just won't .... clean.
11 Prices have .... by ten per cent since last year.
12 The plane still .... well at over twice the speed of sound.

B Complete the pairs of sentences below using the following nouns.

building hand potatoes shirt train vase water window

1 a Has the ....*water*............ boiled yet?
  b Boil the .... in the saucepan and add the sage.
2 a The .... broke when it fell off the shelf.
  b My brother broke a rare ....
3 a His .... caught on a nail and tore.
  b He wiggled and swore, caught his .... on a nail, swore louder.
4 a The whole .... shook in the storm.
  b An earthquake shook the .... where they were meeting.
5 a Her .... rested on the arm of her chair.
  b He rested a .... on Brian's shoulder.
6 a Suddenly the .... opened and a woman poked out her head.
  b He opened the .... of his car and said, 'Come here.'
7 a The .... stopped just outside the station.
  b They stopped the .... less than a mile further down the line.
8 a The .... were cooking in a large pan.
  b Cook the .... over a gentle heat.

Common verb + noun patterns

Main points

Examples are: 'have a bath'; 'give a shout'; 'make promises'; 'take care'.

Common verbs are often used with nouns to describe actions.

You use 'have' with nouns referring to eating, drinking, talking, and washing.

You use 'give' with nouns referring to noises, hitting, and talking.

You use 'make' with nouns referring to talking, plans, and travelling.

1 When you want to talk about actions, you often use common verbs with nouns as their object. The nouns describe the action. For example, if you say 'I had a shower', the noun tells you what the action was. The common verbs have very little meaning.

> *I had a nice rest.*
> *She made a remark about the weather.*

The nouns often have related verbs that do not take an object.

> *Helen went upstairs to rest.*
> *I remarked that it would be better if I came.*

2 Different verbs are used with different nouns. You use 'have' with nouns referring to:

> **meals**: breakfast dinner drink lunch meal taste tea
> **talking**: chat conversation discussion talk
> **washing**: bath shower wash
> **relaxation**: break holiday rest
> **disagreement**: argument fight quarrel trouble

> *We usually have lunch at one o'clock.*
> *He was having his first holiday for five years.*

3 You use 'give' with nouns referring to:

> **human noises**: cry gasp giggle groan laugh scream shout sigh whistle yell
> **facial expressions**: grin smile
> **hitting**: kick punch push slap
> **talking**: advice answer example information interview lecture news report speech talk warning

> *Mr Sutton gave a shout of triumph.*
> *She gave a long lecture about Roosevelt.*

4 You use 'make' with nouns referring to:

> **talking and sounds**: comment enquiry noise point promise remark sound speech suggestion
> **plans**: arrangement choice decision plan
> **travelling**: journey tour trip visit

> *He made the shortest speech I've ever heard.*
> *In 1978 he made his first visit to Australia.*

5 You use 'take' with these nouns:

> | care | chance | charge | decision |
> | interest | offence | photograph | responsibility |
> | risk | time | trouble | turns |

> *He was taking no chances.*
> *She was prepared to take great risks.*

6 You use 'go' and 'come' with '-ing' nouns referring to sports and outdoor activities.

> *She goes climbing in her holidays.*
> *Every morning, he goes jogging with Tommy.*

Note that you can also use 'go for' and 'come for' with 'a jog', 'a run', 'a swim', 'a walk'.

> *They went for a run before breakfast.*

7 You use 'do' with '-ing' nouns referring to jobs connected with the home, and nouns referring generally to work.

> *He wants to do the cooking.*
> *He does all the shopping and I do the washing.*
> *The man who did the job had ten years' training.*
> *He has to get up early and do a hard day's work.*

'Do' is often used instead of more specific verbs. For example, you can say 'Have you done your teeth?' instead of 'Have you brushed your teeth?'

> *Do I need to do my hair?*

Practice

A Say which of the verbs, 'have', 'give', 'take', 'make', 'go', or 'do', are used with nouns referring to:

1 Household jobs. (*cleaning, tidying up*) .... *do* ....
2 Plans and decisions. ....
3 Nouns which involve speaking. (*a speech, talk, lecture*) ....
4 Facial expressions. (*smile*) ....
5 Something which makes you clean. (*a wash*) ....
6 Something to eat or drink. ....
7 Something that hurts. (*a kick*) ....
8 Some form of exercise. (*jogging*) ....

B Complete these sentences using the correct part of 'do' or 'go'.

1 Who .... *does* .... most of the cooking in your house?
2 I'm so busy, I have no time to .... jogging.
3 We .... most of our shopping at the weekend.
4 They often .... climbing in Wales.
5 We .... for a long walk this afternoon.
6 I like to .... water-skiing on my holidays.
7 She always .... the washing on Monday morning.
8 It's a lovely day. Let's .... swimming.

C Complete these sentences using the correct part of 'make' or 'do'.

1 Anyone can .... *make* .... a suggestion.
2 I've got an awful lot of work to ....
3 Have you .... your homework?
4 If you .... a promise, you must keep it.
5 I think there's something wrong with the car. It's .... a dreadful noise.
6 Are you using the word-processor? I need to .... some writing.
7 It wasn't a good speech, but he did .... a few good points.
8 We don't have much time to .... a decision.

D Complete the sentences below using the appropriate part of 'have', 'give', 'take', 'make', or 'do'.

1 She looked up and .... *gave* .... me a friendly smile.
2 I always .... a bit of gardening at the weekend.
3 Skiing is dangerous enough as it is. You shouldn't .... unnecessary risks.
4 I'm awfully nervous. I have to .... a speech after dinner.
5 You must be hot. Would you like to .... a cold shower before supper?
6 It's half past twelve. Let's .... a short break before lunch.
7 Oh dear. I didn't know you were there. You .... such a dreadful scream.
8 The chairman .... a few final remarks before bringing the meeting to a close.
9 We .... some great photographs on holiday this year.
10 I'm not thirsty. I .... a drink just before I left home.
11 A horse can .... you a very nasty kick.
12 They .... arrangements to get everything ready on time.

▸ **Bank**

Auxiliary verbs

Main points

The auxiliaries 'be', 'have', and 'do' are used in forming tenses, negatives, and questions.

The auxiliary 'be' is used in forming the continuous tenses and the passive.

The auxiliary 'have' is used in forming the perfect tenses.

The auxiliary 'do' is used in making negative and question forms from sentences that have a verb in a simple tense.

1 The auxiliary verbs are 'be', 'have', and 'do'. They are used with a main verb to form tenses, negatives, and questions.

He <u>is</u> planning to get married soon.
I <u>haven't</u> seen Peter since last night.
Which doctor <u>do</u> you want to see?

2 'Be' as an auxiliary is used:

• with the '-ing' form of the main verb to form continuous tenses

He <u>is</u> living in Germany.
They <u>were</u> going to phone you.

• with the past participle of the main verb to form the passive

These cars <u>are</u> made in Japan.
The walls of her flat <u>were</u> covered with posters.

3 You use 'have' as an auxiliary with the past participle to form the perfect tenses.

I <u>have</u> changed my mind.
I wish you <u>had</u> met Guy.

The present perfect continuous, the past perfect continuous, and the perfect tenses in the passive, are formed using both 'have' and 'be'.

He <u>has been</u> working very hard recently.
She did not know how long she <u>had been</u> lying there.
The guest-room window <u>has been</u> mended.
They <u>had been</u> taught by a young teacher.

4 'Be' and 'have' are also used as auxiliaries in negative sentences and questions in continuous and perfect tenses, and in the passive.

He <u>isn't</u> going.
<u>Hasn't</u> she seen it yet?
<u>Was</u> it written in English?

You use 'do' as an auxiliary to make negative and question forms from sentences that have a verb in the present simple or past simple.

He <u>doesn't</u> think he can come to the party.
<u>Do</u> you like her new haircut?
She <u>didn't</u> buy the house.
<u>Didn't</u> he get the job?

Note that you can use 'do' as a main verb with the auxiliary 'do'.

He <u>didn't do</u> his homework.
<u>Do</u> they <u>do</u> the work themselves?

You can also use the auxiliary 'do' with 'have' as a main verb.

He <u>doesn't have</u> any money.
<u>Does</u> anyone <u>have</u> a question?

You only use 'do' in affirmative sentences for emphasis or contrast.

I <u>do</u> feel sorry for Roger.

⊖ WARNING: You never use the auxiliary 'do' with 'be' except in the imperative.

<u>Don't be</u> stupid!
<u>Do be</u> a good boy and sit still.

5 Some grammars include modals among the auxiliary verbs. When there is a modal in the verb group, it is always the first word in the verb group, and comes before the auxiliaries 'be' and 'have'.

She <u>might be</u> going to Switzerland for Christmas.
I <u>would have</u> liked to have seen her.

Note that you never use the auxiliary 'do' with a modal.

▶ See Units 79-91 for more information on modals.

Practice

A Use these forms of the auxiliary 'do' to complete the sentences below.

| do | don't | does | doesn't | did | didn't |

1 I ....**didn't**.......................... enjoy the film very much. It was far too long.
2 Where .... you want to go for dinner this evening?
3 .... be silly!
4 How long .... it take you to drive to London last night?
5 How long .... it usually take?
6 .... anyone know the answer?

B Use these auxiliaries to complete the sentences that follow.

| didn't | do (2) | does | don't (2) | had | has |
| hasn't | have been | is (2) | was | will (2) | would have |

1 John .....**has**.................... left home. He ....**is**.................... living in Italy now.
2 .... you still work in the shop, or .... you have another job now?
3 I .... want to be late, so I .... have to take a taxi.
4 We .... waiting for hours, but he still .... phoned.
5 You .... met her, if you .... come earlier.
6 I .... going to write to you, but I .... have time.
7 .... shout! You .... wake the baby.
8 .... anyone know what time the meeting .... going to start?

C Here are some very common question forms in English. First complete the questions by adding 'do', 'does', 'has', or 'have', then match the questions and answers.

1 ...**Do**.......... you know what time it is?   a No. I'll be another ten minutes.
2 .... you finished yet?   b No. I'm afraid my English isn't good enough.
3 .... anyone know where Angelo is?   c Sorry, I haven't got a watch.
4 .... anybody seen Maria?   d The seventeenth, isn't it?
5 .... you think we'll be late?   e Not me. I haven't seen it for ages.
6 .... you ever been abroad?   f In about ten minutes, I think.
7 .... anybody know the date?   g Yes, I've got two fifty-pence pieces.
8 .... you like living in England?   h No. I don't think she's here this morning.
9 .... you ever read any Shakespeare?   i Not yet. But I'm going to America next year.
10 .... anyone here got change for a pound?   j Yes, but I don't like the weather much.
11 .... you know what time the next train leaves?   k He was in the library a minute ago.
12 .... anybody know where the key to this cupboard is?   l Not if we hurry.

The present tenses

Main points

There are four present tenses – present simple ('I walk'), present continuous ('I am walking'), present perfect ('I have walked'), and present perfect continuous ('I have been walking').

All the present tenses are used to refer to a time which includes the present.

Present tenses can also be used for predictions made in the present about future events.

1 There are four tenses which begin with a verb in the present tense. They are the present simple, the present continuous, the present perfect, and the present perfect continuous. These are the present tenses.

2 The present simple and the present continuous are used with reference to present time. If you are talking about the general present, or about a regular or habitual action, you use the present simple.

> *George lives in Birmingham.*
> *They often phone my mother in London.*

If you are talking about something in the present situation, you use the present continuous.

> *He's playing tennis at the University.*
> *I'm cooking the dinner.*

The present continuous is often used to refer to a temporary situation.

> *She's living in a flat at present.*

3 You use the present perfect or the present perfect continuous when you are concerned with the present effects of something which happened at a time in the past, or which started in the past but is still continuing.

> *Have you seen the film at the Odeon?*
> *We've been waiting here since before two o'clock.*

4 If you are talking about something which is scheduled or timetabled to happen in the future, you can use the present simple tense.

> *The next train leaves at two fifteen in the morning.*
> *It's Tuesday tomorrow.*

5 If you are talking about something which has been arranged for the future, you can use the present continuous. When you use the present continuous like this, there is nearly always a time adverbial like 'tomorrow', 'next week', or 'later' in the clause.

> *We're going on holiday with my parents this year.*
> *The Browns are having a party next week.*

6 It is only in the main clauses that the choice of tense can be related to a particular time. In subordinate clauses, for example in 'if'– clauses, time clauses, and defining relative clauses, present tenses often refer to a future time in relation to the time in the main clause.

> *You can go at five if you have finished.*
> *Let's have a drink before we start.*
> *We'll save some food for anyone who arrives late.*

➤ See Unit 65 for more information.

7 The present simple tense normally has no auxiliary verb, but questions and negative sentences are formed with the auxiliary 'do'.

> *Do you live round here?*
> *Does your husband do most of the cooking?*
> *They don't often phone during the week.*
> *She doesn't like being late if she can help it.*

Practice

A In the sentences below, decide if the verb underlined refers to the present (P), the future (F), or to something habitual (H).

1 Joe wants to be a pilot when he <u>grows up.</u> ....F..
2 We always <u>go</u> abroad for our holidays. ....
3 I'm sorry, but I <u>feel</u> tired. ....
4 I just <u>want</u> to go to sleep. ....
5 When <u>do you start</u> at the university next year? ....
6 Oh dear, this milk <u>tastes</u> awful. ....
7 You <u>look</u> really funny in that hat. ....
8 Give my love to Norman if you <u>see</u> him. ....
9 Do your children <u>help</u> about the house? ....
10 It's amazing how many people <u>eat</u> far too much. ....

B Complete these sentences using the correct form of the verb in brackets.

1 We enjoy the theatre but we ....don't go........................... very often. (*not go*)
2 What time .... ? (*the train / leave*)
3 My brother .... at home any more. (*not live*)
4 Where .... nowadays? (*you / work*)
5 I .... Jill .... me very much. (*not think*) (*like*)
6 What time .... after work? (*Ken / get home*)
7 Penny .... Calgary in Canada. (*come from*)
8 How many languages .... ? (*you / speak*)
9 How much .... for a return ticket? (*it / cost*)
10 Anne .... coffee, but she .... tea. (*not drink*) (*like*)

C Look carefully at the verbs in bold. Underline those which refer to the future.

1 A: **Are** you **doing** anything tomorrow?
   B: Not really. We'**re** just **staying** at home.
2 A: **Is** Peter **living** at home now?
   B: No, he **is** still at university in Sheffield.
3 A: How about your exams? **Have** you **passed?**
   B: I **don't know.** I'll let you know as soon as I'**ve heard** the results.
4 A: Is Jack the boy who **is coming** to stay next weekend?
   B: No. Jack **lives** just near us. It's Dan who'**s coming** to stay.
5 A: **Have** you **seen** Jenny recently?
   B: No, but we'll probably see her when we **go** to Leeds.
6 A: Will you come home after you'**ve finished** work?
   B: No. I'**m meeting** Joe in town and we'**re going** to the theatre.

The past tenses

Main points

There are four past tenses – past simple ('I walked'), past continuous ('I was walking'), past perfect ('I had walked'), and past perfect continuous ('I had been walking').

All the past tenses are used to refer to past time.

The past tenses are often used as polite forms.

The past tenses have special meanings in conditional clauses and when referring to imaginary situations.

1 There are four tenses which begin with a verb in the past tense. They are the past simple, the past continuous, the past perfect, and the past perfect continuous. These are the past tenses. They are used to refer to past time, and also to refer to imaginary situations, and to express politeness.

2 The past simple and the past continuous are used with reference to past time. You use the past simple for events which happened in the past.

> I _woke_ up early and _got_ out of bed.

If you are talking about the general past, or about regular or habitual actions in the past, you also use the past simple.

> She _lived_ just outside London.
> We often _saw_ his dog sitting outside his house.

If you are talking about something which continued to happen before and after a particular time in the past, you use the past continuous.

> They _were sitting_ in the kitchen, when they heard the explosion.
> Jack arrived while the children _were having_ their bath.

The past continuous is often used to refer to a temporary situation.

> He _was working_ at home at the time.
> Bill _was using_ my office until I came back from America.

3 You use the past perfect and past perfect continuous tenses when you are talking about the past and you are concerned with something which

happened at an earlier time, or which had started at an earlier time but was still continuing.

> I _had heard_ it was a good film so we decided to go and see it.
> It was getting late. I _had been waiting_ there since two o'clock.

4 You sometimes use a past tense rather than a present tense when you want to be more polite. For example, in the following pairs of sentences, the second one is more polite.

> _Do_ you _want_ to see me now?
> _Did_ you _want_ to see me now?
> I _wonder_ if you can help me.
> I _was wondering_ if you could help me.

I wonder if you can help me.

5 The past tenses have special meanings in conditional clauses and when referring to hypothetical and imaginary situations, for example after 'I wish' or 'What if…?'. You use the past simple and past continuous for something that you think is unlikely to happen.

> If they _saw_ the mess, they would be very angry.
> We would tell you if we _were selling_ the house.

You use the past perfect and past perfect continuous when you are talking about something which could have happened in the past, but which did not actually happen.

> If I _had known_ that you were coming, I would have told Jim.
> They wouldn't have gone to bed if they _had been expecting_ you to arrive.

Practice

A **Make past tense questions and answers using the words given.**

1 a Who / you see / at the meeting? / ...Who did you see at the meeting?...........

  b I see / Jack / not Amy. / ....I saw Jack, but I didn't see Amy....................

2 a Where / you go / in England? / ....

  b We go / London / not Oxford. / ....

3 a What plays / they see / at Stratford? / ....

  b They see / Hamlet / not Julius Caesar. / ....

4 a Angelo / buy some records / in London? / ....

  b He buy / some clothes / not any records. / ....

5 a You enjoy / your holiday? / ....

  b I enjoy / the holiday / not the food. / ....

B **In the sentences below, decide if the modals and past simple verbs, which are underlined, are being used for narrative (N), a hypothetical situation (H), or for politeness (P).**

1 Kathy was looking very well last time I <u>saw</u> her. ....N...................

2 Excuse me. I just <u>wanted</u> to know if you <u>were</u> free at the moment. ....

3 If I <u>wanted</u> to know, I <u>would</u> ask. ....

4 Frank <u>telephoned</u> yesterday and <u>left</u> a message. ....

5 I wish it <u>was</u> time for lunch. ....

6 I first <u>went</u> abroad when I <u>was</u> seventeen. ....

7 I am writing because I <u>wondered</u> if I <u>could</u> offer a useful suggestion. ....

8 Jenny <u>wished</u> she hadn't been so careless. ....

9 We <u>looked</u> everywhere for the money, but we <u>couldn't</u> find it. ....

10 You must take a map with you. Suppose you <u>got</u> lost, then what <u>would</u> you do? ....

11 Do you think I <u>could</u> borrow your bike tomorrow? ....

12 We were expecting a call from John, when Jill <u>phoned.</u> ....

C **Complete these sentences, putting the verbs in the past simple or the past continuous.**

1 I ......was working............ upstairs when the accident ....happened.......... (work) (happen)

2 He .... the book and .... to read. (open) (start)

3 We .... the film, when suddenly the electricity .... off. (enjoy) (go)

4 When she .... the news, she .... to cry. (hear) (begin)

5 Everyone .... quietly. Suddenly the door .... open. (talk) (burst)

6 When I .... the doorbell, I .... downstairs. (hear) (run)

▸ **Bank**

The continuous tenses

Main points

Continuous tenses describe actions which continue to happen before and after a particular time.

Continuous tenses can also indicate duration and change.

1 You use a continuous tense to indicate that an action continues to happen before and after a particular time, without stopping. You use the present continuous for actions which continue to happen before and after the moment of speaking.

> I'm looking at the photographs my brother sent me.
> They're having a meeting.

2 When you are talking about two actions in the present tense, you use the present continuous for an action that continues to happen before and after another action that interrupts it. You use the present simple for the other action.

> The phone always rings when I'm having a bath.
> Friends always talk to me when I'm trying to study.

3 When you are talking about the past, you use the past continuous for actions that continued to happen before and after another action, or before and after a particular time. This is often called the 'interrupted past'. You use the past simple for the other action.

> He was watching television when the doorbell rang.
> At 2.15 we were still waiting for the bus.

⊖ WARNING: If two things happened one after another, you use two verbs in the past simple tense.

> As soon as he saw me, he waved.

4 You can use continuous forms with modals in all their usual meanings.

➤ See Units 79 to 91 for more information on modals.

> What could he be thinking of?
> They might be telling lies.

5 You use continuous tenses to express duration, when you want to emphasize how long something has been happening or will happen for.

> We had been living in Athens for five years.
> They'll be staying with us for a couple of weeks.
> He has been building up the business all his life.
> By 1992, he will have been working for ten years.

Note that you do not have to use continuous tenses for duration.

> We had lived in Africa for five years.
> He worked for us for ten years.

6 You use continuous tenses to describe a state or situation that is temporary.

> I'm living in London at the moment.
> He'll be working nights next week.
> She's spending the summer in Europe.

7 You use continuous tenses to show that something is changing, developing, or progressing.

> Her English was improving.
> The children are growing up quickly.
> The video industry has been developing rapidly.

8 As a general rule, verbs which refer to actions that require a deliberate effort can be used in continuous tenses, verbs which refer to actions that do not require a deliberate effort are not used in continuous tenses.

> I think it's going to rain.
> ('think' = 'believe'. Believing does not require deliberate effort)
> Please be quiet. I'm thinking.
> ('think' = 'try to solve a problem'. Trying to solve a problem does require deliberate effort)

However, many verbs are not normally used in the continuous tenses. These include verbs that refer to thinking, liking and disliking, appearance, possession, and perception.

➤ See Unit 62 for lists of these verbs.

Practice

A Put the verbs in brackets into the present simple or the present continuous.

1 The baby always ....*wakes up*........ when we ....*are trying*........ to go to sleep. (*wake up*) (*try*)

2 It always .... raining when we .... tennis. (*start*) (*play*)

3 I .... a book at the moment so I .... very busy. (*write*) (*be*)

4 Sally always .... as if she .... herself. (*look*) (*enjoy*)

5 John .... with us when he .... London. (*stay*) (*visit*)

6 Mary .... to go on holiday so she .... as little money as possible. (*save up*) (*spend*)

B Complete this dialogue by putting the verbs in brackets into the present continuous.

A: What ....*are you doing,*...................... Angela, now you have left school? (*you do*)

B: I .... in a restaurant. I .... to earn some money before I go to university. (*work*) (*try*)

A: .... at home? (*you live*)

B: No, I .... in a little village. I .... a cottage with some friends. (*live*) (*share*)

C Put the verbs in brackets into the past simple or the past continuous tense to complete the sentences below.

1 He ....*was driving*........ at over 100 kilometres an hour when the accident ....*happened*........ . (*drive*) (*happen*)

2 The thieves .... while we .... (*break in*) (*sleep*)

3 Someone .... with my clothes while I .... (*run off*) (*swim*)

4 I .... in the supermarket when I .... my purse. (*shop*) (*lose*)

5 He .... tennis and he .... his leg. (*play*) (*break*)

6 I first .... my wife when we .... in London. (*meet*) (*work*)

D Complete the following sentences using the present perfect continuous tense of the verbs below.

live   play   study   wait   walk   watch   work

1 We ....*have been living*...................... in England for nearly two years now.

2 Why are you so late? I .... here for hours.

3 I .... German for three years, but I still don't speak it very well.

4 The boys must be tired. They .... football in the garden all afternoon.

5 It's time to do your homework. You .... television all night.

6 John .... in his father's business since he left school.

7 We must be nearly there by now. We .... for over an hour.

▸ **Bank**

The perfect tenses

Main points

You use the present perfect ('I have walked') to relate the past to the present.

You use the past perfect ('I had walked') to talk about a situation that occurred before a particular time in the past.

1 You use the present perfect tense when you are concerned with the present effects of something which happened at an indefinite time in the past.

> *I'm afraid I've forgotten my book.*
> *Have you heard from Jill recently?*

Sometimes, the present effects are important because they are very recent.

> *Karen has just passed her exams.*

You also use the present perfect when you are thinking of a time which started in the past and is still continuing.

> *Have you really lived here for ten years?*
> *I have worked here since 1997.*

You also use the present perfect in time clauses, when you are talking about something which will be done at some time in the future.

> *Tell me when you have finished.*
> *I'll write to you as soon as I have heard from Jenny.*

2 When you want to emphasize the fact that a recent event continued to happen for some time, you use the present perfect continuous.

> *She's been crying.*
> *I've been working hard all day.*

3 You use the past perfect tense when you are looking back from a point in past time, and you are concerned with the effects of something which happened at an earlier time in the past.

> *I apologized because I had forgotten my book.*
> *He felt much happier once he had found a new job.*
> *They would have come if we had invited them.*

You also use the past perfect when you are thinking of a time which had started earlier in the past but was still continuing.

> *I was about twenty. I had been studying French for*

a couple of years.
> *He hated games and had always managed to avoid children's parties.*

4 You use the future perfect tense when you are looking back from a point in the future and you are talking about something which will have happened at a time between now and that future point.

> *In another two years, you will have left school.*
> *Take these tablets, and in twenty-four hours the pain will have gone.*

You also use the future perfect when you are looking back from the present and guessing that an action will be finished.

> *I'm sure they will have arrived home by now.*
> *It's too late to ring Don. He will have left the house by now.*

5 You can also use other modals with 'have', when you are looking back from a point in time at something which you think may have happened at an earlier time.

> *I might have finished work by then.*
> *He should have arrived in Paris by the time we phone.*

➤ For more information on modals with 'have', see Units 79 to 91.

Practice

A Look at these sentences and match questions and answers.

1 Where's Teresa?
2 Are you going to the film tonight?
3 Do you know Michael?
4 Can we go out?
5 May I borrow your book?
6 Do you know London well?
7 How do you feel?
8 Why isn't John at work today?
9 Do you still work at Smith's?
10 Do you live near here?

a No, I've seen it before.
b After I've finished the washing up.
c Yes, I've lived here for years.
d She's gone shopping.
e No, I've never met him before.
f I'm afraid I've left it at home.
g Awful. I think I've caught a cold.
h No, we've just moved to Oxford.
i I don't know. Perhaps he's had an accident.
j Yes, I've worked there ever since 1980.

B Use the information from the sentences above to complete these sentences.

1 He told me Teresa .... *had gone shopping.* ....
2 I didn't go to the film because ....
3 I didn't know Michael. In fact ....
4 We couldn't go out until ....
5 I couldn't lend Sally my book because ....
6 I knew London well ....
7 I felt so bad, I was sure that ....
8 John couldn't go to work because ....
9 We didn't live in Sevenoaks any more. We ....

C Use the following future perfect verb groups to complete the sentences below.

will have driven	will have used up	will have learned	will have run	will have forgotten

1 You may be in love with her now, but in a couple of weeks you *will have forgotten* all about her.
2 By the time we get to Birmingham we .... over two hundred miles.
3 If they start school at four, most children .... to read and write by the age of six.
4 By the end of this century, we .... most of the world's oil supplies.
5 After two hours, the leading competitors .... about thirty kilometres.

D What do you think will have happened by the end of this century? Here are some ideas to help you.

1 Scientists / discover / a cure for cancer. / *Scientists will have discovered a cure for cancer.*
2 Scientists / learn / to control the weather. / ....
3 Third world war / break out. / ....
4 Man / destroy / the planet. / ....
5 World population / grow / to ten billion. / ....
6 Atomic energy / replace / oil and coal. / ....
7 The rhinoceros / become / extinct. / ....
8 Scientists / build / factories in space. / ....

Talking about the present

Main points

For the general present, general truths, and habitual actions, you use the present simple ('I walk').

For something which is happening now, or for temporary situations, you use the present continuous ('I am walking').

1 If you are talking about the present in general, you normally use the present simple tense. You use the present simple for talking about the general present including the present moment.

> My dad <u>works</u> in Saudi Arabia.
> He <u>lives</u> in the French Alps near the Swiss border.

2 If you are talking about general truths, you use the present simple.

> Water <u>boils</u> at 100 degrees centigrade.
> Love <u>makes</u> the world go round.
> The bus <u>takes</u> longer than the train.

3 If you are talking about regular or habitual actions, you use the present simple.

> <u>Do</u> you <u>eat</u> meat?
> I <u>get</u> up early and <u>eat</u> my breakfast in bed.
> I <u>pay</u> the milkman on Fridays.

4 If you are talking about something which is regarded as temporary, you use the present continuous.

> Do you know if she'<u>s</u> still <u>playing</u> tennis these days?
> I'<u>m working</u> as a British Council officer.

5 If you are talking about something which is happening now, you normally use the present continuous tense.

> We'<u>re having</u> a meeting. Come and join in.
> Wait a moment. I'<u>m listening</u> to the news.

6 There are a number of verbs which are used in the present simple tense even when you are talking about the present moment. These verbs are not normally used in the present continuous or the other continuous tenses.

These verbs usually refer to:

thinking:	believe forget imagine know realize recognize suppose think understand want wish
liking and disliking:	admire dislike hate like love prefer
appearance:	appear look like resemble seem
possession:	belong to contain have include own possess
perception:	hear see smell taste
being:	be consist of exist

> I <u>believe</u> he was not to blame.
> She <u>hates</u> going to parties.
> Our neighbours <u>have</u> two cars.

Note that you normally use verbs of perception with the modal 'can', rather than using the present simple tense.

> I <u>can smell</u> gas.

Some other common verbs are not normally used in the present continuous or the other continuous tenses.

concern	deserve	fit	interest	involve
matter	mean	satisfy	surprise	

> What <u>do</u> you <u>mean</u>?

⊖ WARNING: Some of the verbs listed above can be used in continuous tenses in other meanings. For example, 'have' referring to possession is not used in continuous tenses. You do not say 'I am having a car'. But note the following examples.

> We'<u>re having</u> a party tomorrow.
> He'<u>s having</u> problems with his car.
> She'<u>s having</u> a shower.

Practice

A Decide whether these sentences are talking about the present in general or about the present moment. Complete the sentences by putting the verbs in brackets into the present simple or the present continuous.

1 My wife normally ....*works*.............. at home, but she ....*is spending*........ this month in Nottingham. She .....*is teaching*................. in a summer school there. (*work*) (*spend*) (*teach*)

2 A: Look, it .... again.
   B: Yes, it .... most days at this time of year. (*rain*) (*rain*)

3 Goodnight. I .... to bed. I always .... to bed early during the week. (*go*) (*go*)

4 Most days, John .... to work, but since it .... today he ....
   his car to work. So Mary .... her shopping at the local shop
   instead of the supermarket where she usually .... (*cycle*) (*rain*) (*take*) (*do*) (*go*)

5 A: Where are the children?
   B: They .... in the garden. They .... home from school at
   about four and usually .... straight out to play with their friends. (*play*)
   (*get*) (*go*)

6 A: What work .... ?
   B: He .... French and German, and this term he ....
   English as well. (*your husband do*) (*teach*) (*teach*)

7 We usually .... the news on TV at seven o'clock, but tonight
   we .... that new soap opera. (*watch*) (*watch*)

B Choose the form of the verb in brackets which best completes the following sentences.

1 My daughter ...*is working*...... in a restaurant for the summer, but she ....*doesn't like*.......... it
   very much. (*works / is working*) (*doesn't like / isn't liking*)

2 This cheese .... awful. (*smells / is smelling*)

3 I often try to read the newspapers in English but I .... very much.
   (*am not understanding / don't understand*)

4 The children .... very quickly. They .... very like
   their mother now. (*grow up / are growing up*) (*look / are looking*)

5 Sara .... to be very upset. I ....
   she was worried about something. (*seemed / was seeming*) (*think / am thinking*)

6 .... to you? (*Does this coat belong / Is this coat belonging*)

7 No, my coat .... there behind the door. (*hangs / is hanging*)

8 I .... something downstairs. It ....
   as if someone .... to open a window. (*can hear / am hearing*)
   (*sounds / is sounding*) (*tries / is trying*)

125

Talking about the past

Main points

For actions, situations, or regular events in the past, you use the past simple ('I walked'). For regular events in the past, you can also use 'would' or 'used to'.

For events that happened before and after a time in the past, and for temporary situations, you use the past continuous ('I was walking').

For present effects of past situations, you use the present perfect ('I have walked'), and for past effects of earlier events you use the past perfect ('I had walked').

For future in the past, you use 'would', 'was/were going to', or the past continuous ('I was walking').

1 When you want to talk about an event that occurred at a particular time in the past, you use the past simple.

> The Prime Minister _flew_ into New York yesterday.
> The new term _started_ last week.

You also use the past simple to talk about a situation that existed over a period of time in the past.

> We _spent_ most of our time at home last winter.
> They _earned_ their money quickly that year.

2 When you want to talk about something which took place regularly in the past, you use the past simple.

> They _went_ for picnics most weekends.
> We usually _spent_ the winter at Aunt Meg's house.

⊖ WARNING: The past simple always refers to a time in the past. A time reference is necessary to say what time in the past you are referring to. The time reference can be established in an earlier sentence or by another speaker, but it must be established.

When you want to talk about something which occurred regularly in the past, you can use 'would' or 'used to' instead of the past simple.

> We _would_ normally _spend_ the winter in Miami.
> People _used to believe_ that the world was flat.

⊖ WARNING: You do not normally use 'would' with this meaning with verbs which are not used in the continuous tenses.

➤ For a list of these verbs, see Unit 62.

3 When you want to talk about something which continued to happen before and after a given time in the past, you use the past continuous.

> I hurt myself when I _was mending_ my bike.
> It was midnight. She _was driving_ home.

You also use the past continuous to talk about a temporary state of affairs in the past.

> Our team _were losing_ 2-1 at the time.
> We _were staying_ with friends in Italy.

➤ For more information on continuous tenses, see Unit 60.

4 When you are concerned with the present effects or future effects of something which happened at an indefinite time in the past, you use the present perfect.

> I'm afraid I'_ve forgotten_ my book, so I don't know.
> _Have_ you _heard_ from Jill recently? How is she?

You also use the present perfect when you are thinking of a time which started in the past and still continues.

> _Have_ you ever _stolen_ anything? (= at any time up to the present)
> He _has been_ here since six o'clock. (= and he is still here)

5 When you are looking back from a point in past time, and you are concerned with the effects of something which happened at an earlier time in the past, you use the past perfect.

> I apologized because I _had left_ my wallet at home.
> They would have come if we _had invited_ them.

6 When you want to talk about the future from a point of view in past time, you can use 'would', 'was / were going to', or the past continuous.

> He thought to himself how wonderful it _would taste._
> Her daughter _was going to_ do the cooking.
> Mike _was taking_ his test the week after.

Practice

A Complete the following sentences with one verb in the past simple and the other in the past continuous.

1 I ..<u>was reading</u>.. the newspaper, when suddenly I ...<u>heard</u>.. a loud knock on the door. (*read*) (*hear*)

2 I .... George an hour ago. He .... his homework. (*phone*) (*do*)

3 I first .... Mary a couple of years ago. She .... at the Royal Hospital at the time. (*meet*) (*work*)

4 We .... Peter to come with us, but he .... the football on TV. (*ask*) (*watch*)

5 While I .... to work this morning, I almost .... a serious accident. (*drive*) (*have*)

6 When we .... the shopping last week, we .... a nice place to have coffee. (*do*) (*found*)

B Complete the following sentences, putting one verb in the present perfect and one in the past simple.

1 We ..<u>lived</u>.. in Manchester from 1985 to 1990, but we ..<u>have moved</u>.. to Liverpool now. (*live*) (*move*)

2 A: There's a great film at the Odeon this week. .... it? (*you see*)
  B: Not this week. I .... it in London last year. (*see*)

3 When we were kids, we .... to Blackpool for our holidays, but I .... back there for years. (*go*) (*not be*)

4 A: This is Mary. I don't think you .... (*meet*)
  B: Oh yes. We know each other well. We .... at school together. (*be*)

5 A: I .... to phone John, but he's not at home. (*try*)
  B: He should be. He .... work an hour ago. (*leave*)

C Complete these sentences with one verb in the past simple and the other in the past perfect.

1 I ......<u>was</u>...................... late. The meeting ......<u>had started</u>............ an hour ago. (*be*) (*start*)

2 They .... , even though we .... them a special invitation. (*not come*) (*send*)

3 It .... a good story, but I .... it before. (*be*) (*hear*)

4 We .... our way. We .... what to do. (*lose*) (*not know*)

5 As soon as we .... work, we .... home. (*finish*) (*go*)

D Rewrite the sentences below using 'be going to'.

1 He didn't play football. He forgot his boots. / ..<u>He was going to play football, but he forgot</u>....... ..<u>his boots.</u>..

2 They didn't visit Oxford. They didn't have time. / ....
....

3 He didn't see the play. There were no seats left. / ....
....

4 I couldn't do my homework. I had forgotten my books. / ....
....

5 We didn't watch TV. There was nothing interesting on. / ....
....

▶ **Bank**

'Will' and 'going to'

Main points

When you are making predictions about the future or talking about future intentions, you can use either 'will' ('I will walk') or 'going to' ('I am going to walk').

For promises and offers relating to the future, you use 'will' ('I will walk').

For future events based on arrangements, you use the future continuous ('I will be walking').

For events that will happen before a time in the future, you use the future perfect ('I will have walked').

1 You cannot talk about the future with as much certainty as you can about the present or the past. You are usually talking about what you think might happen or what you intend to happen. This is why you often use modals. Although most modals can be used with future reference, you most often use the modal 'will' to talk about the future.

Nancy will arrange it.
When will I see them?

2 When you are making predictions about the future that are based on general beliefs, opinions, or attitudes, you use 'will'.

The weather tomorrow will be warm and sunny.
I'm sure you will enjoy your visit to the zoo.

This use of 'will' is common in sentences with conditional clauses.

You'll be late, if you don't hurry.

When you are using facts or events in the present situation as evidence for a prediction, you can use 'going to'.

It's going to rain. (I can see black clouds)
I'm going to be late. (I have missed my train)

When you are saying what someone has decided to do, you use 'going to'.

I'm going to stay at home today.
They're going to have a party.

⊖ WARNING: You do not normally use 'going to' with the verb 'go'. You usually just say 'I'm going' rather than 'I'm going to go'.

'What are you going to do this weekend?' – 'I'm going to the cinema.'

When you are announcing a decision you have just made or are about to make, you use 'will'.

I'm tired. I think I'll go to bed.

4 In promises and offers relating to the future, you often use 'will' with the meaning 'be willing to'.

I'll do what I can.
I'll help with the washing-up.

Note that you can use 'will' with this meaning in an 'if'-clause.

I'll put you through, if you'll hang on for a minute.
(= if you are willing to hang on for a minute)

⊖ WARNING: Remember that you do not normally use 'will' in 'if'-clauses.

➤ See Unit 66 for more information on 'if'-clauses.

If you do that, you will be wasting your time.
The children will call out if they think he is wrong.

5 When you want to say that something will happen because arrangements have been made, you use the future continuous tense.

I'll be seeing them when I've finished with you.
I'll be waiting for you outside.
She'll be appearing at the Royal Festival Hall.

6 When you want to talk about something that has not happened yet but will happen before a particular time in the future, you use the future perfect tense.

By the time we phone he'll already have started.
By 2010, he will have worked for twelve years.

Practice

A Complete the following sentences with the correct form of the verb in brackets. Use 'going to' if present evidence is given, and 'will' if the statement is based on a general belief.

1 They are playing really well. I think they ....*are going to win*........................ . (*win*)
2 I feel awful. I think I .... (*faint*)
3 It's a very difficult climb. If you're not careful you .... (*fall*)
4 I can't hang on. I .... (*fall*)
5 Have you told Kate about your new job? She .... delighted. (*be*)
6 They've invited a lot of people. It .... very crowded. (*be*)
7 It's Saturday morning. The shops .... crowded. (*be*)
8 John starts his new school tomorrow. I'm sure he .... it. (*enjoy*)
9 The referee is looking at his watch. He .... his whistle. (*blow*)

B Complete the dialogues below using the verb in brackets with 'will' or 'going to'.

1 A: Have you decided how to spend the prize money?
   B: Well I think we ....*will buy*........................ a new car, but we haven't really decided yet. (*buy*)
2 A: Have you decided how to spend the prize money?
   B: Yes. We .... a new car. (*buy*)
3 A: Did you know Sue is in hospital? Do you think you could send her a get-well card?
   B: I didn't know that. Of course I .... her a card. (*send*)
4 A: I heard yesterday that Sue is in hospital.
   B: Yes I know. We .... some money at work to send her some flowers. (*collect*)
5 A: Have you got tickets for the concert?
   B: No. But we saw the advert in the paper and we .... some this afternoon. (*buy*)
6 A: Have you heard about the concert on Saturday?
   B: No! That sounds like a good idea. I think we .... this afternoon and buy some tickets. (*go out*)

C Maggie is trying to make arrangements to meet her friend Carol. Complete their conversation using either the future continuous or the future perfect tense of the verb in brackets.

Carol: Hi Maggie, it's Carol. I was wondering if you'd like to meet up for a drink some time this week?
Maggie: Yes, that would be lovely. When were you thinking of?
Carol: What about Monday? Are you busy?

1 Maggie: Let's see. Well, Monday's a bit difficult. I ....*will be coming*......... back from Manchester in the morning and in the afternoon I .... my bank manager. (*come, see*)
2 Carol: What time are you seeing your bank manager? .... by 3? (*finish*)
3 Maggie: No, I'm afraid not. My meeting's at 3.30, so I .... until about 4.30. (*not finish*)
   Carol: OK. Well, what about Wednesday? Are you free then at all?
4 Maggie: Well, in the morning I .... to the gym, and then after that I .... lunch with Jen. The only other time I'm free is Sunday. Are you free in the afternoon? (*go, have*)
   Carol: That sounds good. 3 o'clock?
   Maggie: 3 o'clock's great. I'll meet you at the tube station. See you then!
   Carol: See you then. Bye!

Present tenses for future

Main points

When you are talking about the future in relation to official timetables or the calendar, you use the present simple ('I walk').

When talking about people's plans and arrangements for the future, you use the present continuous ('I am walking').

In 'if'-clauses, time clauses, and defining relative clauses, you can use the present simple ('I walk') to refer to the future.

1 When you are talking about something in the future which is based on an official timetable or calendar, you use the present simple tense. You usually put a time adverbial in these sentences.

> *My last train <u>leaves</u> Euston <u>at 11.30.</u>*
> *The UN General Assembly <u>opens</u> in New York <u>this</u> <u>month.</u>*
> *Our next lesson <u>is on Thursday.</u>*
> *We <u>set off early tomorrow morning.</u>*

2 In statements about fixed dates, you normally use the present simple.

> *Tomorrow <u>is</u> Tuesday.*
> *It'<u>s</u> my birthday next month.*
> *Monday <u>is</u> the seventeenth of July.*

3 When you want to talk about people's plans or arrangements for the future, you use the present continuous tense.

> *I'<u>m meeting</u> Bill next week.*
> *They'<u>re getting married</u> in June.*

4 You often talk about the future using the present tense of verbs such as 'hope', 'expect', 'intend', and 'want' with a 'to'-infinitive clause, especially when you want to indicate your uncertainty about what will actually happen.

> *We <u>hope to see</u> you soon.*
> *Bill <u>expects to be</u> back at work tomorrow.*

After the verb 'hope', you often use the present simple to refer to the future.

> *I hope you <u>enjoy</u> your holiday.*

5 In subordinate clauses, the relationships between tense and time are different. In 'if'-clauses introduced by 'if', 'unless', 'in case', 'provided' or 'providing', and time clauses introduced by words such as 'after', 'before', 'when', and 'until', you normally use the present simple for future reference.

> *If he <u>comes</u>, I'll let you know.*
> *Please start when you <u>are</u> ready.*
> *We won't start until everyone <u>arrives.</u>*
> *Lock the door after you finally <u>leave.</u>*

6 In defining relative clauses, you normally use the present simple, not 'will', to refer to the future.

> *Any decision <u>that you make</u> will need her approval.*
> *Give my love to any friends <u>you meet.</u>*
> *There is a silver cup for the runner <u>who finishes</u> <u>first.</u>*

7 If you want to show that a condition has to be the case before an action can be carried out, you use the present perfect for future events.

> *We won't start until everyone <u>has arrived.</u>*
> *I'll let you know when I <u>have arranged</u> everything.*

Practice

A Write out these sentences. If they are based on an official timetable or the calendar, put the verb in the present simple. If they are about plans or arrangements that people have made for the future, put the verb in the present continuous.

1 ....*Simon's plane arrives*.................................... just before midnight. (*Simon's plane / arrive*)

2 .... a barbecue tomorrow if it's fine. (*We / have*)

3 .... at half past two. (*The meeting / start*)

4 .... this evening. (*A few friends / come round*)

5 What time .... ? (*the last bus / leave*)

6 .... at nine so I'll be home by ten. (*The match / finish*)

7 .... Janet for lunch at about one thirty today. (*I / meet*)

8 .... school in September. (*Becky / finish*)

9 .... to the match tomorrow. (*Everybody / go*)

10 .... trains at Manchester. (*We / change*)

B Complete the following sentences, putting one of the verbs in brackets into the future with 'will', and the other into the present simple.

1 I ....*will come*.................. round tomorrow, if I ....*have*............. time. (*come*) (*have*)

2 If I .... Jack I .... him the message. (*see*) (*give*)

3 I .... you a call from the first phone box I .... (*give*) (*see*)

4 There .... presents for all the children who .... to the party. (*be*) (*come*)

5 If it ...., we .... the party indoors. (*rain*) (*have*)

6 There .... lots of games. I hope you .... yourselves. (*be*) (*enjoy*)

7 I .... to the cinema, unless you .... too. (*not go*) (*go*)

8 Keep a diary, then you .... all the places you .... (*remember*) (*visit*)

9 Until it .... raining, I think I .... here. (*stop*) (*stay*)

C Complete the following sentences by putting one verb in the future with 'will', and putting the other verb in the present perfect.

1 I .....*will write*............. to you as soon as I ......*have heard*.............. from Helen. (*write*) (*hear*)

2 When I ...., I .... you. (*finish*) (*tell*)

3 When I .... watching the film on television, we .... for a walk. (*finish*) (*go*)

4 I .... you with your homework when I .... the washing up. (*help*) (*do*)

5 John says he .... us as soon as he .... the results of his exams. (*call*) (*get*)

D Rewrite the following sentences, using the verbs in brackets with a 'to'-infinitive.

1 We will come and see you soon. / (*hope*) ......*We hope to come and see you soon.*...............

2 We are going to spend our next holiday in Scotland. / (*intend*) ....
   ....

3 I am sure I will be back at work before long. / (*expect*) ....

4 We are going to drive to Glasgow. / (*plan*) ....

Conditionals using 'if'

Main points

You use conditional clauses to talk about a possible situation and its results.

Conditional clauses can begin with 'if'.

A conditional clause needs a main clause to make a complete sentence. The conditional clause can come before or after the main clause.

1 You use conditional clauses to talk about a situation that might possibly happen and to say what its results might be.

You use 'if' to mention events and situations that happen often, that may happen in the future, that could have happened in the past but did not happen, or that are unlikely to happen at all.

> *If the light comes on, the battery is OK.*
> *I'll call you if I need you.*
> *If I had known, I'd have told you.*
> *If she asked me, I'd help her.*

2 When you are talking about something that is generally true or happens often, you use a present or present perfect tense in the main clause and the conditional clause.

> *If they lose weight during an illness, they soon regain it afterwards.*
> *If an advertisement does not tell the truth, the advertiser is committing an offence.*
> *If the baby is crying, it is probably hungry.*
> *If they have lost any money, they report it to me.*

● WARNING: You do not use the present continuous in both clauses. You do not say 'If they are losing money, they are getting angry.'

3 When you use a conditional clause with a present or present perfect tense, you often use an imperative in the main clause.

> *Wake me up if you're worried.*
> *If he has finished, ask him to leave quietly.*
> *If you are very early, don't expect them to be ready.*

4 When you are talking about something which may possibly happen in the future, you use a present or present perfect tense in the conditional clause, and the simple future in the main clause.

> *If I marry Celia, we will need the money.*
> *If you are going to America, you will need a visa.*
> *If he has done the windows, he will want his money.*

● WARNING: You do not normally use 'will' in conditional clauses. You do not say 'If I will see you tomorrow, I will give you the book'.

5 When you are talking about something that you think is unlikely to happen, you use the past simple or past continuous in the conditional clause and 'would' in the main clause.

> *If I had enough money, I would buy the car.*
> *If he was coming, he would ring.*

● WARNING: You do not normally use 'would' in conditional clauses. You do not say 'If I would do it, I would do it like this'.

6 'Were' is sometimes used instead of 'was' in the conditional clause, especially after 'I'.

> *If I were as big as you, I would kill you.*
> *If I weren't so busy, I would do it for you.*

You often say 'If I were you' when you are giving someone advice.

> *If I were you, I would take the money.*
> *I should keep out of Bernadette's way if I were you.*

7 When you are talking about something which could have happened in the past but which did not actually happen, you use the past perfect in the conditional clause. In the main clause, you use 'would have' and a past participle.

> *If he had realized that, he would have run away.*
> *I wouldn't have been so depressed if I had known how common this feeling is.*

● WARNING: You do not use 'would have' in the conditional clause. You do not say 'If I would have seen him, I would have told him'.

Practice

A Match these parts to make conditional sentences.

1 Dan might help you …
2 You are sure to be late …
3 You'll enjoy the Jacques Tati film …
4 They always stay out late …
5 They'll understand it all right …
6 I'll give her a call …
7 Bill will take a message …
8 I'll do the shopping …
9 You can't get in …
10 You needn't come to the party …

a … if they are enjoying themselves.
b … if I can remember her phone number.
c … if you miss the bus.
d … if you don't want to.
e … if you phone while I'm out.
f … if you explain it to them.
g … if I have the time.
h … if you don't have a ticket.
i … if you can understand French.
j … if you ask him.

B Complete these sentences by putting the verb in brackets in the right tense.

1 If you ……………… ask ……………… Liz, she will tell you what to do. (*ask*)
2 He's going to visit some friends in Athens if he ……………………………………… time. (*have*)
3 You shouldn't interrupt them if they ……………………………………… . (*work*)
4 Maria will get you some money if she ……………………………………… to the bank. (*go*)
5 I'll have a word with Jack if he ……………………………………… at home. (*be*)

C Match these parts to make conditional sentences.

1 If I had their address …
2 If you saw her now …
3 If I took more exercise …
4 If you got a new job …
5 If you asked Heather …
6 If I travelled first class …
7 If it was a little warmer …
8 If you went to the doctor …
9 If I stopped off in Ankara …

a … it would cost over £650.
b … you would earn a bit more money.
c … I would probably stay with Mehmet.
d … she would give you a certificate.
e … she would probably give you a lift.
f … we would go for a swim.
g … I would lose a bit of weight.
h … I would write and ask them.
i … you would hardly recognize her.

'If' with modals; 'unless'

Main points

You can use a modal in a conditional clause.
You use 'unless' to mention an exception to what you are saying.

1 You sometimes use modals in conditional clauses. In the main clause, you can still use a present tense for events that happen often, 'will' for events that are quite likely in the future, 'would' for an event that is unlikely to happen, and 'would have' for events that were possible but did not happen.

> If he <u>can't</u> come, he usually phones me.
> If they <u>must</u> have it today, they will have to come back at five o'clock.
> If I <u>could</u> only find the time, I'd do it gladly.
> If you <u>could</u> have seen him, you would have laughed too.

'Should' is sometimes used in conditional clauses to express greater uncertainty.

> If any visitors <u>should</u> come, I'll say you aren't here.

2 You can use other modals besides 'will', 'would' and 'would have' in the main clause with their usual meanings.

> She <u>might</u> phone me, if she has time.
> You <u>could</u> come, if you wanted to.
> If he sees you leaving, he <u>may</u> cry.

Note that you can have modals in both clauses: the main clause and the conditional clause.

> If he <u>can't</u> come, he <u>will</u> phone.

➤ See Units 79 to 91 for more information.

3 In formal English, if the first verb in a conditional clause is 'had', 'should', or 'were', you can put the verb at the beginning of the clause and omit 'if'.

For example, instead of saying 'If he should come, I will tell him you are sick', it is possible to say 'Should he come, I will tell him you are sick'.

> <u>Should</u> ministers decide to hold an inquiry, we would welcome it.
> <u>Were</u> it all true, it would still not excuse their actions.
> <u>Had</u> I known, I would not have done it.

4 When you want to mention an exception to what you are saying, you use a conditional clause beginning with 'unless'.

> You will fail your exams.
> You will fail your exams <u>unless you work harder.</u>

Note that you can often use 'if...not' instead of 'unless'.

> You will fail your exams <u>if</u> you do <u>not</u> work harder.

When you use 'unless', you use the same tenses that you use with 'if'.

> She <u>spends</u> Sundays in the garden unless the weather <u>is</u> awful.
> We usually <u>walk,</u> unless we'<u>re going</u> shopping.
> He <u>will</u> not <u>let</u> you go unless he <u>is forced</u> to do so.
> You <u>wouldn't believe</u> it, unless you <u>saw</u> it.

5 'If' and 'unless' are not the only ways of beginning conditional clauses. You can also use 'as long as', 'only if', 'provided', 'provided that', 'providing', 'providing that', or 'so long as'. These expressions are all used to indicate that one thing only happens or is true if another thing happens or is true.

> I will come <u>only if</u> nothing is said to the press.
> She was prepared to come, <u>provided that</u> she could bring her daughter.
> <u>Providing</u> they remained at a safe distance, we would be all right.
> Detergent cannot harm a fabric, <u>so long as</u> it has been properly dissolved.

We were all right <u>as long as</u> we kept our heads down.

Practice

A Rewrite these sentences as conditionals.

1 I can't write to her because I don't have her address. …*I could write to her, if I had her address.*…

2 I'd like to go abroad but I can't afford it. ....

3 I'm not going to buy that car because it's so expensive. ....

4 We can't go out because it's raining. ....

5 She won't come to the party because she's away on holiday. ....

6 The central heating isn't working so we can't turn it on. ....

B Rewrite these sentences as conditionals.

1 Unfortunately I didn't see him, so I couldn't give him your message.
 If I had seen him, I could have given him your message....

2 Unfortunately he didn't pass his exams or he might have gone to university.
 ....

3 He didn't realize what was happening or he would have run away.
 ....

4 Fortunately I didn't hear what she said or I would have been very angry.
 ....

5 They got in because you didn't lock the door properly.
 ....

6 It only happened because you didn't follow the instructions.
 ....

7 Luckily she didn't find out or she would have been furious.
 ....

8 It's lucky we booked a room or we would have had nowhere to stay.
 ....

9 It's a good job we weren't going any faster or someone could have been killed.
 ....

10 He was so tired that he went home at lunchtime.
 ....

C Match the two parts of these conditional sentences.

1 You can borrow the money, …

2 He'll probably get lost, …

3 Had I known you were coming, …

4 George says he will come, …

5 You are not allowed to park in the school, …

6 Should he telephone while I'm out, …

7 Henry Ford said you could have any colour you wanted, …

8 Fred will be at school next week, …

a … I would have invited you to lunch.

b … would you ask him to call back later?

c … provided he has recovered from his cold.

d … unless you are a member of staff.

e … as long as it was black.

f … provided he can stay overnight.

g … so long as you promise to pay it back.

h … unless someone shows him the way.

▸ **Bank**

I wish, if only, ...as if...

Main points

You use 'I wish' and 'If only' to talk about wishes and regrets.

You use '...as if...' and '...as though...' to show that information in a manner clause is not or might not be true.

1 You can express what you want to happen now by using 'I wish' or 'If only' followed by a past simple verb.

> *I wish he wasn't here.*
> *If only she had a car.*

Note that in formal English, you sometimes use 'were' instead of 'was' in sentences like these.

> *I often wish that I were really wealthy.*
> *If only I were in Sicily now.*

When you want to express regret about past events, you use the past perfect.

> *I wish I hadn't married him.*
> *If only I hadn't taken those drugs.*

When you want to say that you wish that someone was able to do something, you use 'could'.

> *I wish I could pay somebody to do this for me.*
> *If only they could come with us!*

When you want to say that you wish that someone was willing to do something, you use 'would'.

> *I wish you would come for a visit.*
> *If only they would realise how stupid they've been.*

2 When you want to indicate that the information in a manner clause might not be true, or is definitely not true, you use 'as if' or 'as though'.

> *She reacted as if she didn't know about the race.*
> *She acts as though she owns the place.*

After 'as if' or 'as though', you often use a past tense even when you are talking about the present, to emphasize that the information in the manner clause is not true. In formal English, you use 'were' instead of 'was'.

> *Presidents can't dispose of companies as if people didn't exist.*
> *She treats him as though he was her own son.*
> *He looked at me as though I were mad.*

3 You can also use 'as if' or 'as though' to say how someone or something feels, looks, or sounds.

> *She felt as if she had a fever.*
> *He looked as if he hadn't slept very much.*
> *Mary sounded as though she had just run all the way.*

You can also use 'it looks' and 'it sounds' with 'as if' and 'as though'.

> *It looks to me as if he wrote down some notes.*
> *It sounds to me as though he's just being awkward.*

4 When the subject of the manner clause and the main clause are the same, you can often use a participle in the manner clause and omit the subject and the verb 'be'.

> *He ran off to the house as if escaping.*
> *He shook his head as though dazzled by his own vision.*

You can also use 'as if' or 'as though' with a 'to'-infinitive clause.

> *As if to remind him, the church clock struck eleven.*

5 In informal speech, people often use 'like' instead of 'as if' or 'as' to say how a person feels, looks, or sounds. Some speakers of English think that this use of 'like' is incorrect.

> *He felt like he'd won the pools.*
> *You look like you've seen a ghost.*
> *You talk just like my father does.*

You can also use 'like' in prepositional phrases to say how someone does something.

> *He was sleeping like a baby.*
> *I behaved like an idiot, and I'm sorry.*

Practice

A Add comments to these sentences using 'I wish'.

1 I'm afraid your father can't come. / .... I wish he could. ....

2 They always come late. / ....

3 He always complains about everything. / ....

4 He never invites us round. / ....

5 We can't go on holiday this year. / ....

6 She won't listen to anything you say. / ....

7 They can't help out I'm afraid. / ....

8 She never comes home at weekends. / ....

B Rewrite these sentences using 'like'.

1 I felt as if I'd seen him before. / .... I felt like I'd seen him before. ....

2 She looks as if she's having fun. / ....

3 He accepted his punishment as everyone else did. / ....

4 She refused to dress as her colleagues did. / ....

5 He said he would work as the others did if he was paid as they were. / ....

6 They work a five day week as we do. / ....

7 I don't like people who behave as he does. / ....

8 They still farm as their grandfathers did. / ....

C Rewrite these sentences with 'as if' or 'as though'.

1 The place sounds very quiet. I think it's deserted. / .... The place sounds as though it's deserted. ....

2 They look very happy. I think they've got some good news. / ....

3 This milk smells awful. I think it's gone sour. / ....

4 Your engine sounds very bad. I think it's worn out. / ....

5 He looks very angry. I think he's going to make trouble. / ....

6 I feel awful. I think I'm going to be sick. / ....

7 Those clouds look very dark. I think it's going to rain. / ....

8 She sounded very unhappy. I thought she was going to cry. / ....

Verbs with '-ing' clauses

1 Many verbs are followed by an '-ing' clause. The subject of the verb is also the subject of the '-ing' clause. The '-ing' clause begins with an '-ing' form. The most common of these verbs are:

- verbs of saying and thinking

admit	consider	deny	describe
imagine	mention	recall	suggest

> He _denied taking_ drugs.
> I _suggested meeting_ her for a coffee.

Note that all of these verbs except for 'describe' can also be followed by a 'that'-clause. ▶ See Unit 76.

> He _denied that_ he was involved.

- verbs of liking and disliking

adore	detest	dislike	dread	enjoy
fancy	like	love	mind	resent

> Will they _enjoy using_ it?
> I _don't mind telling_ you.

'Like' and 'love' can also be followed by a 'to'-infinitive clause. ▶ See Unit 71.

- other common verbs

avoid	commence	delay	finish	involve	keep
miss	postpone	practise	resist	risk	stop

> I've just _finished reading_ that book.
> _Avoid giving_ any unnecessary information.

- common phrasal verbs

burst out	carry on	end up	give up
go round	keep on	put off	set about

> She _carried on reading._
> They _kept on walking_ for a while.

Note that some common phrases can be followed by an '-ing' clause.

can't help	can't stand	feel like

> I _can't help worrying._

2 After the verbs and phrases mentioned above, you can also use 'being' followed by a past participle.

> They enjoy _being praised._
> I dislike _being interrupted._

After some verbs of saying and thinking, you can use 'having' followed by a past participle.

admit	deny	mention	recall

> Michael _denied having seen_ him.

3 'Come' and 'go' are used with '-ing' clauses to describe the way that a person or thing moves.

> They both _came running out._
> It _went sliding_ across the road out of control.

'Go' and 'come' are also used with '-ing' nouns to talk about sports and outdoor activities. ▶ See Unit 56.

> Did you say they might _go camping?_

4 Some verbs can be followed by an object and an '-ing' clause. The object of the verb is the subject of the '-ing' clause.

catch	find	imagine	leave	prevent	stop	watch

> It is hard _to imagine him existing_ without it.
> He _left them making_ their calculations.

Note that 'prevent' and 'stop' are often used with 'from' in front of the '-ing' clause.

> I wanted to _prevent him from seeing_ that.

Most verbs of perception can be followed by an object and an '-ing' clause or a base form. ▶ See Unit 72.

> I _saw him riding_ a bicycle.
> I _saw a policeman walk over_ to one of them.

▶ See also Unit 94 for '-ing' clauses after nouns.

A Rewrite these sentences using an '-ing' clause instead of the reported clause.

1 He denied that he had done anything illegal. / ......*He denied doing anything illegal.*......

2 Judy remembered she had noticed him behind the building. / ....

3 When his Dad asked, did you mention that you had seen him? / ....

4 I couldn't recall that I had said anything about him at all. / ....

5 May I suggest that we give them a present of £500 each? / ....

6 Sorry, but I can't imagine I would ever agree to that! / ....

7 He then described how he escaped from prison. / ....

8 They ought to admit that they had stolen the fruit. / ....

B Rewrite the sentences using an '-ing' clause as the object of the verb, instead of the noun group.

1 The Watsons were contemplating a week's visit to Egypt. / ....*The Watsons were contemplating*
 visiting Egypt for a week....

2 Could you consider a reduction in price, for example to £6,000? / ....

3 They delayed the start of the game because of the rain. / ....

4 I want to avoid monthly payments if possible. / ....

5 They didn't finish preparations for the party till after 9pm. / ....

6 This new production process might involve an increase in staff. / ....

C Complete these dialogues using the phrases given.

dread going	fancies taking up	adore climbing	detest getting stuck
feel like having	can't bear being told	give up playing	carry on driving

1 A: They go to the mountains every week-end.
   B: Yes, they ....*adore climbing*... .

2 A: Oh dear, only another 3 days' holidays.
   B: Yes, I .... back to school.

3 A: Oh, just look at the traffic ahead.
   B: Oh no. I .... in traffic jams.

4 A: Let's stop for something to eat. There's a restaurant in a few miles.
   B: I don't know. I think we should .... and get home as quickly as possible.

5 A: She's a very good actress, and she's only 15, you know.
   B: Yes. She really .... acting as a career.

6 A: Jack hates being in the army.
   B: Yes, he .... what to do all the time.

7 A: My grandfather's nearly eighty and he still enjoys a game of tennis.
   B: I don't think he'll ever ....

8 A: Are you taking a holiday this summer?
   B: I hope so. I certainly .... a couple of weeks off.

▸ **Bank**

Infinitives

Main points

Some verbs are followed by a 'to'-infinitive clause. Others are followed by an object and a 'to'-infinitive clause.

Some verbs are followed by a 'wh'-word and a 'to'-infinitive clause. Others are followed by an object, a 'wh'-word, and a 'to'-infinitive clause.

Nouns are followed by 'to'-infinitive clauses that indicate the aim, purpose or necessity of something, or that give extra information.

1 Some verbs are followed by a 'to'-infinitive clause. The subject of the verb is also the subject of the 'to'-infinitive clause.

- verbs of saying and thinking

agree	choose	decide	expect	hope	intend
learn	mean	offer	plan	promise	refuse

She had agreed to let us use her flat.
I decided not to go out for the evening.

- other verbs

fail	manage	pretend	tend	want

England failed to win a place in the finals.

2 Some verbs are followed by an object and a 'to'-infinitive clause. The object of the verb is the subject of the 'to'-infinitive clause.

- verbs of saying and thinking

advise	ask	encourage	expect	invite
order	persuade	remind	teach	tell

I asked her to explain.
They advised us not to wait around too long.

- other verbs

allow	force	get	help	want

I could get someone else to do it.
I didn't want him to go.

Note that 'help' can also be followed by an object and a base form.

I helped him fix it.

⊖ WARNING: You do not use 'want' with a 'that'-clause. You do not say 'I want that you do something'.

3 Some verbs are followed by 'for' and an object, then a 'to'-infinitive clause. The object of 'for' is the subject of the 'to'-infinitive clause.

appeal	arrange	ask	long	pay	wait	wish

Could you arrange for a taxi to collect us?
I waited for him to speak.

4 Some link verbs, and 'pretend' are followed by 'to be' and an '-ing' form for continuing actions, and by 'to have' and a past participle for finished actions.

➤ See also Unit 73.

We pretended to be looking inside.
I don't appear to have written down his name.

5 Some verbs are normally used in the passive when they are followed by a 'to'-infinitive clause.

believe	consider	feel	find	know
report	say	think	understand	

He is said to have died a natural death.
Is it thought to be a good thing?

Continued on page 142.

Practice

A **Rewrite these sentences using a 'to'-infinitive.**

1 He said that he would help if he possibly could. / He promised ....*to help*........ if he possibly could.

2 I'll go up to London tomorrow if I can. / I intend .... up to London tomorrow.

3 It wasn't easy but we drove home in two hours. / We managed .... home in two hours.

4 They said that they would sell us the house. / They agreed .... us the house.

5 He looked as if he was sleeping / He seemed .... sleeping.

6 I expect I will hear from Mary before very long. / I expect .... from Mary before very long.

7 He has a habit of being late for meetings. / He tends .... late for meetings.

8 We were not able to finish all the work in time. / We failed .... all the work in time.

B **Complete these sentences using the past tense of these verbs.**

advise allow ask encourage expect invite remind warn

1 If I were you, George, I would ring the police. / He ....*advised*................ George to ring the police.

2 Mary, could you please type a letter for me? / I .... Mary to type a letter for me.

3 I am sure Bill will arrive before dark. / She .... Bill to arrive before dark.

4 I hope you will visit us in England, Maria. / We .... Maria to visit us in England.

5 Okay, children, you can go home early. / She .... the children to go home early.

6 You should take the exam. I'm sure you'd do well. / Our teacher .... us to take the exam.

7 ELECTRIC FENCE. DO NOT TOUCH. / The notice .... people not to touch the fence.

8 Don't forget to take some warm clothes with you. / My mother .... me to take some warm clothes.

C **Rewrite these sentences using 'to be' and an '-ing' form or 'to have' and a past participle.**

1 I think we have lost our way. / We appear ....*to have lost our way.*............................

2 He pretended that he was working. / He pretended .....*to be working.*..................................

3 I think you've broken your leg. / You seem ....

4 It looks as if they've locked everything away. / They appear ....

5 It appears he is waiting for the doctor. / He appears ....

6 Jenny pretended she had spent the money. / She pretended ....

7 I think they are living at home now. / They seem ....

141

6 Some verbs are followed by a 'wh'-word and a 'to'-infinitive clause. These include:

| ask | decide | explain | forget | imagine |
| know | learn | remember | understand | wonder |

> *I didn't know what to call him.*
> *She had forgotten how to ride a bicycle.*

Some verbs are followed by an object, then a 'wh'-word and a 'to'-infinitive clause.

| ask | remind | show | teach | tell |

> *I asked him what to do.*
> *Who will show him how to use it?*

Some verbs only take 'to'-infinitive clauses to express purpose.

➤ See Unit 97.

> *The captain stopped to reload the gun.*
> *He went to get some fresh milk.*

7 You use a 'to'-infinitive clause after a noun to indicate the aim of an action or the purpose of a physical object.

> *We arranged a meeting to discuss the new rules.*
> *He had nothing to write with.*

You also use a 'to'-infinitive clause after a noun to say that something needs to be done.

> *I gave him several things to mend.*
> *'What's this?' – 'A list of things to remember.'*

8 You use a 'to'-infinitive clause after a noun group that includes an ordinal number, a superlative, or a word like 'next', 'last', or 'only'.

> *She was the first woman to be elected to the council.*
> *Mr Holmes was the oldest person to be chosen.*
> *The only person to speak was James.*

9 You use a 'to'-infinitive clause after abstract nouns to give more specific information about them.

> *All it takes is a willingness to learn.*
> *He'd lost the ability to communicate with people.*

The following abstract nouns are often followed by a 'to'-infinitive clause:

ability	attempt	chance	desire
failure	inability	need	opportunity
unwillingness	willingness		

Note that the verbs or adjectives which are related to these nouns can also be followed by a 'to'-infinitive clause. For example, you can say 'I attempted to find them', and 'He was willing to learn'.

➤ See Unit 95 for information on nouns that are related to reporting verbs and can be followed by a 'to'-infinitive clause.

Practice

D Rewrite these sentences using 'not' in front of a 'to'-infinitive.

1 She told me I shouldn't pay so much for a ticket. / She advised me …*not to pay*………… so much for a ticket.

2 He waved but I pretended that I didn't see him. / I pretended ………………………………… him when he waved.

3 They promised they wouldn't miss the meeting. / They promised ………………………………… the meeting.

4 I told the kids they shouldn't make so much noise. / I told the kids ……………………………… so much noise.

5 I was going to write, but John persuaded me I shouldn't. / John persuaded me ……………………… .

6 Jenny reminded Peter that he shouldn't be late. / Jenny reminded Peter ……………………… late.

E Use the following words to complete the sentences below.

| box | key | matches | meeting | money | party | pen | room |

1 We held ……………*a party*………………… to celebrate.

2 Do you have enough ……………………………………… to pay for all the tickets?

3 I have a master ……………………………………… to open all the doors.

4 There's a big ……………………………………… to pack the clothes in.

5 Have you got a ……………………………………… to sign these papers with?

6 Is there a ……………………………………… to hang our coats in?

7 There will be a ……………………………………… tomorrow to elect a new chairman.

8 Do you have any ……………………………………… to light the fire?

▶ **Bank**

Verb + 'to' or '-ing'

Main points

Some verbs take a 'to'-infinitive clause or an '-ing' clause with little difference in meaning. Others take a 'to'-infinitive or '-ing' clause, but the meaning is different.

1 The following verbs can be followed by a 'to'-infinitive clause or an '-ing' clause, with little difference in meaning.

attempt	begin	bother	continue	fear
hate	love	prefer	start	

> It <u>started raining.</u>
> A very cold wind <u>had started to blow.</u>
> The captain <u>didn't bother answering.</u>
> I <u>didn't bother to answer.</u>

Note that if these verbs are used in a continuous tense, they are followed by a 'to'-infinitive clause.

> The company <u>is beginning to export</u> to the West.
> We <u>are continuing to make</u> good progress.

After 'begin', 'continue', and 'start', you use a 'to'-infinitive clause with the verbs 'understand', 'know', and 'realize'.

> I <u>began to understand</u> her a bit better.

2 You can often use 'like' with a 'to'-infinitive or an '-ing' clause with little difference in meaning.

> I <u>like to fish.</u>
> I <u>like fishing.</u>

However, there is sometimes a difference. You can use 'like' followed by a 'to'-infinitive clause to say that you think something is a good idea, or the right thing to do. You cannot use an '-ing' clause with this meaning.

> They <u>like to interview</u> you first.
> I <u>didn't like to ask</u> him.

3 After 'remember', 'forget', and 'regret', you use an '-ing' clause if you are referring to an event after it has happened.

> I <u>remember discussing</u> it once before.
> I'll never <u>forget going out</u> with my old aunt.
> She did not <u>regret accepting</u> his offer.

You use a 'to'-infinitive clause after 'remember' and 'forget' if you are referring to an event before it happens.

> I must <u>remember to send</u> a gift for her child.
> Don't <u>forget to send in</u> your entries.

After 'regret', in formal English, you use a 'to'-infinitive clause with these verbs to say that you are sorry about what you are saying or doing now:

announce	inform	learn	say	see	tell

> I <u>regret to say</u> that it was all burned up.

4 If you 'try to do' something, you make an effort to do it. If you 'try doing' something, you do it as an experiment, for example to see if you like it or if it is effective.

> I <u>tried to explain.</u>
> <u>Have</u> you <u>tried painting</u> it?

5 If you 'go on doing' something, you continue to do it. If you 'go on to do' something, you do it after you have finished doing something else.

> I <u>went on writing.</u>
> He later <u>went on to form</u> a computer company.

6 If you 'are used to doing' something, you are accustomed to doing it. If you 'used to do' something, you did it regularly in the past, but you no longer do it now.

> We <u>are used to working</u> together.
> I <u>used to live</u> in this street.

7 After 'need', you use a 'to'-infinitive clause if the subject of 'need' is also the subject of the 'to'-infinitive clause. You use an '-ing' form if the subject of 'need' is the object of the '-ing' clause.

> We <u>need to ask</u> certain questions.
> It <u>needs cutting.</u>

Practice

A **Complete the sentences below by using the 'to'-infinitive or '-ing' form of these verbs.**

| enjoy   knock   learn   phone   play   rain   shout   stay |

1 I started ....*learning*.......................... French when I went to secondary school.
2 It's awfully cold in winter, but the kids still love .... outside in the snow.
3 The weather was fine when we set off, but it soon started ....
4 I'll be in my office. Don't bother .... , just come straight in.
5 Joe just lost his temper and began .... at everyone.
6 It's a pity we have to go home now. We were just beginning .... ourselves.
7 We don't go out much in the evening. We prefer .... at home.

B **Look at the following pairs of sentences. Complete one sentence in each pair with the 'to'-infinitive of the verb in brackets and the other with the '-ing' form.**

1 Please remember ....*to close*......................... the door when you go out.
    I remember ....*closing*................. the door, but I'm not sure that I locked it. (*close*)
2 I paid the electricity bill, but I don't remember .... the rent.
    Oh dear! I think I forgot .... the rent this month. (*pay*)
3 I tried .... in a department store, but it wasn't a very good job.
    You really must try .... harder. (*work*)
4 She just went on .... about everything.
    She complained about everything else, and then she went on .... about the price. (*complain*)
5 I remember .... the money in the drawer, but it's not there now.
    I must remember .... some money to pay for the repairs. (*leave*)
6 I really regret .... everyone what happened. I should have kept it a secret.
    I regret .... you that there has been a serious accident. (*tell*)
7 I remember .... to the dentist as a child.
    I must remember .... to the dentist on Wednesday. (*go*)
8 I'll never forget .... Paris for the first time.
    We mustn't forget .... Monique when we're in Paris. (*visit*)

C **Make appropriate sentences to match the pictures, using 'need' and the pairs of words given.**

| shoes / polish   shirt / iron   tyre / mend   trousers / shorten   door / paint   pencil / sharpen |

1 ....*The pencil needs sharpening.*....
2 ....
3 ....
4 ....
5 ....
6 ....

Verbs with other clauses

Main points

'Make' and 'let' can be followed by an object and a base form.

Some verbs of perception can be followed by an object and an '-ing' clause, or an object and a base form.

'Have' and 'get' can be followed by an object and a past participle.

'Dare' is followed by a 'to'-infinitive clause or a base form.

1 You can use an object and a base form after 'make' to say that one person causes another person to do something, or after 'let' to say they allow them to do something.

> *My father made me go for the interview.*
> *Jenny let him talk.*

2 Some verbs of perception are used with an object and an '-ing' clause if an action is unfinished or continues over a period of time, and with an object and a base form if the action is finished.

feel	hear	see	watch

> *He heard a distant voice shouting.*
> *Dr Hochstadt heard her gasp.*

You normally use an '-ing' clause after 'notice', 'observe', 'smell', and 'understand'.

> *I could smell Chinese vegetables cooking.*
> *We can understand them wanting to go.*

3 You can use an object and a past participle after 'have' or 'get', when you want to say that someone arranges for something to be done. 'Have' is slightly more formal.

> *We've just had the house decorated.*
> *We must get the car repaired.*

You also use 'have' and 'get' with an object and a past participle to say that something happens to someone, especially if it is unpleasant.

> *She had her purse stolen.*
> *He got his car broken into at the weekend.*

4 You use 'have' followed by an object and an '-ing' clause, or an object and a past participle, when you want to say that someone causes something to happen, either intentionally or unintentionally.

> *Alan had me looking for that book all day.*
> *He had me utterly confused.*

5 You use 'want' and 'would like' with an object and a past participle to indicate that you want something to be done.

> *I want the work finished by January 1st.*
> *How would you like your hair cut, sir?*

6 'Dare' can be followed by a 'to'-infinitive clause or a base form in negative or interrogative sentences:

• when there is an auxiliary or modal in front of 'dare'

> *He did not dare to walk to the village.*
> *What bank would dare offer such terms?*

• when you use the form 'dares' or 'dared' (but not 'dares not' or 'dared not')

> *No one dares disturb him.*
> *No other manager dared to compete.*

You must use a base form in:
• negative or interrogative sentences without an auxiliary or modal before 'dare'

> *I daren't ring Jeremy again.*
> *Nobody dare disturb him.*
> *Dare she go in?*

• negative sentences with 'dares not' or 'dared not'

> *He dares not risk it.*
> *Sonny dared not disobey.*

Note that the phrase 'how dare you' is always followed by a base form.

> *How dare you speak to me like that?*

'Dare' is rarely used in affirmative sentences.

Practice

A Complete the dialogues below filling the gaps with 'let', 'make', or 'made'.

1 A: When I went to school they ....made............... us wear school uniform.

   B: Really? At my school they ....let................. us wear whatever we liked.

2 A: Did you see that film at the Odeon? It was so funny. It really .... me laugh.

   B: No. My parents wouldn't .... me go. They .... me stay

   at home and finish my homework.

3 A: Do you think they'll .... us go home early on Friday?

   B: No. They always .... us work till five, even just before a holiday.

4 A: I think they should .... old people travel free on buses.

   B: Yes. I certainly don't think they should .... them pay the full fare.

5 A: They wouldn't .... us go in until just before the show started.

   B: No. They .... us wait out in the cold until five to eight.

6 A: Please don't make such a noise. You really .... me jump.

   B: Oh please, just .... us finish this game, then we'll be quiet.

B Complete the sentences below using the following words.

burning	lying	making	playing	talking

1 There must be someone at home. I can hear people ....talking................. .

2 Did you turn the stove off in the kitchen? I think I can smell something ....

3 The children are outside. I can see them .... in the garden.

4 Are these your gloves? I found them .... on the table in the hall.

5 This is awful. Can't you stop those kids .... such a dreadful noise?

C Complete these sentences using a form of 'have' with the words in brackets. Remember to use the correct form of the main verb.

1 It'll be a long journey. We'd better ...have the car serviced... before we set out. (*the car / service*)

2 I'll be late back after lunch. I'm going to .... (*my hair / cut*)

3 Doesn't Mike look smart? He .... specially for the wedding. (*that suit / make*)

4 We're planning to .... while we're on holiday. (*the house / redecorate*)

5 This house is too small now the kids are growing up. We should ....
   (*another room / build on*)

6 Poor old Bill .... while he was on holiday. (*a lot of money / steal*)

▶ **Bank**

Link verbs

Main points

Link verbs are used to join the subject with a complement.

Link verbs can have adjectives, noun groups, or 'to'-infinitive clauses as complements.

You can use 'it' and 'there' as impersonal subjects with link verbs.

1 A small but important group of verbs are followed by a complement rather than an object. The complement tells you more about the subject. Verbs that take complements are called 'link' verbs.

appear	be	become	feel	get	go
grow	keep	look	prove	remain	seem
smell	sound	stay	taste	turn	

I am proud of these people.
She was getting too old to play tennis.
They looked all right to me.

2 Link verbs often have adjectives as complements describing the subject.

We felt very happy.
He was the tallest in the room.

➤ See Units 31 to 33 and Unit 47 for more information about adjectives after link verbs.

3 You can use link verbs with noun groups as complements to give your opinion about the subject.

He's not the right man for it.
She seemed an ideal person to look after them.

You also use noun groups as complements after 'be', 'become', and 'remain' to specify the subject.

This one is yours.
He became a geologist.
Promises by MPs remained just promises.

Note that you use object pronouns after 'be'.

It's me again.

4 Some link verbs can have 'to'-infinitive clauses as complements.

appear	get	grow	look	prove	seem

He appears to have taken my keys.
She seemed to like me.

These verbs, and 'remain', can also be followed by 'to be' and a complement.

Mary seemed to be asleep.
His new job proved to be a challenge.

5 You can use 'it' and 'there' as impersonal subjects with link verbs.

It seems silly not to tell him.
There appears to have been a mistake.

➤ See Units 17 and 18 for more information.

You can use 'be' with some abstract nouns as the subject, followed by a 'that'-clause or a 'to'-infinitive clause as the complement.

advice	agreement	answer	decision
idea	plan	problem	solution

The answer is that they are not interested in it.
The idea was to spend more money on training.

Some can only have a 'that'-clause.

conclusion	explanation	fact	feeling
reason	report	thought	understanding

The fact is that I can't go to the party.

Practice

A Use the link verbs below to complete the sentences which follow.

feels   gets   goes   grows   looks   smells   sounds   tastes

1 What's the matter with Chris? He .... *looks* .... very upset.
2 Why is he shouting? He .... very angry.
3 If you keep milk for too long, it .... sour.
4 Jane says she .... hungry.
5 It .... very hot in summer.
6 Are you sure this fish is all right? It certainly .... a bit funny.
7 This cake is a bit old, but it still .... pretty good.
8 Anne is getting much taller as she .... older.

B Make 8 sentences from the following table.

The picture was old and dirty, The fruit smelled awful, The problem seemed simple, It was a long programme It was only a short walk, The animal looked quiet enough, The jacket seemed to be the right size, The food smelled all right,	but it proved to be	extremely difficult. very tasty. much too small. rather tiring. very valuable. quite vicious. uneatable. very interesting.

1 .... The picture was old and dirty, but it proved to be very valuable. ....
2 ....
3 ....
4 ....
5 ....
6 ....
7 ....
8 ....

C Use the phrases below to complete the sentences which follow.

too cold   too dark   too expensive   too hot   too late   too old   too tired   too young

1 I'm afraid I'm getting .... *too old* .... to work such long hours.
2 We'll have to stop. It's .... for us to see what we're doing.
3 Mary looks much .... to be a grandmother.
4 We should have arrived in time, but we proved to be ....
5 Turn the fire off. It's getting .... in here.
6 I'm going to bed. I feel far .... to stay up any longer.
7 You'll be .... if you don't take more warm clothes.
8 We can't afford to stay in a hotel like that. It looks much ....

▶ **Bank**

Reporting the past

Main points

A report structure is used to report what people say or think.

You use the present tense of the reporting verb when you are reporting something that someone says or thinks at the time you are speaking.

You often use past tenses in report structures because a reported clause usually reports something that was said or believed in the past.

1 You use a report structure to report what people say or think. A report structure consists of two parts. One part is the reporting clause, which contains the reporting verb.

> <u>I told him</u> nothing was going to happen to me.
> <u>I agreed</u> that he should do it.

The other part is the reported clause.

> He felt <u>that he had to do something.</u>
> Henry said <u>he wanted to go home.</u>

➤ See Units 75-77 for more information on report structures.

2 For the verb in the reporting clause, you choose a tense that is appropriate at the time you are speaking.

Because reports are usually about something that was said or believed in the past, both the reporting verb and the verb in the reported clause are often in a past tense.

> Mrs Kaur <u>announced</u> that the lecture <u>had begun.</u>
> At the time we <u>thought</u> that he <u>was</u> mad.

The most common tenses used for verbs in the reported clause are summarized below:

direct speech		reported speech
present simple	→	past simple
present continuous	→	past continuous
present perfect	→	past perfect
past simple	→	past perfect
past continuous	→	past perfect continuous
present perfect continuous	→	past perfect continuous
will	→	would
can	→	could
may	→	might

3 Although you normally use past tenses in reports about the past, you can use a present tense in the reported clause if what you are saying is important in the present, for example:

● because you want to emphasize that it is still true

> <u>Did</u> you <u>tell</u> him that this young woman <u>is looking</u> for a job?

● because you want to give advice or a warning, or make a suggestion for the present or future

> I <u>told</u> you they <u>have</u> this class on Friday afternoon, so you should have come a bit earlier.

4 You use a present tense for the reporting verb when you are reporting:

● what someone says or thinks at the time you are speaking

> She <u>says</u> she wants to see you this afternoon.
> I <u>think</u> there's something wrong.

Note that, as in the last example, it may be your own thoughts that you are reporting.

● what someone often says

> He <u>says</u> that no one understands him.

● what someone has said in the past, if what they said is still true

> My doctor <u>says</u> it's nothing to worry about.

5 If you are predicting what people will say or think, you use a future tense for the reporting verb.

> No doubt he <u>will claim</u> that his car broke down.
> They <u>will think</u> we are making a fuss.

6 You very rarely try to report the exact words of a statement. You usually give a summary of what was said. For example, John might say:

'I tried to phone you about six times yesterday. I let the phone ring for ages but there was no answer. I couldn't get through at all so I finally gave up.'

You would probably report this as:

John said he tried to phone several times yesterday, but he couldn't get through.

A The following passage appeared in a children's comic called 'The Eagle' in 1958. It is about a teenager who wanted to be an atomic engineer. Rewrite the passage starting with the verbs given, and changing the tenses of the verbs in bold as necessary.

'Andrew **is** intelligent and go-ahead. He **thinks** there **is** a great future for engineers in this atomic age. As a trainee, Andrew **works** 44 hours in a five day week and **earns** about £3 per week with an allowance of £1.70. His pay **rises** to £8.16 at 21. Hostel accommodation **is** available. Books and instruments **can** be borrowed and there **are** opportunities for sport.'

In 1958, the Eagle published an article about Andrew, who wanted to be an atomic
engineer. It said that Andrew was intelligent and go-ahead.

....

....

....

....

....

....

....

....

B Here are some sayings by well-known people. Look at the sayings, then complete the reports by putting the verbs in brackets in the right tense.

1 When I grow up I want to be a little boy. (*Joseph Heller*)
   When someone asked Joseph Heller what he ....**wanted**................... to be
   when he ....**grew up**............................. he ....**said**.....................
   he ....**wanted**............................. to be a little boy. (*want*) (*grow up*) (*say*) (*want*)

2 I don't like baths. I do not enjoy them in the slightest and if I could I would prefer to go round dirty. (*J.B. Priestley*)
   J.B. Priestley .... baths. He ....
   that if he .... the choice he would prefer to stay dirty. (*hate*) (*say*) (*have*)

3 I am happy to say someone has stolen my wife's credit card. He will probably spend a lot less than she does. (*Anon.*)
   A man .... he .... delighted that
   someone .... his wife's credit card. He ....
   sure the thief .... less money than his wife. (*say*) (*be*) (*steal*) (*be*) (*spend*)

4 His ears are so big, he looks like a taxicab with both doors open. (*Howard Hughes about Clark Gable*)
   After meeting the film star, Clark Gable, Howard Hughes ....
   Gable .... such big ears he ....
   like a taxi with both doors open. (*say*) (*have*) (*look*)

5 I know only two tunes. One is Yankee Doodle and the other isn't. (*Ulysses S. Grant*)
   President Ulysses S. Grant .... that he only .... two tunes.
   One of them .... Yankee Doodle and the other .... (*say*) (*know*) (*be*) (*not be*)

▸ **Bank**

Reported questions

Main points

You use reported questions to talk about a question that someone else has asked.

In reported questions, the subject of the question comes before the verb.

You use 'if' or 'whether' in reported 'yes/no'-questions.

1 When you are talking about a question that someone has asked, you use a reported question.

> She asked me <u>why I was so late.</u>
> He wanted to know <u>where I was going.</u>
> I demanded to know <u>what was going on.</u>
> I asked her <u>if I could help her.</u>
> I asked her <u>whether there was anything wrong.</u>

In formal and written English, 'enquire' (also spelled 'inquire') is often used instead of 'ask'.

> Wilkie had enquired <u>if she did a lot of acting.</u>
> He inquired <u>whether he could see her.</u>

2 When you are reporting a question, the verb in the reported clause is often in a past tense. This is because you are often talking about the past when you are reporting someone else's words.

> She <u>asked</u> me why I <u>was</u> so late.
> Pat <u>asked</u> him if she <u>had hurt</u> him.

However, you can use a present or future tense if the question you are reporting relates to the present or future.

> Mark <u>was asking</u> if you'<u>re enjoying</u> your new job.
> They <u>asked</u> if you'<u>ll be</u> there tomorrow night.

3 In reported questions, the subject of the question comes before the verb, just as it does in affirmative sentences.

> She asked me why <u>I was late.</u>
> I asked what <u>he was doing.</u>

4 You do not normally use the auxiliary 'do' in reported questions.

> She asked him if <u>his parents spoke</u> French.
> They asked us what <u>we thought.</u>

The auxiliary 'do' can be used in reported questions, but only for emphasis, or to make a contrast with something that has already been said. It is not put before the subject as in direct questions.

> She asked me whether I really <u>did</u> mean it.
> I told him I didn't like classical music. He asked me what kind of music I <u>did</u> like.

5 You use 'if' or 'whether' to introduce reported 'yes/no'-questions.

> I asked him <u>if</u> he was on holiday.
> She hugged him and asked him <u>whether</u> he was all right.
> I asked him <u>whether</u> he was single.

'Whether' is used especially when there is a choice of possibilities.

> I was asked <u>whether</u> I wanted to stay at a hotel <u>or</u> at his home.
> They asked <u>whether</u> Tim was <u>or</u> was <u>not</u> in the team.
> I asked him <u>whether</u> he loved me or not.

Note that you can put 'or not' immediately after 'whether', but not immediately after 'if'.

> The police didn't ask <u>whether or not</u> they were in.

► See Units 74, 76, and 77 for more information on reporting.

Practice

A Rewrite the reported questions below as wh-questions.

1 Jennifer asked him why he wanted to know. / *Why do you want to know?*
2 Tim asked me where I lived. / ....
3 Caroline asked him when he had arrived. / ....
4 Chris asked Jane when she had last seen her mother. / ....
5 He asked me what I did for a living. / ....
6 Kevin asked what we were doing there. / ....
7 Rachel asked me how long I'd lived in the flat. / ....
8 Paul asked his sister who she was going to invite to the party. / ....
9 Jackie asked Dan how long he would be staying. / ....
10 Julie wanted to know how much I'd paid for the car. / ....

B Rewrite these as 'yes/no'-questions.

1 He asked her if Maggie liked fish. / *Does Maggie like fish?*
2 Helen asked me if I was happy. / ....
3 John asked Sam if he was coming to the party. / ....
4 Val asked me if I could help her. / ....
5 Daphne asked him whether he had been to London before. / ....
6 Mark asked her whether she had enjoyed the movie. / ....
7 My mother asked me if I'd like a drink. / ....
8 Paula asked me if I'd seen her glasses anywhere. / ....

C Rewrite the following as reported questions.

1 Do you like my new dress? / She asked him *if he liked her new dress.*
2 Do giraffes eat leaves? / Lewis asked his teacher ....
3 Did you find the keys? / Sally asked me ....
4 Could you open the window, please? / My sister asked me ....
5 Are you hungry? / Kate's husband asked ....
6 Why didn't you ask me before? / Beatrice asked Jim ....
7 Where are you going now? / Colin asked me ....
8 Would you like an ice cream? / Susie asked her nephew ....
9 Why won't you help me? / George asked Paul ....
10 Can I have some more, please? / Oliver asked me ....

▶ **Bank**

Reporting: 'that'-clauses

1 When you are reporting what someone said, you do not usually repeat their exact words, you use your own words in a report structure.

> *Jim said he wanted to go home.*

Jim's actual words might have been 'It's time I went' or 'I must go'.

Report structures contain two clauses. The first clause is the reporting clause, which contains a reporting verb such as 'say', 'tell', or 'ask'.

> *She said <u>that she'd been to Belgium</u>.*
> *The man in the shop told me <u>how much it would cost</u>.*

You often use verbs that refer to people's thoughts and feelings to report what people say. If someone says 'I am wrong', you might report this as 'He felt that he was wrong'. ▶ See Unit 77 for more information.

2 The second clause in a report structure is the reported clause, which contains the information that you are reporting. The reported clause can be a 'that'-clause, a 'to'-infinitive clause, an 'if'-clause, or a 'wh'-word clause.

> *She said <u>that she didn't know.</u>*
> *He told me <u>to do it.</u>*
> *Mary asked <u>if she could stay with us.</u>*
> *She asked <u>where he'd gone.</u>*

3 If you want to report a statement, you use a 'that'-clause after a verb such as 'say'.

admit	agree	answer	argue	claim
complain	decide	deny	explain	insist
mention	promise	reply	say	warn

> *He <u>said that</u> he would go.*
> *I <u>replied that</u> I had not read it yet.*

You often omit 'that' from the 'that'-clause, but not after 'answer', 'argue', 'explain', or 'reply'.

> *They <u>said</u> I had to see a doctor first.*
> *He <u>answered that</u> the price would be three pounds.*

You often mention the hearer after the preposition 'to' with the following verbs.

admit	announce	complain	explain	mention
say	suggest			

> *He <u>complained to me</u> that you were rude.*

4 'Tell' and some other reporting verbs are also used with a 'that'-clause, but with these verbs you have to mention the hearer as the object of the verb.

convince	inform	notify	persuade reassure
remind	tell		

> *He <u>told me</u> that he was a farmer.*
> *I <u>informed her</u> that I could not come.*

The word 'that' is often omitted after 'tell'.

> *I <u>told them</u> you were at the dentist.*

You can also mention the hearer as the object of the verb with 'promise' and 'warn'.

> *I <u>promised her</u> that I wouldn't be late.*

5 Note the differences between 'say' and 'tell'. You cannot use 'say' with the hearer as the object of the verb. You cannot say 'I said them you had gone'. You cannot use 'tell' without the hearer as the object of the verb. You cannot say 'I told that you had gone'. You cannot use 'tell' with 'to' and the hearer. You cannot say 'I told to them you had gone'.

6 The reporting verbs that have the hearer as object, such as 'tell', can be used in the passive.

> *She <u>was told</u> that there were no tickets left.*

Most reporting verbs that do not need the hearer as object, such as 'say', can be used in the passive with impersonal 'it' as subject, but not 'answer', 'complain', 'insist', 'promise', 'reply', or 'warn'.

> *<u>It was said</u> that the money had been stolen.*

▶ See also Units 74 and 77.

A Match the reports with the actual words used.

1 They said they had to go.

2 He said he would help if he could.

3 She promised she would visit us.

4 He suggested that we should write to the boss.

5 They insisted we should stay a bit longer.

6 They complained that they were too busy.

7 She mentioned that she had met you.

8 I explained that they should send a letter.

a 'You can't leave yet. It's only eleven o'clock.'

b 'Well, I'll do whatever I can for you.'

c 'If I were you I would get in touch with the manager.'

d 'I bumped into your brother in London yesterday.'

e 'It's no good just telephoning. Put something in writing.'

f 'I'll certainly come and see you some time.'

g 'We have far too much work at the moment.'

h 'I'm afraid it's time for us to leave.'

B Use the appropriate form of these verbs to complete the definitions and examples.

admit	announce	argue	complain	deny	mention	explain	inform

1 If you .... **inform** .... someone that something is the case, you tell them about it.

EG I .... **informed** .... her that I was unwell and could not come to her party.

2 If you .... something, you agree, often reluctantly, that it is true.

EG I must .... that I had my doubts.

3 When you .... something, you say that it is not true.

EG Green .... that he had done anything illegal.

4 If you .... something, you tell people about it publicly or officially.

EG It was .... that the Prime Minister would speak on television that evening.

5 If you .... , you tell someone about a situation affecting you that is wrong or unsatisfactory.

EG He .... that the office was not 'businesslike'.

6 If you .... something, you say it, but do not spend long talking about it.

EG I .... to Tom that I was thinking of going back to work.

7 If you .... something, you describe it so that it can be understood.

EG He .... that they had to buy a return ticket.

8 If you .... that something is the case, you state your opinion about it and give reasons why you think it is true.

EG Some people .... that nuclear weapons have helped to keep the peace.

C Use one of the words given in brackets to complete each of the sentences below.

1 I .... **explained** .... to him that he would have to wait. (*explained / told*)

2 He .... me that it was time to go. (*mentioned / informed*)

3 She .... to them that they should reconsider their decision. (*suggested / persuaded*)

4 We were .... that you would pay the bill. (*told / said*)

5 It was .... that there would be another meeting the following week. (*informed / announced*)

6 George .... to me that he might look in to see me. (*promised / mentioned*)

Other report structures

Main points

When reporting an order, a request, or a piece of advice, the reported clause is a 'to'-infinitive clause, used after an object.

When reporting a question, the reported clause is an 'if'-clause or a 'wh'-word clause.

Many reporting verbs refer to people's thoughts and feelings.

1. If you want to report an order, a request, or a piece of advice, you use a 'to'-infinitive clause after a reporting verb such as 'tell', 'ask', or 'advise'. You mention the hearer as the object of the verb, before the 'to'-infinitive clause.

advise	ask	beg	command
forbid	instruct	invite	order
persuade	remind	tell	warn

> Johnson <u>told her to wake</u> him <u>up.</u>
> He <u>ordered me to fetch</u> the books.
> He <u>asked her to marry</u> him.
> He <u>advised me to buy</u> it.

If the order, request, or advice is negative, you put 'not' before the 'to'-infinitive.

> He had ordered his officers <u>not to use</u> weapons.
> She asked her staff <u>not to discuss</u> it publicly.
> Doctors advised him <u>not to play</u> for three weeks.

If the subject of the 'to'-infinitive clause is the same as the subject of the main verb, you can use 'ask' or 'beg' to report a request without mentioning the hearer.

> I <u>asked to see</u> the manager.
> Both men <u>begged not to be named.</u>

2. If you want to report a question, you use a verb such as 'ask' followed by an 'if'-clause or a 'wh'-word clause.

> I <u>asked if</u> I could stay with them.
> They <u>wondered whether</u> the time was right.
> He <u>asked</u> me <u>where</u> I was going.
> She <u>inquired how</u> Ibrahim was getting on.

Note that in reported questions, the subject of the question comes before the verb, just as it does in affirmative sentences.

➤ See Unit 75.

3. Many reporting verbs refer to people's thoughts and feelings but are often used to report what people say. For example, if someone says 'I must go', you might report this as 'She wanted to go' or 'She thought she should go'.

Some of these verbs are followed by:

• a 'that'-clause

accept	believe	consider	fear
feel	guess	imagine	know
suppose	think	understand	worry

> We both <u>knew</u> that the town was cut off.
> I had always <u>believed</u> that I would see him again.

• a 'to'-infinitive clause

intend	plan	want

> He doesn't <u>want</u> to get up.

• a 'that'-clause or a 'to'-infinitive clause

agree	decide	expect	forget	hope
prefer	regret	remember	wish	

> She <u>hoped she wasn't going to cry.</u>
> They are in love and <u>wish to marry.</u>

'Expect' and 'prefer' can also be followed by an object and a 'to'-infinitive.

> I'm sure she <u>doesn't expect you to take</u> the plane.
> The headmaster <u>prefers them to act</u> plays they have written themselves.

4. A speaker's exact words are more often used in stories than in ordinary conversation.

> 'I knew I'd seen you,' I said.
> 'Only one,' replied the Englishman.
> 'Let's go and have a look at the swimming pool,' she suggested.

Practice

A Rewrite the sentences below as orders or requests with a 'to'-infinitive clause, and the words in brackets.

1 'Do you think you could look after the children?' (*David / ask / Mary*)
   David asked Mary to look after the children.

2 'I think you should try to get more sleep.' (*John's doctor / advise / him*)
   ....

3 'You can come round and see us any time.' (*We / invite / our friends*)
   ....

4 'Will you take the money to the bank, please?' (*Jack / tell / me*)
   ....

5 'Don't forget to come half an hour early on Tuesday.' (*Mr Brown / remind / the students*)
   ....

6 'Please write to me every day.' (*Bill / beg / Maria*)
   ....

Now do these with 'not' and a 'to'-infinitive clause.

7 'You shouldn't play with fire.' (*I / warn / the children*)
   ....

8 'I don't think you should go to England in the winter.' (*My grandfather / advise / me*)
   ....

9 'You really ought not to go out alone after dark.' (*They / tell / the visitors*)
   ....

10 'Please don't make an official complaint.' (*The manager / persuade / her*)
   ....

B Now do these sentences with 'ask' and a 'wh'-word clause.

1 'What time does the match start please?' (*I / a policeman*)
   I asked a policeman what time the match started.

2 'Where are you going to spend the holiday?' (*Joe / Mary*)
   ....

3 'Why are the tickets so expensive?' (*Everybody / us*)
   ....

4 'How old are Mary's children?' (*Frank / his wife*)
   ....

5 'Who's going to buy your house?' (*Mrs Jones / her neighbour*)
   ....

6 'When are you planning to come to Darlington?' (*Bill / his friend*)
   ....

7 'What are you going to do next?' (*I / Maria*)
   ....

8 'Where can I get the bus to Liverpool?' (*Peter / a policeman*)
   ....

▸ **Bank**

The passive voice

Main points

You use the passive voice to focus on the person or thing affected by an action.

You form the passive by using a form of 'be' and a past participle.

Only verbs that have an object can have a passive form. With verbs that can have two objects, either object can be the subject of the passive.

1 When you want to talk about the person or thing that performs an action, you use the active voice.

>   *Mr Smith locks the gate at 6 o'clock every night.*
>   *The storm destroyed dozens of trees.*

When you want to focus on the person or thing that is affected by an action, rather than the person or thing that performs the action, you use the passive voice.

>   *The gate is locked at 6 o'clock every night.*
>   *Dozens of trees were destroyed.*

2 The passive is formed with a form of the auxiliary 'be', followed by the past participle of a main verb.

>   *Two new stores were opened this year.*
>   *The room had been cleaned.*

Continuous passive tenses are formed with a form of the auxiliary 'be' followed by 'being' and the past participle of a main verb.

>   *Jobs are still being lost.*
>   *It was being done without his knowledge.*

3 After modals you use the base form 'be' followed by the past participle of a main verb.

>   *What can be done?*
>   *We won't be beaten.*

When you are talking about the past, you use a modal with 'have been' followed by the past participle of a main verb.

>   *He may have been given the car.*
>   *He couldn't have been told by Jimmy.*

4 You form passive infinitives by using 'to be' or 'to have been' followed by the past participle of a main verb.

>   *He wanted to be forgiven.*
>   *The car was reported to have been stolen.*

5 In informal English, 'get' is sometimes used instead of 'be' to form the passive.

>   *Our car gets cleaned every weekend.*
>   *He got killed in a plane crash.*

6 When you use the passive, you often do not mention the person or thing that performs the action at all. This may be because you do not know or do not want to say who it is, or because it does not matter.

>   *Her boyfriend was shot in the chest.*
>   *Your application was rejected.*
>   *Such items should be carefully packed in tea chests.*

7 If you are using the passive and you do want to mention the person or thing that performs the action, you use 'by'.

>   *He had been poisoned by his girlfriend.*
>   *He was brought up by an aunt.*

You use 'with' to talk about something that is used to perform the action.

>   *A circle was drawn in the dirt with a stick.*
>   *He was killed with a knife.*

8 Only verbs that usually have an object can have a passive form. You can say 'people spend money' or 'money is spent'.

>   *An enormous amount of money is spent on beer.*
>   *The food is sold at local markets.*

With verbs which can have two objects, you can form two different passive sentences. For example, you can say 'The secretary was given the key' or 'The key was given to the secretary'.

>   *They were offered a new flat.*
>   *The books will be sent to you.*

▶ See Unit 52 for more information on verbs that can have two objects.

Practice

A These sentences are from a newspaper story about a stolen painting. There are twelve passive verb groups, not counting the one which has been done for you; can you underline them?

1 Two men tried to sell a painting that <u>had been stolen.</u>

2 The painting was owned by Maimi Gillies, aged 84.

3 She said it had been presented to one of her ancestors by the artist.

4 She had owned it since 1926, when it was given to her as a wedding present.

5 One of the men, Mr X, who cannot be named for legal reasons, pleaded guilty.

6 He told police he was willing to sell it cheap because it was stolen.

7 A meeting was arranged at an airfield near Retford, where the money for the painting was to be flown in and exchanged, but the airfield had been staffed by police officers in plain clothes.

8 Mr X took the painting to the airfield and was shown the money in a suitcase.

9 The buyer was then taken to see the painting in a barn.

10 Mr X was arrested but Mr Henry escaped.

B Match the parts.

1 Petrol prices …   a … to be won.

2 This jacket …   b … have been increased.

3 Competition! 5000 prizes … c … has been disconnected.

4 Five people …   d … will be sent to candidates.

5 The telephone …   e … was made in Hong Kong.

6 It appears the phone bill … f … were killed in the rally.

7 Further information …   g … is not permitted anywhere on this station.

8 Before the storm everyone … h … had not been paid.

9 Smoking …   i … is currently being rebuilt.

10 The old town theatre …   j … was told to stay inside their homes.

Now look at these sentences again. Underline the past participle and note the form of the verb 'be'. How many refer to the past and how many to the future?

C These sentences are taken from job adverts. Put the verb in brackets after the modal in the sentences, using the correct passive form of the verb.

1 Application forms should ……be returned…………………………… by 12 December. (*return*)

2 Further particulars may ……………………………………………… from the Senior Tutor. (*obtain*)

3 Only candidates with relevant experience can ………………………………………… . (*consider*)

4 You would ……………………………………… to take part in some sports. (*expect*)

5 This post will ……………………………………… initially for three years. (*fund*)

6 Names of two referees should ………………………………………… . (*give*)

7 Interviews will ……………………………………… in early January. (*hold*)

8 Applications should ……………………………………… on this form only. (*make*)

9 Teachers might ……………………………………… accommodation in college. (*offer*)

▸ **Bank**

159

Introduction to modals

Main points

The modal verbs are: 'can', 'could', 'may', 'might', 'must', 'ought', 'shall', 'should', 'will', and 'would'.

Modals are always the first word in a verb group.

All modals except for 'ought' are followed by the base form of a verb.

'Ought' is followed by a 'to'-infinitive.

Modals have only one form.

Modals can be used for various different purposes. These are explained in Units 80-91.

1 Modals are always the first word in a verb group. All modals except for 'ought' are followed by the base form of a verb.

> I _must leave_ fairly soon.
> I think it _will look_ rather nice.
> Things _might have been_ so different.
> People _may be watching._

2 'Ought' is always followed by a 'to'-infinitive.

> She _ought to go_ straight back to England.
> Sam _ought to have realized_ how dangerous it was.
> You _ought to be doing_ this.

3 Modals have only one form. There is no '-s' form for the third person singular of the present tense, and there are no '-ing' or '-ed' forms.

> There's nothing _I can_ do about it.
> I'm sure _he can_ do it.

4 Modals do not normally indicate the time when something happens. There are, however, a few exceptions.

'Shall' and 'will' often indicate a future event or situation.

> I _shall_ do what you suggested.
> He _will_ not return for many hours.

'Could' is used as the past form of 'can' to express ability. 'Would' is used as the past form of 'will' to express the future.

> When I was young, I _could_ run for miles.
> He remembered that he _would_ see his mother the next day.

5 In spoken English and informal written English, 'shall' and 'will' are shortened to '-'ll', and 'would' to '-'d', and added to a pronoun.

> I'_ll_ see you tomorrow.
> I hope _you'll_ agree.
> Posy said _she'd_ love to stay.

'Shall', 'will', and 'would' are never shortened if they come at the end of a sentence.

> Paul said he would come, and I hope he _will._

In spoken English, you can also add '-'ll' and '-'d' to nouns.

> My _car'll_ be outside.
> The _headmaster'd_ be furious.

⊖ WARNING: Remember that '-d' is also the short form of the auxiliary 'had'.

> I'_d_ heard it many times.

Practice

A Rewrite these sentences using the modals given.

1 Perhaps he fell. (*may have*) (*could have*)
.....*He may have fallen.*.....
.....*He could have fallen.*.....

2 Perhaps they saw us. (*could have*) (*might have*)
....
....

3 Perhaps he said that. I don't remember. (*might have*) (*could have*)
....
....

4 We're lost. I think we've taken the wrong road. (*must have*)
....

5 I wish you had seen it. It was wonderful. (*should have*)
....

6 I ought to have known that would happen. (*should have*)
....

7 Perhaps when I am fifty I won't remember it. (*will have forgotten*)
....

8 It was possible for me to prevent that, but I didn't. (*could have*)
....

9 You should have listened to her the first time. (*ought to have*)
....

B Rewrite these sentences using 'ought to have' or 'should have'.

1 Why didn't you tell the truth? / ..*You ought to have told the truth.*.....
..*You should have told the truth.*.....

2 Why didn't they go by car? / ....

3 Why didn't you telephone? / ....

4 Why didn't you ask John to help? / ....

5 Why didn't you do the shopping? / ....

Now rewrite these with 'ought not to have' or 'shouldn't have'.

6 Why did you run away? / .....*You ought not to have run away.*.....
.*You shouldn't have run away.*.....

7 Why did you spend so much money? / ....

8 Why did it take you so long? / ....

9 Why did they do that? / ....

10 Why did she leave so early? / ....

11 Why did he make so much noise? / ....

12 Why was he so upset? / ....

Introduction to modals 2

Main points

You use negative words with modals to make negative clauses.

Modals go in front of the subject in questions.

You never use two modals together.

1 To make a clause negative, you put a negative word immediately after the modal.

> You <u>must not</u> worry.
> I <u>can never</u> remember his name.
> He <u>ought not</u> to have done that.

'Can not' is always written as one word, 'cannot'.

> I <u>cannot</u> go back.

However, if 'can' is followed by 'not only', 'can' and 'not' are not joined.

> We <u>can not only</u> book your flight for you, but also advise you about hotels.

2 In spoken English and informal written English, 'not' is often shortened to '-n't' and added to the modal. The following modals are often shortened in this way:

could not:	couldn't
should not:	shouldn't
must not:	mustn't
would not:	wouldn't

> We <u>couldn't</u> leave the farm.
> You <u>mustn't</u> talk about Ron like that.

Note the following irregular short forms:

shall not:	shan't
will not:	won't
cannot:	can't

> I <u>shan't</u> let you go.
> <u>Won't</u> you change your mind?
> We <u>can't</u> stop now.

'Might not' and 'ought not' are sometimes shortened to 'mightn't' and 'oughtn't'.

Note that 'may not' is very rarely shortened to 'mayn't' in modern English.

3 To make a question, you put the modal in front of the subject.

> <u>Could you</u> give me an example?
> <u>Will you</u> be coming in later?
> <u>Shall I</u> shut the door?

Modals are also used in question tags.

➤ See Units 7 and 8 for more information.

4 You never use two modals together. For example, you cannot say 'He will can come'. Instead you can say 'He will be able to come'.

> I <u>shall have to</u> go.
> Your husband <u>might have to</u> give up work.

5 Instead of using modals, you can often use other verbs and expressions to make requests, offers, or suggestions, to express wishes or intentions, or to show that you are being polite.

For example, 'be able to' is used instead of 'can', 'be likely to' is used instead of 'might', and 'have to' is used instead of 'must'.

> All members <u>are able to</u> claim expenses.
> I think that we <u>are likely to</u> see more of this.

These expressions are also used after modals.

> I really thought I <u>wouldn't be able to</u> visit you this week.

6 'Dare' and 'need' sometimes behave like modals.

➤ See Unit 72 for information on 'dare' and Units 71 and 90 for information on 'need'.

Practice

A Complete these pairs of sentences appropriately using the modal given in brackets in one sentence, and its negative form in the other sentence.

1 He certainly ....*won't*.......................... understand if you don't explain it.
I ....*will*........................... come round later if I have time. (*will*)

2 Unfortunately many elderly people .... afford telephones.
You .... borrow my pen if you want to. (*can*)

3 When I was young you .... buy them for under a pound.
They complained that they .... sleep. (*could*)

4 If you don't work harder you .... have your job much longer.
This medicine .... cause sleepiness. (*may*)

5 I thought I .... find you here.
It's a long journey. They .... be here before midnight. (*might*)

6 Schools .... teach children the difference between right and wrong.
Whatever you do you .... tell anyone about it. (*must*)

7 I .... get angry in a moment.
That was a moment I .... forget in a hurry. (*shall*)

8 We can't be certain how an unfamiliar word .... be pronounced.
These birds .... be in a cage. (*should*)

9 I .... be back in a few minutes.
If we're lucky perhaps this time it .... rain. (*will*)

10 If you can manage to help me I .... be very grateful.
I invited her even though I knew she .... come. (*would*)

11 You .... to wait too long.
She .... to see the doctor. (*ought*)

B Rewrite the following sentences to form questions beginning with the modals given.

1 I would like to help you. / Can I ....*help you?*...

2 I'd like to speak to Nicky please. / Can I ....

3 It would help if you could give me a few examples. / Could you ....

4 I'd like to have a word with you please. / May I ....

5 I wish she wouldn't be so nasty to me. / Why must she ....

6 I don't know what to give them for dinner. / What shall I ....

7 Would you like me to shut the door? / Shall I ....

8 I don't know where to meet you tonight. / Where should ....

9 I don't know who to see about my teaching programme. / Who should ....

10 Doctor, can I offer you a drink? / Will you ....

11 Please tell her that Adrian phoned. / Would you ....

Possibility

Main points

You use 'can' to say that something is possible.

You use 'could', 'might', and 'may' to indicate that you are not certain whether something is possible, but you think it is.

1 When you want to say that something is possible, you use 'can'.

> Cooking _can_ be a real pleasure.
> In some cases this _can_ cause difficulty.

You use 'cannot' or 'can't' to say that something is not possible.

> This _cannot_ be the answer.
> You _can't_ be serious.

2 When you want to indicate that you are not certain whether something is possible, but you think it is, you use 'could', 'might', or 'may'. There is no important difference in meaning between these modals, but 'may' is slightly more formal.

> That _could_ be one reason.
> He _might_ come.
> They _may_ help us.

You can also use 'might not' or 'may not' in this way.

> He _might not_ be in England at all.
> They _may not_ get a house with central heating.

Note that 'could not' normally refers to ability in the past.

➤ See Unit 83.

3 When there is a possibility that something happened in the past, but you are not certain if it actually happened, you use 'could have', 'may have', or 'might have', followed by a past participle.

> It _could have been_ tomato soup.
> You _may have noticed_ this advertisement.

You can also use 'might not have' or 'may not have' in this way.

> He _might not have seen_ me.
> They _may not have done_ it.

You use 'could not have' when you want to indicate that it is not possible that something happened.

> He didn't have a boat, so he _couldn't have rowed away._
> It _couldn't have been_ wrong.

You also use 'could have' to say that there was a possibility of something happening in the past, but it did not happen.

> It _could have been_ awful. (But it wasn't awful.)
> You _could have got_ a job last year. (But you didn't get a job.)

4 You also use 'might have' or 'could have' followed by a past participle to say that if a particular thing had happened, then there was a possibility of something else happening.

> She said it _might have been_ all right, if the weather had been good.
> (But the weather wasn't good, so it wasn't all right.)
> If I'd been there, I _could have helped_ you. (But I wasn't there, so I couldn't help you.)

5 'Be able to', 'not be able to', and 'be unable to' are sometimes used instead of 'can' and 'cannot', for example after another modal, or when you want to use a 'to'-infinitive, an '-ing' form, or a past participle.

> When _will I be able to_ pick them up?
> He had _been unable to_ get a ticket.

6 You use 'used to be able to' to say that something was possible in the past, but is not possible now.

> Everyone _used to be able to_ have free eye tests.
> You _used to be able to_ buy cigarettes in packs of five.

7 Note that you also use 'could' followed by a negative word and the comparative form of an adjective to emphasize a quality that someone or something has. For example, if you say 'I couldn't be happier', you mean that you are very happy indeed and cannot imagine being happier than you are now.

> You _couldn't_ be _more wrong._
> He _could hardly_ have felt _more ashamed_ of himself.

Practice

A Make suitable sentences from the table below using 'can'.

Learning English Watching television Visiting relatives Winter sports Going to the dentist Meeting new people Travelling	can	sometimes often occasionally	be	exciting. boring. interesting. painful. hard work. dangerous. good fun.

1 ....Travelling can often be boring...
2 ....
3 ....
4 ....
5 ....
6 ....
7 ....

B Rewrite these sentences using 'may' or 'might'. You can use either.

1 Maybe you are right. I can't be sure. / ....You may be right.....................
2 Perhaps George will help if you give him a ring. / ....
3 Possibly it's a mistake. / ....
4 Perhaps things won't be so bad after all. / ....
5 It's possible that she won't recognize you even if she sees you. / ....
6 Perhaps it's broken. / ....

Now put the sentences above into the past using 'may have' or 'might have'.

C You hear a strange noise at night. What do you think it 'could be?' Write sentences using these ideas.

1 ...a burglar? / ....It could be a burglar...
2 ...a wild animal? / ....
3 ...one of the neighbours? / ....
4 ...the wind in the trees? / ....
5 ...a car passing? / ....
6 ...someone snoring? / ....
7 ...someone at the door? / ....
8 ...a ghost? / ....

Now imagine that you heard the noise last night. Rewrite the sentences using 'could have been'.

D Complete these sentences using either 'may not' or 'can't'.

1 There ....may not........................... be anybody there when you arrive.
2 That .... be true! It's absolutely impossible.
3 I don't know if she will agree. She .... want to.
4 You .... be serious. You've got to be joking.
5 It may very well happen, but on the other hand it ....
6 It .... be done. It's quite out of the question.

▸ **Bank**

Probability and certainty

Main points

You use 'must', 'ought', 'should', or 'will' to express probability or certainty.

You use 'cannot' or 'can't' as the negative of 'must', rather than 'must not' or 'mustn't', to say that something is not probable or is not certain.

1 When you want to say that something is probably true or that it will probably happen, you use 'should' or 'ought'. 'Should' is followed by the base form of a verb. 'Ought' is followed by a 'to'-infinitive.

> We *should* arrive by dinner time.
> She *ought* to know.

When you want to say that you think something is probably not true or that it will probably not happen, you use 'should not' or 'ought not'.

> There *shouldn't* be any problem.
> That *ought not* to be too difficult.

2 When you want to say that you are fairly sure that something has happened, you use 'should have' or 'ought to have', followed by a past participle.

> You *should have* heard by now that I'm leaving.
> They *ought to have* arrived yesterday.

When you want to say that you do not think that something has happened, you use 'should not have' or 'ought not to have', followed by a past participle.

> You *shouldn't have* had any difficulty in getting there.
> This *ought not to have* been a problem.

3 You also use 'should have' or 'ought to have' to say that you expected something to happen, but that it did not happen.

> Yesterday *should have been* the start of the soccer season.
> She *ought to have been* home by now.

Note that you do not normally use the negative forms with this meaning.

4 When you are fairly sure that something is the case, you use 'must'.

> Oh, you *must* be Sylvia's husband.
> He *must* know something about it.

If you are fairly sure that something is not the case, you use 'cannot' or 'can't'.

> This *cannot* be the whole story.
> He *can't* be very old – he's about 25, isn't he?

⊖ WARNING: You do not use 'must not' or 'mustn't' with this meaning.

5 When you want to say that you are almost certain that something has happened, you use 'must have', followed by a past participle.

> This article *must have been* written by a woman.
> We *must have taken* the wrong road.

To say that you do not think that something has happened, you use 'can't have', followed by a past participle.

> You *can't have forgotten* me.
> He *can't have said* that.

6 You use 'will' or '-'ll' to say that something is certain to happen in the future.

> People *will* always say the things you want to hear.
> They'*ll* manage.

You use 'will not' or 'won't' to say that something is certain not to happen.

> You *won't* get much sympathy from them.

7 There are several ways of talking about probability and certainty without using modals. For example, you can use:

• 'bound to' followed by the base form of a verb

> It was *bound to* happen.
> You're *bound to* make a mistake.

• an adjective such as 'certain', 'likely', 'sure', or 'unlikely', followed by a 'to'-infinitive clause or a 'that'-clause

> They were *certain* that you were defeated.
> I am not *likely* to forget it.

▶ See Unit 33 for more information on these adjectives.

Practice

A Use 'should' or 'ought to' with one of these verbs and an appropriate ending to comment on each of the sentences below.

have   get   win   be (x3)   do

| a comfortable trip | easily | a nice day | some peace and quiet |
| fun | really interesting | very well | |

1 We are going to Japan for a holiday this summer. / It ....*should be really interesting.*.....

2 Bill's asked me to his birthday party. / That ....*ought to be fun.*.....

3 There's a good match on this weekend. / Yes, our team ....

4 We couldn't get standard tickets so we're travelling first class. / Well, at least you ....

5 The weather forecast for tomorrow is excellent. / Yes, it ....

6 Jan has just opened a new shop in the High Street. / I know. It ....

7 Our hotel is right out in the country. / That's good. You ....

B Write comments with 'must' or 'can't' after the following sentences.

1 You haven't eaten for a *whole day?* / (*you / hungry*) ....*You must be hungry.*...............

2 But you've just eaten your dinner! / (*you / hungry*) ....*You can't be hungry.*...............

3 They've been travelling all night? / (*they / tired out*) ....

4 It's only six o'clock. / (*you / tired*) ....

5 She doesn't look at all like Mary. / (*she / her sister*) ....

6 He looks just like you! / (*he / your brother*) ....

7 I saw him going in. / (*he / at home*) ....

8 I saw him going out. / (*he / at home*) ....

9 She looks so young. / (*she / your grandmother*) ....

10 She looks like his mother, but older. / (*she / his grandmother*) ....

C Rewrite the parts in bold using 'must have'.

1 He drove all the way from Glasgow. **Obviously it was a long journey.**
   It must have been a long journey...

2 He pretended to be innocent, but **I'm sure he did it.**
   ....

3 George was standing very close to you. **Of course you saw him.**
   ....

4 You look very well. **It seems you enjoyed your holiday.**
   ....

5 There's nobody in. **Probably they've gone shopping.**
   ....

6 My coat isn't there. **Perhaps someone has taken it by mistake.**
   ....

▸ **Bank**

Ability

Main points

You use 'can' to talk about ability in the present and in the future.

You use 'could' to talk about ability in the past.

You use 'be able to' to talk about ability in the present, future, and past.

1 You use 'can' to say that someone has the ability to do something.

> *You can all read and write.*
> *Anybody can become a qualified teacher.*

You use 'cannot' or 'can't' to say that they do not have the ability to do something.

> *He cannot dance.*

2 When you want to talk about someone's ability in the past as a result of a skill they had or did not have, you use 'could', 'could not', or 'couldn't'.

> *He could run faster than anyone else.*
> *A lot of them couldn't read or write.*

3 You also use 'be able to', 'not be able to', and 'be unable to' to talk about someone's ability to do something, but 'can' and 'could' are more common.

> *She was able to tie her own shoelaces.*
> *They are not able to run very fast.*
> *Many people were unable to read or write.*

4 You use 'was able to' and 'were able to' to say that someone managed to do something in a particular situation in the past.

> *After treatment he was able to return to work.*
> *The farmers were able to pay the new wages.*
> *We were able to find time to discuss it.*

⊖ WARNING: You do not normally use 'could' to say that someone managed to do something in a particular situation. However, you can use 'could not' or 'couldn't' to say that someone did not manage to do something in a particular situation.

> *We couldn't stop laughing.*
> *I just couldn't think of anything to say.*

5 When you want to say that someone had the ability to do something in the past, but did not do it, you use 'could have' followed by a past participle.

> *You could have given it all to me.*
> *You know, she could have done French.*

You often use this form when you want to express disapproval about something that was not done.

> *You could have been a little bit tidier.*
> *You could have told me!*

6 You use 'could not have' or 'couldn't have' followed by a past participle to say that it is not possible that someone had the ability to do something.

> *I couldn't have gone with you, because I was in London at the time.*
> *She couldn't have taken the car, because Jim was using it.*

7 In most cases, you can choose to use 'can' or 'be able to'. However, you sometimes have to use 'be able to'. You have to use 'be able to' if you are using another modal, or if you want to use an '-ing' form, a past participle, or a 'to'-infinitive.

> *Nobody else will be able to read it.*
> *…the satisfaction of being able to do the job.*
> *I don't think I'd have been able to get an answer.*
> *You're foolish to expect to be able to do that.*

8 You also use 'can' or 'could' with verbs such as 'see', 'hear', and 'smell' to say that someone is or was aware of something through one of their senses.

> *I can smell gas.*
> *I can't see her.*
> *I could see a few stars in the sky.*
> *There was such a noise we couldn't hear.*

Practice

A Which of these things 'can' you do? Which 'can't' you do? Write three true sentences like this:

......I can play chess, but my sister can't...

And three like this:

......My sister can't play chess, but I can...

count to twenty in Spanish	swim	ride a bike	drive a car
understand sign language	swim like a fish	ride a horse	sail a boat
use a word processor	play chess	run a marathon	ski

....

....

....

....

....

....

Now write down five questions about the things above to ask someone else.

......Can you play chess really well?...

....

....

....

....

....

B How many of the things above 'could' you do when you were ten years old? Write down three things you 'could' do and three things you 'couldn't' do.

....

....

....

....

....

....

Now write down three questions to ask someone else.

......When you were ten, could you ride a bike?..

....

....

....

C Complete these sentences using 'can', 'can't', 'could', or 'couldn't'.

1 There was a woman with a big hat right in front of me. I ....*couldn't*.................... see a thing.

2 I'm sorry, you're in my light. I .... see what I'm doing.

3 It was a huge hall and we were at the back, so we .... hear very well.

4 When she screams, you .... hear her all over the house.

5 She was phoning all the way from Singapore, but I .... hear her very clearly.

6 .... you hear me at the back?

7 Put your hands up if you .... hear me.

▶ **Bank**

169

Permission

Main points

You use 'can' or 'be allowed to' to talk about whether someone has permission to do something or not.

You usually use 'can' to give someone permission to do something.

You usually use 'can' or 'could' to ask for permission to do something.

1 You use 'can' to say that someone is allowed to do something. You use 'cannot' or 'can't' to say that they are not allowed to do it.

> Students <u>can</u> take a year away from university.
> Children <u>cannot</u> bathe except in the presence of two lifesavers.

You use 'could' to say that someone was allowed to do something in the past. You use 'could not' or 'couldn't' to say that they were not allowed to do it.

> We <u>could</u> go to any part of the island we wanted.
> Both students and staff <u>could</u> use the swimming pool.
> We <u>couldn't</u> go into the library after 5 pm.

2 You also use 'be allowed to' when you are talking about permission, but not when you are asking for it or giving it.

> When Mr Wilt asks for a solicitor he will <u>be allowed to</u> see one.
> It was only after several months that I <u>was allowed to</u> visit her.
> You<u>'re</u> not <u>allowed to</u> use calculators in exams.

3 In more formal situations, 'may' is used to say that someone is allowed to do something, and 'may not' is used to say that they are not allowed to do it.

> They <u>may</u> do exactly as they like.
> The retailer <u>may not</u> sell that book below the publisher's price.

4 When you want to give someone permission to do something, you use 'can'.

> You <u>can</u> borrow that pen if you want to.
> You <u>can</u> go off duty now.
> She <u>can</u> go with you.

'May' is also used to give permission, but this is more formal.

> You <u>may</u> speak.
> You <u>may</u> leave as soon as you have finished.

5 When you want to refuse someone permission to do something, you use 'cannot', 'can't', 'will not', 'won't', 'shall not', or 'shan't'.

> 'Can I have some sweets?' – 'No, you <u>can't</u>!'
> 'I'll just go upstairs.' – 'You <u>will not</u>!'
> You <u>shan't</u> leave without my permission.

6 When you are asking for permission to do something, you use 'can' or 'could'. If you ask in a very simple and direct way, you use 'can'.

> <u>Can</u> I ask a question?
> <u>Can</u> we have something to wipe our hands on please?

'Could' is more polite than 'can'.

> <u>Could</u> I just interrupt a minute?
> <u>Could</u> we put this fire on?

'May' is also used to ask permission, but this is more formal.

> <u>May</u> I have a cigarette?

'Might' is rather old-fashioned and is not often used in modern English in this way.

> <u>Might</u> I inquire if you are the owner?

7 You have to use 'be allowed to' instead of a modal if you are using another modal, or if you want to use an '-ing' form, a past participle, or a 'to'-infinitive.

> Teachers <u>will be allowed to</u> decide for themselves.
> I am strongly in favour of people <u>being allowed to</u> put on plays.
> They have not <u>been allowed to</u> come.
> We were going <u>to be allowed to</u> travel on the trains.

Practice

A **All of these sentences can be used to ask for permission. Rewrite each one using 'can'.**

1 Do you mind if I open this window just a little? / ..*Can I open this window just a little?*..........

2 I'd like to ask you just one more question. / ....

3 Is it all right if I give you a ring some time later? / ....

4 Is it okay if we go swimming? / ....

5 Do you mind if I sit down? / ....

6 I'd like an ice-cream please. / ....

7 Do you think I could go home now? / ....

8 I wonder if I could come back later. / ....

Make the requests more formal by changing 'can' to 'may'.
Then make them more polite by changing 'can' to 'could'.

B **Rewrite these sentences asking for permission, starting with the phrases given.**

1 I'd like to have a little more time. / I wonder if ....*I could have a little more time.*....................

2 Can I start now? / Do you think ....

3 Can I listen to the radio while you're working? / Do you mind if ....

4 May I come in now? / Is it all right if ....

5 I'd like to speak next. / Do you think ....

C **Rewrite these sentences giving permission, starting with the words given.**

1 You're allowed to do whatever you want. / You can ......*do whatever you want.*.................

2 It's all right to have visitors after three o'clock. / You're allowed to ....

3 You may all go home as soon as you've finished work. / You can all ....

4 I don't mind you coming back late as long as you don't make too much noise. / You can ....
....

5 With this banker's card you can cash a cheque for up to £250. / With this card you are allowed to
....

6 I'll let you use my pen until I need it myself. / You can ....

D **Read this passage and complete the sentences below.**

In Britain you are not allowed to leave school or to get married until you are at least sixteen years old.
You cannot drive a car until you are seventeen, and you cannot drive a taxi until you are twenty-one. You
are allowed to vote at the age of eighteen.

1 When you are sixteen you can ..*leave school*..... and you can also .... , but you
are not allowed to .... until you are eighteen.

2 You are allowed to .... when you are seventeen, but you can't ....
until you are twenty-one.

3 You can .... at the age of seventeen and you can
.... at the age of eighteen.

4 It seems silly that you are allowed to .... when you are only
sixteen, but you're not allowed to .... until you are
seventeen.

5 I think you should be allowed to .... a year earlier, when you are seventeen.

6 If you can .... at the age of seventeen I don't see why you
shouldn't be allowed to ....

Instructions and requests

Main points

You use 'Could you' to tell someone politely to do something.

Imperatives are not very polite.

You also use 'Could you' to ask someone politely for help.

You use 'I would like', 'Would you mind', 'Do you think you could', and 'I wonder if you could' to make requests.

1 When you want to tell someone to do something, you can use 'Could you', 'Will you', and 'Would you'. 'Could you' is very polite.

> _Could you_ make out her bill, please?
> _Could you_ just switch on the light behind you?

'Will you' and 'Would you' are normally used by people in authority. 'Would you' is more polite than 'Will you'.

> _Would you_ tell her that Adrian phoned?
> _Will you_ please leave the room?

Note that although these sentences look like questions ('Will you', not 'You will'), they are not really questions.

2 If someone in authority wants to tell someone to do something, they sometimes say 'I would like you to do this' or 'I'd like you to do this'.

> Penelope, I _would like_ you to get us the files.
> I _'d like_ you to finish this work by Thursday.

3 You can use an imperative to tell someone to do something, but this is not very polite.

> _Stop_ her.
> _Go_ away, all of you.

However, imperatives are commonly used when talking to people you know very well.

> _Come_ here, love.
> _Sit down_ and let me get you a drink.

You often use imperatives in situations of danger or urgency.

> _Look out!_ There's a car coming.
> _Put_ it _away_ before Mum sees you.

4 When you want to ask someone to help you, you use 'Could you', 'Would you', 'Can you', or 'Will you'. 'Could you' and 'Would you' are used in formal situations, or when you want to be very polite, for example because you are asking for something that requires a lot of effort. 'Could you' is more polite than 'Would you'.

> _Could you_ show me how to do this?
> _Would you_ do me a favour?

'Will you' and 'Can you' are used in informal situations, especially when you are not asking for something that requires a lot of effort.

> _Will you_ post this for me on your way to work?
> _Can you_ make me a copy of that?

5 You also use 'I would like' or 'I'd like', followed by a 'to'-infinitive or a noun group, to make a request.

> _I would like_ to ask you one question.
> _I'd like_ steak and chips, please.

6 You can also make a request by using:

• 'Would you mind', followed by an '-ing' form

> _Would you mind_ doing the washing up?
> _Would you mind_ waiting a moment?

• 'Do you think you could', followed by the base form of a verb

> _Do you think you could_ help me?

• 'I wonder if you could', followed by the base form of a verb

> _I wonder if you could_ look after my cat for me while I'm away?

Practice

A **Make six requests from this table, using 'could I', 'may I', and 'could you'.**

Could I May I Could you let me	have	another cup of coffee a look at your newspaper something to eat one of those biscuits a bit of advice a little more time	please?

1 .... May I have something to eat, please? ....
2 ....
3 ....
4 ....
5 ....
6 ....

Rewrite two of your requests beginning with 'could you give me'.

....
....

B **Make these requests more polite by starting them with 'would you mind'.**

1 Could you come back later, please? / Would you mind coming back later please? ....
2 Will you help this lady with her bags? / ....
3 Can you pay cash, please? / ....
4 Would you tell them that I called? / ....
5 Can you close the door behind you, please? / ....
6 Do you think you could do the shopping on your way home? / ....
7 I wonder if you could help me, please? / ....
8 Will you do the cooking tonight? / ....
9 Can you come ten minutes before the meeting starts? / ....
10 Could you tell me when you're ready? / ....

C **Turn these instructions into polite requests by starting with the words given.**

1 I can't hear very well. Speak up. / I can't hear very well. Do you think ... you could speak up? ....
2 Give Joan a message. / I wonder if ....
3 Give me your full name. / Would you mind ....
4 Repeat that. / Do you think ....
5 Stand up. / I wonder if ....
6 Hold this for me. / Would you mind ....
7 Open the door. / Do you think ....
8 Do it again. / Would you mind ....
9 All of you sit down quietly. / I wonder if ....
10 Give me a little more time. / Do you think ....

Suggestions

Main points

You use 'could', 'couldn't', or 'shall' to make a suggestion.

You use 'Shall we' to suggest doing something with someone.

You use 'You might like' or 'You might want' to make polite suggestions.

You use 'may as well' or 'might as well' to suggest a sensible action.

You use 'What about', 'Let's', 'Why don't', and 'Why not' to make suggestions.

1 You use 'could' to suggest doing something.

> You *could* phone her.
> She *could* go into research.
> We *could* go on Friday.

You also use 'couldn't' in a question to suggest doing something.

> *Couldn't* you just build some more factories?
> *Couldn't* we do it at the weekend?

2 You use 'Shall we' to suggest doing something with somebody else.

> *Shall we* go and see a film?
> *Shall we* talk about something different now?

You use 'Shall I' to suggest doing something yourself.

> *Shall I* contact the Chairman?

3 You use 'You might', followed by a verb meaning 'like' or 'want', to make a suggestion in a very polite way.

> I thought perhaps *you might like* to come along with me.
> *You might want* to try another shop.

You can also do this using 'It might be', followed by a noun group or an adjective, and a 'to'-infinitive.

> I think *it might be a good idea* to stop recording now.
> *It might be wise* to get a new car.

4 You use 'may as well' or 'might as well' to suggest doing something, but only because it seems the sensible thing to do, or because there is no reason not to do it.

> You *may as well* open them all.
> He *might as well* take the car.

5 You can also make a suggestion by using:

- 'What about' or 'How about' followed by an '-ing' form

> *What about going* to Judy's?
> *How about using* my car?

- 'Let's' followed by the base form of a verb

> *Let's go* outside.

- 'Why don't I', 'Why don't you' or 'Why don't we' followed by the base form of a verb

> *Why don't I pick* you *up* at seven?
> *Why don't you write* to her yourself?
> *Why don't we just give* them what they want?

- 'Why not' followed by the base form of a verb

> *Why not bring* him along?
> *Why not try* both?

Why not try both?

Practice

A Rewrite these suggestions to make them more direct.

1 Most people try to get there a bit earlier. / Couldn't you ....*try to get there a bit earlier?*............

2 I always use a word processor. / You should ....

3 My mother borrowed the money from the bank. / Couldn't you ....

4 My father always gets the information from the local library. / You could ....

5 A lot of people take a later train. / Why not ....

B Rewrite these suggestions starting with the words given.

1 Let's go to the theatre. / How about ....*going to the theatre?*................................

2 We should get started as soon as possible. / It might be a good idea ....

3 You could write and ask her yourself. / You might like to ....

4 Why don't we take a winter holiday for a change? / What about ....

5 Couldn't you just pay at the end of the month? / You could ....

6 We could take a week off in July. / Let's ....

7 You could ask Bill to help. / What ....

8 Why don't you ring and tell them you're coming? / You ....

9 We could borrow the equipment from Peter. / Couldn't ....

10 Why don't we keep quiet about that? / It might ....

C Join the parts to make sentences and then fit the suggestions to the pictures.

1 Shall we call …   a … something to eat.
2 Why don't you send her …   b … eat out tonight.
3 Perhaps you could give him …   c … a taxi?
4 Shall we ask her to …   d … before they get back?
5 Do you think we could mend it …   e … back to the shop.
6 I suppose we could …   f … a get-well card.
7 Couldn't you give him …   g … a bone?
8 You could always take it …   h … take it off?

▸ **Bank**

Offers and invitations

Main points

You use 'Would you like' to offer something to someone or to invite them to do something.

You use 'Can I', 'Could I', and 'Shall I' when you offer to help someone.

1 When you are offering something to someone, or inviting them to do something, you use 'Would you like'.

> _Would you like_ a drink?
> _Would you like_ to come for a meal?

You can use 'Will you' to offer something to someone you know quite well, or to give an invitation in a fairly informal way.

> _Will you_ have another biscuit, Dave?
> _Will you_ come to my party on Saturday?

2 You use 'Can I' or 'Could I' when you are offering to do something for someone. 'Could I' is more polite.

> _Can I_ help you with the dishes?
> _Could I_ help you carry those bags?

You also use 'Shall I' when you are offering to do something, especially if you are fairly sure that your offer will be accepted.

> _Shall I_ shut the door?
> _Shall I_ spell that for you?

3 You use 'I can' or 'I could' to make an offer when you want to say that you are able to help someone.

> _I have a car. I can_ take Daisy to the station.
> _I could_ pay some of the rent.

4 You also use 'I'll' to offer to do something.

> _I'll_ give them a ring if you like.
> _I'll_ show you the hotel.

5 You use 'You must' if you want to invite someone very persuasively to do something.

> _You must_ come round for a meal some time.
> _You must_ come and visit me.

6 There are other ways of making offers and giving invitations without using modals. For example, you can use 'Let me' when offering to help someone.

> _Let me_ take you to your room.
> _Let me_ drive you to London.

You can make an offer or give an invitation in a more informal way by using an imperative sentence, when it is clear that you are not giving an order.

> _Have_ a cigar.
> _Come_ to my place.

You can add emphasis by putting 'do' in front of the verb.

> _Do have_ a chocolate biscuit.
> _Do help_ yourselves.

You can also give an invitation by using 'Why don't you' or 'How about'.

> _Why don't you_ come to lunch tomorrow?
> _How about_ coming with us to the party?

Practice

A Join the part sentences below to make offers to fit the situations in the pictures.

1 Would you like me to open…   a …you with the cooking?
2 Let me carry…   b …the children for you.
3 Can I help…   c …the door for you?
4 Shall I post…   d …those bags for you.
5 Could I give you…   e …these letters for you?
6 I'll look after…   f …a lift?
7 Can I telephone…   g …those parcels for you.
8 I can hold…   h …for a taxi?

B Make these invitations very welcoming by starting with 'you must'.

1 Can you come to our party next week? / You must come to our party next week.
2 Would you like to come round for a game of chess some time? / ....
3 Why don't you bring your wife with you next time? / ....
4 I'd like you to meet my brother next time he's here. / ....
5 Do have another cup of coffee. / ....
6 Can't you stay a little longer? / ....
7 Would you like to see my holiday photographs? / ....
8 Why don't you come to the theatre with me some time next week? / ....
9 Will you stay for lunch? / ....
10 Would you like another piece of cake? / ....

C Match the sentences with the offers.

1 You look thirsty.   a I'll get lunch.
2 It's hot in here.   b I can give you a lift.
3 I've got plenty of time.   c Let me give you a bit more.
4 It's a long way to town.   d I'll turn it down.
5 The radio's a bit noisy.   e I could turn it up a bit.
6 Can't you hear the record player?   f We could go to the cinema.
7 There's plenty to eat.   g Perhaps I can get you something to drink.
8 I've got nothing to do this evening.   h Shall I open the window?

Wants and wishes

Main points

You use 'would like' to say what you want.

You use 'wouldn't like' to say what you do not want.

You use 'would rather' or 'would sooner' to say what you prefer.

You also use 'wouldn't mind' to say what you want.

1 You can say what someone wants by using 'would like' followed by a 'to'-infinitive or a noun group.

> I _would like_ to know the date of the next meeting.
> John _would like_ his book back.

When the subject is a pronoun, you often use the short form '-'d' instead of 'would'.

> I_'d like_ more information about the work you do.
> We_'d like_ seats in the non-smoking section, please.

In spoken English, you can also use the short form '-'d' instead of 'would' when the subject is a noun.

> Sally_'d like_ to go to the circus.

2 You can say what someone does not want by using 'would not like' or 'wouldn't like'.

> I _would not like_ to see it.
> They _wouldn't like_ that.

3 You use 'would like' followed by 'to have' and a past participle to say that someone wishes now that something had happened in the past, but that it did not happen.

> I _would like to have felt_ more relaxed.
> She_'d like to have heard_ me first.

You use 'would have liked', followed by a 'to'-infinitive or a noun group, to say that someone wanted something to happen, but it did not happen.

> Perhaps he _would have liked_ to be a teacher.
> I _would have liked_ more ice cream.

Note the difference. 'Would like to have' refers to present wishes about past events. 'Would have liked' refers to past wishes about past events.

4 You can also use 'would hate', 'would love', or 'would prefer', followed by a 'to'-infinitive or a noun group.

> I _would hate_ to move to another house now.
> I _would prefer_ a cup of coffee.

Note that 'would enjoy' is followed by a noun group or an '-ing' form, not by a 'to'-infinitive.

> I _would enjoy a bath_ before we go.
> I _would enjoy seeing_ him again.

5 You can use 'would rather' or 'would sooner' followed by the base form of a verb to say that someone prefers one situation to another.

> He_'d rather_ be playing golf.
> I_'d sooner_ walk than take the bus.

6 You use 'I wouldn't mind', followed by an '-ing' form or a noun group, to say that you would like to do or have something.

> I _wouldn't mind_ being the manager of a store.
> I _wouldn't mind_ a cup of tea.

Practice

A Form a question using 'would you like' and the first of the phrases given below. Then form an answer using 'I'd like' or 'I'd rather' and the second of the phrases given below.

1 have another drink / get home early
  Would you like to have another drink? No thanks, *I'd rather get home early.*

2 to go with me / go alone
  ....

3 start now / wait a few minutes
  ....

4 go shopping this morning / go this afternoon
  ....

5 pay cash / pay by cheque.
  ....

Change three sentences with 'I'd rather' to 'I'd sooner'.
  I'd sooner get home early.
  ....
  ....
  ....

B Rewrite these sentences using 'would like'.

1 I wish I lived in the country. / I would like ...... *to live in the country.* ....
2 I wish I could find a better job. / I would like ....
3 I bet she wishes she could start all over again. / I bet she'd like ....
4 I suppose you wish you saw them more often. / I suppose you'd like ....
5 They all wish they understood more about it. / They'd all like ....
6 My wife often wishes we had a bigger garden. / My wife would like ....

C Rewrite these sentences using 'wouldn't mind'.

1 I'd quite like to live in London. / I wouldn't mind .... *living in London.* ....
2 She said she'd quite like to learn English. / She said she wouldn't mind ....
3 Bill agreed that he would quite like to be chairman. / Bill agreed he wouldn't mind ....
  ....
4 We all agreed we'd quite like to go back to work. / We all agreed we wouldn't mind ....
  ....
5 I'd quite like to go into politics. / I wouldn't mind ....
6 We'd quite like to catch an early train. / We wouldn't mind ....

▸ **Bank**

Obligation and necessity 1

Main points

You use 'have to', 'must', and 'mustn't' to talk about obligation and necessity in the present and future.

You use 'had to' to talk about obligation and necessity in the past.

You use the auxiliary 'do' with 'have to' to make questions.

You use 'have got to' in informal English.

1 When you want to say that someone has an obligation to do something, or that it is necessary for them to do it, you use 'must' or 'have to'.

> You _must_ come to the meeting tomorrow.
> The plants _must_ have plenty of sunshine.
> I enjoy parties, unless I _have to_ make a speech.
> He _has to_ travel to find work.

2 There is sometimes a difference between 'must' and 'have to'. When you are stating your own opinion that something is an obligation or a necessity, you normally use 'must'.

> I _must_ be very careful not to upset him.
> We _must_ eat before we go.
> He _must_ stop working so hard.

When you are giving information about what someone else considers to be an obligation or a necessity, you normally use 'have to'.

> They _have to_ pay the bill by Thursday.
> She _has to_ go now.

Note that you normally use 'have to' for things that happen repeatedly, especially with adverbs of frequency such as 'often', 'always', and 'regularly'.

> I always _have to_ do the shopping.
> You often _have to_ wait a long time for a bus.

3 You use 'must not' or 'mustn't' to say that it is important that something is not done or does not happen.

> You _must not_ talk about politics.
> They _mustn't_ find out that I came here.

Note that 'must not' does not mean the same as 'not have to'. If you 'must not' do something, it is important that you do not do it.

If you 'do not have to' do something, it is not necessary for you to do it, but you can do it if you want.

⊖ WARNING: You only use 'must' for obligation and necessity in the present and the future. When you want to talk about obligation and necessity in the past, you use 'had to' rather than 'must'.

> She _had to_ catch the six o'clock train.
> I _had to_ wear a suit.

4 You use 'do', 'does', or 'did' when you want to make a question using 'have to' and 'not have to'.

> How often _do_ you _have to_ buy petrol for the car?
> _Does_ he _have to_ take so long to get ready?
> What _did_ you _have to_ do?
> _Don't_ you _have to_ be there at one o'clock?

⊖ WARNING: You do not normally form questions like these by putting a form of 'have' before the subject. For example, you do not normally say 'How often have you to buy petrol?'

5 In informal English, you can use 'have got to' instead of 'have to'.

> You've just _got to_ make sure you tell him.
> She's _got to_ see the doctor.
> _Have_ you _got to_ go so soon?

⊖ WARNING: You normally use 'had to', not 'had got to', for the past.

> He _had to_ know.
> I _had to_ lend him some money.

6 You can only use 'have to', not 'must', if you are using another modal, or if you want to use an '-ing' form, a past participle, or a 'to'-infinitive.

> They _may have to_ be paid by cheque.
> She grumbled a lot about _having to_ stay abroad.
> I would have _had to_ go through London.
> He doesn't like _to have to_ do the same job every day.

Practice

A List the things you have to do if you join the army, using 'have to'.

1 ......You have to keep your hair short..
2 ....
3 ....
4 ....
5 ....
6 ....
7 ....
8 ....

B Sally is feeling very ill. What advice does her doctor give her? Write sentences using 'You must' or 'You mustn't', using the prompts given.

1 You .... / (medicine/before every meal)
2 You .... / (bed/not get out)
4 You .... / (sleep/plenty)
5 You .... / (food/not eat)
6 You .... / (lots of water)

C Match these clauses with the 'have got to' clauses.

1 It's getting late…   a … so I'm afraid we've got to walk.
2 You broke the window…   b … so I've got to start all over again.
3 The car has broken down…   c … so we've got to look after ourselves.
4 Mother is away…   d … so you've got to pay for it.
5 I've got it all wrong…   e … so we've got to go.

Obligation and necessity 2

Main points

You use 'need to' to talk about necessity.

You use 'don't have to', 'don't need to', 'haven't got to', or 'needn't' to say that it is not necessary to do something.

You use 'needn't' to give someone permission not to do something.

You use 'need not have', 'needn't have', 'didn't need to', or 'didn't have to' to say that it was not necessary to do something in the past.

1 You can use 'need to' to talk about the necessity of doing something.

> You might <u>need to</u> see a doctor.
> A number of questions <u>need to</u> be asked.

2 You use 'don't have to' when there is no obligation or necessity to do something.

> Many women <u>don't have to</u> work.
> You <u>don't have to</u> learn any new typing skills.

You can also use 'don't need to', 'haven't got to', or 'needn't' to say that there is no obligation or necessity to do something.

> You <u>don't need to</u> buy anything.
> I <u>haven't got to</u> go to work today.
> I can pick John up. You <u>needn't</u> bother.

3 You also use 'needn't' when you are giving someone permission not to do something.

> You <u>needn't</u> say anything if you don't want to.
> You <u>needn't</u> stay any longer tonight.

4 You use 'need not have' or 'needn't have' and a past participle to say that someone did something which was not necessary. You are often implying that the person did not know at the time that their action was not necessary.

> I <u>needn't have</u> waited until the game began.
> Nell <u>needn't have</u> worked.
> They <u>needn't have</u> worried about Reagan.

5 You use 'didn't need to' to say that something was not necessary, and that it was known at the time that the action was not necessary. You do not know if the action was done, unless you are given more information.

> They <u>didn't need</u> to talk about it.
> I <u>didn't need</u> to worry.

6 You also use 'didn't have to' to say that it was not necessary to do something.

> He <u>didn't have to</u> speak.
> Bill and I <u>didn't have to</u> pay.

7 You cannot use 'must' to refer to the past, so when you want to say that it was important that something did not happen or was not done, you use other expressions.

You can say 'It was important not to', or use phrases like 'had to make sure' or 'had to make certain' in a negative sentence.

> It was <u>necessary</u> that no one was aware of being watched.
> You <u>had to make sure</u> that you didn't spend too much.
> We <u>had to</u> do our best to <u>make certain</u> that it wasn't out of date.

It was <u>important</u> not to take the game too seriously.

Practice

A Bill has just left the army. List five things he 'doesn't need to' do any more.

1 ...He doesn't need to wear a uniform...
2 ....
3 ....
4 ....
5 ....

See the pictures at Unit 89 if you need more ideas.

B Sally is better now. List four things she 'doesn't have to' do now.

1 ..She doesn't have to stay in bed..
2 ....
3 ....
4 ....

See Unit 89 for more ideas.

C Match the sentences and comments.

1 My trousers are creased.   a I need to get it mended.
2 My computer's broken.   b I need to get it painted.
3 My torch won't work.   c I need to take a taxi.
4 The house looks awful.   d I need to get it cut.
5 My hair is too long.   e I need to get a new battery.
6 My car has broken down.   f I need to get them pressed.

D Add comments to these sentences, using 'needn't have'.

1 The letter was so untidy, I wrote it out again
...Really? You needn't have written it out again...........................

2 He was so worried about being late that he sent the letter by fax.
....

3 She was so worried about not getting a seat that she bought a first-class ticket.
....

4 We weren't sure about sheets and towels, so we brought our own.
....

5 The old people thought the room was dirty, so they cleaned it out themselves.
....

6 I didn't know you were coming home, so I cooked my own supper.
....

Now rewrite the comments using 'didn't need to'.

1 ....You didn't need to write it out again..............................
2 ....
3 ....
4 ....
5 ....
6 ....

Mild obligation and advice

Main points

You use 'should' and 'ought' to talk about mild obligation.

You use 'should have' and 'ought to have' to say that there was a mild obligation to do something in the past, but it was not done.

You can also use 'had better' to talk about mild obligation.

1 You can use 'should' and 'ought' to talk about a mild obligation to do something. When you use 'should' and 'ought', you are saying that the feeling of obligation is not as strong as when you use 'must'.

'Should' and 'ought' are very common in spoken English.

'Should' is followed by the base form of a verb, but 'ought' is followed by a 'to'-infinitive.

When you want to say that there is a mild obligation not to do something, you use 'should not', 'shouldn't', 'ought not', or 'oughtn't'.

2 You use 'should' and 'ought' in three main ways:

• when you are talking about what is a good thing to do, or the right thing to do.

    We <u>should</u> send her a postcard.
    We <u>shouldn't</u> spend all the money.
    He <u>ought</u> to come more often.
    You <u>ought not</u> to see him again.

• when you are trying to advise someone about what to do or what not to do.

    You <u>should</u> claim your pension 3-4 months before you retire.
    You <u>shouldn't</u> use a detergent.
    You <u>ought</u> to get a new TV.
    You <u>oughtn't</u> to marry him.

• when you are giving or asking for an opinion about a situation. You often use 'I think', 'I don't think', or 'Do you think' to start the sentence.

    I think that we <u>should</u> be paid more.
    I don't think we <u>ought</u> to grumble.
    Do you think he <u>ought not</u> to go?
    What do you think we <u>should</u> do?

3 You use 'should have' or 'ought to have' and a past participle to say that there was a mild obligation to do something in the past, but that it was not done. For example, if you say 'I should have given him the money yesterday', you mean that you had a mild obligation to give him the money yesterday, but you did not give it to him.

    I <u>should have</u> finished my drink and gone home.
    You <u>should have</u> realised that he was joking.
    We <u>ought to have</u> stayed in tonight.
    They <u>ought to have</u> taken a taxi.

You use 'should not have' or 'ought not to have' and a past participle to say that it was important not to do something in the past, but that it was done. For example, if you say 'I should not have left the door open', you mean that it was important that you did not leave the door open, but you did leave it open.

    I <u>should not have</u> said that.
    You <u>shouldn't have</u> given him the money.
    They <u>ought not to have</u> told him.
    She <u>oughtn't to have</u> sold the ring.

4 You use 'had better' followed by a base form to indicate mild obligation to do something in a particular situation. You also use 'had better' when giving advice or when giving your opinion about something. The negative is 'had better not'.

    I think I <u>had better</u> show this to you now.
    You<u>'d better</u> go tomorrow.

⊖ WARNING: The correct form is always 'had better' (not 'have better'). You do not use 'had better' to talk about mild obligation in the past, even though it looks like a past form.

I'<u>d better not</u> look at this.

Practice

A **Complete the following sentences using 'you ought to' or 'you ought not to'.**

1 ..*You ought to*............................ drive carefully on a busy road.
2 ..*You ought not to*........................ eat between meals if you want to lose weight.
3 .... pay your bills regularly.
4 .... be selfish.
5 .... smoke too heavily.
6 .... go to the dentist's regularly.
7 .... lie in bed late every day.
8 .... clean your teeth at least twice a day.
9 .... eat a lot of sugar.
10 .... be more careful.

B **Match these situations with the advice you might give in each one.**

1 It's raining.
2 It's too far to walk.
3 Someone doesn't know which way to go.
4 Someone is going to live overseas.
5 Someone has to get up early in the morning.
6 Someone hasn't got any money with them.
7 It's going to be a cold day.
8 Someone is tired out.
9 Someone has seen someone breaking into a shop window.
10 Someone is feeling hot and has a headache.

a You should take a rest.
b You should ask a policeman.
c You should take an umbrella.
d You should wear an overcoat.
e You should see a doctor.
f You should learn the language before you go.
g You should pay by cheque.
h You should take a taxi.
i You should set your alarm clock.
j You should call the police.

C **Rewrite these sentences using 'should have' or 'shouldn't have'.**

1 Why didn't you phone to say you'd be late? / ..*You should have phoned to say you'd be late.*....
2 I wish they hadn't made such a mess. / ....*They shouldn't have made such a mess.*.............
3 I wish I had got home earlier. / ....
4 We didn't read the instructions carefully. / ....
5 Why did you spend so much money? / ....
6 I wish you had told me you were coming. / ....
7 It was very bad of them to make such a noise. / ....
8 John left the restaurant without paying his bill. / ....
9 I wish Jack had explained what he was doing. / ....
10 Why didn't you send Mary a birthday card? / ....

Now rewrite the first five sentences using 'ought to have' or 'ought not to have'.

1 ....
2 ....
3 ....
4 ....
5 ....

▶ **Bank**

Defining relative clauses

Main points

You use defining relative clauses to say exactly which person or thing you are talking about.

Defining relative clauses are usually introduced by a relative pronoun such as 'that', 'which', 'who', 'whom', or 'whose'.

A defining relative clause comes immediately after noun, and needs a main clause to make a complete sentence.

1 You use defining relative clauses to give information that helps to identify the person or thing you are talking about.

> The man _who you met yesterday_ was my brother.
> The car _which crashed into me_ belonged to Paul.

When you are talking about people, you use 'that' or 'who' in the relative clause.

> He was the man _that_ bought my house.
> You are the only person here _who_ knows me.

When you are talking about things, you use 'that' or 'which' in the relative clause.

> There was ice cream _that_ Mum had made herself.
> I will tell you the first thing _which_ I can remember.

2 'That', 'who', or 'which' can be:

- the subject of the verb in the relative clause

> The thing _that_ really surprised me was his attitude.
> The woman _who_ lives next door is very friendly.
> The car _which_ caused the accident drove off.

- the object of the verb in the relative clause

> The thing _that_ I really liked about it was its size.
> The woman _who_ you met yesterday lives next door.
> The car _which_ I wanted to buy was not for sale.

In formal English, 'whom' is used instead of 'who' as the object of the verb in the relative clause.

> She was a woman _whom_ I greatly respected.

3 You can leave out 'that', 'who', or 'which' when they are the object of the verb in the relative clause.

> The woman you met yesterday lives next door.
> The car I wanted to buy was not for sale.
> The thing I really liked about it was its size.

⊖ WARNING: You cannot leave out 'that', 'who', or 'which' when they are the subject of the verb in the relative clause. For example, you say 'The woman who lives next door is very friendly'. You do not say 'The woman lives next door is very friendly'.

4 A relative pronoun in a relative clause can be the object of a preposition. Usually the preposition goes at the end of the clause.

> I wanted to do the job _which_ I'd been training _for._
> The house _that_ we lived _in_ was huge.

You can often omit a relative pronoun that is the object of a preposition.

> Angela was the only person _I could talk to._
> She's the girl _I sang the song for._

The preposition always goes in front of 'whom', and in front of 'which' in formal English.

> These are the people _to whom_ Catherine was referring.
> He was asking questions _to which_ there were no answers.

5 You use 'whose' in relative clauses to indicate who something belongs to or relates to. You normally use 'whose' for people, not for things.

> A child _whose_ mother had left him was crying loudly.
> We have only told the people _whose_ work is relevant to this project.

6 You can use 'when', 'where', and 'why' in defining relative clauses after certain nouns. You use 'when' after 'time' or time words such as 'day' or 'year'. You use 'where' after 'place' or place words such as 'room' or 'street'. You use 'why' after 'reason'.

> There had been _a time when_ she hated all men.
> This is _the year when_ profits should increase.
> He showed me _the place where_ they work.
> That was _the room where_ I did my homework.
> There are several _reasons why_ we can't do that.

Practice

A Complete the following sentences using a relative clause with 'that' as the subject.

1 The train leaves at 2.15. / You're too late to catch the train …..*that leaves at 2.15*………… .

2 Mary has two brothers. One lives in America. / Do you know the one ……………………………
…… ?

3 Some things were stolen. / Have you got back the things ………………………………… ?

4 A man plays James Bond. / What's the name of the man ………………………………… ?

5 A woman answered the phone. / The woman …………………………………………………
………………………………………… asked me to call back later.

6 A book was left behind on the desk. / The book ………………………………………………
………………………………………… belongs to John.

7 Some people live in glass houses. / People …………………………………………………
………………………………………… shouldn't throw stones.

Now do the same with these using 'that' as the object of the relative clause.

8 I read a book last week. / I really enjoyed the book …*that I read last week*………………… .

9 I met someone on the train. / Someone …………………………………………………………
………………………………………… gave me some good advice.

10 We took some photographs on holiday. / Have you seen the photographs …………………
…………………………………………………………… ?

11 You read things in the newspaper. / You shouldn't believe all the things …………………
…… .

12 I left some money on the table. / The money …………………………………………………
………………………………………… seems to have disappeared.

13 The Beatles recorded this song in 1966. / This is one of the songs ………………………
………………………………………… .

14 You asked for some information. / We cannot provide the information ……………………
………………………………………… .

B Look at the sentences above. In some the relative pronoun 'that' stands for a person and can be replaced by 'who'. In others 'that' stands for a thing and can be replaced by 'which'. Write 'who' or 'which' in brackets after each sentence to show which word could replace 'that'.

1 You're too late to catch the train …*that leaves at 2.15*…………… …*(which)*………… .

C Complete these sentences by adding 'when', 'where', 'whose', or 'why'.

1 This is definitely the place ……*where*…………………………………… I left it.

2 Do you remember the time ………………………………………………… we got lost?

3 There must be a good reason ……………………………………………… he's late.

4 They are building a hospital on the street ……………………………………… we live.

5 Peter? Is he the one ……………………………………………………… car you borrowed?

6 Can you give me any reason ………………………………………… I should help you?

7 Carl is the one ………………………………………………… desk is next to mine.

▶ **Bank**

Non-defining clauses

1 You use non-defining relative clauses to give extra information about the person or thing you are talking about. The information is not needed to identify that person or thing.

> Professor Marvin, <u>who was always early,</u> was there already.

'Who was always early' gives extra information about Professor Marvin. This is a non-defining relative clause, because it is not needed to identify the person you are talking about. We already know that you are talking about Professor Marvin.

Note that in written English, a non-defining relative clause is usually separated from the main clause by a comma, or by two commas.

> I went to the cinema with Mary, who I think you met.
> British Rail, which has launched an enquiry, said one coach was badly damaged.

2 You always start a non-defining relative clause with a relative pronoun. When you are talking about people, you use 'who'. 'Who' can be the subject or object of a non-defining relative clause.

> Heath Robinson, <u>who</u> died in 1944, was a graphic artist and cartoonist.
> I was in the same group as Janice, <u>who</u> I like a lot.

In formal English, 'whom' is sometimes used instead of 'who' as the object of a non-defining relative clause.

> She was engaged to a sailor, <u>whom</u> she had met at Dartmouth.

3 When you are talking about things, you use 'which' as the subject or object of a non-defining relative clause.

> I am teaching at the Selly Oak centre, <u>which</u> is just over the road.
> He was a man of considerable inherited wealth, <u>which</u> he ultimately spent on his experiments.

⊖ WARNING: You do not normally use 'that' in non-defining relative clauses.

4 You can also use a non-defining relative clause beginning with 'which' to say something about the whole situation described in a main clause.

> I never met Brando again, <u>which</u> was a pity.
> She was a little tense, <u>which</u> was understandable.
> Small computers need only small amounts of power, <u>which</u> means that they will run on small batteries.

5 When you are talking about a group of people or things and then want to say something about only some of them, you can use one of the following expressions:

many of which	many of whom	most of which
most of whom	neither of which	neither of whom
none of which	none of whom	one of which
one of whom	some of which	some of whom

> They were all friends, <u>many of whom</u> had known each other for years.
> He talked about several very interesting people, <u>some of whom</u> he was still in contact with.

6 You can use 'when' and 'where' in non-defining relative clauses after expressions of time or place.

> This happened in 1957, <u>when</u> I was still a baby.
> She has just come back from a holiday in Crete, <u>where</u> Alex and I went last year.

Practice

A Join the sentences below using 'who', 'whose', or 'which'. Make sure that the relative clause goes next to the word it gives extra information about.

1 I met Jane's father. He works at the university.
I met Jane's father, who works at the university.

2 Peter is studying French and German. He has never been abroad.
Peter, who is studying French and German, has never been abroad.

3 You've all met Michael Wood. He is visiting us for a couple of days.

4 Michael Wood is one of my oldest friends. He has just gone to live in Canada.

5 We are moving to Manchester. Manchester is in the north-west.

6 Manchester is in the north-west. It is one of England's fastest growing towns.

7 I'll be staying with Adrian. His brother is one of my closest friends.

8 This is Adrian. We stayed in Adrian's house for our holidays.

B Match the first clauses with the non-defining relative clauses.

1 I had to travel first class, …   a … which meant we had to cancel the match next day.
2 It snowed heavily all night, …   b … which meant we had to eat out in the evenings.
3 The car uses very little petrol, …   c … which really annoyed everyone.
4 He didn't get up until after eight o'clock, …   d … which certainly pleased her mother.
5 The food in the hotel was not very good, …   e … which means it is quite cheap to run.
6 He kept complaining about everything, …   f … which meant he was almost late for work.
7 Both the girls were late, …   g … which meant we had to leave without them.
8 Michelle always did very well at school, …   h … which was very expensive.

C Rewrite these sentences using phrases with 'of which' or 'of whom'.

1 I got four books for my birthday. I had read three of them before.
I got four books for my birthday, three of which I had read before.

2 Only two people came to look at the house, and neither of them wanted to buy it.

3 He had a lot to say about his new computer. None of it interested me very much.

4 There were some noisy people in the audience. One of them kept interrupting the speaker.

5 She made all kinds of suggestions. I couldn't understand most of them.

189

Participle clauses

Main points

Nouns are followed by '-ing' clauses that say what a person or thing is doing.

Nouns are followed by '-ed' clauses that show that a person or thing has been affected or caused by an action.

1 You can often give more information about a noun, or an indefinite pronoun such as 'someone' or 'something', by adding a clause beginning with an '-ing' form, an '-ed' form, or a 'to'-infinitive.

> He gestured towards <u>the box lying on the table.</u>
> I think <u>the idea suggested by Tim</u> is the best one.
> She wanted <u>someone to talk to.</u>

2 You use an '-ing' clause after a noun to say what someone or something is doing or was doing at a particular time.

> The young girl <u>sitting opposite him</u> was his daughter.
> Most of the people <u>strolling in the park</u> were teenagers.

3 You can also use an '-ing' clause after a noun to say what a person or thing does generally, rather than at a particular time.

> Problems <u>facing parents</u> should be discussed.
> The men <u>working there</u> were not very friendly.

4 You often use an '-ing' clause after a noun which is the object of a verb of perception, such as 'see', 'hear', or 'feel'.

➤ See also Unit 72.

> Suddenly we saw Amy <u>walking down the path.</u>
> He heard a distant voice <u>shouting.</u>
> I could feel something <u>touching my face and neck,</u> something ice-cold.

5 You use an '-ed' clause after a noun to show that someone or something has been affected or caused by an action.

> He was the new minister <u>appointed by the President.</u>
> The man <u>injured in the accident</u> was taken to hospital.

Remember that not all verbs have regular '-ed' forms.

> A story <u>written by a young girl</u> won the competition.
> She was wearing a dress <u>bought in Paris.</u>

Practice

A Complete the following sentences using the correct part of the verb in brackets. One sentence in each pair should have an '-ing' form and the other an '-ed' form.

1 a There was a table ....*covered*................................ by a clean white cloth.
   b There was a clean white cloth .....*covering*.............................. the table. (*cover*)

2 a The man .... by the dog was seriously injured.
   b The dog .... my friend was pulled off by its owner. (*attack*)

3 a Everyone went home early .... a dreadful mess behind.
   b We cleared up the things .... behind after the party. (*leave*)

4 a I saw a man .... a heavy wooden box.
   b We lost most of the luggage .... in the plane. (*carry*)

5 a The problems .... by the government are growing more serious every day.
   b There are a lot of problems .... us at the moment. (*face*)

6 a I heard someone .... French.
   b Tagalog is one of the languages .... in the Philippines. (*speak*)

B Use these '-ing' forms to complete the sentences below.

burning   climbing   crying   drowning   lying   screaming   standing

1 If I saw someone ....*climbing*.................... in my neighbour's window, I would call the police.
2 If I smelled something .... , I would check in the kitchen.
3 If I saw a disabled man .... in a train, I would offer him my seat.
4 If I saw a child .... , I would ask what was the matter.
5 If you saw someone .... , would you try to rescue them?
6 If you found a lot of money .... in the street, would you take it to the police station?
7 If you heard someone .... , what would you do?

C Join the two sentences to make one sentence, using an '-ing' or '-ed' clause.

1 A car was parked at the side of the road. It had been stolen. / .*The car parked at the side of*......
   ..*the road had been stolen.*..

2 A man was walking towards me. I recognized him. / ....
   ....

3 A boy stole some chocolate from the shop. I saw him. / ....
   ....

4 The woman lives next door to me. She is very friendly. / ....
   ....

5 The soldiers stole some money. It was found in the farmhouse. / ....
   ....

6 A fire engine was coming up the road. I heard it. / ....

7 My mother wrote a book. It won a prize. / ....

▸ **Bank**

191

Adding to a noun group

1 You can use some adjectives after a noun to give more information about it, but the adjectives are usually followed by a prepositional phrase, a 'to'-infinitive clause, or an adverbial.

> This is a warning to people _eager for a quick profit._
> These are the weapons _likely to be used._
> For a list of the facilities _available here,_ ask the secretary.
> You must talk to the people _concerned._

▶ See Unit 31 for more information on adjectives used after nouns.

2 When you want to give more precise information about the person or thing you are talking about, you can use a defining relative clause after the noun.

> The man _who had done it_ was arrested.
> There are a lot of things _that are wrong._
> Nearly all the people _I used to know_ have gone.

Note that you can also use defining relative clauses after indefinite pronouns such as 'someone' or 'something'.

> I'm talking about somebody _who is really ill._

▶ See Unit 92 for more information on defining relative clauses.

3 You can use an adverbial of place or time after a noun.

> People _everywhere_ are becoming more selfish.
> This is a reflection of life _today._

4 You can add a second noun group after a noun. The second noun group gives you more precise information about the first noun.

> Her mother, _a Canadian,_ died when she was six.

Note that the second noun group is separated by commas from the rest of the clause.

5 Nouns such as 'advice', 'hope', and 'wish', which refer to what someone says or thinks, can be followed by a 'that'-clause. Here are some examples:

advice	agreement	belief	claim
conclusion	decision	feeling	hope
promise	threat	warning	wish

> It is my firm _belief that_ more women should stand for Parliament.
> I had a _feeling that_ no-one thought I was good enough.

Note that all these nouns are related to reporting verbs, which also take a 'that'-clause. For example, 'information' is related to 'inform', and 'decision' is related to 'decide'.

Some of these nouns can also be followed by a 'to'-infinitive clause.

agreement	decision	hope	order
promise	threat	warning	wish

> The _decision to go_ had not been an easy one.
> I reminded Barnaby of his _promise to buy his son a horse._

6 A few other nouns can be followed by a 'that'-clause.

advantage	confidence	danger
effect	evidence	fact
idea	impression	news
opinion	possibility	view

> He didn't want her to get the _idea that_ he was rich.
> I had no _evidence that_ Jed was the killer.
> He couldn't believe the _news that_ his house had just burned down.

Note that when a noun group is the object of a verb, it may be followed by different structures.

▶ See Units 69 to 72 for more information.

Practice

A **Complete these sentences by adding one of the names below.**

Abraham Lincoln	Amazon	Canada	Kyoto	Marilyn Monroe	Yuri Gagarin

1 ....Abraham Lincoln................. , the sixteenth US president, was assassinated in 1865.
2 .... , the Russian cosmonaut, was born in 1934.
3 The woman who was born Norma Jean Mortenson later became .... , the glamorous film star.
4 .... , the second largest country in the world, has a population of less than 25 million.
5 .... , a city in central Japan, was the nation's capital until 1868.
6 The .... , the longest river in the world, flows from the Peruvian Andes to the Atlantic Ocean.

B **Write six sentences from the table below.**

People Life	in the twenty-first century in most parts of the world in Britain today	are much better off than they used to be. is much easier than it used to be. was often difficult. has changed very rapidly. have lived through difficult times. is changing very rapidly.

....
....
....
....
....
....

C **Complete these sentences using 'that' or 'to'.**

1 The decision ....to................................ raise prices was bound to be unpopular.
2 Nobody accepted his claim .... he was the clear winner of the contest.
3 I have a feeling .... things will get worse before they get better.
4 The army attacked the plane in spite of the terrorists' threat .... kill the hostages.
5 There is a distinct possibility .... we will be late for the meeting.
6 They gave us a promise .... provide whatever help we needed.
7 There was a danger .... the building might catch fire.

Time clauses

Main points

You use time clauses to say when something happens.

Time clauses can refer to the past, present, or future.

Time clauses are introduced by words such as 'after', 'when', or 'while'.

A time clause needs a main clause to make a complete sentence. The time clause can come before or after the main clause.

1 You use time clauses to say when something happens. The verb in the time clause can be in a present or a past tense.

I look after the children <u>while</u> she <u>goes</u> to London.
I haven't given him a thing to eat <u>since</u> he <u>arrived</u>.

⊖ WARNING: You never use a future tense in a time clause. You use one of the present tenses instead.

Let me stay here <u>till</u> Jeannie <u>comes</u> to bed.
I'll do it <u>when</u> I<u>'ve finished</u> writing this letter.

2 When you want to say that two events happen at the same time, you use a time clause with 'as', 'when', or 'while'.

We arrived <u>as they were leaving.</u>

Sometimes the two events happen together for a period of time.

She wept bitterly <u>as she told her story.</u>

Sometimes one event interrupts another event.

He was having his dinner <u>when</u> the telephone rang.
John will arrive <u>while</u> we are watching the film.

Note that you often use a continuous tense for the interrupted action. ➤ See Unit 60.

3 When you want to say that one event happens before or after another event, you use a time clause with 'after', 'as soon as', 'before', or 'when'.

<u>As soon as</u> we get tickets, we'll send them to you.
Can I see you <u>before</u> you go, Helen?
<u>When</u> he had finished reading, he looked up.

Note that you use the past perfect to indicate an event that happened before another event in the past.

4 When you want to mention a situation which started in the past and continued until a later time, you use a time clause with 'since' or 'ever since'. You use a past simple or a past perfect in the time clause, and a past perfect in the main clause.

He hadn't cried <u>since he was</u> a boy of ten.
Janine had been busy <u>ever since she had heard</u> the news.
I<u>'d wanted</u> to come ever since I was a child.

If the situation started in the past and still continues now, you use a past simple in the time clause, and a present perfect in the main clause.

I've been in politics <u>since I was</u> at university.
Ever since you arrived <u>you've been causing</u> trouble.

Note that after impersonal 'it' and a time expression, if the main clause is in the present tense, you use 'since' with a past simple.

It <u>is</u> two weeks now since I <u>wrote</u> to you.

If the main clause is in the past tense, you use 'since' with a past perfect.

It <u>was</u> nearly seven years since I<u>'d seen</u> Toby.

➤ For 'since' as a preposition, see Unit 40.

5 When you want to talk about when a situation ends, you use a time clause with 'till' or 'until' and a present or past tense.

We'll support them <u>till they find</u> work.
I stayed there talking to them <u>until I saw</u> Sam.
She waited <u>until he had gone.</u>

6 When you want to say that something happens before or at a particular time, you use a time clause with 'by the time' or 'by which time'.

<u>By the time</u> I went to bed, I was exhausted.
He came back later, <u>by which time</u> they <u>had gone.</u>

7 In written or formal English, if the subject of the main clause and the time clause are the same, you sometimes omit the subject in the time clause and use a participle as the verb.

I read the book <u>before going</u> to see the film.
The car was stolen <u>while parked</u> in a London street.

Practice

A Complete the following sentences using the past simple or past continuous of the verbs given.

1 We played chess from 6.30 to 8.30. Margaret arrived at 7.15. / We …… *were playing* …………… chess when Margaret ……*arrived*…………… . (*play*) (*arrive*)

2 Bill arrived at 7.45, so we all sat down to dinner. / As soon as Bill ………………………… we all ………………………… down to dinner. (*arrive*) (*sit*)

3 I worked in the kitchen until 7.15. My mother phoned at 7.05. / My mother ……………………………… while I ……………………………………………… in the kitchen. (*phone*) (*work*)

4 I wrote letters in my study all afternoon. I heard the explosion at about 3 pm. / When I ……………………………… the explosion I ……………………………… a letter in my study. (*hear*) (*write*)

5 I heard the explosion and immediately telephoned the police. / I ………………………… the police immediately after I ……………………………… the explosion. (*telephone*) (*hear*)

B Complete these sentences using the present simple in the time clause, and either 'will' or 'will be' and an '-ing' form in the main clause.

1 I work from 8 am until 6 pm every Wednesday. Mary will arrive at about 4 pm. / I … *will be working* …. when Mary …………… *arrives* ………………………… . (*work*) (*arrive*)

2 Bill is going to phone me on Wednesday, so I will let you know then. / I ……………………………… you know as soon as Bill ……………………………………………… me. (*let*) (*phone*)

3 According to the weather forecast, it's going to rain all day tomorrow. We are going to set out at nine o'clock. / According to the weather forecast, it …………………… when we ………………………… tomorrow. (*rain*) (*set out*)

4 I'll be seeing Helen next week. I'll tell her then. / I ……………………………… Helen when I ……………………………………… her. (*tell*) (*see*)

5 I'm going to the supermarket soon. I always buy bread at the supermarket. / I ………………………… some bread when I ……………………………………… to the supermarket. (*buy*) (*go*)

C Complete the sentences using the 'since' clauses given below.

1 George and I have been close friends …
2 We haven't been to the cinema …
3 He hasn't been able to play the piano …
4 They have lived next door to us …
5 Fred has been working at home …
6 Mary has been looking after the children …

a … since they moved here in 1987.
b … ever since he left his job at the factory.
c … since we saw Dracula at the Odeon last year.
d … since we were at school together.
e … since he had his accident a month ago.
f … ever since their mother went into hospital.

Rewrite your sentences using the past perfect.

George and I had been close friends since we were at school together.

………………………………………………………………………………………………………
………………………………………………………………………………………………………
………………………………………………………………………………………………………
………………………………………………………………………………………………………
………………………………………………………………………………………………………

▶ **Bank**

Purpose and reason clauses

Main points

Purpose clauses are introduced by conjunctions such as 'so', 'so as to', 'so that', 'in order to' or 'in order that'.

Reason clauses are introduced by conjunctions such as 'as', 'because', or 'in case'.

A purpose or reason clause needs a main clause to make a complete sentence.

A purpose clause usually comes after a main clause. A reason clause can come before or after a main clause.

1 You use a purpose clause when you are saying what someone's intention is when they do something. The most common type of purpose clause is a 'to'-infinitive clause.

> *The children sleep together <u>to keep</u> warm.*
> *They locked the door <u>to stop</u> us from getting in.*

Instead of using an ordinary 'to'-infinitive, you often use 'in order to' or 'so as to' with an infinitive.

> *He was giving up his job <u>in order to stay</u> at home.*
> *I keep the window open, <u>so as to let</u> fresh air in.*

To make a purpose clause negative, you have to use 'in order not to' or 'so as not to' with an infinitive.

> *I would have to give myself something to do <u>in order not to</u> be bored.*
> *They went on foot, <u>so as not to</u> be heard.*

Another way of making purpose clauses negative is by using 'to avoid' with an '-ing' form or a noun group.

> *I had to turn away <u>to avoid letting</u> him see my smile.*
> *They drove through town <u>to avoid the motorway.</u>*

2 Another type of purpose clause begins with 'in order that', 'so', or 'so that'. These clauses usually contain a modal.

When the main clause refers to the present, you usually use 'can', 'may', 'will', or 'shall' in the purpose clause.

> *Any holes should be fenced <u>so that</u> people <u>can't</u> fall down them.*
> *I have drawn a diagram <u>so that</u> my explanation <u>will</u> be clearer.*

When the main clause refers to the past, you usually use 'could', 'might', 'should', or 'would' in the purpose clause.

> *She said she wanted tea ready at six <u>so</u> she <u>could</u> be out by eight.*
> *Someone lifted Philip onto his shoulder <u>so that</u> he <u>might</u> see the procession.*

You use 'in order that', 'so', and 'so that', when the subject of the purpose clause is different from the subject of the main clause. For example, you say 'I've underlined it so that it will be easier.' You do not say 'I've underlined it to be easier'.

3 You can also talk about the purpose of an action by using a prepositional phrase introduced by 'for'.

> *She went out <u>for a run.</u>*
> *They said they did it <u>for fun.</u>*
> *I usually check, just <u>for safety's sake.</u>*

4 You use a reason clause when you want to explain why someone does something or why it happens. When you are simply giving the reason for something, you use 'because', 'since', or 'as'.

> *I couldn't see Helen's expression, <u>because</u> her head was turned.*
> *<u>Since</u> it was Saturday, he stayed in bed.*
> *<u>As</u> he had been up since 4 am, he was very tired.*

You can also use 'why' and a reported question to talk about the reason for an action.

▶ See Unit 75.

> *I asked him <u>why</u> he had come.*

5 When you are talking about a possible situation which explains the reason why someone does something, you use 'in case' or 'just in case'.

> *I've got the key <u>in case</u> we want to go inside.*
> *I am here <u>just in case</u> anything unusual happens.*

⊖ WARNING: You do not use a future tense after 'in case'. You do not say 'I'll stay behind in case she'll arrive later'.

Practice

A Rewrite these sentences to include a 'to'-infinitive purpose clause introduced by the words given in brackets.

1 Everyone was pushing because they wanted to get to the front of the queue. (*in order to*)
   Everyone was pushing in order to get to the front of the queue.

2 Try to write clearly. That way you will avoid being misunderstood. (*so as to*)

3 A lot of people learn English because they want to study in English. (*in order to*)

4 What do I need to know, if I want to be a good doctor? (*in order to*)

5 She turned up early because she wanted to get the room ready. (*in order to*)

6 If you want to have a hundred students, you will need at least three teachers. (*in order to*)

7 I came to live in the country because I wanted to have trees around me instead of buildings. (*so as to*)

8 They had to eat grass and drink melted snow if they wanted to stay alive. (*in order to*)

9 He wanted to keep his car out of sight so he left it in the road. (*in order to*)

10 I wanted to get to Madrid so I had to travel overnight from Barcelona. (*to*)

B Rewrite these sentences to include a negative purpose clause using 'to avoid'.

1 We spoke quietly because we didn't want to disturb anyone.
   We spoke quietly to avoid disturbing anyone.

2 She moved carefully because she didn't want to wake the children.

3 He sat in the furthest corner because he didn't want to be seen.

4 I gave up sugar and butter because I didn't want to put on weight.

5 He used both hands because he didn't want to drop anything.

6 We went over everything carefully because we didn't want to make any mistakes.

7 She left quietly because she didn't want to make any trouble.

8 We covered the furniture because we didn't want to get paint all over it.

▶ **Bank**

Result clauses

Main points

You use result clauses to talk about the result of an action or situation.

Result clauses are introduced by conjunctions such as 'so', 'so…(that)', or 'such…(that)'.

A result clause needs a main clause to make a complete sentence. The result clause always comes after the main clause.

1 You use 'so' and 'so that' to say what the result of an action or situation is.

He speaks very little English, so I talked to him through an interpreter.
My suitcase had become damaged on the journey home, so that the lid would not stay closed.

2 You also use 'so…that' or 'such…that' to talk about the result of an action or situation.

He dressed so quickly that he put his boots on the wrong feet.
She got such a shock that she dropped the bag.

'That' is often omitted.

They were so surprised they didn't try to stop him.
They got such a fright they ran away again.

3 You only use 'such' before a noun, with or without an adjective.

They obeyed him with such willingness that the strike went on for over a year.
Sometimes they say such stupid things that I don't even bother to listen.

If the noun is a singular count noun, you put 'a' or 'an' in front of it.

I was in such a panic that I didn't know it was him.

Note that you only use 'so' before an adjective or an adverb.

It all sounded so crazy that I laughed out loud.
They worked so quickly that there was no time for talking.

4 When you want to say that a situation does not happen because someone or something has an excessive amount of a quality, you use 'too' with an adjective and a 'to'-infinitive. For example, if you say 'They were too tired to walk', you mean that they did not walk because they were too tired.

He was too proud to apologise.
She was too weak to lift me.

You also use 'too' with an adverb and a 'to'-infinitive.

They had been walking too silently to be heard.
She spoke too quickly for me to understand.

5 When you want to say that a situation happens or is possible because someone or something has a sufficient amount of a quality, you use 'enough' after adjectives and adverbs, followed by a 'to'-infinitive.

He was old enough to understand.
I could see well enough to know we were losing.

You normally put 'enough' in front of a noun, not after it.

I don't think I've got enough information to speak confidently.

6 You also use 'and as a result', 'and so', or 'and therefore' to talk about the result of an action or situation.

He had been ill for six months, and as a result had lost his job.
She was having great difficulty getting her car out, and so I had to move my car to let her out.
We have a growing population and therefore we need more and more food.

You can also put 'therefore' after the subject of the clause. For example, you can say 'We have a growing population and we therefore need more food'.

'As a result' and 'therefore' can also be used at the beginning of a separate sentence.

In a group, they are not so frightened. As a result, patients reveal their problems more easily.
He lacks money to invest in improving his tools. Therefore he is poor.

Practice

A Look at these pairs of sentences. Complete one sentence with 'so' and the other with 'such a'.

1 He was .... *such a* .... fool that no one took any notice of him.

He was .... *so* .... silly that no one took any notice of him.

2 The room was in .... mess it took two hours to tidy.

The room was .... untidy it took three hours to sort out.

3 We were .... tired we went straight to bed when we got home.

We had had .... tiring day that we went straight to bed.

4 It took us .... long to get home that we missed our supper.

It took us .... long time to get home that we missed our supper.

5 Her throat was .... sore that she could hardly speak.

She had .... sore throat she could hardly speak.

6 He spoke in .... soft voice we could hardly hear him.

His voice was .... soft we could hardly hear him.

7 I got .... shock when I heard the news I didn't know what to say.

I was .... shocked when I got the news I didn't know what to say.

8 He lived .... long way off that we hardly ever saw him.

He lived .... far away that we hardly ever saw him.

9 He was .... badly injured that they took him straight to the hospital.

He had suffered .... serious injury that they took him straight to hospital.

10 The children made .... noise we could hardly hear ourselves speak.

The kids were .... noisy we could hardly hear ourselves speak.

B Rewrite these sentences with 'so...that'.

1 The hill was very steep. I had to get off my bike and walk.

...*The hill was so steep that I had to get off my bike and walk.*............................

2 Her writing was very small. I could hardly read it. ....

3 The winter was bitterly cold. All the streams were frozen. ....

4 His favourite shoes were very badly worn. He had to throw them away ....

5 He looked very young. Everyone took him for a student. ....

6 Ken got very excited. He kept jumping up and down. ....

C Now rewrite these sentences with 'such...that'.

1 The hill was very steep. I had to get off my bike and walk.

.....*It was such a steep hill that I had to get off my bike and walk.*...............................

2 He was a dreadful liar. Nobody believed anything he said. ....

3 It proved to be a very difficult problem. Nobody could solve it. ....

4 We had a very good time. We didn't want to go home. ....

5 His clothes were very old. They were falling apart. ....

6 The food was very good. We all ate far too much. ....

▶ **Bank**

Contrast clauses

Main points

These are clauses introduced by 'although', 'in spite of' and 'though'.

You use contrast clauses when you want to make two statements, and one statement makes the other seem surprising.

Contrast clauses are introduced by conjunctions such as 'although', 'in spite of', or 'though'.

A contrast clause needs a main clause to make a complete sentence. The contrast clause can come before or after the main clause.

1 When you simply want to contrast two statements, you use 'although', 'though' or 'even though'.

Although he was late, he stopped to buy a sandwich.
Though he has lived for years in London, he writes in German.
I used to love listening to her, even though I could only understand about half of what she said.

Sometimes you use words like 'still', 'nevertheless', or 'just the same' in the main clause to add emphasis to the contrast.

Although I was shocked, I still couldn't blame him.
Although his company is profitable, it nevertheless needs to face up to some serious problems.
Although she hated them, she agreed to help them just the same.

When the subject of the contrast clause and the main clause are the same, you can often omit the subject and the verb 'be' in the contrast clause.

Although poor, we still have our pride. (Although we are poor…)
Though dying of cancer, he painted every day.
(Though he was dying of cancer…)

2 Another way of making a contrast is to use 'despite' or 'in spite of', followed by a noun group.

Despite the difference in their ages they were close friends.
In spite of poor health, my father was always cheerful.

⊖ WARNING: You say 'in spite of' but 'despite' without 'of'.

3 You can also use an '-ing' form after 'despite' or 'in spite of'.

Despite working hard, I failed my exams.
Conservative MPs are against tax rises, in spite of wanting lower inflation.

4 You can also use 'despite the fact that' or 'in spite of the fact that', followed by a clause.

Despite the fact that it sounds like science fiction, most of it is technically possible at this moment.
They ignored this order, in spite of the fact that they would probably get into trouble.

It is possible to omit 'that', especially in spoken English.

He insisted on playing, in spite of the fact he had a bad cold.

He insisted on playing, in spite of the fact he had a bad cold.

Practice

A The sentences below all have 'though', 'although', or 'even though'. Use one of these phrases to complete them.

we only arrived just in time	he was difficult to understand	she kept her coat on
I used to when I was younger	we had no time for lunch	the weather was awful
you're not as tall as he was	I really like John	he still wasn't tired

1 Although we were desperately hungry, ...*we had no time for lunch*............................. .
2 We enjoyed our holiday, even though ....
3 .... , even though it was very warm.
4 I don't play the piano now, although ....
5 You look very like your grandfather, although ....
6 Though he hadn't stopped working all day, ...
7 .... , even though his English was very good.
8 .... , although he can be very annoying at times.
9 Although we set off early, ...

B The sentences below all have 'in spite of' or 'despite'. Use one of the noun groups given to complete them.

the high cost of living	his injury	the unpopularity of his decision	all his precautions
the difference in their ages	the rain	her fear the heavy traffic	his recent illness

1 The air was fresh and clean in spite of ....*the heavy traffic*.............................. .
2 He looked very well in spite of ....
3 Despite .... she did her best to smile bravely.
4 He refused to change his mind despite ....
5 Despite .... they were very close friends.
6 I didn't earn much in Japan in spite of ....
7 In spite of .... his money was still stolen.
8 He continued the race despite ....
9 We still had our picnic in spite of ....

▶ **Bank**

Manner clauses

Main points

You use manner clauses to talk about how something is done.

Manner clauses are introduced by conjunctions such as 'as', 'as if', 'as though', or 'like'.

A manner clause needs a main clause to make a complete sentence. The manner clause always comes after the main clause.

1 When you want to say how someone does something, or how something is done, you use 'as'.

> He behaves _as_ he does, because his father was really cruel to him.
> The bricks are still made _as_ they were in Roman times.

You often use 'just', 'exactly', or 'precisely' in front of 'as' for emphasis.

> It swims on the sea floor _just as_ its ancestors did.
> I like the freedom to plan my day _exactly as_ I want.
> Everything was going _precisely as_ she had planned.

2 When you want to indicate that the information in the manner clause might not be true, or is definitely not true, you use 'as if' or 'as though'.

> Almost _as if_ she'd read his thought, she straightened her back and returned to her seat.
> Just act _as though_ everything's normal.

After 'as if' or 'as though', you often use a past tense even when you are talking about the present, to emphasize that the infomation in the manner clause is not true. In formal English, you use 'were' instead of 'was'.

> You talk about him _as if_ he _were_ dead.
> It is Malcolm's 37th birthday, but he and his mother both behave _as if_ he _were_ 7.

➤ See also Unit 68 for more information on '…as if…' and '…as though…'

3 You also use 'the way (that)', 'in a way (that)', or 'in the way (that)' to talk about how someone does something, or how something is done.

> I was never allowed to sing _the way_ I wanted to.
> They did it _in a way that_ I had never seen before.
> We make it move _in the way that_ we want it to.

4 You can use 'how' in questions and reported questions to talk about the method used to do something, and sometimes to indicate your surprise that it was possible to do it.

> '_How_ did he get in?' – 'He broke a window.'
> I wondered _how_ he could afford a new car.

Sometimes, you can use 'how' to talk about the manner in which someone does something.

> I watched _how_ he did it, then tried to copy him.
> Tell me _how_ he reacted when he saw you.

Practice

Unit 100

A **Rewrite these sentences with 'just as'.**

1 I knew he would complain about everything, and he did. / ...He complained about everything...
   ...just as I knew he would.

2 You said they would arrive late, and they did. / ....

3 Everyone believed he would run away, and he did. / ....

4 Most people thought the play would be a success, and it was. / ....

5 We hoped he would do well at school, and he did. / ....

6 We all thought Mary would win, and she did. / ....

7 Her father worked at the bank, and now she works there. / ....

8 We used these ingredients in the past, and we use them today. / ....

B **Rewrite these sentences with 'the way'.**

1 I don't like people who behave as he does. / ...I don't like people who behave the way he does.

2 They still farm as their grandfathers did. / ....

3 He accepted his punishment, as everyone else did. / ....
   ....

4 She refused to dress as her colleagues did. / ....

5 He said he would work as the others did if he was paid as they were. / ....
   ....

6 They work a five day week, as we do. / ....

7 Her piano teacher taught her to play as the other pupils did. / ....
   ....

C **Match the questions and answers.**

1 I wonder how he got into the house.   a Maybe his father gave him a lift.
2 How do you think he got there so quickly?   b They were at University together.
3 Do you know how she became so wealthy?   c He must have worked very hard.
4 I wonder how Maria heard the news.   d He must have climbed through a window.
5 Do you know how they met?   e Perhaps she won the state lottery.
6 I wonder how he's been so successful.   f I think her husband told her about it.

Main points

You can sometimes change the focus of a sentence by moving part of the sentence to the front.

You can also change the focus of a sentence by using an expression such as 'The fact is', 'The thing is', or 'The problem is'.

You can also use impersonal 'it' to change the focus of a sentence.

1 In most affirmative clauses, the subject of the verb comes first.

> *They went to Australia in 1956.*
> *I've no idea who it was.*

However, when you want to emphasize another part of the sentence, you can put that part first instead.

> *In 1956 they went to Australia.*
> *Who it was I've no idea.*

2 One common way of giving emphasis is by placing an adverbial at the beginning of the sentence.

> *At eight o'clock I went down for my breakfast.*
> *For years I'd had to hide what I was thinking.*

Note that after adverbials of place and negative adverbials, you normally put the subject after the verb.

> *She rang the bell for Sylvia. In came a girl she had not seen before.*
> *Scarcely had they left before soldiers arrived.*
> *Never had he been so free of worry.*

After adverbials of place, you can also put the subject before the verb. You must do so, if the subject is a pronoun.

> *The door opened and in she came.*
> *He'd chosen Japan, so off we went to the Japanese Embassy.*

3 When you want to say that you do not know something, you can put a reported question at the beginning of the sentence.

> *What I'm going to do next I don't quite know.*
> *How he managed I can't imagine.*

4 Another way of focusing on information is to use a structure which introduces what you want to say by using 'the' and a noun, followed by 'is'. The nouns most commonly used in this way are:

answer	conclusion	fact	point
problem	question	rule	solution
thing	trouble	truth	

The second part of the sentence is usually a 'that'-clause or a 'wh'-clause, although it can also be a 'to'-infinitive clause or a noun group.

> *The problem is that she can't cook.*
> *The thing is, how are we going to get her out?*
> *The solution is to adopt the policy which will produce the greatest benefits.*
> *The answer is planning, timing, and, above all, practical experience.*

It is also common to use a whole sentence to introduce information in following sentences.

➤ See Unit 102 for more information.

5 You can also focus on information by using impersonal 'it', followed by 'be', a noun group, and a relative clause.

The noun group can be the subject or object of the relative clause.

> *It was Ted who broke the news to me.*
> *It is usually the other vehicle that suffers most.*
> *It's money that they want.*
> *It was me Dookie wanted.*

There are many other ways of focusing on information:

> *Ted was the one who broke the news to me.*
> *Money is what we want.*
> *What we want is money.*

6 You can also focus on the information given in the other parts of a clause, or a whole clause, using impersonal 'it'. In this case, the second part of the sentence is a 'that'-clause.

> *It was from Francis that she first heard the news.*
> *It was meeting Peter that really started me off on this new line of work.*
> *Perhaps it's because he's a misfit that I get along with him.*

Practice

A Rewrite the sentences below starting with the words given.

1 I had scarcely finished speaking when Henry jumped to his feet.
Scarcely ...... *had I finished speaking when Henry jumped to his feet.* ......

2 I have never heard such a lot of nonsense before.
Never before ....

3 We got in the bus and went off to Brighton.
We got in the bus and off ....

4 She opened the box and a live mouse jumped out.
She opened the box and out ....

5 She did not tell me once that she would be coming round.
Not once ....

6 They not only spent all my money, they also wasted a good deal of my time.
Not only .... , but they also wasted a good deal of my time.

B Match these sentences.

1 I bought a beautiful pair of shoes.   a The fact is I haven't eaten for twenty-four hours.
2 I'm more than hungry, I'm starving.   b The question is can we afford one?
3 Everything's in an awful mess.   c The problem now is how to get into the house.
4 I know we need a new car.   d The only trouble is they were rather too tight.
5 I've forgotten my key.   e The only answer is to start all over again.

C Answer these questions using 'it was' or 'it is' with the words given in brackets.

1 Did Mike take this message for me? (*Jenny*)
.... *No, it was Jenny who took the message.* ....

2 Did Peter leave the message? (*Ken*)
No, ...

3 Does he usually come in before nine? (*just after nine*)
No, ...

4 Did he call in this morning? (*this afternoon*)
No, ...

5 Did he want to see Helen? (*Becky*)
No, ...

6 Is he going to call back today? (*tomorrow*)
No, ...

▸ **Bank**

Cohesion

Main points

You can use pronouns and determiners to refer back to something that has already been mentioned.

You use coordinating conjunctions to link clauses.

1 When you speak or write, you usually need to make some connection with other things that you are saying or writing. The most common way of doing this is by referring back to something that has already been mentioned.

2 One way of referring back to something is to use a personal pronoun such as 'she', 'it', or 'them', or a possessive pronoun such as 'mine' or 'hers'.

> *My father is fat. He weighs over fifteen stone.*
> *Mary came in. She was a good-looking woman.*
> *'Have you been to London ?' – 'Yes, it was very crowded.'*
> *'Have you heard of David Lodge ?' – 'Yes, I've just read a novel of his.'*
> *'Would you mind moving your car, please?' – 'It's not mine.'*

3 You can also use a specific determiner such as 'the' or 'his' in front of a noun to refer back to something.

> *A man and a woman were walking up the hill. The man wore shorts, a T-shirt, and basketball sneakers. The woman wore a print dress.*
> *'Thanks,' said Brody. He put the telephone down, turned out the light in his office, and walked out to his car.*

4 The demonstratives 'this', 'that', 'these' and 'those' are also used to refer back to a thing or fact that has just been mentioned.

> *In 1973 he went on a caravan holiday. At the beginning of this holiday he began to experience pain in his chest.*
> *There's a lot of material there. You can use some of that.*

5 The following general determiners can also be used to refer back to something:

another	both	each	either	every	neither	other

> *Five officials were sacked. Another four were arrested.*
> *There are more than two hundred and fifty species of shark, and every one is different.*

6 Another common way of making connections in spoken or written English is by using one of the following coordinating conjunctions:

and	but	nor	or	so	then	yet

> *Anna had to go into town and she wanted to go to Bride Street.*
> *I asked if I could borrow her bicycle but she refused.*
> *He was only a boy then, yet he was not afraid.*

You can use a coordinating conjunction to link clauses that have the same subject. When you link clauses which have the same subject, you do not always need to repeat the subject in the second clause.

> *She was born in Budapest and raised in Manhattan.*
> *He didn't yell or scream.*
> *When she saw Morris she went pale, then blushed.*

7 Most subordinating conjunctions can also be used to link sentences together, rather than to link a subordinate clause with a main clause in the same sentence.

> *'When will you do it?' – 'When I get time.'*
> *'Can I borrow your car?' – 'So long as you drive carefully.'*
> *We send that by airmail. Therefore, it's away on Thursday and our client gets it on Monday.*

8 When people are speaking or writing, they often use words that refer back to similar words, or words that refer back to a whole sentence or paragraph.

> *Everything was quiet. Everywhere there was the silence of the winter night.*
> *'What are you going to do?' – 'That's a good question.'*

Practice

A Use these words and phrases to complete the story which follows.

> her   her friend   it   the first student   the first student   the second

A student went to ....**her**..................... first lecture at the university, and
mentioned this to a friend, another student.
'What was .... about?' asked ....'I don't know,'
.... replied.'Why not?' asked ....'Weren't you listening?'
'Of course I was listening,' .... replied,'but he didn't tell us what it was about.'

Now do the same with this story.

> the customer   the curious bank manager   it   the car park   it   the car   he
> a wealthy man   his bank manager   he   the customer   it   his car   he

...**A wealthy man**...................... was told by .... that he owed the
bank £100 and that .... would have to pay 12% interest per year. ....
.... agreed to pay, and said he would leave .... , a
Rolls Royce, as security. He then drove .... round to the bank, and left
.... in the car park.
A month later, ... returned to collect the car. ....
asked why .... had insisted on leaving ....
in ....
Where else could I park .... for a month, for only £1?' replied ....

B Rearrange these clauses to tell a story.

1 the psychiatrist asked him what his problem was
2 'Well, doctor, I don't really know what's wrong with me.'
3 one day a man went to see a psychiatrist
4 and the patient explained
5 'Can you tell me how long you've had this trouble?'
6 'My main problem is, I always forget what I've said as soon as I've said it.'
7 'How long I've had what trouble?' replied the patient
8 'I see,' said the doctor

C Now rearrange these clauses to tell a story.

1 'Would you like it with or without cream?' she asked
2 The waitress asked him if he would take coffee
3 The waitress went off, but soon came back.
4 'but there's no more cream.
5 After a long wait, the waitress came back again.
6 'Without cream,' replied the customer.
7 A man was just finishing his lunch in a restaurant.
8 Would you mind having it without milk?'
9 and the customer replied that he would.
10 'I'm sorry, sir,' she said,

BANK OF FURTHER EXERCISES

1 The imperative (▶ see Unit 4)

Make these polite requests more emphatic by using 'do'.

1 Would you like to come in and take a seat? / ......*Do come in and take a seat.*......

2 Why don't you come and see us at the weekend? / ....

3 It would be nice if you could bring the children too. / ....

4 Would you like to have some more tea? / ....

5 Could you write to me when you get home? / ....

Now use 'do' to make these into emphatic orders.

6 You should stop making so much noise. / ......*Do stop making so much noise.*......

7 You ought to listen carefully. / ....

8 You should be more careful. / ....

9 Please be quiet while I'm talking. / ....

10 Sit down and behave yourself. / ....

2 Questions (▶ see Unit 5)

Rearrange these phrases to make questions.

1 your homework / finished / yet / have you? / ..*Have you finished your homework yet?*..

2 French / how well / speak / do you? / ....

3 next Friday / will you / at school / be? / ....

4 who / next to you / in class / sits? / ....

5 who / next to / do you / in class / sit? / ....

3 'Wh-'words (▶ see Unit 6)

Match the questions and answers.

1 What's the longest word in the dictionary?

2 Where does Thursday come before Wednesday?

3 Which is easier to spell, seventeen or eighteen?

4 What begins with a 't', ends with a 't', and has 't' in it?

5 Why is an island like the letter 't'?

6 Why is the letter 'e' lazy?

7 How should you dress on a cold day?

8 Why is there plenty of food in the desert?

a Because of all the sandwiches (*sand which is*) there.

b In a dictionary.

c A teapot.

d Because it's always in bed.

e Smiles – because it's a mile from beginning to end.

f Seventeen, because it's spelt with more ease. (*more 'e's*)

g Because it's in the middle of water.

h As quickly as possible.

BANK OF FURTHER EXERCISES

4 Question tags (► see Unit 8)

Use question tags to complete these sentences.

1 Everyone was there, ...*weren't they*... ?
2 Nobody was watching, ... ?
3 Everybody knew, ... ?
4 Nothing really matters, ... ?
5 Something funny happened, ... ?
6 There was nobody there, ... ?
7 There's no time to spare, ... ?
8 Nobody understands, ... ?
9 Everything is all right, ... ?
10 Everyone has arrived, ... ?

5 Statements, questions, and commands (► see Units 4–12)

Mark these sentences affirmative (A), interrogative (?) or imperative (!).

1 Don't look now. ....*!*..
2 What time did you have dinner. ....
3 I think it's time to go. ....
4 Ask your father to give you the answer. ....
5 Who's that knocking on the door. ....
6 Nobody knows what to do. ....
7 Please try to find out where to go. ....
8 Can you find out where to go. ....
9 You should find out where to go. ....

6 Review of mood (► see Units 4–12)

Add question tags to these statements to make them into questions asking someone to confirm what you are saying, or to agree with you.

1 You've met George, ...*haven't you*... ?
2 They won't be too late, ... ?
3 Helen left a message for me, ... ?
4 There isn't time for another game, ... ?
5 Nobody saw what happened, ... ?
6 Something's wrong, ... ?
7 Somebody has made a mistake, ... ?
8 You didn't do it, ... ?
9 I'll see you tomorrow, ... ?
10 He knows where you are, ... ?
11 Don't do it again, ... ?
12 Everybody is in agreement, ... ?

BANK OF FURTHER EXERCISES

7 **Review of mood** (▶ see Units 4–12)

Make negative questions using the modals given.

1 You didn't stop at the traffic lights. (*should*) / Shouldn't you have stopped at the traffic lights?

2 You didn't send me a letter. (*could*) / ....

3 Perhaps they went home earlier. (*might*) / ....

4 We didn't pay in advance. (*should*) / ....

5 Why didn't you take a bus? (*could*) / ....

8 **Review of mood** (▶ see Units 4–12)

Complete these short answers using the verbs in brackets.

1 A: Do you think we'll be on time.
   B: Yes, ... I hope so. .... (*hope*)

2 A: Will Jacky be there?
   B: No, ... (*think*)

3 A: Will you be going abroad this year?
   B: Yes, ... (*suppose*)

4 A: Has the newspaper come yet?
   B: Yes, ... (*expect*)

5 A: Did you do the shopping on your way home?
   B: No, ... (*afraid*)

6 A: Did Jenny get my letter?
   B: Yes, ... (*think*)

9 **Plural nouns** (▶ see Unit 14 paragraph 3)

Choose the correct phrase to answer each of the questions below.

What might you use ...

1 ... to cut paper?   a ... a pair of binoculars.

2 ... if you can't see very well?   b ... a pair of pliers.

3 ... when you go to bed?   c ... a pair of pyjamas.

4 ... to see something a long way off?   d ... a pair of scissors.

5 ... instead of stockings?   e ... a pair of shorts.

6 ... to pull nails out of a piece of wood?   f ... a pair of spectacles.

7 ... if you were going jogging?   g ... a pair of sunglasses.

8 ... if the sun is shining very brightly?   h ... a pair of tights.

10 **'It' as impersonal subject** (▶ see Unit 17 paragraph 6)

Rewrite these sentences with 'it' and a 'that'-clause.

1 The earth was generally believed to be flat. / It was generally believed that the earth was flat.

2 He is known to be a dangerous man. / ....

3 Charlie Chaplin is said to have been a great comedian. / ....

4 She is understood to be arriving later today. / ....

5 They are rumoured to have escaped. / ....

11 'There' as impersonal subject (► see Unit 18)

Match these phrases to describe the picture.

1 There's a little boy ...   a ... looking at the little girl.

2 There's an old man ...   b ... reading a newspaper.

3 There's a young woman ...   c ... on the wall.

4 There's a girl ...   d ... looking round the door.

5 There are some flowers ...   e ... sitting next to the old man.

6 There's a NO SMOKING notice ... f ... sitting on his mother's knee.

7 There's a nurse ...   g ... in a vase by the window.

8 There's a young man ...   h ... sitting on the floor.

12 Reflexive pronouns (► see Unit 20 paragraph 6)

Complete these sentences using a suitable tense of the verb in brackets and a reflexive pronoun for emphasis.

1 Where did you buy those beautiful flowers?

   We didn't buy them. We ...*grew them ourselves.*.. (*grow*)

2 It must have been pretty expensive having the house decorated.

   No it was very cheap. We .... (*do*)

3 Your hair looks great. Who did it for you?

   Thank you. Actually I .... (*cut*)

4 Do you have the newspaper delivered on Sundays?

   No, I usually go and .... (*get*)

5 That bag looks awfully heavy. Let me take it for you.

   It's okay thanks. I can .... (*carry*)

6 Are you going to send a taxi to collect your wife from the airport?

   No. I always like to .... (*meet*)

13 Possession (► see Unit 22)

Rewrite these sentences using 'a...of' instead of 'one of'.

1 Neil is one of my friends. / ....*Neil is a friend of mine.*..................................

2 That book is one of Mary's favourites. / ....

3 Mr White is one of my father's colleagues. / ....

4 Angela is one of her classmates. / ....

5 I'm one of their employees. / ....

6 Jack is one of your neighbours. / ....

BANK OF FURTHER EXERCISES

14 Determiners (► see Units 23–30)

Complete these sentences by putting the determiner in the right place.

1 I'll lend you my new bicycle if you like. (*my*)
2 Children have left school now. (*both*)
3 Could you carry bag for me? (*this*)
4 I'd like to buy brown shoes please. (*those*)
5 I have to go to bank this afternoon. (*the*)
6 They live in big new house. (*a*)
7 I'm afraid I haven't got money left. (*much*)
8 I'd like to buy fruit. (*some*)
9 People enjoy going to the theatre. (*most*)
10 You can buy soap at supermarket. (*any*)

15 'a', 'an', 'the' (► see Units 24–26)

Look at this passage. If you see a noun phrase with a singular count noun but no determiner, put in 'a' or 'an'.

Psychiatrist greeting new patient noticed that she was carrying live duck under her arm. He invited her to take seat and asked how he could help her. 'Oh, I don't need any help, thank you,' she replied. 'My husband is the one who has problem. He thinks he's duck.'

This time put in either 'a', 'an', or 'the'.

Young man was out for a walk in large city when he met penguin. Penguin seemed to like him and began to follow him. Young man didn't know what to do so he went up to policeman to ask for advice. 'Take it to zoo,' said policeman.

Next day policeman saw same young man again still followed by penguin. 'What are you doing with that penguin?' he asked. 'I told you to take it to zoo.'

'Yes,' said young man, 'we went to zoo yesterday. Today we are going to museum.'

16 'all of' (► see Unit 27 paragraph 4)

Answer these questions using a phrase with 'all of' and a pronoun.

1 How many of you saw the thief? / .... *All of us.* ....
2 How many students passed the exam? / ....
3 How much milk have you drunk? / ....
4 How many of us have won a prize? / ....
5 How many of these books have you read? / ....

BANK OF FURTHER EXERCISES

17 'all', 'none', 'both', 'neither' (➤ see Units 27–28)

Look at the shapes. Make true sentences using 'all of the', 'all the', 'none of the', 'both of the', 'both the' or 'neither of the'.

1 .....*None of the*.......................... large triangles is white.
2 .... big triangles are black.
3 .... big squares are white.
4 .... big squares are black.
5 .... large circles are black.
6 .... circles are green.

18 Review of determiners (➤ see Units 23–30)

Complete the passages below by choosing a determiner from the brackets, or leaving a blank if a determiner is not needed.

1 When I was (- / a / the) ....*a*............ young man (a / the / my) ...... father gave me (- / an / some) .... advice. He told me that (- / an / the) .... honesty is always (- / a / the) .... best policy. It was (- / a / the) .... best advice I have ever had.

2 I recently bought (- / a / the) .... lot of (- / an / the) .... electronic equipment. (It was / They were) .... very expensive.

3 He is very popular. He has (lot of / many of / a lot of) .... friends and (few / a few / some) .... enemies.

4 When we were on holiday in (- / the) .... Iran we visited (- / the) .... Isfahan and stayed in (- / a-the) .... Shah Abbas Hotel near (- / a / the) .... centre of town.

5 Because the Hodja was believed to be (- / a / the) .... wisest man in (- / a / the) .... country, many people used to go and ask him (- / the) .... difficult questions. One day, a man asked him which was more useful, (- / a / the) .... sun or (- / a / the) .... moon. The Hodja thought for (a few / few / the few) .... minutes then said '(- / A / The) .... moon is more useful because (- / a / the) .... sun only shines during (- / a / the) .... day when it is light, but (- / a / the) .... moon shines at (- / a / the) .... night when it is dark.'

19 Review of determiners (➤ see Units 23–30)

Use one of the determiners below to complete the sentences which follow.

all	both	either	neither	none	no

1 A: Have you seen Jane or Richard? They were ....*both*............................... here a minute ago.
B: No, I haven't seen .... of them.
C: No. .... of them was here when I arrived.

2 A: Six of us went to see the film, but it was dreadful. .... of us enjoyed it very much. We were .... very disappointed.
B: We were planning to see it tomorrow, but we have .... free time.

BANK OF FURTHER EXERCISES

20 Position of adjectives (► see Unit 31 paragraph 6)

Complete these sentences using adjectives describing size or age.

1 He's tiny. He's only about four feet ....*tall*.. .

2 You can drive a car when you're seventeen years ....

3 The sea was about thirty feet .... at this point.

4 The wall was over ten feet ....

5 The lake is ten miles .... and two miles ....

6 When the baby was born it was over four kilos ....

21 Adjectives ending in '-ing' (► see Unit 34 paragraphs 1,2,4)

Complete each of the following dialogues with one of the '-ing' adjectives given below.

| alarming | amazing | exhausting | fascinating | terrifying | thrilling |

1 A: It was surprising, wasn't it? / B: Yes, absolutely .....*amazing*........................... .

2 A: Was it interesting? / B: Yes, it was ....

3 A: Did you find it frightening? / B: Yes, it was ....

4 A: Was it tiring? / B: Tiring? It was ....

5 A: It was worrying, wasn't it? / B: Yes, very ....

6 A: Was it an exciting game? / B: Yes, it was ....

22 '-ing' and '-ed' adjectives (► see Unit 34)

Choose one of the adjectives in brackets to complete each of the following sentences.

1 I was so ....*bored*........................... I could hardly stay awake. (*bored / boring*)

2 I think it's very .... the way people keep complaining about everything.
(*annoyed / annoying*)

3 The children did really well. I thought they were .... (*amazed / amazing*)

4 The children behaved very badly. I was very .... (*embarrassed / embarrassing*)

5 I am .... I was right. (*convinced / convincing*)

6 The boy .... the car looked about twelve years old. (*driven / driving*)

23 Comparative adjectives (► see Unit 36 paragraph 4)

Read the following passage and then make six correct sentences using the table below.

John is twenty years old. He's nearly two metres tall, and weighs nearly one hundred kilos. Mary is twenty-two. She's only one metre sixty, and weighs less than fifty kilos. Peter is forty-five. He's one metre ninety-five, and weighs one hundred and eighty kilos.

John	far (very) much a lot	older		John.
Mary	is a good deal slightly	taller	than	Mary.
Peter	a bit a little	heavier		Peter.

1 ...Peter is a lot older than John..

2 ....

3 ....

4 ....

5 ....

6 ....

24 Superlative adjectives (► see Unit 36 paragraph 6)

Complete the following sentences using superlative adjectives in front of the nouns.

1 Everest is ...... the highest mountain .... in the world. (*high mountain*)

2 The Pacific is .... in the world. (*big ocean*)

3 China is .... in the world. (*populated country*)

4 Oxford is .... in Britain. (*old university*)

5 The Nile is .... in Africa. (*long river*)

6 The Amazon is .... in the world. (*long river*)

25 Comparative adjectives and other ways of comparing (► see Units 36–37)

Look at the pictures and complete these sentences about John, Mike, and Peter.

1 ...John............... is taller than ...Mike...........

   and ......Peter........................... .

2 .... is taller than .... ,

   but he isn't as tall as ....

3 .... is older than .... ,

   but he isn't as old as ....

4 .... is younger than ....,

   but he isn't as young as ....

5 .... is younger than .... and ....

6 .... is nearly as old as ....

7 .... is nearly as tall as ....

8 .... is much taller than........................... .

John 18   Mike 19   Peter 15

215

BANK OF FURTHER EXERCISES

26 Comparison (▶ see Units 35–37)

Rewrite these sentences using the comparative of the adjectives in brackets.

1 I prefer my new school to the one I went to before. (*good*)
   My new school is better than the one I went to before.
   ....

2 I prefer staying in a hotel to camping. (*comfortable*)
   ....

3 I prefer eating out to cooking for myself. (*easy*)
   ....

4 I prefer living in the country to living in a town. (*peaceful*)
   ....

5 I prefer cycling to driving. (*healthy*)
   ....

27 Position of adverbials (▶ see Unit 38 paragraph 3)

Rewrite these sentences with the adverbials in the normal place at the end of the clause.

1 Quickly I hid the bag under the table. / ...*I hid the bag quickly under the table.*...................

2 On Saturday morning our holiday began. / ....

3 Unhappily she shook her head. / ....

4 Slowly and sadly he walked back home. / ....

5 Before going home he locked up the office. / ....

6 In the box there was a gold ring. / ....

7 Quietly he whispered his name. / ....

8 Early in the morning she went for a jog. / ....

9 Too late I tried to stop him. / ....

10 At exactly seven o'clock the film began. / ....

28 Adverbials of time (▶ see Unit 40 paragraphs 3–5)

Complete the following sets of sentences using 'ago', 'for', or 'since' once each.

1 I'll be staying in Newcastle ....*for*.. about a couple of weeks.
   I've been waiting here ....*since*.. five o'clock.
   I got here about an hour ....*ago*.. .

2 George had already worked on the farm .... over five years.
   He had started work there five years ....
   He had been in charge .... the summer of 1988.

3 It was about ten years .... that I started learning English.
   I have been learning English .... I started secondary school.
   I studied English .... five years at school.

4 Judith has lived with us ever .... she was seven.
   She has been with us .... nearly five years now.
   She first came to live with us about five years ....

5 .... October the weather has been awful.

Fortunately we had our holiday months ....

We went to Italy .... ten days.

6 I first met Jan at a party about six months ....

I have known Jan .... just over six months.

I have known Jan .... we met at your Christmas party.

7 We will be at home .... the next hour or so.

I got home about ten minutes ....

I've been at home .... just before five.

8 Ten years .... very few people knew much about computers.

My kids have been using a home computer .... the last five years.

The youngest one has been using a computer .... the age of four.

29 Adverbials of degree (➤ see Unit 43 paragraph 3)

Use these phrases, which consist of adverbs of degree that are being used to modify adjectives, to complete the sentences.

| really angry   awfully good   very happy   extremely intelligent   pretty tired |

1 You must be ....*pretty tired*.................................... . You've been working all day.

2 I'm .... I'm really enjoying myself.

3 His new book is .... I think it's one of his best.

4 The children behaved badly. Finally their father got .... with them.

5 Mary may seem a bit slow when you first meet her, but she's actually ....

30 Adverbials of degree (➤ see Unit 43 paragraph 7)

Match the questions with the answers, which contain emphasizing adverbs.

1 Were you very frightened?   a Yes. We were absolutely furious.

2 Was it a very exciting match?   b It was really thrilling.

3 Did she get very good exam results?   c He's quite brilliant.

4 Is he a very good scientist?   d It was quite fascinating.

5 Is it very big?   e He's absolutely awful.

6 Were you very angry?   f Yes. We were completely terrified.

7 Was it a very interesting play?   g Yes. They were absolutely brilliant.

8 Were her parents very pleased?   h Yes. They were absolutely delighted.

9 Is he a very bad student?   i Yes. It's absolutely enormous.

31 Review of adverbials (➤ see Units 38–43)

Choose the adjective or adverb from the brackets to complete these sentences.

1 Be as ....*quick*.................................... as you can. (*quick / quickly*)

2 Fortunately, he was driving very .... at the time of the accident. (*slow / slowly*)

BANK OF FURTHER EXERCISES

3 Try to be .... with that vase. It's very valuable. (*careful / carefully*)

4 We lived very .... abroad for nearly five years. (*happy / happily*)

5 How are you? I hope you're .... (*good / well*)

6 Where's Henry nowadays? I haven't seen him .... (*late / lately*)

7 Don't worry about Francis. She always arrives .... (*late / lately*)

8 You'll find it if you look .... enough. (*hard / hardly*)

32 Prepositions of place (▶ see Unit 45)

Fill the gaps in these paragraphs using 'at', 'in', or 'on'.

1 Liz lives ......*in*...... Harton. She has a flat .... the third floor of Conway House, ... Church Street. It's on the left, opposite the bank, as you drive along the road towards the traffic lights .... the end of the street.

2 There's a picture .... the wall .... the top of the stairs and Liz's flat is on the left with her name .... the door.

3 There was a good film .... the Odeon last week. The Odeon is .... the corner of the High Street. I met Judy .... the entrance to the cinema after work, but I was rather late so we didn't get very good seats. We had to sit .... the front row, right .... the end on the left.

33 Review of adverbials (▶ see Units 38–46)

Choose one of the prepositions in brackets to fill each gap in the sentence, or leave the gap empty if you think a preposition is not needed.

1 I start work (*- / in / on / at*) ......*at*...... eight o'clock (*- / in / on / at*) .... the morning (*- / in / on / at*) .... every day, except (*in / on / at / until*) .... Saturday, when I don't start (*in / on / at / until*) .... nine thirty.

2 It's nearly two o'clock and we have had nothing to eat (*at / for / since / until*) .... six o'clock (*- / in / on / at*) .... this morning.

3 I asked him (*- / in / on / at*) .... yesterday, and he said the car will be ready (*- / since / until / by*) .... lunchtime (*in / on / at*) .... Friday.

4 The last time I saw Jan was (*in / on / at / for*) .... Christmas three years (*before / since / ago / last*) .... We were at a party together (*- / in / on / at*) .... Christmas Eve.

5 George worked in France (*- / for / since / until*) .... three months (*- / during / for / at*) .... the summer, but he's been back home (*- / for / since / until*) .... October.

6 I will be (*- / in / at / to*) .... abroad (*- / in / from / until*) .... October (*- / at / to / since*) .... Christmas.

7 Have you finished your essay (*still / any more / yet / since*) .... , or are you (*still / yet / already / any more*) .... working on it?

8 Jack hasn't phoned (*still / since / until / yet*) .... last month. Perhaps he (*still / yet / now / already*) .... isn't back from his holidays.

9 A: We have been waiting (*until / since / for / already*) .... more than an hour. Do you think

218

they are coming? B: I don't know. Perhaps they have (*just / already / since / now*) .... left.

10 Look at the time. It's (*already / until / before / yet*) .... eight o'clock and we haven't even started (*already / until / any more / yet*) ....

34 Review of adverbials (▶ see Units 38–46)

Use one of the following prepositions to fill each of the gaps below. You may use the same word more than once.

above	at	by	in	off	on	opposite	out of	to

1 Do you usually go to school ....*by*............ bus or .... your bike?

2 John's not .... home. He went out .... work an hour ago.

3 There was a big picture .... the wall just .... the fireplace.

4 They live .... the big house on the left .... the end of our street.

5 He was so badly injured he couldn't get .... the car by himself.

6 Meet me .... the entrance .... your way in.

7 Get .... the bus .... the end of the High Street, and you'll see my office just .... the bus stop.

8 He drove me to the hospital .... his car.

35 Nouns with prepositions (▶ see Unit 48 paragraph 3)

Complete these sentences by changing the clause in brackets into a noun phrase with 'of'. Use these nouns.

arrival	behaviour	death	departure	invasion	theft

1 Trouble was prevented by ..*the sudden arrival of the police*......... . (*the police suddenly arrived*)

2 The meeting was postponed following .... (*the chairman died unexpectedly*)

3 British Rail apologized for .... (*the train departed late*)

4 She rang the police to report .... (*her jewellery had been stolen*)

5 Mrs Green apologized for .... (*the children behaved dreadfully*)

6 War was inevitable after .... (*the island was invaded*)

36 Verbs with prepositions (▶ see Unit 49)

Complete these sentences using 'of' or 'on'.

1 We thought ....*of*..... asking James to design it, but I'm not sure if you can count .... him to get it done.

2 I know .... two or three designers you could really depend ....

3 I'm relying .... Alphaco for the construction work. Have you heard .... them?

4 I'm depending .... you to think .... something, before the boss gets here.

5 Talking .... holidays, where were you planning .... going?

37 **Verbs with prepositions** (➔ see Unit 49)

Which one of these verbs with prepositions means the same as the underlined word or phrase in the sentences below?

apologize for	ask for	laugh at	rely on	talk about

1 They rang the ambulance service to <u>request</u> help. / .... *ask for* ....
2 I feel silly in these clothes. Everyone will <u>make fun of</u> me. / ....
3 I would just like to say that I <u>am sorry for</u> the trouble I have caused. / ....
4 If you want help, you can always <u>depend on</u> me. / ....
5 Let's leave that for the time being. We can <u>discuss</u> it later. / ....

38 **Phrasal verbs** (➔ see Unit 50)

Complete the following sentences using the phrasal verb given in brackets. You will need to use an appropriate pronoun as object.

1 Their parents were overseas so their grandparents ...... *brought them up* .... (*bring up*)
2 I want to put these blankets away. Could you help me to .... ? (*fold up*)
3 I want to fold these blankets up and .... (*put away*)
4 When we come to Henry's house, I'll .... (*point out*)
5 He never read my letters, he just .... (*tore up*)
6 You mean he tore up your letters and .... ? (*threw away*)
7 These papers are in a dreadful mess. Have you got time to .... ? (*sort out*)
8 The vase was lying there broken. Someone must have .... (*knock down*)
9 It's my money. Please .... (*hand over*)
10 The garage is falling apart. The best thing is to .... and build another. (*pull down*)

39 **Phrasal verbs** (➔ see Unit 50)

Write these sentences in two ways. First use the phrasal verb and noun group given in brackets in this structure: verb followed by noun and particle ('v+n+p'). Then rewrite the clause in the structure: verb followed by particle and noun ('v+p+n').

1 Can I help you to (*the blankets / fold up*)?
   v+n+p: .... *Can I help you to fold the blankets up?* ....
   v+p+n: .... *Can I help you to fold up the blankets?* ....
2 We never found out who (*the vase / knock over*).
   v+n+p: ....
   v+p+n: ....
3 He refused to (*the money / hand over*).
   v+n+p: ....
   v+p+n: ....
4 Can you help me to (*the papers / sort out*)?
   v+n+p: ....
   v+p+n: ....

5 It would be useful if someone could (*my mistakes / sort out*).

v+n+p: ....

v+p+n: ....

6 It's very hard work (*children / bringing up*).

v+n+p: ....

v+p+n: ....

7 They're planning to (*all the houses / pull down*).

v+n+p: ....

v+p+n: ....

8 Andrew never remembers to (*his books / put away*).

v+n+p: ....

v+p+n: ....

40 Verbs with two objects (▶ see Unit 52)

Rewrite these sentences using 'for' or 'to'.

1 I have reserved your friends a table.
   I have reserved a table for your friends.
   ....

2 He offered his next door neighbour a lot of help.

   ....

3 I have cooked the children a special supper.

   ....

4 Please send us your reply as soon as possible.

   ....

5 I'll try to save you a place.

   ....

6 Show your uncle that book you've just bought.

   ....

41 Common verbs with nouns for actions (▶ see Unit 56)

Use these verbs to complete the sentences which follow. You may use each verb more than once.

did	gave	had	made	took	went

1 George ....*made*.................... a useful suggestion.

2 It wasn't working, so I .... it a good kick.

3 You obviously .... a lot of trouble over this.

4 They .... a dreadful fight when they got home.

5 I .... the washing up before going to bed.

6 We .... for a swim every morning before breakfast.

7 John .... me some useful advice.

8 We .... a short break over the weekend.

BANK OF FURTHER EXERCISES

42 Past simple and past perfect (► see Unit 59 paragraphs 2,3)

Look at this narrative of a day at school.

I left home early and finished my homework at school. I had a hard morning, with tests in maths and English, then at lunchtime I got a surprise.

Now the narrative starts at lunchtime and looks back. What happens to the tenses of the verbs?

It was lunchtime and I was tired. I ......*had left*...... home early and .... my homework at school. I .... a hard morning, with tests in maths and English. Then I got a surprise.

Now complete the following narrative, using the past simple or past perfect of the verbs given.

| get | ask | choose | tell | be | be | rush | happen |

I ....*got*.................... a message from the headmaster. Earlier in the week, the local TV station .... him to send a student to appear in a quiz show. After talking to several teachers, he .... me. He .... me I .... going to represent the school. I .... so excited, I .... home as fast as I could to tell my parents what ....

43 Past continuous (► see Unit 60 paragraph 3)

Complete this past tense narrative, using each of the following verbs once.

| work | share | try | live |

Angela ...*was working*........ in a restaurant. She had just left school and she .... to save some money before going to university. She .... in a little village in the country where she .... a cottage with some friends.

44 Continuous tenses (► see Unit 60)

Use one of the following verbs in a continuous tense to complete each of the sentences below. You may use each verb more than once.

| change | get | grow up | improve | increase |

1 Jean has been very ill but she ....*is getting*............................ better now.
2 The world's population .... by 100% every year.
3 My French isn't very good but it ....
4 Scientists believe that the world's climate .... It .... warmer every year.
5 John is a good player and he .... all the time.
6 The weather had been dreadful that year, and it .... worse.
7 My father has retired from his job now. He .... old.

222

8   The children .... quickly now that they have reached their teens.

9   Unemployment is still high in Britain but things .... slowly.

10 Office work .... rapidly with the introduction of computers.

45 Talking about the past (► see Unit 63)

Use these verbs and verb groups to complete the paragraph below.

| offered   didn't ask   had never played   asked   used to go   used to go |
| would practise   had had   wanted   was playing   couldn't play |

When I was a boy, I .....*wanted*.............. to be a jazz musician. I used to play the drums. I ....
.... for hours every evening, and I would spend almost every weekend practising
too. I .... to my local jazz club every week to listen. One night a group
called The Rollers .... there. Unfortunately, their drummer ....
an accident on his way to the club, so he ....They .... me to
take his place, and of course I agreed. It was awful. I felt that I .... so badly
before. After that, I still .... to the club, but I never ....
to play again, and they certainly .... me.

46 Review of tenses (► see Units 57-65)

Choose the right form of the verb to complete the following sentences.

1   I ....*usually go*.......................... (*usually go / am usually going / have usually gone*) to
    work by car, but I .... (*go / am going / have gone*) on the bus
    this week while my car .... (*is / is being / has been*) mended.

2   A: .... (*Do you know / Are you knowing / Can you know*)
    where Brian is?
    B: I .... (*don't see / am not seeing / haven't seen*) him since
    lunch. I .... (*think / am thinking / can think*) he's in the
    kitchen. He .... (*probably do / probably does / is probably doing*) the washing up.

3   My daughter is a vegetarian. She .... (*doesn't eat / isn't eating / hasn't eaten*)
    meat. It is sometimes difficult in a restaurant when she ....
    (*finds / is finding / will find*) that they .... (*don't have / aren't having / won't
    have*) any vegetarian dishes. That's why she .... (*usually telephones / is usually
    telephoning / will usually telephone*) beforehand to find out what's on the menu.

4   A: How long .... (*do you live / are you living / have you been living*) in Liverpool?
    B: Only three weeks. We .... (*stay / are staying / have been staying*) in a hotel
    until we .... (*are finding / will find / have found*) a house to buy.

5   A: I .... (*met / was meeting / have meeting*) George while I ....
    (*waited / was waiting / have waited*) for the bus tonight.
    B: How is he? I .... (*am not seeing / haven't seen / didn't see*) him for months.
    A: He .... (*was seeming / seemed / has seemed*) to be very well.

BANK OF FURTHER EXERCISES

B: I .... (*think / am thinking*) he .... (*was just getting / just got / has just got*) a new job, ... (*wasn't he / didn't he / hasn't he*)? A: Well, he .... (*is just leaving / has just left / just left*) his old job about a month ago, but he .... (*doesn't find / hasn't found / didn't find*) anything else yet. He .... (*still looks / is still looking*) for something.

6 Everyone in the Hodja's village .... (*knew / was knowing*) that the Hodja was well educated and .... (*went / was going / had been*) to the finest schools. They .... (*were often going / had often gone / would often go*) to him for advice. One day a poor illiterate farmer .... (*wants / was wanting / wanted*) the Hodja to write a letter for him.

'Where .... (*will you / do you / are you going to*) send this letter?' the Hodja .... (*asked / was asking / had asked*). 'To Cairo,' said the farmer. 'I'm afraid I .... (*can't / couldn't / don't*) help you,' said the Hodja, 'I .... (*don't go / am not going*) to Cairo.' 'But you .... (*don't need / are not needing / didn't need*) to go there,' said the farmer, 'I .... (*just want / am just wanting / will just want*) to send the letter there.' 'Yes,' said the Hodja, 'but my writing is so bad that nobody else .... (*is reading / reads / can read*) it so if I .... (*write / am writing / will write*) the letter, I .... (*have / will have / am having*) to go there and read it myself.'

7 When the farmer asked the Hodja if he .... (*will write / would write*) the letter, the Hodja asked him where the letter .... (*goes / is going / was going*). The man said that it .... (*is / was*) to a friend in Cairo. Then the Hodja explained that he .... (*cannot / could not / does not*) write the letter because he .... (*is not going / was not going / does not go*) to Cairo. He said his writing .... (*is / was*) so bad that nobody else .... (*can / could*) read it. So if he .... (*writes / wrote / is writing*) the letter he .... (*has / will have / would have*) to go to Cairo himself to read it.

8 One day the Hodja .... (*hears / heard / was hearing*) some soldiers telling stories about how brave they .... (*are / were / have been*). 'Well,' said the Hodja, 'I .... (*am remembering / remember / remembered*) when I was a soldier, I .... (*have once cut / once cut / was once cutting*) the arm right off my enemy.' 'Really?' asked one of the soldiers. 'Why .... (*haven't you cut / didn't you cut / weren't you cutting*) off his head?' 'Well,' said the Hodja, 'somebody .... (*was already doing / already did / had already done*) that.

47 Conditional clauses (▶ see Unit 67)

Match these parts to make conditional sentences.

1 If one of the dogs attacked, …	a … you could always go by bus.
2 If you were late for the train, …	b … I can take you by car.
3 If you moved to the country, …	c … there's sure to be an accident.
4 If the dog had attacked, …	d … you would certainly have been late.
5 If the train is late, …	e … it could have killed one of the children.
6 If you move to London, …	f … you could buy a bigger house.
7 If you drive too fast, …	g … you'll be closer to the office.
8 If you had missed your connection, …	h … you would get a nasty bite.

48 I wish – wants and wishes (▶ see Unit 68)

Match the comments with the wishes.

1 I feel so old.	a I wish it would rain.
2 The plants in the garden are dying.	b I wish you had told me.
3 We never hear from Angela.	c I wish we lived nearer the office.
4 I didn't know you were ill.	d I wish you could come more often.
5 I can't afford to go out.	e I wish I hadn't told anyone.
6 It takes hours to get to work.	f I wish I were younger.
7 She looked absolutely lovely.	g I wish she would write more often.
8 We don't see you very often nowadays.	h I wish I had more money.
9 Now everyone knows the secret.	i I wish I could have taken a photograph.

49 Verbs with '-ing' clauses (▶ see Unit 69)

Use the correct forms of the verbs in brackets to complete these sentences.

1 All right, children, …… *stop* …… talking please and …… *start* …… writing. (*start / stop*)
2 Dan never ……………… talking. I hate the way he…………… interrupting everyone. (*stop / keep*)
3 It ……………… raining early in the morning and ……………… pouring down until late afternoon. (*go on / start*)
4 He ……………… shouting and waving, until we all ……………… talking and ……………… taking notice of him. (*start / keep on / stop*)
5 We had ……………… discussing his case, but he still ……………… complaining about it, until the chairman told him to ……………… making such a fuss and ……………… behaving sensibly. (*go on / finish / start / stop*)

50 Verbs with '-ing' clauses (▶ see Unit 69 paragraph 1)

Complete the following to make true sentences.

1 I loathe ……………………………………………………………………………………
2 I detest ……………………………………………………………………………………
3 I can't stand ……………………………………………………………………………………

BANK OF FURTHER EXERCISES

4 I dislike ....

5 I quite enjoy ....

6 I enjoy ....

7 I really enjoy ....

Here are some ideas to help you.

being late for something	going to the dentist	learning English	going to the doctor
lying in bed in the morning	reading	listening to rock music	watching tennis on TV
playing football			

51 Verbs with '-ing' clauses (➤ see Unit 69 paragraph 4)

Use these verbs to complete the sentences which follow.

catch	feel	hear	imagine	prevent	see	stop

1 You can't ....*stop*.................... people wasting their money, if that's what they want to do.

2 It was so quiet that I could .... people talking at the other end of the field.

3 Look over there. I think I can .... something moving.

4 If you put your hand here, you can .... the baby's heart beating.

5 You'll be in a lot of trouble, if they .... you driving without a licence.

6 They tied his hands to .... him escaping.

7 He is so serious, it's difficult to .... him playing a joke on anyone.

52 Nouns with 'to'-infinitive clauses (➤ see Unit 70 paragraph 9)

Use the following nouns to complete the sentences below.

decision	inability	need	opportunity	refusal	willingness	attempt	order

1 I was surprised that he couldn't understand.
   I was surprised at his ....*inability*................................ to understand.

2 We were angry when he made up his mind to withdraw from the competition.
   We were angry at his .... to withdraw from the competition.

3 John's father arranged for him to work abroad.
   John's father gave him the .... to work abroad.

4 It is not necessary to send the books by air mail.
   There is no .... to send the books by air mail.

5 We were disappointed when she said she wouldn't help.
   We were disappointed at her .... to help.

6 We thanked the headmaster when he offered to help.
   We thanked the headmaster for his .... to help.

7 He failed by two seconds when he tried to break the record.
   He failed by two seconds in his .... to break the record.

8 The soldiers did not obey when they were told to advance.

The soldiers did not obey the .... to advance.

53 Verbs with 'to'-infinitive clauses (▶ see Unit 70 paragraph 5)

Rewrite these sentences, using the first verb in the passive voice.

1 At one time everybody believed that the world was flat. /

At one time the world ......*was believed to be flat.*......................................

2 I suppose that their new house cost a million pounds. /

Their new house ....

3 Our correspondent reported that the city had been hit by an earthquake early this morning. /

The city ....

4 Everyone knows that he is a brilliant politician. /

He ....

5 The police allege that the prisoner brought dangerous drugs into the country. /

The prisoner ....

6 We understand that the man is armed and dangerous. /

The man ....

54 Verbs with 'to'-infinitive clauses (▶ see Unit 70 paragraph 6)

Rewrite these sentences using a 'wh'-word and a 'to'-infinitive clause.

1 What shall I wear? / I can't decide ....*what to wear*......................... .

2 Who shall I ask? / I don't know ....

3 Where shall we go? / Can you tell us ....?

4 How do you open it? / Can you explain ....?

5 When should I start? / Tell me ....

6 I want to play tennis. / Can you teach me ....?

7 I can't swim. / I never learned ....

55 Verbs with 'to'-infinitive or '-ing' clauses (▶ see Units 69–71)

Complete the following sentences, using the verb in brackets in a 'to'-infinitive or '-ing' clause.

1 He expects ....*to come*............................ round about six this evening. (*come*)

2 He kept .... while we were talking. (*interrupt*)

3 We asked him to stop .... , but he took no notice. (*shout*)

4 I managed .... everything ready in time. (*get*)

5 The key is on the shelf. I remember .... it there. (*leave*)

6 Remind me .... that letter on my way to work. (*post*)

7 You'll have to wait for someone .... and mend it. (*come*)

8 Maria suggested .... Fred to help. (*ask*)

BANK OF FURTHER EXERCISES

56 Verbs with other types of clauses (▶ see Unit 72 paragraph 2)

Complete these sentences using the appropriate form of these verbs.

move	play	speak	steal	leave

1 They say Pele was the greatest footballer ever. I'm afraid I was too young to see him ..... play ....
2 Please stop making such a noise. We can hardly hear ourselves ....
3 I think it's still alive. I'm sure I felt it ....
4 I saw the shoplifter .... the necklace and pass it to his friend.
5 A: Is Joe still here? B: No. I saw him .... half an hour ago.

57 Verbs with other types of clauses (▶ see Unit 72 paragraph 3)

Complete these sentences using a form of 'get' with the words in brackets.

1 It's dreadful. You can hardly see out. We must ..get the windows cleaned... . (the windows / clean)
2 I have to .... for a new passport. (my photograph / take)
3 The television is very bad. We really ought to .... (it / mend)
4 These trousers are too long. I think I'll .... (them / shorten)
5 John Brown .... playing football last week. (his nose / break)

58 Link verbs (▶ see Unit 73)

Match the two clauses or sentences.

1 She looks just like her sister, ...   a ... but she became a doctor instead.
2 She wanted to be a pop singer, ...   b ... but she caused a lot of trouble.
3 She always seemed very quiet, ...   c ... but she doesn't look very happy.
4 She looked exhausted, ...   d ... so let's offer her the job.
5 She sounds cheerful, ...   e ... but she's much younger.
6 She seems well qualified, ...   f ... but she soon felt better.

59 Reporting the past (▶ see Unit 74)

Here is part of a story told in the present tense.

Late that night, as I am sitting on my bed reading, there is a knock on my door. It turns out to be the daughter of the hotel manager. He has told her I am English, and she asks if I will help her do a translation that she's been set for homework.

Imagine you are telling the author's story to someone else. Use the appropriate tense of one the following verbs to complete the story below.

sit	knock	tell	be	want	be

As Eric .....sat............. on his bed reading, the hotel manager's daughter ....
on the door. Her father .... her that Eric .... English, and she
.... him to help her with the translation she .... set for homework.

228

60 **Reporting the past** (► see Unit 74)

Below there are reports of some famous sayings. Decide whether they contain advice, or things that are still true. Then complete the original sayings by putting the verbs in brackets into the right tenses.

1 Anatole France said that you should never lend books out, because no one ever returns them. He said the only books in his library were the ones that other folk had lent him.
Never lend books, because no one ever ......*returns*.......... them. The only books I ....*have*........ in my library are books that other people ....*have lent*............ me. (*return*) (*have*) (*lend*)

2 Someone once defined a banker as a man who lends you an umbrella when the weather's good, and takes it away when it starts to rain.
A banker is a man who .... you an umbrella when the weather .... fine and .... it away from you when it .... (*lend*) (*be*) (*take*) (*rain*)

3 Somerset Maugham said that if you want to eat well in England, you should eat three breakfasts. That was what he always did, and he had had no cause to regret it.
If you .... to eat well in England, eat three breakfasts. That's what I always .... , and I .... no cause to regret it. (*want*) (*do*) (*have*)

61 **Reported questions** (► see Unit 75 and Unit 9)

Make these questions into indirect questions. Do each one first in the present and then in the past.

1 What time will Helen be home?
He wants to know ....*what time Helen will be home.*...
He wanted to know ....*what time Helen would be home.*.............................

2 Does Joe still live in Liverpool?
She would like to know ....
She asked me ....

3 Have you mended the roof?
They are asking ....
They wanted to know ....

4 When will Harry be moving to Manchester?
She wants to know ....
She asked ....

5 What time does the concert finish?
They would like to know ....
They wanted to know ....

6 Will Peggy be coming too?
Everyone keeps asking ....
Everyone kept asking ....

7 Will we have to speak English all the time?
They want to know ....
They wanted to know ....

8   Who did you speak to on the phone?

She is asking me ....

She asked me ....

62 Reporting (▶ see Unit 77 paragraph 1)

Use the appropriate form of these verbs to complete the sentences below.

advise   beg   command   forbid   instruct   invite   remind   warn

1   If you ......*forbid*.......................... someone to do something, you order that it must not be done.

EG I ......*forbid*.. you to tell her.

2   If you .... someone to do something, you advise them to do it in
order to avoid possible danger or punishment.

EG I .... him not to lose his temper.

3   If you .... someone to do something, you ask them very seriously.

EG She .... the doctor not to tell her husband how ill she was.

4   If someone .... you to do something or take part in
something, they ask you to do it.

EG I was .... by a friend to attend the committee meeting.

5   When someone .... you to do something, they say
something to make you remember to do it.

EG .... me to speak to you about that later.

6   If you .... someone to do something, you order them to do it.

EG He .... them to lie down.

7   If you .... someone to do something, you tell them to do it in a formal or severe way.

EG I've been .... to take you to London.

8   If you .... someone to do something, you say that you think they ought to do it.

EG His doctor .... him to change his job.

63 Reporting (▶ see Unit 77 paragraph 2)

Rewrite these sentences with 'ask' and an 'if'-clause using the words given.

1   'Do you think you will be able to come back later?' (*We / everyone*)
    .....*We asked everyone if they would be able to come back later.*.................................

2   'Are you ready to go?' (*John / Jill*)
    ....

3   'Can we go on the school picnic?' (*The children / their parents*)
    ....

4   'Is there a bus to Piccadilly?' (*I / the policeman*)
    ....

5   'Do you think we can afford to take a taxi?' (*My wife / me*)
    ....

6   'Have you anything to declare?' (*The customs officer / Joe*)
    ....

64 **The passive voice (▶ see Unit 78 paragraph 8)**

Some passive sentences can be expressed in two ways. Look at the example, then find another way to write the remaining five sentences.

1 I was shown their letters of appointment. / ...*Their letters of appointment were shown to me.*...

2 I was sent full details of the job. / ....

3 They were all presented with signed certificates. / ....
....

4 A free sightseeing trip is offered to all passengers. / ....
....

5 Drinks and snacks have been given to everyone in our group. / ....
....

6 She was brought the news of their success yesterday evening. / ....
....

65 **Could – possibility (▶ see Unit 81 paragraph 2)**

Complete these sentences using 'could'.

1 If you don't take a map, you might easily get lost.
Without a map, ... *you could get lost.* ....

2 Even though it sounds unlikely, it may be true.
It sounds unlikely, but ....

3 If you aren't careful, you might cut yourself.
Be careful. ....

4 If they are lucky, they might easily win.
With a bit of luck, ...

5 If she gets the job, she might earn as much as £50,000 a year.
She ....

6 It's a dangerous bend. It is likely to cause a serious accident.
That bend is really dangerous. ....

7 It's possible to get there in time, if you take a taxi.
If you take a taxi, ...

8 The telephone's ringing. Perhaps it's for you.
There's the telephone. ....

9 The police said the man was armed and that he might be dangerous.
It was reported that the man was armed and ....

10 There will be rain which might turn to snow on high ground.
There is likely to be rain, ...

BANK OF FURTHER EXERCISES

66 Could have, couldn't have – possibility (▶ see Unit 81 paragraph 3)

Which of these things 'could' you 'have done' if you had lived a hundred years ago? Which things 'couldn't' you 'have done?' Write six sentences like this one, using the information in the box below.

A hundred years ago I could have ridden a horse, but I couldn't have flown in an aeroplane.

....

....

....

....

....

....

flown in an aeroplane	gone to the cinema	learnt English	listened to Beethoven
listened to The Beatles	played chess	played computer games	read Ernest Hemingway
read Shakespeare	ridden a horse	travelled by train	watched television

67 Couldn't, couldn't have – possibility (▶ see Unit 81 paragraph 7)

Match the sentences with the comments, which contain 'couldn't' or 'couldn't have' and a comparative adjective.

1 I'm absolutely delighted.   a She couldn't have felt better.

2 He was terrified.   b He couldn't have been more frightened.

3 She was as fit as a fiddle.   c I couldn't feel more tired.

4 I'm exhausted.   d I couldn't be happier.

5 She was thrilled to bits.   e He couldn't have been worse.

6 He was desperately ill.   f She couldn't have been more excited.

68 Must, must have – probability and certainty (▶ see Unit 82 paragraphs 4,5)

Rewrite the parts of the sentence in bold, using either 'must' or 'must have'.

1 Our house is in Bradford Road too. **We probably live very close to you.**
   We must live very close to you.
....

2 His car's not in the garage. **I suppose he has taken it to work.**
   He must have taken it to work.
....

3 Peter has worked here for ages. **I'm sure he knows the answer.**
....

4 The children aren't at home. **They've probably left for school.**
....

5 It's a very well known book. **I'm sure you've read it.**
....

6 It's dreadfully busy. **I suppose this is the rush hour.**
....

BANK OF FURTHER EXERCISES

69 **Be able to – ability** (▶ see Unit 83 paragraphs 3,4,7)

Complete these sentences using the correct form of 'be able to'.

1 If you sit at the back, you ....*won't be able to*........................ see very well.

2 Fortunately, she .... give the police a good description of the mugger.

3 I'm sorry. We're busy on Sunday, so we .... come.

4 Experiments suggest that some dolphins .... use a complicated system of sounds for communication.

5 We got there in good time, so we .... help Janet get everything ready.

6 I hope we .... produce better results in the future.

7 The chairman sends his apologies that he .... be with us this evening.

70 **Could have – ability** (▶ see Unit 83 paragraph 6)

Read the following passage.

My friend Tom had an eventful week last week. On Sunday he had a bad car accident. Tom wasn't seriously injured, but the other driver wasn't so fortunate. His leg was broken. On Monday evening, Tom played tennis. On Tuesday, he drove to the supermarket and did the shopping. On Wednesday, he went for a long walk in the country. On Thursday he mowed the lawn and weeded the garden, on Friday he cleaned the windows and tidied the garden shed, and on Saturday he cycled to the next village, where he refereed a football match. If he had broken his leg, Tom couldn't have done any of these things.

Now list six things Tom couldn't have done if he had broken his leg.

1 ....*He couldn't have driven to the supermarket.*........................

2 ....

3 ....

4 ....

5 ....

6 ....

71 **Can, can't – ability** (▶ see Unit 83 paragraph 8)

Use these phrases with 'can' and 'can't' to complete the sentences below.

can hear	can't hear	can see	can't see (x 2)	can smell	can't smell

1 I've got a really bad cold. I ....*can't smell*................ anything.

2 I .... you, but I .... you.

3 There's something good in the kitchen. You .... it from here.

4 Turn the radio up a bit. I .... it very clearly.

5 There's a lovely view. On a clear day you .... for miles.

6 Can you move over a bit? I .... anything when you're in the way.

BANK OF FURTHER EXERCISES

72 **Might – suggestions** (➤ see Unit 86 paragraphs 3,4)

Use the following phrases to complete the sentences below.

| buy a new one   come too   come round and meet him   come with me |
| enjoy it   go home   go together   see a doctor |

1 There's a good film on this evening. I thought perhaps you might .... *enjoy it.* ....

2 If we're all going to London, we might as well ....

3 If your bike has been stolen, you might want to ....

4 If you're still feeling ill, it might be wise to ....

5 The party's over. We might as well ....

6 We're having a few friends round. I thought you might like to ....

7 I'm driving to Birmingham tomorrow. You might as well ....

8 George is coming tomorrow. You might like to ....

73 **Ought to have – mild obligation** (➤ see Unit 91 paragraph 3)

Rewrite these sentences using 'ought to have' or 'ought not to have'.

1 I wish I had known what was going to happen. /
  ..*I ought to have known what was going to happen.*..

2 It was silly of John to leave home without telling us. /
  ..*John ought not to have left home without telling us.*..

3 Why didn't you ask for permission? /
  ....

4 I wish we hadn't stayed so late. /
  ....

5 Why didn't you go to the doctor's earlier? /
  ....

6 It's a pity you didn't meet Jenny while you were here. /
  ....

7 I'm sorry I got so angry about what happened. /
  ....

8 It would have been better if you had come on your own. /
  ....

9 It's a pity we didn't reserve seats. /
  ....

10 Why didn't you stop at the traffic lights? /
  ....

74 **Had better – mild obligation and advice** (➤ see Unit 91 paragraph 4)

Rewrite these sentences using 'had better' or 'had better not'.

1 I think you should come back tomorrow. / .... *You had better come back tomorrow.* ....

2 He's busy. I don't think you should disturb him. / ... *You had better not disturb him.* ....

3 I think I ought to ask my father first. / ....

4 I think we should be going home now. / ....

5 I hope they won't make any trouble. / ....

6 You ought to get a return ticket. / ....

7 Don't go out alone at night. / ....

8 You ought to go to bed. / ....

9 We should get something to eat. / ....

10 We shouldn't waste any more time. / ....

75 Review of modals (➤ see Units 79–91)

Rewrite these sentences using the modals given.

1 Don't stay out too late. (*ought*) / .....*You ought not to stay out too late.*.....................

2 Come home before midnight. (*must*) / ....

3 Don't go out in the rain. (*should*) / ....

4 Don't complain so much. (*ought*) / ....

5 Don't spend too much money. (*must*) / ....

76 Review of modals (➤ see Units 79–91)

Write sentences with 'I wish'.

1 It's raining very hard. / ....*I wish it wasn't raining so hard.*..............................

2 We haven't time to stop. / ....

3 John didn't pass his examination. / ....

4 It's very cold in here. / ....

5 There's no time to spare. / ....

6 George won't help. / ....

7 Mary didn't come. / ....

8 I didn't see the match last week. / ....

77 Defining relative clauses (➤ see Unit 92 paragraph 3,4)

When the relative pronouns 'that', 'who', or 'which' are the object of the relative clause, you can leave them out if you want to. Make these sentences into relative clauses with the relative pronoun left out.

1 I bought a car. / ....*the car I bought*..

2 You met a friend. / ....

3 He sent a message home. / ....

4 Jack is going to give a lecture. / ....

5 Bill had hoped to meet some friends. / ....

6 We decided to offer a prize. / ....

Now do these, in which the relative pronoun is the object of a preposition.

7 We lived in an old house. / ....*the old house we lived in*.................................

8 You asked for some money. / ....

9 He was looking at the picture. / ....

10 They had waited for a bus. / ....

11 She is looking after some children. / ....

12 I picked up a coin. / ....

78 Time clauses (➤ see Unit 96 paragraph 7)

Rewrite these sentences, replacing the underlined verb group with an '-ing' form on its own.

1 I <u>was getting</u> ready for bed, when I heard someone downstairs.
   While .... *getting ready for bed, I heard someone downstairs.* ....

2 When I <u>heard</u> the noise, I immediately telephoned the police.
   On ....

3 As soon as they <u>heard</u> my report, they promised to send two policemen round.
   On ....

4 When they <u>arrived</u> at my house, one policeman found that a window had been broken.
   ....

5 When he <u>saw</u> this, he rang the doorbell.
   ....

6 When he <u>heard</u> the bell, a burglar ran out through the back door.
   On ....

7 When he <u>saw</u> the burglar escaping, the second policeman chased after him.
   ....

8 The unlucky burglar was hit by a car as he <u>ran</u> across the road.
   ....

9 After they <u>had arrested</u> the man, the police called for an ambulance.
   After ....

10 When they <u>arrived</u> at the hospital, they found the man had made his escape.
   On ....

79 Purpose and reason clauses (➤ see Unit 97 paragraph 1)

Rewrite these sentences using 'in order not to'.

1 We spoke quietly, because we didn't want to disturb anyone.
   .... *We spoke quietly in order not to disturb anyone.* ....

2 She moved carefully, because she didn't want to wake the children.
   ....

3 He sat in the furthest corner, because he didn't want to be seen.
   ....

4 I gave up sugar and butter, because I didn't want to put on weight.
   ....

236

BANK OF FURTHER EXERCISES

Now rewrite these sentences using 'so as not to'.

5   He used both hands, because he didn't want to drop anything.
   He used both hands, so as not to drop anything.

6   We went over everything carefully, because we didn't want to make any mistakes.
   ....

7   She left quietly, because she didn't want to make any trouble.
   ....

8   We covered the furniture, because we didn't want to get paint all over it.
   ....

80 Purpose and reason clauses (➤ see Unit 97 paragraph 2)

Rewrite these sentences with a purpose clause containing a modal.

1   I couldn't see what was happening, until he lifted me up.
   He lifted me up, so that I could see what was happening.

2   The houses were knocked down and replaced by car parks and office blocks.
   ....

3   I sat next to the window, because I wanted to see out.
   ....

4   He tied a knot in his handkerchief, because he didn't want to forget.
   ....

5   I waved my arms, because I wanted them to see me.
   ....

6   He wanted the report early, because he wanted to discuss it with colleagues.
   ....

7   We will take a telescope, because we want to see the birds without getting too close.
   ....

8   I'll fasten the donkey, because I don't want it to escape.
   ....

9   She left her address, because she wanted us to forward her letters.
   ....

10   He wore a disguise, because he didn't want even his friends to recognize him.
    ....

81 Result clauses (➤ see Unit 98 paragraph 4)

Use 'too' with one of the following adjectives or adverbs to complete each of the sentences below.

expensive	far	late	many	old	quickly	small	tired	young

1   I was ....*too tired*........................ to stay awake any longer.

2   The children are only three and four. They're .... to go to school.

3 You'd better take a bus to the city centre. It's .... to walk.

4 My French isn't very good. People always speak .... for me to understand.

5 This jacket doesn't fit properly. It's far .... for me.

6 I can't afford to go abroad this year. The air fares are much ....

7 We missed most of the party. We arrived much ....

8 There are .... students in my class. The room gets very crowded.

9 John still enjoys a game of golf, but he's getting .... to play tennis.

82 Result clauses (▶ see Unit 98 paragraph 5)

The sentences below all have 'enough' and a 'to'-infinitive. Use these nouns and adjectives to complete them.

Chinese	clean	food	lucky	money	noisy	old	room	well	work

1 Most students have hardly enough .... *money* .... to live on.

2 I couldn't speak Japanese .... enough to make myself understood.

3 I hope I'll be .... enough to get a place at University when I finish school.

4 You'll soon be able to speak enough .... to get around on your own.

5 The disco is close by, and it's .... enough to be a nuisance at night.

6 There would be enough .... to feed the whole world if we ate less meat and more of other things.

7 It's a tiny place. There's hardly enough .... to swing a cat.

8 I'll be glad when the kids are .... enough to go to school.

9 I'm not sure if that water's .... enough to drink.

10 Have you got enough .... to keep you busy?

83 Contrast clauses (▶ see Unit 99 paragraph 3)

Complete the rewritten sentences below using 'in spite of' or 'despite' and an '-ing' form.

1 He arrived on time, even though he stopped for lunch on the way. /
   He arrived on time .... *in spite of stopping for lunch* .... on the way.

2 He died poor, although he had worked hard all his life. /
   He died poor .... all his life.

3 She finished the race, even though he had a bad fall. /
   She finished the race ....

4 Even though I have studied French for three years, I still find it difficult to speak. /
   .... for three years, I still find it difficult to speak.

5 Even though she's over sixty, she's still very fit. /
   .... she's still very fit.

6 John is still very cheerful, even though he has lost his job. /
   John is still very cheerful ....

238

BANK OF FURTHER EXERCISES

84 Contrast clauses (► see Unit 99 paragraph 4)

These sentences have 'in spite of the fact that' or 'despite the fact that'. Use one of the following phrases to complete them.

we warned them not to	I've known him for years	I've done nothing all day
we lived next door to a police station		most of the employees were working mothers
they tend to live longer	they live in the same house	it wasn't very well written
we didn't have very good seats		everyone else disagreed with him

1 The company refused to provide nursery facilities in spite of the fact that ...*most of the employees* ...*were working mothers.*...

2 I quite enjoyed his last book in spite of the fact that ....

3 Despite the fact that .... , we were burgled three times.

4 I really enjoyed the play despite the fact that ....

5 Women retire earlier than men in spite of the fact that ....

6 Despite the fact that .... , they hardly ever speak to each other.

7 I'm exhausted in spite of the fact that ....

8 He insisted that he was right despite the fact that ....

9 They went ahead and swam in the bay despite the fact that ....

10 I can never remember his face in spite of the fact that ....

85 Changing the focus of a sentence (► see Unit 101 paragraph 5)

Answer these questions using the name in brackets and 'the one who'.

1 Does Sue keep the list of books? (*Liz*)
   No, ...*Liz is the one who keeps the list of books.*................................

2 Did Mike take the dictionary? (*Jack*)
   No, ...

3 Was Peter waiting to borrow it? (*Bill*)
   No, ...

4 Did Jane promise to bring it back? (*Helen*)
   No, ...

5 Is Helen going to look after it for me? (*Diana*)
   No, ...

Verb Forms

APPENDIX

Regular verbs have four forms: the base form, the third person singular form of the present simple, the '-ing' form or present participle, and the '-ed' form used for the past simple and for the past participle. The base form is used in the present tense, and for the imperative, and in the 'to'-infinitive. The base form is always given first in dictionaries and is the form used in the lists in this grammar.

REGULAR VERBS

	base form	'-s' form	'-ing' form or present participle	past form and past participle	EXCEPTIONS
		add '-s'	add '-ing'	add '-ed'	
	join	joins	joining	joined	
ending in '-sh' ending in '-ch' ending in '-ss' ending in '-x' ending in '-z' ending in '-o'	finish reach pass mix buzz echo	add '-es' finishes reaches passes mixes buzzes echoes	finishing reaching passing mixing buzzing echoing	finished reached passed mixed buzzed echoed	
ending in '-e'	dance	dances	omit '-e' before adding '-ing' or '-ed' dancing	danced	age, agree, disagree, dye, free, knee, referee, singe, tiptoe
ending in '-ie'	tie	ties	change '-ie' to '-y' before adding '-ing' tying	omit '-e' before adding '-ed' tied	
ending in consonant + '-y'	cry	change '-y' to '-ies' cries	crying	change '-y' to '-ied' cried	
one syllable ending in single vowel + consonant	dip	dips	double final consonant before adding '-ing' or '-ed' dipping	dipped	not '-w', '-x', '-y': rowing, boxing, playing
last syllable stressed	refer	refers	double final consonant before adding '-ing' or '-ed' referring	referred	
two syllables ending in single vowel + '-l'	travel	travels	double final consonant before adding '-ing' or '-ed' travelling	travelled	optional in American English: traveling, traveled
the following verbs: equip, handicap, hiccup, kidnap, progam, refer, worship	equip	equips	double final consonant before adding '-ing' or '-ed' equipping	equipped	optional in American English for: handicap, hiccup, kidnap, program, worship
ending in '-ic'	panic	panics	add '-k' before adding '-ing' or '-ed' panicking	panicked	

REGULAR/IRREGULAR VERBS

Irregular verbs do not add '-ed' for the past form, and some have different forms for the past simple and past participle. Some verbs have two forms for the past participle.

base form	past simple	past participle	base form	past simple	past participle
mow	mowed	mowed, mown	shear	sheared	shorn, sheared
prove	proved	proved, proven	sow	sowed	sown, sowed
saw	sawed	sawed, sawn	swell	swelled	swelled, swollen

APPENDIX

Some verbs have two forms for the past simple and two forms for the past participle. If there is a regular form, it is given first, but it may not be the most common one.

base form	past simple	past participle	base form	past simple	past participle
bet	bet, betted	bet, betted	learn	learnt, learned	learnt, learned
bid	bid, bade	bid, bidden	light	lit, lighted	lit, lighted
burn	burned, burnt	burned, burnt	quit	quit, quitted	quit, quitted
bust	busted, bust	busted, bust	smell	smelled, smelt	smelled, smelt
dream	dreamed, dreamt	dreamed, dreamt	speed	speeded, sped	speeded, sped
dwell	dwelled, dwelt	dwelled, dwelt	spell	spelled, spelt	spelled, spelt
hang	hanged, hung	hanged, hung	spill	spilled, spilt	spilled, spilt
kneel	kneeled, knelt	kneeled, knelt	spoil	spoiled, spoilt	spoiled, spoilt
lean	leaned, leant	leaned, leant	wake	waked, woke	waked, woken
leap	leaped, leapt	leaped, leapt			

Note that 'gotten' is sometimes used instead of 'got' as the past participle of 'get' in American English. With a few verbs, different forms are used in different meanings. For example, the past form and the past participle of the verb 'hang' is normally 'hung'. However, 'hanged' is used when it means 'executed by hanging'.

Below is a list of irregular verbs which have one form for the past simple and another form for the past participle.

IRREGULAR VERBS

base form	past simple	past participle	base form	past simple	past participle	base form	past simple	past participle
arise	arose	arisen	give	gave	given	shut	shut	shut
awake	awoke	awoken	go (goes)	went	gone	sing	sang	sung
be	was, were	been	grind	ground	ground	sink	sank	sunk
bear	bore	born(e)	grow	grew	grown	sit	sat	sat
beat	beat	beaten	hang	hung	hung	sleep	slept	slept
become	became	become	hang (execute)	hanged	hanged	slide	slid	slid
begin	began	begun	have	had	had	sling	slung	slung
bend	bent	bent	hear	heard	heard	slit	slit	slit
bind	bound	bound	hide	hid	hidden	speak	spoke	spoken
bite	bit	bitten	hit	hit	hit	spend	spent	spent
bleed	bled	bled	hold	held	held	spin	spun	spun
blow	blew	blown	hurt	hurt	hurt	spit	spat	spat
break	broke	broken	keep	kept	kept	spread	spread	spread
breed	bred	bred	know	knew	known	spring	sprang	sprung
bring	brought	brought	lay	laid	laid	stand	stood	stood
build	built	built	lead	led	led	steal	stole	stolen
burst	burst	burst	leave	left	left	stick	stuck	stuck
buy	bought	bought	lend	lent	lent	sting	stung	stung
cast	cast	cast	let	let	let	stink	stank	stunk
catch	caught	caught	lie (lying)	lay	lain	stride	strode	stridden
choose	chose	chosen	lose	lost	lost	strike	struck	struck
cling	clung	clung	make	made	made	string	strung	strung
come	came	come	may	might	–	strive	strove	striven
cost	cost	cost	mean	meant	meant	swear	swore	sworn
creep	crept	crept	meet	met	met	sweep	swept	swept
cut	cut	cut	mistake	mistook	mistaken	swim	swam	swum
deal	dealt	dealt	pay	paid	paid	swing	swung	swung
dig	dug	dug	put	put	put	take	took	taken
do (does)	did	done	read	read	read	teach	taught	taught
draw	drew	drawn	rid	rid	rid	tear	tore	torn
drink	drank	drunk	ride	rode	ridden	tell	told	told
drive	drove	driven	ring	rang	rung	think	thought	thought
eat	ate	eaten	rise	rose	risen	throw	threw	thrown
fall	fell	fallen	run	ran	run	thrust	thrust	thrust
feed	fed	fed	say	said	said	tread	trod	trodden
feel	felt	felt	see	saw	seen	understand	understood	understood
fight	fought	fought	seek	sought	sought	wear	wore	worn
find	found	found	sell	sold	sold	weave	wove	woven
flee	fled	fled	send	sent	sent	weep	wept	wept
fling	flung	flung	set	set	set	win	won	won
fly	flew	flown	sew	sewed	sewn	wind	wound	wound
forbid	forbad(e)	forbidden	shake	shook	shaken	wring	wrung	wrung
forecast	forecast	forecast	shed	shed	shed	write	wrote	written
forget	forgot	forgotten	shine	shone	shone			
forgive	forgave	forgiven	shoot	shot	shot			
freeze	froze	frozen	show	showed	shown			
get	got	got, (US) gotten	shrink	shrank	shrunk			

INDEX

Note: numbers refer to Units and paragraphs, not to pages; entries in **bold** are grammar terms; entries in *italics* are actual words and forms; an arrow ➤ tells you to look at another entry.

A

a/an 26
ability 83
able
   be able to 83.3–4, 83.7
abstract nouns 15.1, 70.9, 73.5
active voice 78.1
adjectives 31–34
   position of adjectives 31
   as complements following link verbs 31.2–3, 33.1, 34.5, 47.1, 73.1
   in front of nouns 31.4–5, 31.8
   following nouns 31.6–8, 95.1
   order of adjectives 32
   followed by prepositions 47
   followed by 'to'-infinitive clauses 33.1, 33.3–4, 33.6
   followed by 'that'-clauses 33.1–2, 33.5
   comparative adjectives 32.4, 35–36
   descriptive adjectives 32.3
   '-ed' adjectives 34.3–5
   '-ing' adjectives 34.1–2, 34.4
   opinion adjectives 32.2
   possessive adjectives 22.1–2
   superlative adjectives 32.4, 35–36
   the and adjectives 25.3–4
   modified by adverbs of degree 43.3, 43.7
adverbials 38–43
   position of adverbials 38.3–5, 41.3
   order of adverbials 38.5
   adverbials of manner 39
   adverbials of time 40
   adverbials of frequency 41
   adverbials of probability 41
   adverbials of duration 42
   adverbials of place 44–45
adverb phrases 38
adverbs
   following nouns 95.3
   in comparisons 35–37
   adverbs of degree 43
   adverbs of place and direction 44.4
   adverbs of manner 39
   indefinite adverbs 21.8–9
advice
   followed by a 'that'-clause 95.5
advise
   followed by a 'to'-infinitive clause 77.1
affirmative clauses
   with indefinite pronouns 21
   choice of determiners 29–30
   with adverbials 41–42
afraid
   followed by prepositions 47.1, 47.3
   followed by a 'to'-infinitive or 'that'-clause 33.1
   I'm afraid so, I'm afraid not 10.7
after
   in adverbials of time 40.5
   in time clauses 96

ago 40.6
all 27
   all of 27.4
   all the 27.5
   all used for emphasis 27.6
already 42
although 99
always 41.1, 41.3
answers
   see **short answers**
any 30
   any of 30.5
   any longer 42.5
anybody, anyone, anything 21
anywhere 12, 21.8
apostrophe s 22.4–8
   with indefinite pronouns 21.4
articles 24–26
as
   in time clauses 96
   in reason clauses 97.4
   in manner clauses 100.1
   as…as 37.1–3
   the same as 37.4
   as soon as 96.3
   as long as, so long as 67.5
   so as to 97.1
   as if, as though 68.2–3
ask 77
at
   in adverbials of time 40.1–2
   in adverbials of place 45
   contrasted with *in* 45.4
auxiliary verbs 3.3–5, 57
   in questions 5, 9
   in question tags 7
   in short answers 10
   in negatives 11
avoid
   followed by an '-ing' clause 69.1
   in negative purpose clauses 97.1

B

base form 3.2
   following a verb and object 72.1
   following modals 79.1
be
   forms 3.2
   as a link verb 73
   as an auxiliary verb 57
   used in passives 78
   used in question tags 7–8
   used in short answers 10
   with impersonal *it* as subject 17
   with *there* as impersonal subject 18
because 97.4
before 40.5, 96.3
begin
   followed by a 'to'-infinitive or '-ing' clause 71.1

INDEX

better
  comparative of *good* 35.6
    had better 91.4
both 28
    both of 28.6
    both…and 28.7
by
    with the passive voice 78.7
    with reflexive pronouns 20.7
    in adverbials of time 40.5
    with forms of transport 46

C

can, can't
    indicating possibility 81
    indicating probability and certainty 82
    indicating ability 83
    giving permission 84
    in instructions and requests 85
    in offers and invitations 87
    with verbs of perception 62.6
certainty 82
clauses
    clause structure 1
    ➤ conditional clauses
    ➤ contrast clauses
    ➤ main clauses
    ➤ manner clauses
    ➤ purpose clauses
    ➤ reason clauses
    ➤ relative clauses
    ➤ result clauses
    ➤ 'that'-clauses
    ➤ time clauses
    ➤ 'to'-infinitive clauses
    ➤ 'wh-'word clauses
come
    with '-ing' nouns 56.6
    with '-ing' clauses 69.3
comparatives 35–36
    forms of comparatives 35
    uses of comparatives 36
complements 1.2–3, 2.1, 3.6, 73
compound sentences 1.5
complex sentences 1.6
conditional clauses
    using *if* 66
    using modals and *unless* 67
conjunctions 1.6, 97, 102
contrast clauses 99
coordinating conjunctions 102
could, couldn't
    indicating possibility 81
    indicating ability 83
    giving permission 84
    in instructions and requests 85
    making suggestions 86
    in offers and invitations 87
count nouns 13
    plural count nouns 13.1, 26.6, 27.1–3, 29.2, 30.1–2
    singular count nouns 13.1, 26.1, 27.3, 30.2–4
    the and singular count nouns 24.5–6

D

dare 72.6
definite article 24–25
demonstratives 19
descriptive adjectives 32
despite 99.2–4
determiners 13.4–5, 23–30
    position of determiners 23.1
    specific determiners 23.2, 24, 25, 28.5
    general determiners 23.3–4, 26–30
    determiners as pronouns 23.5
direct objects 51, 52
    object pronouns as direct objects 16.4
    reflexive pronouns as direct objects 20.2, 53
direct speech 77
do
    as an auxiliary 57
    in questions 5
    in question tags 7.4, 7.6
    in negatives 11.3, 11.5
    for emphasis 87.6
    with '-ing' nouns 56.7
during 40.5

E

each 19.4, 23.5, 30.4–5, 102.5
    each other 54
'-ed'
    '-ed' forms of verbs 3.2, 57
    '-ed' adjectives 34
    '-ed' clauses following nouns 94
either 10.6, 28, 102.5
emphasizing adverbs 43
else 21.9
enjoy 43.2
    with a reflexive pronoun 53.5
    followed by an '-ing' clause 69.1
    would enjoy 88.4
enough
    following adjectives and adverbs 43.6
    as determiner followed by nouns 23.4
    with result clauses 98.5
ergative verbs 55
even though 99.1
ever 41.4
every 30.4–5
everybody, everyone, everything 21, 8.5
everywhere 21.8
expect
    expressing the future 65.4
    in short answers 10.7
    followed by 'to'-infinitive clauses 70.1–2
    in reporting 77.3

F

fairly 43.3
feel
    as a link verb 73
    as link verb followed by adjectives 31.2, 34.5
    with object and '-ing' clause or base form 72.2
    used in reporting 77.3
    feel as if 68.3

feel for 50.4
feel like 37.5, 68.5
few 29
  a few 29.5
  so few, too few 43.5–6
for
  following adjectives 33.6, 47.3
  following nouns 48.6
  in adverbials of time 40.3
  with verbs to indicate purpose or reason 49.3
forget 71.3
frequently 41
future
  using *will* and *going to* 64
  using present tenses to talk about the future 65

G

get
  followed by an object and a past participle 72.3
  used as a link verb 39.6, 73
  used to form the passive 78.5
  used with impersonal 'it' 17.3
give
  with two objects 52
  with nouns for actions 56
go
  followed by '-ing' nouns 56.6
  followed by '-ing' clauses 69.3
  go on followed by an '-ing' or 'to'-infinitive clause 71.5
going to
  in predictions 64.2
  in intentions 64.3
good
  followed by a preposition 47.3
  followed by a 'that'-clause 33.5
  better and *best* in comparisons 35.6
  related adverb *well* 39.5

H

habitual actions
  using present simple 58.2, 62.3
  using past simple 59.2
had
  short form 79.5
  in conditional clauses 67.3
  had better 91.4
have
  as auxiliary 57
  as main verb in questions 5.3
  in question tags 7.6
  with nouns for actions 56
  followed by an object and an '-ing' clause 72.4
  followed by an object and a past participle 72.3–4
have got to 89.5
have to
  indicating obligation 89.1
  with modals or auxiliaries 89.6
hear
  not used in continuous tenses 62.6
  used with *can* and *could* 83.8
  followed by prepositions 49.3
  followed by '-ing' clause or base form 72.2
help 70.2

hope
  as noun followed by a 'that'-clause 95.5
  as verb with a 'to'-infinitive clause 65.4, 70.1
  as verb with 'that'-clause 77.3
  I hope so, I hope not 10.7
  hope for 49.1
how
  as 'wh'-word 5.7, 6
  how about 86.5

I

if
  in conditional clauses 66–67
  in reporting 75, 76.2, 77.2
  used with *ever* 41.4
  used with *already* 42.2
  used to talk about the future 64–65
imperative 4
  with question tags 8.3
  with negatives 12.3
  imperatives in conditional sentences 66.3
impersonal *it* 16.6, 17, 33.6, 47.4, 73, 76.6, 96.4, 101.5–6
  main uses of impersonal *it* 17
impersonal use of *there* as subject 18, 73
in
  as a preposition of time 40
  as a preposition of place 45
  with forms of transport 46
  in case 97.5
indefinite article 26
indefinite adverbs 21.8–9
indefinite pronouns 21
  followed by '-ing', '-ed', or 'to'-infinitive clauses 94.1
  followed by defining relative clauses 95.2
indirect objects 52
  pronouns as indirect objects 16.4
  reflexive pronouns as indirect objects 20.2
indirect questions 9
indirect speech
  see **report structures**
infinitive
  see **'to'-infinitive**
'-ing'
  '-ing' forms of verbs 3.2
  '-ing' adjectives 34
  '-ing' clauses following nouns 94
  '-ing' clauses following verbs 69, 71, 72.2
in order to 97
in spite of 99.2–4
instructions 85
  expressed by imperatives 4.5
intentions
  using *will* and *going to* 64
  expressed by purpose clauses 97.1
interrogative pronouns 6
interrogative sentences 5–6
intransitive verbs 51
invitations 87

J

just
  as adverbial of degree 43.4
  just as...as in comparisons 37.3–5

just as in manner clauses 100.1
just in case 97.5
just the same 99.1

K

keep
  with two objects 52.4
  as a link verb 73.1
  followed by an '-ing' clause 69.1
  keep on followed by an '-ing' clause 69.1
kind 47.3–4

L

let
  as an imperative 4
  followed by an object and a base form 72.1
  like
  as verb followed by an '-ing' or 'to'-infinitive clause 69.1, 71.2
  as preposition in comparisons following link verbs 37.5
  as preposition in adverbials of manner 39.7
  as conjunction in manner clauses 68.5
  would like 88
link verbs 73
  followed by adjectives 47.1
  followed by '-ed' adjectives 34.5
  followed by *like* 37.5
little
  with uncount nouns 29
  a little 29.5, 36.4, 37.5
look
  followed by prepositions 49.3
  in phrasal verbs 50
  as a link verb 73
  look as if 68.3
  look like 37.5, 62.6, 68.5
lot
  a lot 36.4
  a lot of 29.3
  lots of 29.3
love
  followed by an '-ing' form or 'to'-infinitive 69.1, 71.1

M

main clause 1
main verbs 3, 5, 57
make
  with nouns for actions 56
  with object and base form 72.1
manner
  adverbials of manner 39
  manner clauses 100
many
  with plural count nouns 26.6, 29
  so many 43.5
  too many 43.6
may
  indicating possibility 81
  indicating permission 84
  making suggestions 86
  in purpose clauses 97.2
mean
  as verb with 'to'-infinitive 70.1
might
  indicating possibility 81
  making suggestions 86
mind
  followed by '-ing' clauses 69.1
  would you mind 85.6
  wouldn't mind 88.6
modals 79–91
  form and position of modals 79
  in negatives and questions 80
  indicating possibility 81
  indicating probability and certainty 82
  indicating ability 83
  giving permission 84
  in instructions and requests 85
  making suggestions 86
  in offers and invitations 87
  indicating wants and wishes 88
  indicating obligation and necessity 89–91
  giving advice 91
  expressing the future 64.1
  in conditional clauses 67.1–2
  in purpose clauses 97.2
  with *there* as impersonal subject 18.6
  with continuous tenses 60.4
  with the perfect tenses 61.5
  used in question tags 7–8
more
  with plural count nouns and uncount nouns 29.6
  in comparatives 35
most
  with plural count nouns and uncount nouns 27
  in superlatives 35
much
  with uncount nouns 29
  so much 43.5
  too much 43.6
must
  expressing probability or certainty 82
  expressing obligation and necessity 89, 90.7, 91.1
  used in invitations 87.5

N

necessity 89, 90
  expressed by nouns with 'to'-infinitive clauses 70.7
negatives 11, 12
  in short forms of modals 80
  negative imperative 4.2
  auxiliaries in negative sentences 11, 57
neither 10.6, 12.8, 102.5
never 4, 12.2–3
no
  as a general determiner 19.6, 23.4–5, 27
  with comparatives 30.2
  in 'yes/no' questions 5
nobody, no one, nothing 8.5, 12.6–7, 21
none 12.5, 23.5
nor 10.6, 12.8, 102.6
normally 41.1, 41.3
not 11
  position in verb group 3.4
  shortened to '-n't' 11
  short forms with modals 80.2
  not any with comparatives 30.2

INDEX

noun group 1.1–2, 2
  as adverbials 38.1
  as adverbials of manner 39.7
  as adverbials of time 40.1
nouns 13–15, 48, 70.7–9, 94, 95
  with determiners 23–30
  with adjectives 31, 95.1
  followed by prepositions 48
  followed by '-ing', '-ed', and 'to'-infinitive clauses
    70.7–9, 94
  followed by defining relative clauses 95.2
  followed by adverbs 95.3
  related to reporting verbs 95.5
  followed by 'that'-clauses 95.6
  used for actions with *do, give, have, make,* and *take* 56
  count nouns 13
  singular nouns 14
  plural nouns 14
  collective nouns 14
  uncount nouns 15
nowhere 12.6–7, 21.8
numbers
  in noun groups 2.5, 22.2, 23.1, 31.1, 31.6
  with count nouns 13.3
  with *a* or *an* 26.5
  with *another* 30.3

O

object
  see **direct object, indirect object**
object pronouns 16
obligation 89–91
of
  indicating possession 22
  following adjectives 47
  following nouns 48
offers 87
  using *some* 30.1
  using *will* 64.4
  using *let* 4.6
often 41.1, 41.3
on
  following nouns 48.6
  in time expressions 40
  as preposition of place 45
one 19, 23.5
opinion adjectives 32
or 1.5, 102.6
other 30, 102.5
ought
  always followed by 'to'-infinitive 79
  indicating probability and certainty 82
  giving advice 91
own 5.3, 20.7, 22.8

P

participles
  see **'-ing'** and **'-ed'**
particles 50
passive 78
  form of the passive 78
  form of the passive with *get* 78.5
  followed by 'to'-infinitive clauses 70.5

past participles
  see **'-ing'**
past tenses 59–61, 63, 74
  verb forms: see the Appendix
  use of auxiliaries 57
  with adverbials of time 40
  with adverbials of duration 42
  used in reporting 74–5
  in time clauses 96
  in conditional clauses 66–68
  past simple 59, 63
  past continuous 60, 63
  past perfect 61, 63
  past perfect continuous 60, 63
perfect tenses 61
perhaps 41.2
permission 84, 90.3
personal pronouns 16, 102.2
  as subject 16.3
  as object 16.3–4
phrasal verbs 50
  with '-ing' clauses 69.1
plenty of 29.3
plural 2, 13, 14
plural nouns 14
possession 22
possessive pronouns 22, 37.6
possessives 22–23
possibility 81
predictions 64.2
prefer
  as a transitive verb 51.2
  with '-ing' or 'to'-infinitive clauses 71.1
  in reporting 77.3
  would prefer 88.4
prepositional phrases 38
  as adverbials of manner 39.7
  as adverbials of time 40.2, 40.5
  modified by adverbs of degree 43.4
  expressing possession 22.7
  expressing purpose 97.3
  expressing manner 68.5
prepositions 44–50
  prepositions of place and direction 44
  prepositions and forms of transport 46
  with relative pronouns 92.4
  with interrogative pronouns 5.7
  followed by indirect objects 52.3
  following adjectives 34.5, 47, 95.1
  following nouns 48
  followed by object pronouns 16.4
  followed by reflexive pronouns 20.4
  following verbs 49, 54.4–5
  following superlatives 36.6
  in phrasal verbs 50
present participles
  see **'-ing'**
present tenses 58, 60–62
  verb forms: see the Appendix
  use of auxiliaries 57
  with adverbials of time 40
  with adverbials of duration 42
  used to talk about the future 65

INDEX

used in reporting 74–5
in time clauses 96
in conditional clauses 66–8
present simple 58, 62
present continuous 58, 60, 62
present perfect 58, 61–3
present perfect continuous 58, 60–62
probability 82
  adverbials of probability 41.2–3
  position of adverbials of probability 38.4
  using modals 82
  other ways of expressing probability 82.7
probably 41.2
pronouns 16–21
  ➤ demonstrative pronouns
  ➤ indefinite pronouns
  ➤ interrogative pronouns
  ➤ personal pronouns
  ➤ possessive pronouns
  ➤ relative pronouns
  use of *one* as a pronoun 19.4–5
proper nouns with *the* 25
provided that, providing that 67.5
purpose clauses 97

Q

quantity
  quantity and uncount nouns 15.6
  using determiners 27, 29–30
question tags 7–8
  be in question tags 7
  do, does, did in question tags 7
  form of question tags 7
  have and question tags 7.6
  imperatives and question tags 8
  use of auxiliaries and modals in question tags 7
questions 5–6
  'yes/no' questions 5
  do in questions 5
  have in questions 5
  be in questions 5
  'wh'-words in questions 5–6
  indirect questions 9
  reported questions 75
  present simple in questions 58
  questions and modals 80
  negative questions 11.7
quite
  with superlatives 36.4
  quite as…as in comparisons 37.3
  a quite and *quite a* 43.3

R

rarely 41.1
rather
  as adverb of degree 36.4, 43.3
  with *like* 37.5
  a rather and *rather a* 43.3
  would rather 88.5
reason clauses 97
reciprocal verbs 54
reflexive pronouns 20
  as direct object 20.2

as indirect object 20.2
  following prepositions 20.4
reflexive verbs 53
  used for emphasis 53.3
regret 71.3
relative clauses 92–3
  defining relative clauses 92
  defining relative clauses following nouns 95.2
  non-defining relative clauses 93
relative pronouns
  in defining relative clauses 92
  in non-defining relative clauses 93
remember
  with or without object 51.2–3
  followed by 'wh'-word 70.6
  followed by '-ing' or 'to'-infinitive clause 71.3
  as reporting verb followed by 'to'-infinitive or 'that'-clause 77.3
remind
  followed by 'to'-infinitive clause 70.2, 77.1
  followed by 'that'-clause 76.4
reported clauses 74–77
reported questions 75
  position of subject 75.4
  using *if* or *whether* to report questions 75.5
  verb tenses in reported questions 74, 75.2
reporting clauses 74, 76
reporting verbs 74, 76–77
report structures 76–77
  reporting what someone said 76.1
  reported clauses 76.2
  reporting a statement 76.3
  'that'-clauses in report structures 76.3–4
  'that'-clauses, 'to'-infinitive clauses, 'if'-clauses, and 'wh'-clauses in report structures 76.2–3
  say and *tell* contrasted 76.5
  reporting verbs used in the passive 76.6
  reporting orders, requests, or advice 77.1
  reporting thoughts or feelings 77.3
  verb tenses in report structures 74
requests 85
  requests using *some* 30.1
  requests using question tags 8.1
  reporting requests 77
result clauses 98

S

say 76
  contrasted with *tell* 76.5
see
  not used in continuous tenses 62.6
  used with *can* and *could* 83.8
  followed by '-ing' clause or base form 72.2
seem
  in comparisons 37.5
  as a link verb 73
  with *there* as impersonal subject 18.7
sentence structure 1, 66–68, 92–102
  simple sentence 1.1
  compound sentence 1.5
  complex sentence 1.6
shall
  making suggestions 86

in offers and invitations 87
in purpose clauses 97
in question tags 8
short answers 10
short forms 11, 80.2
should
  indicating probability and certainty 82
  giving advice 91
  in conditional clauses 67
  in purpose clauses 97
simple tenses 58–60
since
  in adverbials of time 40.4
  in time clauses 96.4
  in reason clauses 97.4
singular nouns 14
so
  as adverb of degree 43.5
  in result clauses 98.2–3
  in short answers 10.6
  used to refer back 102.6
  so that in purpose clauses 97.2
some 30
somebody, someone, something 21
somewhere 21.8
still
  as adverbial of duration 42.3
  in contrast clauses 99.1
subject pronouns 16
subjects
  in clauses 1
  position in clause 3, 38, 10, 80
  subjects and verbs 13, 15, 21, 25
  personal pronouns as subjects 16
  position in indirect questions 9
  position in questions 5
  position in reported questions 75
  subjects of ergative verbs 55
  subjects of '-ing' clauses 69
  subjects of 'to'-infinitive clauses 70–71, 77
  it as impersonal subject 17, 76
  there as impersonal subject 18
  linking clauses which have the same subject 102
subordinate clauses 66–68, 92–100
  in complex sentences 1
  see also **adverbials, reporting clauses**
subordinating conjunctions 102
such
  as adverb of degree 43.5
  in result clauses 98.2–3
suggestions 86
  using *let* 4
superlatives
  position of superlatives 32
  forms of superlatives 35
  uses of superlatives 36
  followed by 'to'-infinitive clauses 70.8

T

take 56
tell 76
  contrasted with *say* 76.5
tenses 57–65

present tenses 58, 62, 65
past tenses 59, 63, 74
continuous tenses 60
perfect tenses 61
future tenses 64
in conditional clauses 66–67
than
  following comparatives 36
that
  as demonstrative 19, 23
  in defining relative clauses 92
'that'-clauses
  following adjectives 33, 95
  following '-ed' adjectives 34.5
  following nouns 95
  in report structures 76–7
the 24–5
  with nouns 24
  with places 25.1
  with adjectives 25.3–4
  with superlatives 25.5
there
  as adverb of place 44.4
  as impersonal subject 18
though
  in contrast clauses 99.1
  as though 68.2–4
  even though 99.1
till
  in adverbials of time 40.5
  in time clauses 96.5
time clauses 96
time expressions 40
to
  following adjectives 47.3–4
  following nouns 48.6
  with indirect object 52.3
  following verbs 49.3
  with reporting verbs 76.3
'to'-infinitive clauses
  following adjectives 33, 95
  following '-ed' adjectives 34
  following nouns 70, 95
  following verbs, to express the future 65.4
  following verbs 70–1
  following *not* 11.6
  following *ought* 79, 82, 91
  following link verbs 73
  in report structures 76–7
  as purpose clause 97
  in result clauses 98
too 43.6
  followed by 'to'-infinitive 98.4
transitive verbs 51
try
  followed by an '-ing' form or 'to'-infinitive 71.4

U

uncount nouns 15
  following *the* 24
  used with determiners 27, 29–30
understand
  followed by a 'to'-infinitive clause 71.1

followed by an '-ing' clause 72.2
unless 67
until
  in adverbials of time 40.5
  in time clauses 96.5
used to
  for habitual action in the past 63.2
  followed by '-ing' form or infinitive 71.6
usually 41.1, 41.3

V

verb group 1.1–2, 3
  auxiliaries in verb groups 57
  modals in verb groups 79
  in questions 5–9
  with negatives 11–12
verbs
  regular and irregular verb forms: see the Appendix
  passive voice 78
  tenses 57–65
  answers 10
  imperative 4
  intransitive verbs 51
  transitive verbs 51
  verbs with two objects 52
  reflexive verbs 53
  reciprocal verbs 54
  ergative verbs 55
  using *do, give, have, make,* and *take* with nouns to describe actions 56
  verbs followed by prepositions 49
  phrasal verbs 50
  link verbs 73
  verbs followed by an '-ing' form 69, 71–72
  verbs of saying and thinking 60, 69, 76–77
  verbs of perception 60, 62, 72
  verbs followed by a 'to'-infinitive clause 70–71
  verbs followed by a base form of other verbs 72
  verbs not normally used in the continuous tenses 60
  reporting verbs 75–7
very
  with determiners 29.5
  with superlative adjectives 36.4
  as adverb of degree 43.3
  very much with verbs 43.2

W

want
  with 'to'-infinitive 65.4
  with object and past participle 72.5
were
  in wishes 68.1
  in conditional clauses 66.6, 67.3
  in manner clauses 68.2
what 5–6
  what about 86.5
  what for 6.3
'wh'-questions 5–6
  used in reporting 75
'wh'-words 5–6
  followed by 'to'-infinitive clauses 70.6
  in reported clauses 77.2

in reported questions 75
in relative clauses 92–3
will
  referring to the future 64
  in promises and offers 64
  expressing intentions 64
  indicating probability or certainty 82
  refusing permission 84
  in offers and invitations 87
  in question tags 8
  in short answers 10
  in conditional clauses 66–67
  in purpose clauses 97
  will not, won't as negative forms 80
wish
  noun followed by 'that'-clause 95.5
  verb followed by 'to'-infinitive 70
  verb in conditional sentences 59.5
  verb not used in continuous tenses 62
  verb in reporting clauses 77.3
wishes 68, 88
with
  following adjectives 47.3–4
  following nouns to express qualities 48.5–6
  following reciprocal verbs 54.6
  following verbs expressing agreement 49.3
  in passive sentences 78.7
word order 1
  order of adjectives 32
  order of adverbials 38
  position of adjectives 31
  position of comparative and superlative adjectives 36.3
  position of adverbials 38.3, 38.5
  position of adverbials of frequency 38.4, 41.3
  position of adverbials of probability 38.4
  position of adverbs of degree 43.2
  position of determiners 2.2, 23.1
  position of direct objects 51
  position of indirect objects 52
  position of modals 79
  position of subject in clause 3, 10, 38, 80
  position of subject in questions 5
  position of subject in reported questions 75
would
  referring to regular actions in the past 63
  used for the future in the past 63
  in question tags 8
  in instructions and requests 85
  in offers and invitations 87
  expressing wants and wishes 88
  in conditional clauses 66–7
  in purpose clauses 97

Y

'yes/no' questions 5
  with question tags 7.1
  indirect and reported 'yes/no' questions 9, 75
  short answers to 'yes/no' questions 10.1
yet 42, 102.6

ANSWER KEY – MAIN TEXT

Unit 1

A

2 The horse kicked Charlie Brown.
3 Jonah ate a big fish.
4 My father taught Mrs Jackson.
5 Jack killed the giant.

B

2 Everybody worked hard.
3 The cat caught the mouse.
4 Children love kittens.
5 Nobody knows the answer.
6 Mary bought a new dress yesterday.
7 All of us enjoyed the film last night.
8 John Black went to the supermarket.
9 Janet Black drove her car to the airport.
10 Mike drank a cup of coffee after lunch.

C

2 S + V + A
3 S + V + O + A
4 S + V + A
5 S + V + O + A
6 S + V + O + A

D

2 Didn't you see Jill last Friday?
3 Haven't they arrived yet?
4 Won't Peter help you?
5 Can't Henry speak French?
6 Doesn't he smoke anymore?
7 Didn't they understand him?
8 Hasn't John met Mary yet?

Unit 2

A

2 There's a big dog.
    There's a big dog running out of the shop.
    There's a big dog carrying a bone running out of the shop.
    There's a big dog running out of the shop carrying a bone.
3 There's a fat man.
    There's a fat man with a knife in his hand.
    There's a fat man with a knife in his hand running after the dog.
4 There's a young woman.
    There's a young woman with long hair.
    There's a young woman with long hair standing outside the shop.

B

2 to do.
3 to play.
4 to meet.
5 to post.
6 to read.
7 to wear.
8 to carry.
9 to catch.
10 to visit…to drive through.

Unit 3

A

2 come
3 heard…went
4 told…asked
5 walk…go
6 stayed…known…coming
7 said…know…coming
8 woke up…heard
9 do…tells
10 do…tells

B

2 haven't
3 were
4 are…have
5 had
6 Do…are
7 Do…haven't
8 be…are
9 has been
10 have been
Note the modal use of 'will' in 8 and 10.

C

2 'll…can
3 will…can
4 Could
5 would…could
6 should…can
7 might…might (not)
8 may…can
9 should…would
10 would…could

Unit 4

A

2 an insect spray
3 a bottle of cough mixture
4 a tube of toothpaste
5 a bottle of orange squash
6 a packet of breakfast cereal
7 a bottle of cooking oil
8 a tin of milk
9 a box of cheese biscuits

B

First you dial 999 for emergency, wait for the emergency service to answer, and tell the operator which service you want. Then you give the telephone number shown on the phone, give the address where help is needed, and give any other necessary information.

C

2 don't wake her up
3 Don't keep him waiting
4 Don't tell anyone.
5 Don't bother me now.

D

3 Let me carry that bag for you.
4 Let's telephone for help.
5 Let me help you.
6 Let's start now.

Unit 5

A

2 Have you read the newspaper?
3 Do you often go for a walk in the park?
4 Does Becky live near here?
5 Have your children gone back to school?
6 Will Sally and Peter be home for lunch?
7 Could you have eaten a bit more?
8 Will Sandra have arrived by noon?
9 Did you ever learn German at school?
10 Do you do most of the cooking at home?
11 Is Joe here?
12 Are Alan and Tina here?

B

2 Which team won first prize at the weekend?
3 What happened when you were late for work this morning?
4 Who told you the answer to the exam question?
5 Who lives next door to you?
6 What is the right answer to this question?
7 Whose car is that red one over there?
8 How many students come to your English class?

C

2 Which chocolates do you like best?
3 How did you come?
4 How far can Jim swim?
5 How many cards did you get?
6 What time will Mary and Bill be there?
7 When did Kathy arrive?
8 When will you have finished work by? / What time will you have finished work by?

D

2 Who are you going to the dance with?
3 Who is your letter from?
4 Which university does your brother go to?
5 What is this afternoon's lecture about? / What is the afternoon lecture about?

Unit 6

A

2 Who
3 Which
4 What
5 How
6 Where
7 When
8 Whose
9 how
10 How
11 Where

12 why
13 Which / What
14 Why

B

3 Who have they invited?
4 Who have you lent that book to?
5 What did they give to Peter?
6 Who answered the telephone?
7 What did the manager say?
8 Who did you ask to help?
9 What can we send?
10 Who will be at home?

C

2 How long had / has your young brother been playing outside?
3 What did he ask for?
4 What did you give him?
5 How did he hold the bread?
6 Why did he look so puzzled?
7 Why couldn't he open the door?
8 What did he do with the bread?
9 Where did he go then?

Unit 7

A

2 f
3 d
4 a/e
5 a/e
6 b
7 j
8 i
9 h
10 g

B

2 have you
3 can you
4 have you
5 will it
6 did we
7 do we
8 do we
9 will there

C

2 haven't you
3 wasn't it
4 didn't we
5 won't we
6 can't you
7 mustn't it
8 wasn't it
9 didn't it
10 don't they
11 didn't we
12 had we
13 aren't they
14 isn't there
15 aren't I

Unit 8

A

2 You don't know what time the next train leaves, do you?
3 You wouldn't look after the children, would you?
4 You couldn't tell me what to do, could you?
5 You wouldn't lend me your car, would you?
6 You couldn't come round tomorrow, could you?
7 You haven't got time to help me out, have you?
8 You couldn't do the shopping while you're out, could you?
10 You won't spend too much, will you?
11 You won't drive too fast, will you?
12 You won't be angry with him, will you?

B

2 did you
3 were you
4 was it
5 were you
6 did it
7 did you
8 are you
9 will you
10 will you

Unit 9

A

2 Where do Tom and Mary live?
3 What work does Tom do?
4 How can I get to the post office?
5 How old is she?
6 Who is in charge here?
7 What do I have to do?
8 Who has left his car in front of our house?
9 Where have they gone?
10 When will they be here?

B

2 Is the shop still open?
3 Will Mary be coming?
4 Can I book a room?
5 Is this seat free?
6 Has anyone left any messages for me?
7 Will you be staying long?
8 Did Bill call this evening?

C

2 Do you know where Bill and Tessa live?
3 I wonder if you would look after the children this evening.
4 Could you tell me where the nearest post office is?
5 I wonder if you could give me Peter's address.
6 Do you know where Simon will be staying?

7 I wonder why Jack and Jill left so suddenly.
8 Can you tell me whether the shops open at the weekend?
9 Do you know what he would like for his birthday?
10 I wonder whether you would like to come round for a cup of coffee sometime?

Unit 10

A

2 No, it isn't
3 Yes, he was
4 Yes, it will
5 No, I don't
6 Yes, I am
7 No, I don't
8 No, it isn't
9 No, he wasn't
10 Yes, I have!

B

2 a
3 f
4 b
5 g
6 c
7 d
8 h

C

2 f
3 b
4 c
5 g
6 d
7 h
8 e

D

2 I expect so
3 I suppose so
4 I'm afraid so
5 I imagine so
6 I hope so

E

2 I hope not
3 I don't expect so
4 I don't suppose so
5 I'm afraid not

Unit 11

A

2 We haven't been there often.
3 Mary wasn't very happy.
4 English isn't easy to understand.
5 I haven't been to San Francisco.
6 We mightn't be late.
7 He doesn't know her name.
8 They won't be arriving in time for lunch.
9 We can't go by train.
10 John may not be coming with his wife.

B

2 They probably won't have telephoned.
3 Mary shouldn't have told you.
4 I couldn't have arrived earlier.
5 You shouldn't have asked Peter.

C

2 She doesn't have any friends in London.
3 He doesn't have any brothers or sisters.
4 I don't have any money.
5 They didn't have any new clothes to wear.
6 We don't have anything to eat.

D

2 Doesn't he earn more than that?
3 Didn't they give you more than that?
4 Can't you stay later than that?
5 Haven't you met his brother too?

E

2 I didn't
3 I haven't
4 they will
5 I can
6 she hasn't
7 I am
8 I hadn't

Unit 12

A

2 None…no
3 Nothing
4 Nowhere
5 Nobody…none
6 Neither
7 never
8 no-one
9 neither
10 neither…nor

B

2 anybody
3 no one
4 anything
5 something
6 ever
7 never
8 any
9 none
10 nobody

Unit 13

A

cows	children	teeth
glasses	wishes	lorries
stories	friends	buses
tomatoes	parents	monkeys
boxes	pianos	houses
mice	keys	ways

B

2 Lions are dangerous animals.

3 Lawyers generally earn more than teachers.
4 Computers are expensive pieces of equipment.
5 Students have to work hard.
6 Policemen only do what they are told.
7 Cats are supposed to have nine lives.
8 Buses are the best way of getting into town(s).
9 Women tend o live longer than men.
10 Good books help to pass the time.

C

2 children
3 dishes
4 tomatoes
5 box
6 man
7 people
8 tooth
9 dishes
10 boy

D

2 is
3 smells
4 have eaten
5 were
6 was hanging
7 goes
8 were
9 has
10 have

Unit 14

A

2 a rest
3 a bath / a shower…a wash
4 a bath / a shower
5 a ride
6 a jog
7 a drink
8 a fight
9 a go
10 a move

B

2 goods
3 refreshments
4 clothes
5 feelings
6 holidays
7 pictures
8 papers
9 belongings
10 sights

C

2 team
3 family
4 government
5 crew
6 staff

7 gang
8 audience
9 public
10 media

Unit 15

A

2 knowledge
3 information
4 equipment
5 money
6 advice
7 traffic
8 electricity
9 help
10 happiness

B

2 U; C
3 C; U
4 U; C
5 U; C
6 U; C

C

2 the advice you gave me
3 the strength to go on
4 the information you need
5 The traffic in London
6 the news about Bill

Unit 16

A

2 Mary
3 Tom and Jane
4 Mr and Mrs Jackson

B

2 Tom and Jane
3 Mr and Mrs Jackson
4 Mr Brown

C

The other day when I was shopping a woman stopped me and asked me the way to the post office. I gave her directions and she thanked me politely, then ran off quickly in the opposite direction. I put my hand in my pocket and found that my wallet was missing. She must have taken it while we were talking. I shouted and ran after her but it was no good. She had disappeared in the crowd.

Unit 17

A

2 It is a village near Birmingham.
3 but it is very difficult to understand
4 It opened about a month ago. We went there last week but it was very expensive and we didn't like it very much.
5 I think it is in the kitchen. I put it back in the drawer.

ANSWER KEY – MAIN TEXT

6 she tried not to show it
7 I really enjoyed it.
  Yes I enjoyed it too. I thought it was very interesting.
  I didn't see it. I went to bed before it started.

B

Example sentences:
It is difficult travelling in the rush hour.
It can be fun meeting new people.

C

2 It's very annoying to miss a train.
3 It's nice to get a letter from an old friend.
4 It's fun to go for a good night out.
5 It's interesting to learn another language.
6 It's unhealthy to eat too much.
7 It's tiring to look after children.
8 It's very dangerous to drive too fast.

Unit 18

A

2 to sleep
3 to eat
4 to spare
5 to help
6 to do
7 to read
8 to ask
9 to watch
10 to see

B

2 There is a class every Friday.
3 There will be a meeting at three o'clock on Tuesday.
4 There will be lots of children at the concert.
5 There will be a few friends coming round.
6 There are lots of parties (given by people) at Christmas.
7 There will be an accident if you are not careful.
8 There must have been a mistake.

C

3 There appears to be something wrong with the engine.
4 There seems to be nothing left.
5 There seems to have been an accident.
6 There appears to have been a lot of trouble.
7 There seems to be no one at home.
8 There appears to have been a fire.
Note that in all these sentences it is possible to use either 'appears' or 'seems'.

Unit 19

A

2 He's always complaining

3 George had just got a new job
4 I've mended the radiator
5 she was tired of him
6 she doesn't like him
7 the brakes are useless
8 the children sometimes stay awake all night
9 The traffic was dreadful
10 the light goes on

B

2 ones…ones
3 one…one
4 ones…one
5 one…one

C

1 There are five books.
2 Red, green and blue.
3 Green and blue.

Unit 20

A

3 herself
4 her
5 themselves
6 himself
7 you
8 you
9 themselves
10 themselves

B

2 by herself
3 by ourselves
4 by themselves
5 by themselves
6 by yourselves
7 by myself
8 by themselves
9 by himself
10 by myself

C

2 myself
3 ourselves
4 herself
5 themselves

D

2 the Chief of Police himself who made the arrest.
3 Rembrandt himself who painted this picture.
4 was written by Shakespeare himself.
5 by the captain himself.

Unit 21

A

2 Everyone…nobody
3 No one
4 somebody
5 Nobody

6 anybody
7 Anybody

B

2 arrives
3 likes
4 wants
5 lives
6 asks

C

2 them
3 they
4 They
5 them

D

2 everything
3 nothing
4 something
5 anything

E

2 anyone
3 nobody
4 anything
5 anything
6 nothing
7 anybody
8 nothing
9 Nobody

Unit 22

A

2 her
3 his
4 their
5 your
6 our
8 their own
9 His own
10 my own
11 its own
12 your own

B

2 parents'
3 David and Neil's
4 James's
5 friends'
6 John and Jean's
7 Sylvia's
8 a week's
9 a couple of days'
10 two weeks'

C

2 They're mine.
3 No, I think it's yours.
4 Yes, I think it's his.
5 Yes, I'm sure it's hers.
6 Yes, it's theirs.

Unit 23

A

2 many...the ...our...each
3 another...this...a
4 Most...this
5 Every...the...a
6 your...the
7 a...the...a...several
8 another...your...this
9 little...the...Few...any...the
10 another...the...much

B

2 Each
3 A: your
  B: that...the...my...the
4 Most...both
Note that 'either' is used as a pronoun in 4.
5 several...the
6 my
7 any...my
8 another...the...a
Note that 'some' is used as a pronoun in 8.
9 that...the
Note that 'another' is used as a pronoun in 9.
10 Most...the...the

Unit 24

A

2 Turkey
3 The three learned Christian monks
4 The Turkish sultan
5 The sultan's palace
6 The first monk
7 The centre of the earth
9 The front right foot of Hodja's donkey
10 The first monk
11 The second monk
13 The third monk
14 Hodja's donkey
15 The hairs in the third monk's beard
16 The hairs in the donkey's tail
17 The donkey's tail
8, 12, 18 Because there is only one.

Unit 25

A

2 The Amazon in Brazil is the longest river in South America.
3 Japan and the United States are separated by the Pacific Ocean.
4 Liverpool is in the north of England, fairly close to Wales.
5 I would love to go to Jamaica, the Bahamas or somewhere else in the Caribbean.
6 The Suez Canal flows through the north of Egypt from Port Said to Suez, joining the Mediterranean to the Gulf of Suez and the Red Sea.
7 Lake Windermere in the north-west of England is one of the largest lakes in the British Isles.
8 Mont Blanc is in the Alps on the border between France and Italy.
9 Biarritz stands on the mouth of the Adour river which flows into the Gulf of Gascony in the Bay of Biscay.

B

2 On the first morning we went to the British Museum and had lunch at MacDonald's in Church Street.
3 In the evening we went to a pub just off Leicester Square then we went to a play at the National Theatre.
4 Next day we went to the Houses of Parliament and Westminster Abbey and had lunch at the Peking Restaurant.
5 We looked in the Evening Standard newspaper and found there was a good film at the Odeon cinema near Piccadilly Circus.

C

2 the disabled
3 the rich...the poor
4 the blind
5 the unemployed

Unit 26

A

2 A lawyer usually earns more than a policeman.
3 I love reading a good book.
4 You don't often see a good programme on TV nowadays.
5 A son is always a lot more trouble than a daughter.
6 I often have an egg for breakfast.
7 Nowadays you can buy a computer-controlled washing machine.
8 I hate to hear a baby crying or a dog barking.

B

2 We have just bought a new house with a large garden.
3 My brother is a teacher and I have a cousin who works with young children as well.
4 Would you like a biscuit or a piece of cake?
5 I spoke to an official and he gave me very good advice.

C

2 a; the
3 a; the
4 the; a
5 the; a
6 a; the
7 a; the
8 a; The
9 an; the
10 a; the

Unit 27

A

2 All cars
3 All old people
4 all alcoholic drinks
5 All banks
6 All doctors

B

2 in a library
3 in a restaurant
4 in a department store
5 at an airport
6 in a bank
7 at a railway station
8 in a hotel

C

2 Most of the children were fast asleep.
3 Most of the students passed the exam.
4 All of my friends came to the party.
5 All of the clothes were very expensive.
6 Most of the seats were booked.
7 Most of the ice cream was finished.
8 Most of the garden was full of weeds.

D

2 John had no money left.
3 He has no friends.
4 There's no milk in the fridge.
5 We got no letters today.
6 There were no girls in the class.

Unit 28

A

2 is/are
3 was
4 like...likes/like
5 come...gives/give
6 have...has/have

B

2 New York, Washington
3 London, Milan, Rome
4 London, Rome, Washington
5 Milan, Rome
6 London, Milan, Rome

C

2 Neither of them is
3 All of them are...None of them are
4 None of them are
5 All of them are...None of them are
6 Both of them are...Neither of them is

Unit 29

A

2 many...much
3 many...plenty of

4 few...little
5 a lot of...much
6 a little...a few
7 much...little
8 lots of...few

B

2 Few
3 little
4 few
5 little

C

2 a few
3 a few
4 a little
5 a few

D

2 very little
3 a few
4 very little / a little
5 a little
6 very little
7 a few
8 very little
9 A few
10 a little

Unit 30

A

2 some...any
3 A: any
  B: some
4 some...any
5 some...any
6 A: any
  B: some
7 some...any
8 any

B

2 Some of the children understood.
3 I will be free any day next week.
4 Any bus will take you to the city centre.
5 Some people said that they would be late.
6 You can buy it at any good bookshop.
7 I'd like to give you some advice.
8 Any of the guides will show you the way.
9 Some of the children missed the bus.
10 I like any fruit except bananas.

C

2 a few...every
3 each
4 any
5 another...any
6 any...other
7 some
8 every
9 every
10 any

Unit 31

A

2 atomic power
3 a digital watch
4 the introductory paragraph
5 the maximum number
6 the northern border
7 neighbouring countries
8 an outdoor party
9 indoor plants
10 countless people

B

2 glad
3 unable
4 due
5 sorry
6 sure
7 aware
8 asleep
9 ready
10 content

C

2g 3a 4i 5d 6b 7e 8f 9c

Unit 32

A

opinion: good, ugly, lovely, handsome
descriptive: golden, wood, tiny, young,
plastic, modern, Japanese, triangular,
enormous, square

B

2 large 3 round 4 wooden 8
3 nice 1 intelligent 2 young 5
4 old 5 Spanish 7
5 big 3 square 4 metal 8
6 horrible 1 stinking 2
7 small 3 brown 6 paper 8
8 valuable 2 ancient 5 Egyptian 7
9 huge 3 red 6 American 7

C

2 old green German
3 famous nineteenth-century French
4 big new timber
5 long wavy brown
6 big, round black pearl

Unit 33

A

2 a I was happy to meet George again.
  b I was pleased that George was waiting
  to meet me.
3 a I was sorry that Mary was ill.
  b She was unhappy to hear the news.
4 a We were surprised to see them.
  b We were delighted that everyone had
  enjoyed the picnic.
5 a Peter was disappointed to miss the match.

b Peter was disappointed that Anne
  missed the match.
6 a She was ashamed to tell the children
  b She was ashamed that the children
  didn't tell her.

B

2 important
3 unlikely
4 bound
5 willing
6 due
7 impossible
8 wrong

C

2 It was brave of them to stop the thief.
3 I was very careless of you to forget to lock
  the door.
4 It was kind of her to look after the
  children
5 It was very generous of Mary to pay the
  bill.
6 It was clever of you to solve the problem.
7 It was kind of Joe to send us the flowers.
8 It was mean of him to keep everything for
  himself.

D

2 It's very important for them to succeed.
3 It will be very difficult for me to do it.
4 It's very common for them to complain.
5 It's very easy for me to give you a lift.
6 It's unnecessary for you to come early.

Unit 34

A

2 increasing
3 existing
4 living
5 ageing
6 growing

B

2 depressed
3 astonished
4 alarmed
5 satisfied
6 bored

C

2 a interesting ; b interested
3 a depressing ; b depressed
4 a terrifying ; b terrified
5 a disappointed ; b disappointing
6 a embarrassing ; b embarrassed
7 a amazed ; b amazing
8 a exciting ; b excited

Unit 35

A

One syllable adjectives: black, great, long, old,
short, slow, small, warm

Adjectives using 'more' and 'most': careful, certain, difficult, fashionable, intelligent, useful

B

2 more valuable - most valuable
3 more important - most important
4 funnier - funniest

C

2 finer - finest
3 bigger - biggest
4 fitter - fittest
5 better - best
6 hotter - hottest
7 whiter - whitest
8 slimmer - slimmest

D

2 simpler - simplest
3 angrier - angriest
4 more convenient - most convenient
5 colder - coldest
6 wider - widest
7 fatter - fattest
8 thinner - thinnest
9 more slender - most slender
10 more generous - most generous
11 more friendly - most friendly
12 gentler - gentlest

Unit 36

A

2 My sister is older than me.
3 Our new house is bigger than the one we used to live in.
4 Travelling by train is more comfortable than travelling by bus.
5 Shopping at a supermarket is cheaper than going to the local shops.

B

2 more interested…than
3 more exciting than
4 noisier than
5 older than

C

2 a younger man
3 a bigger house
4 a better idea
5 a better job

D

2 the most expensive hotel
3 the most tiring journey
4 the tastiest meal
5 the best game

Unit 37

A

2 Jean is as generous as her mother.
3 Neil is as mischievous as his brother.

4 Helen drives as fast as Mary.
5 Your home is as comfortable as ours.
6 This summer is as hot as last summer.
7 Becky works as hard as Jenny.
8 Jill can run as fast as Jack.

B

2 as cheap as
3 as well as
4 as clever as
5 as cold as
6 as much as
7 as quick as
8 as long as

C

2 They're the same height.
3 We're the same height.
4 They're the same size.
5 They're the same length.

D

2a 3f 4b 5d 6c

Unit 38

A

2 We enjoyed the concert last night very much.
3 I met Mary in the supermarket yesterday.
4 Last year we had a holiday in Greece.
5 In London most people start work about nine o'clock.
6 This morning I got to work very late.
7 Next year they are building a new school in our town.
8 You can buy most things cheaply in the supermarket.
9 Andreas speaks five languages fluently.
10 Jack spoke very angrily at the meeting yesterday.
11 It rained very heavily in London last night.
12 He wrote his name neatly at the bottom of the page.

B

2 Quietly he opened the door.
3 Several times I have tried to call you.
4 For over an hour we waited for him.
5 By mistake he posted the wrong letter.
6 As quickly as possible she drove to town.
7 Carefully he folded the paper.
8 Only yesterday I spoke to him about it.
9 In the National Gallery there are some wonderful paintings.
10 Angrily he walked out of the room.

Unit 39

A

2 slow…slowly
3 angrily…angry
4 comfortably…comfortable
5 beautifully…beautiful
6 nervous…nervously

7 sad…sadly
8 happily…happy
9 carelessly…careless
10 unexpected…unexpectedly

B

2 well
3 carefully…fast
4 fast…late
5 slowly
6 quietly
7 hard…badly
8 anxiously
9 lately
10 quietly…suddenly

Unit 40

A

2 in…in
3 on
4 at…in… –
5 in…at… –
6 in…on
7 at…at…at
8 at…on
9 on…in… –
10 at…at…on…at

B

2 since
3 for
4 for
5 ago
6 since
7 ago
8 since
9 ago
10 since

C

1 from…until
2 in…for
3 ago…by…on
4 in…ago…since
5 from…until…By

Unit 41

C

2 My brother normally goes swimming twice a week.
3 On Sundays Peter often went to visit his grandparents./Peter often went to visit his grandparents on Sundays.
4 The British are always talking about the weather.
5 I'll probably be back in a couple of minutes.
6 He will probably be at home at lunchtime.
7 He should certainly have telephoned by now./He certainly should have telephoned by now.
8 I definitely locked the door last night./Last

night I definitely locked the door.
9 He usually phoned home every day.
10 Perhaps they didn't get there in time.
11 We hardly ever go to the theatre nowadays./Nowadays we hardly ever go to the theatre.
12 John will probably call round tomorrow.

Unit 42

A

2 any longer
3 yet
4 yet
5 yet
6 any longer / any more

B

2 still
3 still
4 still…already
5 still
6 already

C

2 yet…still
3 A: still
  B: already
4 yet…still
5 yet…still
6 still
7 still…any more
8 already
9 any more
10 A: yet…still
  B: already

Unit 43

A

2 Wrong ; right
3 Right ; wrong
4 Right ; wrong
5 Right ; wrong

B

2 His success was largely the result of hard work.
3 They finally came to an agreement simply because they were tired of arguing.
4 You can often get what you want simply by asking.
5 He usually disagreed with the majority just to make things difficult.
6 I missed my flight to Cairo partly owing to a traffic hold-up.
7 He finally got what he wanted but it was mainly by good luck.
8 He used to play the fool just to annoy his father.

C

2 quite a big house.
3 quite an exciting film.
4 rather a sad childhood.

5 rather an expensive car.
6 quite a good school.
7 quite an interesting man.
8 rather a naughty child.
9 rather a difficult problem.
10 quite a rude letter.
4 She had a rather sad childhood.
5 It was a rather expensive car.
9 It was a rather difficult problem.

Unit 44

A

True sentences:
2b 3a 4a 5a 6b 7a 8b 9a 10b

B

2 round…across…down
3 opposite…round
4 at…in
5 next to…behind
6 in the middle of…close to

Unit 45

A

2 picture…corner
3 back
4 corner…phone box
5 left…front row
6 flat…Park Street…floor
7 table…bottom
8 car…bus

B

2 in…at
3 at…on…in
4 at…at
5 in…on
6 in…at…on
7 on…in
8 on…at
9 at…in
10 at…in
11 in…at

Unit 46

A

2 a by luxury liner
  b on a luxury liner
3 a on a jumbo jet
  b by fighter plane
4 a on a double-decker bus
  b by bus
5 a by coach
  b in an air-conditioned coach
6 a by car ferry
  b on a car ferry

B

1 …by
2 on…by
3 in…on

4 on…on
5 by…on
6 by…out of
7 off
8 out of
9 by…on
10 in

Unit 47

A

2 stupid
3 used
4 different
5 surprised
6 delighted
7 responsible
8 bored
9 fond
10 senior

B

2 loyal
3 similar
4 identical
5 generous
6 good / excellent

C

2 furious with
3 sensible of
4 suspicious of
5 jealous of
6 kind to
7 engaged to

D

2 I was proud of the way she played.
3 Everyone was very critical of the way he behaved.
4 I was delighted with the way they looked.
5 We were very happy about the way they treated us.

Unit 48

A

2 contribution
3 reply
4 invitation
5 solution
6 cure
7 room
8 sympathy
9 recipe
10 demand

B

2 comment
3 relationship
4 contact
5 increase
6 cause
7 advantage
8 difficulty

9 decision
10 difference

C
2 on
3 in
4 of
5 for
6 on
7 to
8 for
9 of
10 with

Unit 49

A
2 suffered from
3 resulted in
4 appealing to/for
5 sympathize with
6 belonged to
7 depend on
8 hoping for
9 insist on
10 pay for

B
2 to…about
3 about…about
4 to…about…about
5 about…to
6 to…about…about

C
2 at
3 at
4 into
5 at

D
2 with…for
3 for
4 for…with
5 for

Unit 50

A
2 stay on
3 wait up
4 give in
5 keep up
6 speak up
7 Watch out
8 cool off
9 catch up
10 fall behind

B
2 ask us in
3 call him back
4 pull them apart
5 invite you in
6 get it back

7 catch her out
8 invite them out
9 work it out
10 show you out

C
3 bumped into an old friend
4 looking after the house
5 invite them out
6 take after my mother

Unit 51

A
2 T a car ; I
3 T anyone ; I
4 I ; T human nature
5 T a course ; I
6 I ; T chemistry
7 I ; T the handle
8 I ; T me
9 I ; T what
10 T the bus ; I

B
2 choose
3 know
4 phone
5 remember
6 forget
7 understand
8 leave
9 watch
10 heard

Unit 52

A
2 John sold his old car to Mary.
3 Could you show those old photographs to your grandfather?
4 Save something to eat for the rest of us.
5 I'm going to book a really good table for your guests.
6 We've prepared a light snack for you.
7 We'll leave some food in the fridge for you.
8 I taught French to Peter's children when they were younger.
9 I'll try to find those books for you.
10 We must remember to send a card to George and Alice.

B
2 She cooked them a wonderful meal.
3 He passed him the money.
4 Cut them some bread.
5 Give her this letter.
6 She used to teach them arithmetic.
7 I'd like to keep them something.
8 You must show them these papers.
9 He always reads her a story before she

goes to sleep.
10 I'm going to write her a short note.

C
2 Mrs Brown left some money for the milkman.
3 We sent a Christmas card to the people we met on holiday.
4 He gave her some flowers on her birthday.
5 Jack and Mary promised the children a day at the seaside.
6 Nobody told us what to do.

Unit 53

A
2 Help yourself / yourselves
3 behave themselves
4 repeating himself
5 enjoy myself
6 introduce myself
7 teaching herself
8 describe myself
9 blame yourself / yourselves
10 express himself
11 excelled themselves
12 kill herself

B
2 You ought to behave yourself / yourselves better than that.
3 You must learn to adapt yourself / yourselves to new ideas.
4 The children tried to hide themselves in the cupboard.
5 You can dry yourself on that towel.
6 Billy undressed himself before going to bed.

Unit 54

A
2 attack
3 fight
4 cooperate
5 argue
6 talk
7 bumped
8 communicate
9 part

B
2 of
3 to
4 with
5 at
6 to
7 into
8 at / to
9 of
10 at
11 on
12 on

ANSWER KEY – MAIN TEXT

C

3 each other
4 themselves
5 each other
6 themselves
7 each other
8 themselves

Unit 55

A

2 tear
3 crack
4 boiled
5 sell
6 stops
7 cook
8 began
9 rang
10 wash
11 increased
12 handles

B

2 vase
3 shirt
4 building
5 hand
6 window
7 train
8 potatoes

Unit 56

A

2 make
3 give
4 give
5 have
6 have
7 give
8 go

B

2 go
3 do
4 go
5 are going
6 go
7 does
8 go

C

2 do
3 done
4 make
5 making
6 do
7 make
8 make

D

2 do
3 take

4 give / make
5 have
6 have
7 gave
8 made
9 took
10 had
11 give
12 made

Unit 57

A

2 do
3 Don't
4 did
5 does
6 Does

B

2 Do…do
3 don't…will
4 have been…hasn't
5 would have…had
6 was…didn't
7 Don't…will
8 Does…is

C

2 Have a
3 Does k
4 Has h
5 Do l
6 Have i
7 Does d
8 Do j
9 Have b
10 Has g
11 Do f
12 Does e

Unit 58

A

2 H
3 P
4 P
5 F
6 P
7 P
8 F
9 H
10 H

B

2 does the train leave
3 doesn't live
4 do you work
5 don't think…likes
6 does Ken get home
7 comes from
8 do you speak
9 does it cost
10 doesn't drink coffee…likes

C

Verbs that refer to the future:
3 B: 've heard
4 A: is coming
   B: 's coming
5 B: go
6 A: 've finished
   B: I'm meeting…'re going

Unit 59

A

2 a Where did you go in England?
   b We went to London, but we didn't go to Oxford.
3 a What plays did they see at Stratford?
   b They saw Hamlet but they didn't see Julius Caesar.
4 a Did Angelo buy some records in London?
   b He bought some clothes but he didn't buy any records.
5 a Did you enjoy your holiday?
   b I enjoyed the holiday but I didn't enjoy the food.

B

2 P ; H
3 H ; H
4 N ; N
5 H
6 N ; N
7 P ; P
8 N
9 N ; N
10 H ; H
11 P
12 N

C

2 opened…started
3 were enjoying…went
4 heard…began
5 was talking…burst
6 heard…ran

Unit 60

A

2 starts…are playing
3 am writing…am
4 looks…is enjoying
5 is staying…visits
6 is saving up…is spending

B

B: am working…am trying
A: Are you living
B: am living…am sharing

C

2 broke in…were sleeping
3 ran off…was swimming
4 was shopping…lost

5 was playing tennis…broke
6 met…were working

D

2 have been waiting
3 have been studying
4 have been playing
5 have been watching
6 has been working
7 have been walking

Unit 61

A

2 a
3 e
4 b
5 f
6 c
7 g
8 i
9 j
10 h

B

2 I had seen it before.
3 I had never met him before.
4 I had finished the washing up.
5 I had left it at home.
6 because I had lived there for years.
7 I had caught a cold.
8 he had had an accident.
9 had just moved to Oxford.

C

2 will have driven
3 will have learned
4 will have used up
5 will have run

D

2 Scientists will have learned to control the weather.
3 The Third world war will have broken out.
4 Man will have destroyed the planet.
5 The world population will have grown to ten billion.
6 Atomic energy will have replaced oil and coal.
7 The rhinoceros will have become extinct.
8 Scientists will have built factories in space.

Unit 62

A

2 is raining…rains
3 am going…go
4 cycles…is raining…is taking…is doing…goes
5 are playing…get…go
6 does your husband do…teaches…is teaching
7 watch…are watching

B

2 smells
3 don't understand
4 are growing up…look
5 seemed…think
6 Does this coat belong
7 is hanging
8 can hear…sounds…is trying

Unit 63

A

2 phoned…was doing
3 met…was working
4 asked…was watching
5 was driving…had
6 were doing…found

B

2 A: Have you seen
   B: saw
3 went…haven't been
4 A: have met
   B: were
5 A: have tried
   B: left

C

2 didn't come…had sent
3 was…had heard
4 had lost…didn't know
5 had finished…went

D

2 They were going to visit Oxford, but they didn't have time.
3 He was going to see the play, but there were no seats left.
4 I was going to do my homework, but I had forgotten my books.
5 We were going to watch TV, but there was nothing interesting on.

Unit 64

A

2 am going to faint
3 will fall
4 am going to fall
5 will be
6 is going to be
7 will be
8 will enjoy
9 is going to blow

B

2 are going to buy
3 will send
4 are going to collect
5 are going to buy
6 will go out

C

1 will be seeing

2 will you have finished
3 won't have finished
4 will be going…will be having

Unit 65

A

2 We're having
3 The meeting starts
4 A few friends are coming round
5 does the last bus leave
6 The match finishes
7 I'm meeting
8 Becky finishes
9 Everybody is going
10 We change

B

2 see…will give
3 will give…see
4 will be…come
5 rains…will have
6 will be…enjoy
7 won't go…go
8 will remember…visit
9 stops…will stay

C

2 have finished…will tell
3 have finished…will go
4 will help…have done
5 will call…has got

D

2 We intend to spend our next holiday in Scotland.
3 I expect to be back at work before long.
4 We are planning to drive to Glasgow.

Unit 66

A

2 c
3 i
4 a
5 f
6 b
7 e
8 g
9 h
10 d

B

2 has
3 are working
4 goes
5 is

C

2 i
3 g
4 b
5 e
6 a

7 f
8 d
9 c

Unit 67

A

2 I would go abroad if I could afford it.
3 I could buy that car if it wasn't so expensive.
4 We could go out if it wasn't raining.
5 She would come to the party if she wasn't away on holiday.
6 If the central heating was working we could turn it on.

B

2 If he had passed his exams he might have gone to university.
3 If he had realized what was happening he would have run away.
4 If I had heard what she said I would have been very angry.
5 They wouldn't have got in if you had locked the door properly.
6 It wouldn't have happened if you had followed the instructions.
7 If she had found out she would have been furious.
8 If we hadn't booked a room we would have had nowhere to stay.
9 If we had been going any faster someone could have been killed.
10 If he hadn't been so tired he wouldn't have gone home at lunchtime.

C

2 h
3 a
4 f
5 d
6 b
7 e
8 c

Unit 68

A

2 I wish they wouldn't.
3 I wish he wouldn't.
4 I wish he would.
5 I wish we could.
6 I wish she would.
7 I wish they could.
8 I wish she would.

B

2 She looks like she's having fun.
3 He accepted his punishment like everyone else did.
4 She refused to dress like her colleagues did.
5 He said he would work like the others did if he was paid like were.

6 They work a five day week like we do.
7 I don't like people who behave like he does.
8 They still farm like their grandfathers did.

C

2 They look as if they've got some good news.
3 This milk smells as though it's gone sour.
4 Your engine sounds as if it's worn out.
5 He looks as if he's going to make trouble.
6 I feel as if I'm going to be sick.
7 It looks as if it's going to rain.
8 She sounded as if she was going to cry.
Note that it is possible to use 'as if' or 'as though' in all these sentences.

Unit 69

A

2 Judy remembered noticing him behind the building.
3 When his Dad asked, did you mention seeing him?
4 I couldn't recall saying anything about him at all.
5 May I suggest giving them a present of £500 each?
6 Sorry, But I can't imagine ever agreeing to that!
7 He then described escaping from prison.
8 They ought to admit stealing the fruit.

B

2 Could you consider reducing the price, for example to £6,000?
3 They delayed starting the game because of the rain.
4 I want to avoid paying monthly if possible.
5 They didn't finish preparing for the party until after 9 pm.
6 This new production process might involve increasing staff.

C

2 dread going
3 detest getting stuck
4 carry on driving
5 fancies taking up
6 can't bear being told
7 give up playing
8 feel like having

Unit 70

A

2 to go
3 to drive
4 to sell
5 to be
6 to hear
7 to be
8 to finish

B

2 asked
3 expected
4 invited
5 allowed
6 encouraged
7 warned
8 reminded

C

3 to have broken your leg.
4 to have locked everything away.
5 to be waiting for the doctor.
6 to have spent the money.
7 to be living at home now.

D

2 not to see
3 not to miss
4 not to make
5 not to write
6 not to be

E

2 money
3 key
4 box
5 pen
6 room
7 meeting
8 matches

Unit 71

A

2 playing
3 raining / to rain
4 knocking / to knock
5 shouting / to shout
6 to enjoy
7 staying

B

2 paying…to pay
3 working…to work
4 complaining…to complain
5 leaving…to leave
6 telling…to tell
7 going…to go
8 visiting…to visit

C

2 The shoes need polishing.
3 The shirt needs ironing.
4 The tyre needs mending.
5 The trousers need shortening.
6 The door needs painting.

Unit 72

A

2 A: made
    B: let…made
3 A: let

B: make
4 A: let
   B: make
5 A: let
   B: made
6 A: made
   B: let

B
2 burning
3 playing
4 lying
5 making

C
2 have my hair cut
3 had that suit made
4 have the house redecorated
5 have another room built on
6 had a lot of money stolen

Unit 73

A
2 sounds
3 goes
4 feels
5 gets
6 smells
7 tastes
8 grows

B
2 The fruit smelled awful, but it proved to be very tasty.
3 The problem seemed simple, but it proved to be extremely difficult.
4 It was a long programme, but it proved to be very interesting.
5 It was only a short walk, but it proved to be rather tiring.
6 The animal looked quiet enough, but it proved to be quite vicious.
7 The jacket seemed to be the right size, but it proved to be much too small.
8 The food smelled all right, but it proved to be uneatable.

C
2 too dark
3 too young
4 too late
5 too hot
6 too tired
7 too cold
8 too expensive

Unit 74

A
Andrew was intelligent and go-ahead. He thought there was a great future for engineers in this atomic age. As a trainee, Andrew worked 44 hours in a five day week and earned about £3 per week with an allowance of £1.70. His pay

rose to £8.16 at 21. Hostel accommodation was available. Books and instruments could be borrowed and there were opportunities for sport.

B
2 hated…said…had
3 said…was…had stolen…was…would spend
4 said…had…looked
5 said…knew…was…wasn't

Unit 75

A
2 Where do you live?
3 When did you arrive?
4 When did you last see your mother?
5 What do you do for a living?
6 What are you doing here?
7 How long have you lived in the flat?
8 Who are you going to invite to the party?
9 How long will you be staying?
10 How much did you pay for the car?

B
2 Are you happy?
3 Are you coming to the party?
4 Can you help me?
5 Have you been to London before?
6 Did you enjoy the movie?
7 Would you like a drink?
8 Have you seen my glasses anywhere?

C
2 if giraffes ate leaves.
3 if I had found the keys.
4 if I could open the window.
5 her if she was hungry.
6 why he hadn't asked her before.
7 where I was going now.
8 if he would like an ice cream
9 why he wouldn't help him.
10 if he could have some more.

Unit 76

A
2 b
3 f
4 c
5 a
6 g
7 d
8 e

B
2 admit…admit
3 deny…denied
4 announce…announced
5 complain…complained
6 mention…mentioned
7 explain…explained
8 argue…argue

C
2 informed
3 suggested
4 told
5 announced
6 mentioned

Unit 77

A
2 John's doctor advised him to get more sleep.
3 We invited our friends to come round and see us any time.
4 Jack told me to take the money to the bank.
5 Mr Brown reminded the students to come half an hour early on Tuesday.
6 Bill begged Maria to write to him every day.
7 I warned the children not to play with fire.
8 My grandfather advised me not to go to England in the winter.
9 They told the visitors not to go out alone after dark.
10 The manager persuaded her not to make an official complaint.

B
2 Joe asked Mary where she was going to spend the holiday.
3 Everybody asked us why the tickets were so expensive.
4 Frank asked his wife how old Mary's children were.
5 Mrs Jones asked he neighbour who was going to buy their house.
6 Bill asked his friend when he was planning to come to Darlington.
7 I asked Maria what she was going to do next.
8 Peter asked a policeman where he could get the bus to Liverpool.

Unit 78

A
2 was owned
3 had been presented
4 was given
5 cannot be named
6 was stolen
7 was arranged…was to be flown in…exchanged…had been staffed
8 was shown
9 was taken
10 was arrested

B
2 e made PAST
3 a won FUTURE
4 f killed P
5 c disconnected P
6 h paid P

7 d sent F
8 j told P
9 g permitted
10 i rebuilt

C

2 be obtained
3 be considered
4 be expected
5 be funded
6 be given
7 be held
8 be made
9 be offered

Unit 79

A

2 They could have seen us.
   They might have seen us
3 He might have said that, I don't
   remember.
   He could have said that, I don't remember.
4 We're lost. I think we must have taken the
   wrong road.
5 You should have seen it. It was wonderful.
6 I should have known that would happen.
7 Perhaps when I am fifty I will have
   forgotten it.
8 I could have prevented that, but I didn't.
9 You ought to have listened to her the first
   time.

B

2 They ought to have gone by car./They
   should have gone by car.
3 You ought to have telephoned./You
   should have telephoned.
4 You ought to have asked John to
   help./You should have asked John to help.
5 You ought to have done the
   shopping./You should have done the
   shopping.
7 You ought not to have spent so much
   money./You shouldn't have spent so
   much money.
8 It ought not to have taken you so long./It
   shouldn't have taken you so long.
9 They ought not to have done that./They
   shouldn't have done that.
10 She ought not to have left so early./She
   shouldn't have left so early.
11 He ought not to have made so much
   noise./He shouldn't have made so much
   noise.
12 He ought not to have been so upset./He
   shouldn't have been so upset.

Unit 80

A

2 cannot…can
3 could…couldn't
4 may not…may

5 might…might not
6 must…mustn't
7 shall…shan't
8 should…shouldn't
9 will…won't
10 would…wouldn't
11 oughtn't…ought

B

2 speak to Nicky please?
3 give me a few examples?
4 have a word with you please?
5 be so nasty to me?
6 give them for dinner?
7 shut the door?
8 I meet you tonight?
9 I see about my teaching programme?
10 have a drink, Doctor?
11 please tell her that Adrian phoned?

Unit 81

A

Example sentences:
Learning English can often be hard work.
Going to the dentist can sometimes be
painful.

B

2 George may/might help if you give him a
   ring.
3 It may/might be a mistake.
4 Things may not/might not be so bad after
   all.
5 She may not/might not recognize you
   even if she sees you.
6 It may/might be broken.
   Past:
2 George may/might have helped if you
   had given him a ring.
3 It may/might have been a mistake.
4 Things may not/might not have been so
   bad after all.
5 She may not/might not have recognized
   you even if she had seen you.
6 It may/might have been broken.

C

2 It could be a wild animal.
3 It could be one of the neighbours.
4 It could be the wind in the trees.
5 It could be a car passing.
6 It could be someone snoring.
7 It could be someone at the door.
8 It could be a ghost.
Last night:
2 It could have been a wild animal.
3 It could have been one of the neighbours.
4 It could have been the wind in the trees.
5 It could have been a car passing.
6 It could have been someone snoring.
7 It could have been someone at the door.
8 It dould have been a ghost.

D

2 can't
3 may not
4 can't
5 may not
6 can't

Unit 82

A

3 ought to win / should win easily.
4 should have / ought to have a
   comfortable trip.
5 ought to be / should be a nice day.
6 should do / ought to do very well.
7 ought to get / should get some peace
   and quiet.

B

3 They must be tired out.
4 You can't be tired.
5 She can't be her sister.
6 He must be your brother.
7 He must be at home.
8 He can't be at home.
9 She can't be your grandmother.
10 She must be his grandmother.

C

2 He must have done it.
3 You must have seen him.
4 You must have enjoyed your holiday.
5 They must have gone shopping.
6 Someone must have taken it by mistake.

Unit 83

A

Example sentences:
I can count to twenty in Spanish, but my
daughter can't.
My friend John can run a marathon, but I can't.
My son can't swim, but I can.
I can't play chess, but my brother can.
Example questions:
Can you swim like a fish?
Can you understand sign language?

B

Example sentence:
When I was ten years old, I could swim, but I
couldn't ride a bike.

C

2 can't
3 couldn't
4 can
5 could
6 Can
7 can

Unit 84

A

2 Can I ask you just one more question?

3 Can I give you a ring sometime later?
4 Can we go swimmimg?
5 Can I sit down?
6 Can I have an ice-cream please?
7 Can I go home now?
8 Can I come back later?
Example request with 'may':
3 May I give you a ring sometime later?
Example request with 'could':
8 Could I come back later?

B

2 Do you think I could start now?
3 Do you mind if I listen to the radio while you're working?
4 Is it all right if I come in now?
5 Do you think I could speak next?

C

2 You're allowed to have visitors after three o'clock.
3 You can all go home as soon as you've finished work.
4 You can come back late as long as you don't make too much noise.
5 With this card you are allowed to cash a cheque for up to £250.
6 You can use my pen until I need it myself.

D

1 get married…vote
2 drive a car…drive a taxi
3 drive a car…vote
4 get married / leave school…drive a car
5 vote
6 drive a car…drive a taxi

Unit 85

A

Example requests:
Could I have a look at you newspaper please?
May I have one of those biscuits please?
Could you let me have a little more time please?
Could you give me another cup of coffee please?

B

2 Would you mind helping this lady with her bags?
3 Would you mind paying cash, please?
4 Would you mind telling them that I called?
5 Would you mind closing the door behind you, please?
6 Would you mind doing the shopping on the way home?
7 Would you mind helping me, please?
8 Would you mind doing the cooking tonight?
9 Would you mind coming ten minutes before the meeting starts?
10 Would you mind telling me when you are ready?

C

2 you could give Joan a message?
3 giving me your full name?
4 you could repeat that?
5 you could stand up?
6 holding this for me?
7 you could open the door?
8 doing it again?
9 all of you could sit down quietly?
10 you could give me a little more time?

Unit 86

A

2 always use a word processor.
3 borrow the money from the bank?
4 get the information from the local library.
5 take a later train?

B

2 to get started as soon as possible.
3 write and ask her yourself.
4 taking a winter holiday for a change?
5 just pay at the end of the month.
6 take a week off in July.
7 about asking Bill to help?
8 could ring and tell them you're coming.
9 we borrow the equipment from Peter?
10 be a good idea to keep quiet about that.

C

2 f
3 g / a
4 h
5 d
6 b
7 a / g
8 e

Unit 87

A

2 d
3 a
4 e
5 f
6 b
7 h
8 g

B

2 You must come round for a game of chess some time.
3 You must bring your wife with you next time.
4 You must meet my brother next time he's here.
5 You must have another cup of coffee.
6 You must stay a little longer.
7 You must see my holiday photographs.
8 You must come to the theatre with me some time next week.
9 You must stay for lunch.
10 You must have another piece of cake.

C

2 h
3 a
4 b
5 d
6 e
7 c
8 f

Unit 88

A

2 Would you like to go with me?
   No thanks, I'd like to go alone./I'd rather go alone.
3 Would you like to start now?
   No thanks, I'd like to wait a few minutes./I'd rather wait a few minutes.
4 Would you like to go shopping this morning?
   No thanks, I'd like to go this afternoon./I'd rather go this afternoon.
5 Would you like to pay cash?
   No thanks, I'd like to pay by cheque./I'd rather pay by cheque.

B

2 to find a better job.
3 to start all over again.
4 to see them more often.
5 to understand more about it.
6 to have a bigger garden.

C

2 learning English.
3 being chairman.
4 going back to work.
5 going into politics.
6 catching an early train.

Unit 89

A

2 You have to stand to attention.
3 You have to keep your boots clean.
4 You have to get up early.
5 You have to keep fit. / You have to do exercises.
6 You have to salute your superiors.
7 You have to learn to use a rifle. / You have to learn to shoot.
8 You have to keep your equipment clean. / You have to clean your equipment.

B

2 You must take this medicine before every meal.
3 You mustn't get out of bed.
4 You must get plenty of sleep.
5 You mustn't eat any food.
6 You must drink lots of water.

C

2 d

3 a
4 c
5 b

Unit 90

A

2 He doesn't need to keep his hair short.
3 He doesn't need to keep his boots clean.
4 He doesn't need to get up early.
5 He doesn't need to keep fit.

B

1 She doesn't have to stay in bed.
2 She doesn't have to take any more medicine.
3 She doesn't have to get plenty of sleep.
4 She doesn't have to drink lots of water.

C

2 a
3 e
4 b
5 d
6 c

D

2 What? He needn't have sent it by fax.
3 Really? She needn't have bought a first-class ticket.
4 Oh? You needn't have brought your own.
5 What? They needn't have cleaned it out themselves.
6 Really? You needn't have cooked your own supper.

Note that in 2–6 you can use any of the exclamations given.

2 You didn't need to send it by fax.
3 She didn't need to buy a first-class ticket.
4 You didn't need to bring your own.
5 They didn't need to clean it out themselves.
6 You didn't need to cook your own supper.

Unit 91

A

3 You ought to
4 You ought not to
5 You ought not to
6 You ought to
7 You ought not to
8 You ought to
9 You ought not to
10 You ought to

B

2 h
3 b
4 f
5 i
6 g
7 d
8 a
9 j
10 e

C

3 I should have got home earlier.
4 We should have read the instructions carefully.
5 You shoudn't have spent so much money.
6 You should have told me you were coming.
7 They shouldn't have made such a noise.
8 John should have paid his bill. / John shouldn't have left the restaurant without paying his bill.
9 Jack should have explained what he was doing.
10 You should have sent Mary a birthday card.
1 You ought to have phoned.
2 They oughtn't to have made such a mess.
3 I ought to have got home earlier.
4 We ought to have read the instructions carefully.
5 You oughtn't to have spent so much money.

Unit 92

A

2 that lives in America
3 that were stolen
4 that plays James Bond
5 that answered the phone
6 that was left behind on the desk
7 that live in glass houses
9 that I met on the train
10 that we took on holiday
11 that you read in the newspaper
12 that I left on the table
13 that The Beatles recorded in 1966
14 that you asked for

B

2 who
3 which
4 who
5 who
6 which
7 who
8 which
9 who
10 which
11 which
12 which
13 which
14 which

C

2 when
3 why
4 where
5 whose
6 why
7 whose

Unit 93

A

3 You've all met Michael Wood, who is

visiting us for a couple of days.
4 Michael Wood, who is one of my oldest friends, has just gone to live in Canada.
5 We are moving to Manchester, which is in the north-west.
6 Manchester, which is in the north-west, is one of England's fastest growing towns.
7 I'll be staying with Adrian, whose brother is one of my oldest friends.
8 This is Adrian, whose house we stayed in for our holidays.

B

2 a
3 e
4 f
5 b
6 c
7 g
8 d

C

2 Only two people came to look at the house, neither of whom wanted to buy it.
3 He had a lot to say about his new computer, none of which interested me very much.
4 There were some noisy people in the audience, one of whom kept interrupting the speaker.
5 She made all kinds of suggestions, most of which I couldn't understand.

Unit 94

A

2 a attacked ; b attacking
3 a leaving ; b left
4 a carrying ; b carried
5 a faced ; b facing
6 a speaking ; b spoken

B

2 burning
3 standing
4 crying
5 drowning
6 lying
7 screaming

C

2 I recognized the man walking towards me.
3 I saw a boy stealing some chocolate from the shop.
4 The woman living next door to me is very friendly.
5 The money stolen by the soldiers was found in the farmhouse.
6 I heard the fire engine coming up the road.
7 A book written by my mother won a prize.

Unit 95

A

2 Yuri Gagarin

ANSWER KEY – MAIN TEXT

3 Marilyn Monroe
4 Canada
5 Kyoto
6 Amazon

B

2 Example sentence:
   Life in the twenty-first century is
   changing very rapidly.

C

2 that
3 that
4 to
5 that
6 to
7 that

Unit 96

A

2 arrived…sat
3 phoned…was working
4 heard…was writing
5 telephoned…heard

B

2 will let…phones
3 will be raining…set out
4 will tell…see
5 will buy…go

C

2 c
3 e
4 a
5 b
6 f

2 We hadn't been to the cinema since we had
   seen Dracula at the Odeon the year before.
3 He hadn't been able to play the piano since
   he had had his accident a month before.
4 They had lived next door to us since they
   had moved here in 1987.
5 Fred had been working at home ever
   since he had left his job at the factory.
6 Mary had been looking after the children
   ever since their mother had gone into
   hospital.

Unit 97

A

2 Try to write clearly so as to avoid being
   misunderstood.
3 A lot of people learn English in order to
   study in English.
4 What do I need to know in order to be a
   good doctor?
5 She turned up early in order to get the
   room ready.
6 In order to have 100 students you will
   need at least three teachers.
7 I came to live in the country so as to have

trees around me instead of buildings.
8 They had to eat grass and drink melted
   snow in order to stay alive.
9 In order to keep his car out of sight he left
   it in the road.
10 To get to Madrid I had to travel overnight
   from Barcelona.

B

2 She moved carefully to avoid waking the
   children.
3 He sat in the furthest corner to avoid
   being seen.
4 I gave up sugar and butter to avoid
   putting on weight.
5 He used both hands to avoid dropping
   anything.
6 He went over everything carefully to
   avoid making any mistakes.
7 She left quietly to avoid making any trouble.
8 We covered the furniture to avoid getting
   paint all over it.

Unit 98

A

2 such a ; so
3 so ; such a
4 so ; such a
5 so ; such a
6 such a ; so
7 such a ; so
8 such a; so
9 so ; such a
10 such a; so

B

2 Her writing was so small that I could
   hardly read it.
3 The winter was so bitterly cold that all the
   streams were frozen.
4 His favorite shoes were so badly worn
   that he had to throw them away.
5 He looked so young that everyone took
   him for a student.
6 Ken got so excited that he kept jumping
   up and down.

C

2 He was such a dreadful liar that nobody
   believed anything he said.
3 It proved to be such a difficult problem
   that nobody could solve it.
4 We had such a good time that we didn't
   want to go home.
5 They were such old clothes that they were
   falling apart.
6 It was such good food that we all ate far
   too much.

Unit 99

A

2 the weather was awful

3 She kept her coat on
4 I used to when I was younger
5 you're not as tall as he was
6 he still wasn't tired
7 He was difficult to understand
8 I really like John
9 we only arrived just in time

B

2 his recent illness
3 her fear
4 the unpopularity of his decision
5 the difference in their ages
6 the high cost of living
7 all his precautions
8 his injury
9 the rain

Unit 100

A

2 They arrived late, just as you said they
   would.
3 He ran away, just as everyone believed he
   would.
4 The play was a success, just as most
   people thought it would be.
5 He did well at school, just as we hoped he
   would.
6 Mary won, just as we thought she would.
7 She works at the bank just as her father
   did.
8 We use these ingredients today, just as we
   did in the past.

B

2 They still farm the way their grandfathers
   did.
3 He accepted his punishment the way
   everyone else did.
4 She refused to dress the way her
   colleagues did.
5 He said he would work the way others did
   if he was paid the way they were.
6 They work a five day week the way we do.
7 Her piano teacher taught her to play the
   way the other pupils did.

C

2 a
3 e
4 f
5 b
6 c

Unit 101

A

2 have I heard such a lot of nonsense.
3 we went to Brighton.
4 jumped a live mouse.
5 did she tell me that she would be coming
   round.
6 did they spend all my money

266

B

2 a

3 e

4 b

5 c

C

2 it was Ken who left the message.

3 it is usually just after nine when he comes in.

4 it is this afternoon that he is calling in

5 it was Becky who he wanted to see.

6 it is tomorrow that he is going to call back

Unit 102

A

A student went to her first lecture at the university, and mentioned this to a friend, another student. 'What was it about?' asked her friend. 'I don't know,' the first student replied. 'Why not?' asked the second. 'Weren't you listening?' 'Of course I was listening,' the first student replied, 'but he didn't tell us what it was about.'

A wealthy man was told by his bank manager that he owed the bank £100 and that he would have to pay 12% interest per year. The customer agreed to pay, and said he would leave his car, a Rolls-Royce, as security. He then drove the car round to the bank, and left it in the car park. A month later, he returned to collect the car. The curious bank manager asked why he had insisted on leaving it in the car park. 'Where else could I park it for a month, for only £1?' replied the customer.

B

3, 1, 4, 2, 6, 8, 5, 7

C

7, 2, 9, 3, 1, 6, 5, 10, 4, 8

Exercise 1

2 Do come and see us at the weekend.
3 Do bring the children too.
4 Do have some more tea.
5 Do write to me when you get home.
7 Do listen carefully.
8 Do be more careful.
9 Do be quiet while I'm talking.
10 Do sit down and behave yourself.

Exercise 2

2 How well do you speak French?
3 Will you be at school next Friday?
4 Who sits next to you in class?
5 Who do you sit next to in class?

Exercise 3

2 b
3 f
4 c
5 g
6 d
7 h
8 a

Exercise 4

2 were they
3 didn't they
4 does it
5 didn't it
6 was there
7 is there
8 do they
9 isn't it
10 haven't they

Exercise 5

2 ?
3 A
4 !
5 ?
6 A
7 !
8 ?
9 A

Exercise 6

2 will they
3 didn't she
4 is there
5 did they
6 isn't it
7 haven't they
8 did you
9 won't I
10 doesn't he
11 will you
12 aren't they

Exercise 7

2 Couldn't you have sent me a letter?

3 Mightn't they have gone home earlier?
4 Shouldn't we have paid in advance?
5 Couldn't you have taken a bus?

Exercise 8

2 I don't think so.
3 I suppose so.
4 I expect so.
5 I'm afraid not.
6 I think so.

Exercise 9

2 f
3 c
4 a
5 h
6 b
7 e
8 g

Exercise 10

2 It is known that he is a dangerous man.
3 It is said that Charlie Chaplin was a great comedian.
4 It is understood that she is arriving later today.
5 It is rumoured that they have escaped.

Exercise 11

2 b
3 e
4 h
5 g
6 c
7 d
8 a

Exercise 12

2 did it ourselves
3 cut it myself
4 get it myself
5 carry it myself
6 meet her myself

Exercise 13

2 That book is a favourite of Mary's.
3 Mr White is a colleague of my father's.
4 Angela is a classmate of hers.
5 I'm an employee of theirs.
6 Jack is a neighbour of yours.

Exercise 14

2 Both children have left school now.
3 Could you carry this bag for me?
4 I'd like to buy those brown shoes please.
5 I have to go to the bank this afternoon.
6 They live in a big new house.
7 I'm afraid I haven't got much money left.
8 I'd like to buy some fruit.
9 Most people enjoy going to the theatre.
10 You can buy soap at any supermarket.

Exercise 15

A psychiatrist greeting a new patient noticed that she was carrying a live duck under her arm. He invited her to take a seat and asked how he could help her. 'Oh, I don't need any help, thank you doctor,' she replied. 'My husband is the one who has a problem. He thinks he's a duck.'

A young man was out for a walk in a large city when he met a penguin. The penguin seemed to like him and began to follow him. The young man didn't know what to do so he went up to a policeman to ask for advice. 'Take it to the zoo,' said the policeman.
Next day, the policeman saw the same young man again still followed by the penguin. 'What are you doing with that penguin?' he asked. 'I told you to take it to the zoo.'
'Yes said the young man, 'we went to the zoo yesterday. Today, we are going to the museum.'

Exercise 16

2 All of them.
3 All of it.
4 All of us.
5 All of them.

Exercise 17

2 All of the/All the
3 Both of the/Both the
4 Neither of the
5 Both of the/Both the
6 None of the

Exercise 18

1 my, some, -, the, the
2 a, -, It was
3 a lot of, few
4 -, -, the, the
5 the, the, -, the, the, a few, The, the, the, the, -

Exercise 19

either, Neither
None, all, no

Exercise 20

2 old
3 deep
4 high/thick
5 long, wide
6 in weight

Exercise 21

2 fascinating
3 terrifying
4 exhausting
5 alarming
6 thrilling

Exercise 22

2 annoying
3 amazing
4 embarrassed

ANSWER KEY – FURTHER EXERCISES

5 convinced
6 driving

Exercise 23

Example sentences:
2 John is a good deal taller than Mary.
3 Mary is a little older than John.
4 Peter is far taller than Mary.
5 John is a good deal heavier than Mary.
6 Peter is far heavier than Mary.

Exercise 24

2 the biggest ocean
3 the most populated country
4 the oldest university
5 the longest river
6 the longest river

Exercise 25

2 Mike, Peter, John
3 John, Peter, Mike
4 John, Mike, Peter
5 Peter, John, Mike
6 John, Mike
7 Mike, John
8 John, Peter

Exercise 26

2 Staying in a hotel is more comfortable than camping.
3 Eating out is easier than cooking for myself.
4 Living in the country is more peaceful than living in a town.
5 Cycling is healthier than driving.

Exercise 27

2 Our holiday began on Saturday morning.
3 She shook her head unhappily.
4 He walked back home slowly and sadly.
5 He locked up the office before going home.
6 There was a gold ring in the box.
7 He whispered his name quietly.
8 She went for a jog early in the morning.
9 I tried to stop him too late.
10 The film began at exactly seven o'clock.

Exercise 28

2 for, ago, since
3 ago, since, for
4 since, for, ago
5 since, ago, for
6 ago, for, since
7 for, ago, since
8 ago, for, since

Exercise 29

2 very happy
3 awfully good
4 really angry
5 extremely intelligent

Exercise 30

2 b
3 g
4 c
5 i
6 a
7 d
8 h
9 e

Exercise 31

2 slowly
3 careful
4 happily
5 well
6 lately
7 late
8 hard

Exercise 32

1 on, in, at
2 on, at, on
3 at, on, at, in, at

Exercise 33

1 in, -, on, until
2 since, -
3 -, by, on
4 at, ago, on
5 for, during, since
6 -, from, to
7 yet, still
8 since, still
9 for, just
10 already, yet

Exercise 34

1 on
2 at, to
3 on, above
4 in, at
5 out of
6 at, on
7 off, at, opposite
8 in

Exercise 35

2 the unexpected death of the chairman
3 the late departure of the train
4 the theft of her jewellery
5 the dreadful behaviour of the children
6 the invasion of the island

Exercise 36

1 on
2 of, on
3 on, of
4 on, of
5 of, on

Exercise 37

2 laugh at

3 apologize for
4 rely on
5 talk about

Exercise 38

2 fold them up
3 put them away
4 point it out
5 tore them up
6 threw them away
7 sort them out
8 knocked it down
9 hand it over
10 pull it down

Exercise 39

2 We never found out who knocked the vase over./ We never found out who knocked over the vase.
3 He refused to hand the money over./ He refused to hand over the money.
4 Can you help me to sort the papers out?/ Can you help me to sort out the papers?
5 It would be useful if someone could sort my mistakes out./It would be useful if someone could sort out my mistakes.
6 It's very hard work bringing children up./It's very hard work bringing up children.
7 They're planning to pull all the houses down./They're planning to pull down all the houses.
8 Andrew never remembers to put his books away./Andrew never remembers to put away his books.

Exercise 40

2 He offered a lot of help to his next door neighbour.
3 I have cooked a special supper for the children.
4 Please send your reply to us as soon as possible.
5 I'll try to save a place for you.
6 Show that book you've just bought to your uncle.

Exercise 41

2 gave
3 took
4 had
5 did
6 went
7 gave
8 had

Exercise 42

had finished, had had

had asked, had chosen, told, was, was, rushed, had happened

Exercise 43

was trying, was living, was sharing

ANSWER KEY – FURTHER EXERCISES

Exercise 44

2 is increasing
3 is improving
4 is changing, is getting
5 is improving
6 was getting
7 is getting
8 are growing up
9 are improving
10 is changing

Exercise 45

When I was a boy, I wanted to be a jazz musician. I used to play the drums. I would practise for hours every evening, and I would spend almost every weekend practising too. I used to go to my local jazz club every week to listen. One night a group called The Rollers was playing there. Unfortunately, their drummer had had an accident on his way to the club, so he couldn't play. They asked me to take his place, and of course I agreed. It was awful. I felt that I had never played so badly before. After that, I still used to go to the club, but I never offered to play again, and they certainly didn't ask me.

Exercise 46

1 am going, is being
2 Do you know, haven't seen, think, is probably doing
3 doesn't eat, finds, don't have, usually telephones
4 have you been living, are staying, have found
5 met, was waiting, haven't seen, seemed, think, has just got, hasn't he, just left, hasn't found, is still looking
6 knew, had been, would often go, wanted, are you going to, asked, can't, am not going, don't need, just want, can read, write, will have
7 would write, was going, was, could not, was not going, was, could, wrote, would have
8 heard, were, remember, once cut, didn't you cut, had already done

Exercise 47

2 a
3 f
4 e
5 b
6 g
7 c
8 d

Exercise 48

2 a
3 g
4 b
5 h
6 c

7 i
8 d
9 e

Exercise 49

2 stops, keeps
3 started, went on
4 kept on, stopped, started
5 finished, went on, stop, start

Exercise 50

Example sentence: I loathe going to the dentist.

Exercise 51

2 hear
3 see
4 feel
5 catch
6 prevent
7 imagine

Exercise 52

2 decision
3 opportunity
4 need
5 refusal
6 willingness
7 attempt
8 order

Exercise 53

2 is supposed to have cost a million pounds.
3 was reported to have been hit by an earthquake early this morning.
4 is known to be a brilliant politician.
5 is alleged to have brought dangerous drugs into the country.
6 is understood to be armed and dangerous.

Exercise 54

2 who to ask
3 where to go
4 how to open it
5 when I should start
6 how to play tennis
7 to swim

Exercise 55

2 interrupting
3 shouting
4 to get
5 leaving
6 to post
7 to come
8 asking

Exercise 56

2 speak
3 move
4 steal
5 leave

Exercise 57

2 get my photograph taken
3 get it mended
4 get them shortened
5 got his nose broken

Exercise 58

2 a
3 b
4 f
5 c
6 d

Exercise 59

As Eric sat on his bed reading, the hotel manager's daughter knocked on the door. Her father had told her that Eric was English, and she wanted him to help her with the translation she had been set for homework.

Exercise 60

2 lends, is, takes, rains/is raining
3 want, do, have had

Exercise 61

2 if/whether Joe still lives in Liverpool.
  if/whether Joe still lived in Liverpool.
3 if/whether you have mended the roof.
  if/whether you had mended the roof.
4 when Harry will be moving to Manchester.
  when Harry would be moving to Manchester.
5 what time the concert finishes.
  what time the concert finished.
6 if/whether Peggy will be coming too.
  if/whether Peggy would be coming too.
7 if/whether they will have to speak English all the time.
  if/whether they would have to speak English all the time.
8 who I spoke to on the phone.
  who I had spoken to on the phone.

Exercise 62

2 warn, warned
3 beg, begged
4 invites, invited
5 reminds, remind
6 command, commanded
7 instruct, instructed
8 advise, advised

Exercise 63

2 John asked Jill if she was ready to go.
3 The children asked their parents if they could go on the school picnic.
4 I asked the policeman if there was a bus to Piccadilly.
5 My wife asked me if we could afford to take a taxi.
6 The customs officer asked Joe if he had anything to declare.

ANSWER KEY – FURTHER EXERCISES

Exercise 64

2 Full details of the job were sent to me.
3 Signed certificates were presented to all of them.
4 All passengers are offered a free sightseeing trip.
5 Everyone in our group has been given drinks and snacks.
6 News of their success was brought to her yesterday evening.

Exercise 65

2 it could be true.
3 You could cut yourself.
4 they could win.
5 could earn as much as £50,000 if she gets the job.
6 It could cause a serious accident.
7 you could get there in time.
8 It could be for you.
9 could be dangerous.
10 which could turn to snow on high ground.

Exercise 66

Example sentence: A hundred years ago I could have read Shakespeare, but I couldn't have read Ernest Hemingway.

Exercise 67

2 b
3 a
4 c
5 f
6 e

Exercise 68

3 He must know the answer.
4 They must have left for school.
5 You must have read it.
6 This must be the rush hour.

Exercise 69

2 was able to
3 won't be able to
4 are able to
5 were able to
6 will be able to
7 won't be able to

Exercise 70

Example sentence: He couldn't have driven to the supermarket.

Exercise 71

2 can hear, can't see
3 can smell
4 can't hear
5 can see
6 can't see

Exercise 72

2 go together.

3 buy a new one.
4 see a doctor.
5 go home.
6 come too.
7 come with me.
8 come round and meet him.

Exercise 73

3 You ought to have asked for permission.
4 We ought not to have stayed so late.
5 You ought to have gone to the doctor's earlier.
6 You ought to have met Jenny while you were here.
7 I ought not to have got so angry about what happened.
8 You ought to have come on your own.
9 We ought to have reserved seats.
10 You ought to have stopped at the traffic lights.

Exercise 74

3 I had better ask my father first.
4 We had better be going home now.
5 They had better not make any trouble.
6 You had better get a return ticket.
7 You had better not go out alone at night.
8 You had better go to bed.
9 We had better get something to eat.
10 We had better not waste any more time.

Exercise 75

2 You must come home before midnight.
3 You shouldn't go out in the rain.
4 You ought not to complain so much.
5 You mustn't spend too much money.

Exercise 76

2 I wish we had time to stop.
3 I wish he had passed his exam.
4 I wish it wasn't so cold in here.
5 I wish there was more time.
6 I wish George would help.
7 I wish Mary had come.
8 I wish I had seen the match last week.

Exercise 77

2 the friend you met
3 the message he sent home
4 the lecture Jack is going to give
5 the friends Bill had hoped to meet
6 the prize we decided to offer
8 the money you asked for
9 the picture he was looking at
10 the bus they had waited for
11 the children she is looking after
12 the coin I picked up

Exercise 78

2 hearing the noise, I immediately telephoned the police.
3 hearing my report, they promised to send two policemen round.

4 Arriving at my house, one policeman found that a window had been broken.
5 Seeing this, he rang the doorbell.
6 On hearing the bell, a burglar ran out through the back door.
7 Seeing the burglar escaping, the second policeman chased after him.
8 Running across the road, the unlucky burglar was hit by a car.
9 After having arrested the man, the police called for an ambulance.
10 On arriving at the hospital, they found the man had made his escape.

Exercise 79

2 She moved carefully in order not to wake the children.
3 He sat in the furthest corner in order not to be seen.
4 I gave up sugar and butter in order not to put on weight.
6 We went over everything so as not to make any mistakes.
7 She left quietly so as not to make any trouble.
8 We covered the furniture so as not to get paint all over it.

Exercise 80

2 The houses were knocked down so that they could be replaced by car parks and office blocks.
3 I sat next to the window so that I could see out.
4 He tied a knot in his handkerchief so that he wouldn't forget.
5 I waved my arms so that they would see me.
6 He wanted the report early so that he could discuss it with colleagues.
7 We will take a telescope so that we can see the birds without getting too close.
8 I'll fasten the donkey so that it can't escape.
9 She left her address so that we could forward her letters.
10 He wore a disguise so that even his friends wouldn't recognise him.

Exercise 81

2 too young
3 too far
4 too quickly
5 too small
6 too expensive
7 too late
8 too many
9 too old

Exercise 82

2 well
3 lucky
4 Chinese

ANSWER KEY – FURTHER EXERCISES

5 noisy
6 food
7 room
8 old
9 clean
10 work

Exercise 83

2 despite working hard
3 in spite of having a bad fall.
4 Despite learning French
5 In spite of being over sixty

6 despite having lost his job.
Note: it is possible to use 'in spite of' or 'despite'
in all these sentences.

Exercise 84

2 it wasn't very well written.
3 we lived next door to a policeman
4 we didn't have very good seats.
5 they tend to live longer.
6 they live in the same house
7 I've done nothing all day.
8 everyone else disagreed with him.

9 we warned them not to.
10 I've known him for years.

Exercise 85

2 Jack was the one who took the dictionary.
3 Bill was the one who was waiting to
   borrow it.
4 Helen was the one who promised to bring
   it back.
5 Diana is the one who is going to look
   after it for you.